LAW, MORALITY AND RIGHTS

VOLUME 162

ROYAL INSTITUTE OF PHILOSOPHY CONFERENCES
VOLUME 1979

LAW, MORALITY AND RIGHTS

Edited by

M. A. STEWART
Department of Philosophy,
University of Lancaster

D. REIDEL PUBLISHING COMPANY
A MEMBER OF THE KLUWER ACADEMIC PUBLISHERS GROUP
DORDRECHT / BOSTON / LANCASTER

Library of Congress Cataloging in Publication Data
Main entry under title:

Law, morality, and rights.
(Royal Institute of Philosophy conferences ; v. 79)
(Synthese library ; v. 162)
Includes index.
1. Jurisprudence—Congresses. 2. Law—Philosophy—Congresses. 3. Law and ethics—Congresses. I. Stewart, M. A. (Michael Alexander), 1937– . II. Series.
K225.L38 1983 340'.1 82-24118
ISBN 90-277-1519-X

Published by D. Reidel Publishing Company,
P.O. Box 17, 3300 AA Dordrecht, Holland

Sold and distributed in the U.S.A. and Canada
by Kluwer Boston Inc.,
190 Old Derby Street, Hingham, MA 02043, U.S.A.

In all other countries, sold and distributed
by Kluwer Academic Publishers Group,
P.O. Box 322, 3300 AH Dordrecht, Holland

Printed in The Netherlands

TABLE OF CONTENTS

PART V: REVERSE DISCRIMINATION

PART VI: DURESS

PART VII: PUNISHMENT

SERIES PREFACE

The Royal Institute of Philosophy has been sponsoring conferences in alternate years since 1969. These have from the start been intended to be of interest to persons who are not philosophers by profession. They have mainly focused on interdisciplinary areas such as the philosophies of psychology, education and the social sciences. The volumes arising from these conferences have included discussions between philosophers and distinguished practitioners of other disciplines relevant to the chosen topic.

Beginning with the 1979 conference on 'Law, Morality and Rights' and the 1981 conference on 'Space, Time and Causality' these volumes are now constituted as a series. It is hoped that this series will contribute to advancing philosophical understanding at the frontiers of philosophy and areas of interest to non-philosophers. It is hoped that it will do so by writing which reduces technicalities as much as the subject-matter permits. In this way the series is intended to demonstrate that philosophy can be clear and worthwhile in itself and at the same time relevant to the interests of lay people.

Honorary Assistant Director
Royal Institute of Philosophy

STUART BROWN

M. A. Stewart (ed.), Law, Morality and Rights, vii.

PREFACE

"I am afraid of Lord Kaims's Law Tracts," wrote David Hume, tongue in cheek, to Adam Smith in 1759. "A man might as well think of making a fine Sauce by a Mixture of Wormwood & Aloes as an agreeable Composition by joining Metaphysics & Scotch Law." In point of fact, the common interests of philosophers and jurists were as extensive then as now; and it is a pleasure to record that there was no shortage of Scots and other lawyers to mix with English and other metaphysicians at the University of Lancaster conference organized by the Royal Institute of Philosophy from 14 to 17 September 1979.

The meetings were devoted to commissioned symposia and a number of individual seminar papers submitted by participants. The symposia brought together distinguished philosophers and jurists, drawn from both sides of the Atlantic, addressing subjects of common professional concern. The topics were chosen so as to include both some questions of traditional jurisprudence and some issues of current social interest. They include the working of the judicial mind, and the concept of a "claim"; the present state of British, especially English, law on obscenity and duress; and problems of social justice and fair punishment within the context of the American Constitution.

It has not been possible, within the limits of this volume, to reproduce the fruitful and lively debate from the floor that attended most of these sessions. We print the opening papers by the protagonist and respondent for each symposium, and, where available, the chairman's commentary and some concluding comments by the first speaker; the concluding comments were written after the conference and some of the other papers have been revised, particularly in their topical documentation, before publication. There are two small deviations from this format: in Part VI

Lord Kilbrandon did not wish to exercise his right of reply and in Part VII Professor W. L. Twining's chairman's comments were not available for publication. We are grateful to two of the other participants in these debates, Mr Mackie and Dr Cottingham, for developing their remarks into short papers specially for this volume, to fill these spaces. Certain of the papers from Parts I, III, IV and VI of this volume have appeared in whole or in part in *Law and Philosophy* **1** (1982), by agreement between the Institute and the editor of that journal. Special permission was given to enable Professor Murphy to include an earlier text of his paper on 'Cruel and Unusual Punishments' in his own book *Retribution, Justice and Therapy* (Reidel, 1979) ahead of publication in the present volume.

We could not offer to print all of the individual seminar papers. Part II contains two of those submitted, selected because they bring to bear fresh philosophical perspectives (those of the philosopher of science and of Wittgensteinian philosophy) on the current debates on the theoretical understanding of the judicial process sparked off by the recent writings of H. L. A. Hart and R. M. Dworkin. Three other papers presented in seminars at the conference have been published elsewhere: R. A. Duff's 'Implied and Constructive Malice in Murder' has appeared in *Law Quarterly Review* **95** (1979): 418–444; Frederick Schauer's 'Free Speech and the Paradox of Tolerance' in *Values in Conflict*, edited by Burton M. Leiser (New York: Macmillan, 1981); and an early text of Frank Marsh's paper on 'Synthetic Competency' (co-authored with G. C. Graber under the title 'Ought a Defendant Be Drugged to Stand Trial?') in *Hastings Center Report* **9** (1979): 8–10.

The slight delay in publishing these proceedings is not the responsibility of any of the parties to this volume, and I am grateful both to the publishers and to the contributors for the speed, efficiency and good humour with which they have cooperated in dealing with the few problems that came to light after the signing of the publishing contract. The work of editing the volume for the press has occupied part of my time as a visiting fellow at the

Institute for Advanced Studies in the Humanities at the University of Edinburgh. I should like to record my thanks to Professors Neil MacCormick, Alan White and John Benson for their help in planning the original programme, and to all those whose attendance contributed to the great success of the meetings.

M. A. S.

PART I

WORKING CONCEPTIONS OF "THE LAW"

ROBERT S. SUMMERS

WORKING CONCEPTIONS OF "THE LAW"

1. PREFATORY NOTE

This exploratory essay is an admixture of amateur psychology, moral theory, and jurisprudence. It grows out of seminars I have given for judges, and reflects that focus.[1] Co-theorists will now see some of what I have been telling practitioners. And error in my story may be exposed. But one can have no qualms about this. It is especially important to have things put right for judges.

2. INTRODUCTION

I will consider the work of judges in civil law cases, and will begin with one of *many* possible examples. In 1809, English judges decided a now famous case, one with extraordinarily wide-ranging influence. The full original report of the case reads as follows:

Butterfield v. *Forrester*
(1809) 11 East 60 (KB)

This was an action on the case for obstructing a highway, by means of which obstruction the plaintiff, who was riding along the road, was thrown down with his horse, and injured, &c. At the trial before *Bayley J.* at *Derby*, it appeared that the defendant, for the purpose of making some repairs to his house, which was close by the road side at one end of the town, had put up a pole across this part of the road, a free passage being left by another branch or street in the same direction. That the plaintiff left a public house not far distant from the place in question at 8 o'clock in the evening in *August*, when

[1] Several ideas in this essay were presented in June 1978 to judges in seminars at Madison, Wisconsin, and at the Harvard Law School. I am indebted to these judges for comments. I am grateful to Professors David Lyons and Roger C. Cramton for helpful criticism. I also wish to thank Mr Leigh Kelley and Mr Erik M. Jensen, Cornell Law School classes of 1980 and 1979, respectively, for valuable research and editorial assistance.

M. A. Stewart (ed.), Law, Morality and Rights, 3–29.

they were just beginning to light candles, but while there was light enough left to discern the obstruction at 100 yards distance: and the witness, who proved this, said that if the plaintiff had not been riding very hard he might have observed and avoided it: the plaintiff however, who was riding violently, did not observe it, but rode against it, and fell with his horse and was much hurt in consequence of the accident; and there was no evidence of his being intoxicated at the time. On this evidence *Bayley J.* directed the jury, that if a person riding with reasonable and ordinary care could have seen and avoided the obstruction; and if they were satisfied that the plaintiff was riding along the street extremely hard, and without ordinary care, they should find a verdict for the defendant: which they accordingly did. [The plaintiff moved for a new trial.]

Bayley J. The plaintiff was proved to be riding as fast as his horse could go, and this was through the streets of *Derby*. If he had used ordinary care he must have seen the obstruction; so that the accident appeared to happen entirely from his own fault.

Lord Ellenborough C. J. A party is not to cast himself upon an obstruction which has been made by the fault of another, and avail himself of it, if he do not himself use common and ordinary caution to be in the right. In cases of persons riding upon what is considered to be the wrong side of the road, that would not authorise another purposely to ride up against them. One person being in fault will not dispense with another's using ordinary care for himself. Two things must concur to support this action, an obstruction in the road by the fault of the defendant, and no want of ordinary care to avoid it on the part of the plaintiff. [New trial denied.]

As interpreted by most subsequent judges (though not without some license), the foregoing precedent stands for the so-called "complete bar" rule to the effect that if a plaintiff is contributorily negligent, he may not recover *any* compensation from a defendant whose negligent act or omission also contributed to the plaintiff's loss. (There are qualifications but we need not go into them here.)

Now consider a second case (my summary of the report):

Maki v. *Frelk*
Supreme Court of Illinois, 1968
239 N.E.2d 445

Decedent was killed in an auto collision at an intersection. The plaintiff was administratrix of the decedent's estate and was suing the defendant, driver of the other car, for wrongful death. In counts one and two of the complaint, the plaintiff alleged that the decedent exercised due care for his own safety (was *not* contributorily negligent), and that the defendant negligently caused the accident by driving too fast, failing to keep a proper lookout, failing to keep his car under control, and operating a car without adequate brakes. In the third count, the plaintiff did not allege the decedent's own freedom from contributory negligence, but did allege the defendant's negligence, and alleged that if there was any negligence on the part of the decedent, the plaintiff could still win because the decedent's negligence, if any, "was less than the negligence of the defendant, when compared."

The trial judge granted the defendant's motion to strike this third count on the basis of Illinois case law following *Butterfield* v. *Forrester*. The intermediate court of appeals reversed, and thus repudiated *Butterfield* v. *Forrester*. However, on appeal to the highest court of Illinois, the trial judge's ruling was affirmed.

Thus, in 1968, a majority of judges of the Illinois Supreme Court in *Maki* v. *Frelk* purported to follow *Butterfield* v. *Forrester* and its progeny faithfully.[2] Yet one of the acknowledged leaders among American scholars of tort law had already called the "complete bar" rule the "harshest doctrine known to the common law,"[3] a characterization that may be justified especially since the doctrine precludes even a slightly negligent plaintiff from recovering anything from a grossly negligent defendant. In 1945 the English had abandoned this precedent by a statute apportioning recoverable damages in accord with estimates of each negligent party's share of responsibility for the loss.[4] By 1968, several American state legislatures had followed suit.[5] Subsequently, the highest state courts of a few American states (e.g. Florida, 1973

---

[2] One justification the judges offered for this course of action was that, in their view, any change should come from the legislature. I cannot go into this complex issue here.

[3] L. Green, 'Illinois Negligence Law', *Illinois Law Review* 39 (1944): 36.

[4] See generally Glanville L. Williams, 'The Law Reform (Contributory Negligence) Act, 1945', *Modern Law Review* 9 (1946): 105–186.

[5] Victor E. Schwartz, *Comparative Negligence* (Indianapolis: Allen Smith, 1974), pp. 12–15.

and California, 1975) acted on their own to abandon the complete bar rule.[6]

What explains *Maki* v. *Frelk*? The various factors that influence judges are numerous and complex, and they vary somewhat from judge to judge. For my purposes, however, it is not necessary to try to offer a comprehensive account. There are at least four possible explanations for the Illinois court's refusal in *Maki* v. *Frelk* to abandon the "harshest doctrine known to the common law": (1) the judges believed (what, in my view, would be mistaken) that only the Illinois legislature had power to modify the "complete bar" rule, or (2) the judges simply failed to reason through the conflicting considerations as they should have and decided against the plaintiff, even though, according to the allegations, the defendant was partly responsible, or (3) the judges, in deciding the case, were unduly influenced by a particular *working conception* of "the law," and this led them to uphold the harsh doctrine, or (4) some combination of the foregoing.

The working conception most likely figuring here in an explanation of the third possible kind is easy enough to identify: "The law" governing an issue to be decided consists of a pre-existing rule[7] – the "complete bar" rule of *Butterfield* v. *Forrester.* Judges unduly influenced by this working conception would vote to uphold the harshest doctrine known to the common law. Of course, such a working conception does not itself *require* this result. It is only a *working* conception, and judges not obsessed with it would not give it an undue or disproportionate place in their thinking. Instead, they would vote to overrule a case like *Butterfield* v. *Forrester* (unless they rightly believed that the matter should be left only to the legislature). In voting to overrule,

---

[6] *Li* v. *Yellow Cab Co.*, 13 Cal.3d 804, 119 Cal. Rptr. 858, 532 P.2d 1226 (1975); *Hoffman* v. *Jones*, 280 So.2d 431 (Fla. 1973).

[7] The most influential of American Judges, Oliver Wendell Holmes, Jr., once put it this way: "My job is to play the game according to the rules." (L. Hand, 'Address', in *Continuing Legal Education for Professional Competence and Responsibility* (Philadelphia: Joint Committee on Continuing Legal Education, 1959), p. 119.)

these judges would be abandoning, for this case, "the law" that their working conception had put them on to and would be turning to other normative phenomena of "the law" that should here have primacy. These other phenomena include (1) the law's commitment to the reassessment of precedent in light of reason and (2) the discretionary power of common law judges to overrule unsound precedent.

In this essay, I will concentrate on the roles of working conceptions in judicial decisions. I will not try to prove that this factor actually helps explain the decision in *Maki* v. *Frelk*. Nor, of course, will I try to establish the general extent to which judges are influenced by their working conceptions. But from my reading of opinions over many years, and from numerous discussions with judges, I have concluded that such conceptions do play important roles, both for good and for ill. They can facilitate sound decision making. Indeed, one would hope that this is the usual result. Some judges, however, become preoccupied with their working ideas of "the law." And there is evidence that this sometimes affects outcomes. These conclusions should surprise no one. Working conceptions are useful (in ways I will try to explain). Indeed, they are pragmatic necessities for most judges. That some proportion of judges will become preoccupied with such conceptions seems more or less inevitable.

It would help if judges were more conscious of the possible adverse effects of becoming preoccupied with a working conception of "the law," and I offer this essay partly to that end. Judges conscious of the limits of their working conceptions will be far less likely to become imprisoned in them. I also offer this essay as a partial account of what it is for a judge to have a philosophy of law. But my main purpose here is to explore whether there is an alternative working conception that might be better than the influential notion that law consists of pre-existing rules – better in that (1) it would be a more serviceable working conception as such; or (2) its normative effects would be preferable; or (3) the consequences of judicial obsession with it would be less untoward; or (4) some combination of the foregoing. I believe there is a better alternative working conception, and it is one in which morality plays a major part.

3. THE NATURE OF A WORKING CONCEPTION

I must first discuss what I take a working conception to be, and I will continue to use the notion of "law as pre-existing rule" for illustrative purposes.

As I conceive it, a working conception is not the same as what Professor Hart has called a "criterion of legal validity."[8] Such a conception might specify a feature required for a form of law to be valid within a system, but it need not. Thus a criterion of legal validity within a society might, for example, be that the law, whatever form it happens to take, must be promulgated by Rex. And judges might have a working conception of the law as "rules made by Rex." Yet judges in this society might hold a working conception of the law devoid of any reference to Rex, too. Virtually all all of them might conceive of "the law" simply as pre-existing rules (and there might be few other social rules). Furthermore, as I conceive it, a working notion of the law is not as such *binding* upon a judge, whereas a true criterion of legal validity is.

A working conception is not the same as a working hypothesis as to the likely actual substantive content of relevant law.[9] Rather, it is "prior" to any such hypothesis. It is a kind of conceptual schema, and it *may* be one that can accommodate almost any particular substantive content.

Nor is a working notion necessarily the same as an "ideal type" of law.[10] It is possible to imagine, for example, an ideal type of a

---

[8] H. L. A. Hart, *The Concept of Law* (Oxford: Clarendon Press, 1961), chapter 6.

[9] Similarly, it is not the same as a "hunch" as to the right result in a case. See Joseph C. Hutcheson, Jr., 'The Judgment Intuitive: The Function of the "Hunch" in Judicial Decision', *Cornell Law Quarterly* 14 (1928/9): 274–288.

[10] I refer here to Weber's notion of an "ideal type." See his 'Religious Rejections of the World and their Directions', in *From Max Weber: Essays in*

legal rule – one that is precise, clear, prospective, and in still other ways formally ideal. A notion of "the law as pre-existing rule" could, however, qualify as a working conception even if the concept of a rule embodied in it did not have such features.

My notion of a working idea is one in which "the law" is conceptualized in terms of one, or at most two types of recurrent normative phenomena of "the law." These phenomena may also be thought of as "justificatory resources"; they are themselves varied and complex, and, in Anglo-American systems, include:

(a) pre-existing rules,
(b) actual reasons for those rules,
(c) equities between the parties outside any relevant rules,
(d) discretionary judgment (including that involved in the overruling or modification of precedent),
(e) the bearing of ideas of justice and the common good characteristically found in some forms of law,
(f) the general dictates of reason, including "goal" reasons and "rightness" reasons, relevant to the justification of judicial decisions, and
(g) fiat.

A working conception, however, leaves things out; it is only a partial schematization. Thus, for example, judges who adopt a working conception of "the law" as pre-existing rules adopt a notion that leaves out the foregoing other important normative phenomena of the law that may also be relevant to issues for decision. (Many judges who hold a rule conception also incorporate the reason or reasons for the rules, too.)

But that a particular conception leaves out important phenomena of "the law" is in itself not a criticism of that notion as a *working* conception. In my view, to be serviceable to the usual judge, such a notion must be partial and selective. Only the ablest

---

Sociology, edited by H. H. Gerth and C. Wright Mills (New York: Oxford University Press, 1946), pp. 323–359. The editors of this volume also discuss Weber's notion at pp. 59–61 of their Introduction.

judge could wield a working conception *qua* working conception that encompasses all normative phenomena of "the law." (On this, more later.) Furthermore, a conception that meets the five threshold requirements of a viable working conception (soon to be set forth) will, *on its own*, serve a judge well in a substantial proportion of cases. That is, he will not have to resort to other phenomena of the law to dispose of these cases appropriately. Indeed, this is one factor that accounts for the widespread judicial resort to a rule conception. The phenomena of the law relevant to decision just do consist, in a significant proportion of cases, of pre-existing rules (and the reasons therefor). Thus in all such cases the inevitably partial nature of a working conception can hardly be prejudicial or dysfunctional. Indeed that characterization may be thought of as part of the very "beauty" of a viable working conception. Of course, even in the cases to which a working conception readily applies and which would lead to an analysis that ought to be determinative, it is still possible for judges to go wrong. A working conception is not a *guarantee*.

It does not follow, however, that if a judge brings a serviceable working conception to an issue for decision this judge must, ought to, or will decide that issue solely in light of the general feature or features of phenomena of "the law" embodied in that conception. On the contrary, the judge *ought* to decide in light of phenomena of the law that emerge as relevant and appropriate bases for decision, even when these phenomena turn out, in the circumstances, *not* to be incorporated in his working conception. And, on my account, the judge who is not unduly influenced by his working conception will generally so decide. After all, his conception is only a *working* idea.

In my view, a viable working conception of the law is, however, a *pragmatic* necessity for the usual judge. When performing intellectual operations with the law, this judge needs *some general notion* of what he is performing them on, and for. A working conception of "the law" is such a notion. Note that I do not claim that a working conception is a *conceptual* necessity. And some judges may get along without any such idea.

In a related way, a viable working idea of the law is functionally serviceable. One conception may be preferable to another on grounds of comparative serviceability. First, it might facilitate the identification of pre-existing law better than some other general idea. For example, in Anglo-American systems, a rule conception would more often lead judges to relevant authoritative materials than would an "unfettered discretion" notion of law. Second, one conception may put the judge on to a better interpretational method than another. Thus a notion of the law as a reasoned reconciliation of conflicting considerations would lead the usual judge to interpret statutes, for example, in accord with their rationales more readily than would a rule conception (at least if the latter itself omitted rationales). Third, one conception might, better than any other, facilitate the identification and resolution of issues calling for the creation of new law. It should be evident, for example, that the notion of law as pre-existing rule provides little sustenance to the judge who must decide a case of first impression. A working conception may be serviceable in still other ways, too.

Before a conception can be at all adequately serviceable in the foregoing ways, it must satisfy five "criteria of viability" which I will now sketch (and only that). Since the idea of law as pre-existing rule satisfies these criteria, I will illustrate each criterion with it.

First, an idea cannot qualify if not faithful to law's reality. Obviously, ideas of space exploration, or of the modern novel, are essentially foreign to law and thus cannot count as, or figure in, what I call a working notion of the law. Pre-existing rules, on the other hand, are not at all foreign to the law, and thus readily qualify. (Of course, this is not to say that the whole of the law consists of rules or that rules are law.)

Second, the notion must be sufficiently unitary. Otherwise, it cannot be serviceable as a working conception (at least for the ordinary judge). Again, the pre-existing rule idea qualifies, even if reasons for the rules are included. Such a conception would thus embody three related elements: rule, reasons, and pre-existence.

Of course, an unusually able judge might have a conception that is "total" and thus embodies all phenomena of the law. But any such all-encompassing conception could not be of service to the usual judge. It would be too complex, and thus too cumbersome for him to "wield all at once." And it would not be sufficiently "selective."

Third, since in our systems, law ranges over nearly every nook and cranny of social life, a serviceable working idea of "the law" must be widely applicable – not narrowly pocketed or restricted to specific varieties of social relations. Again, a rule conception qualifies. This is not to say that pre-existing rules exist for, or are justifiably applicable to, all, or even the overwhelming majority of, issues arising for decision.

Fourth, the phenomenon, or phenomena, of the law picked out by a working conception must be sufficiently represented or instantiated numerically within the totality of legal phenomena. Thus, a phenomenon that rarely recurs could not qualify. For example, the relation of circular priority in mortgage law could not. Nor could "adverse possession." But pre-existing rules could. Rules are ubiquitous in the law.

Fifth, the conception must not be vacuous or unduly indeterminate. The notion of law as pre-existing rules satisfies this criterion, too. (On this, more later.)

A *viable* working conception is one that is functionally serviceable. It facilitates the identification of relevant law, the adoption of sound interpretational method, the application of reason afresh when called for, and more. To be serviceable in such ways, a working conception must sufficiently satisfy the foregoing criteria of viability.

It does not follow, however, that a serviceable working conception is one with which no judge can become obsessed. On the contrary, a judge may be unduly influenced by *any* working conception. There are two basic forms that this can take in the case of a judge who holds a rule conception. First, let us assume that the rule notion is *prima facie* applicable to the issue at hand (the issue *is* one to which some version of a pre-existing rule is actually relevant). Even so, it may be that in the end the particular rule should not control; yet our judge may fail to see this. For example, reason may reveal that the rule is the harshest doctrine of the common law and require that it be overruled. Or, for example, it may be that equities between the parties have arisen in the particular case (for which the rule does not provide) and these ought to control.[11] Second, our preoccupied judge may fail to see that his working conception of the law as pre-existing rule is not even *prima facie* applicable to the issue at hand, for the case is a genuine case of first impression, or a statutory *casus omissus.* In these cases there is no pre-existing rule, yet our judge acts as if there were, by, for example, invoking a far-fetched analogy.

4. POSSIBLE WORKING CONCEPTIONS

I have already said that a conception of "the law" as pre-existing rule qualifies as one possiblê working conception and that many judges actually hold this idea. I have also said that some judges become obsessed with it, and that this helps account for some bad outcomes. But in my view, nothing inherent in the nature of law, or of the judge's role, requires that a judge hold this particular working idea. I will now consider whether certain other possibilities also satisfy the relevant qualifying criteria of viability. Among these are the following (each of which, except perhaps the first, has some actual subscribers among judges):

(1) The law is whatever the equities between the parties dictate in the particular case.

This possible working conception fails to qualify for lack of sufficient numerical significance (fourth criterion). In a very high proportion of cases, there are no relevant "equities" between the parties (or the equities are not appropriately determinative).

(2) The law is whatever the official organs of final application within the system say it is.

---

[11] On the nature of such equities, see Robert S. Summers, 'General Equitable Principles under Section 1–103 of the Uniform Commercial Code', *Northwestern Law Review* 72 (1978): 906.

This candidate might be called the "unfettered discretion" or "free law" idea. Although popular in some jurisprudential circles, it cannot qualify either. At least in Anglo-American systems, it lacks the required phenomenological felicity (first criterion). The law in these systems is not (and never has been) a game of scorer's discretion. A judge is almost never free to take the view that the law is entirely "up to me."

(3) The law consists of certain characteristic substantive ideas of justice and of the common good.

Of course, we do have certain received ideas of justice and the common good, and some of these may even be more or less characteristic of the content of much law, at least in Anglo-American legal systems. But this candidate fails, nonetheless. The relevant ideas do not have sufficient range and bearing, given the diverse, and detailed, nature of the issues judges must face (third and fifth criteria). Moreover, some notions of justice and the common good have been (and are) more ideal than real and thus lack sufficient phenomenological felicity (first criterion). Laws applicable to blacks in the Southern United States until after World War II are perhaps most dramatically illustrative (within recent Anglo-American legal history).

(4) The law is a reasoned reconciliation of conflicting considerations.

Hereafter I will refer to the foregoing as the "reason conception" or as the notion of "law as reason" (not to be confused with that of Aquinas). Does this notion qualify as a viable working conception?

First, it is phenomenologically felicitous. Reasoned resolutions are not at all foreign to the law. Of course, this is not to say that these resolutions are always sound. Nor is it to say that reason properly rules all. Some role for fiat in the law is inevitable (as, for example, in determining the number of years required for an adverse possessor to get title).[12]

---

[12] See generally Lon L. Fuller, 'Reason and Fiat in Case Law', *Harvard Law Review* 59 (1945/6): 376–395.

Second, a reason conception is sufficiently unitary.

Third, the scope and potential bearing of the notion of law as reason is sufficient. Indeed, it may be the most wide-ranging of candidates.

Fourth, the relevance of the idea of reasoned resolution is sufficiently recurrent to qualify as a working conception. That is, it would regularly "come into play."

Fifth, the notion of law as reason is not unduly indeterminate or vague. Over a wide range of issues, the weight of reason is often heavily on one side.[13] It is also possible to define and analyse the types of substantive reasons that rationally figure in deciding and justifying court decisions (something I have attempted elsewhere).[14] These types are twofold: "goal reasons" and "rightness reasons." A goal reason derives its justificatory force from the fact that, at the time it is given, the decision it supports can be predicted to have effects that serve a good goal. (The goal may or may not have been previously recognized in the law.) A good rightness reason does not derive its justificatory force from predicted goal-serving effects of the decision it supports. Rather, it draws its force from the way in which the decision accords with a moral norm of rightness as applied to a party's actions or to a state of affairs resulting from those actions. Most rightness reasons are past-regarding – they have to do with how the case *came about.* All goal reasons are future-regarding. (Of course, a goal reason may have to do with bringing about more rightness.) Judges know how to construct and evaluate reasons of both types. Thus, "reason" is not a vague and vacuous category that frees judges to import their own personal prejudice and bias in the guise of reason. Moreover, a judge committed to a working conception in the form of a reasoned reconciliation of conflicting considerations will be opposed to deciding cases on the basis merely of personal prejudice, bias, or idiosyn-

---

13 *ibid.*

14 Robert S. Summers, 'Two Types of Substantive Reasons: The Core of a Theory of Common-Law Justification', *Cornell Law Review* 63 (1977/8): 707–788.

cratic views. It does not follow that such a judge will, by virtue of his commitment, always reach the best justified result in the case. Again, a working conception is not a guarantee.

It may forestall misunderstanding if I stress once more that a judge who rationally depends upon a working conception does not, however, ignore phenomena of the law not embodied in his conception. Thus a judge who harbors a reason conception ought to abandon its dictates if reason and the legal materials relevant to the problem turn out to counsel as much. For example, such a judge may end up applying a pre-existing rule. Just because a judge typically thinks in the first instance of law as reason it does not follow that he cannot also believe in rules or the rule of law. Similarly, a judge who harbors a rule conception may even end up overruling a precedent that he in the end thinks goes beyond the bounds of reason (e.g., the complete bar rule of *Butterfield* v. *Forrester*). It is one thing to have a working conception and another to be unduly influenced by it. A judge who is not obsessed will depart from the dictates of his working notion as circumstances demand. A working notion is only that. It is only a partial and nonbinding schematization of the law, and the methodologically selfconscious judge will treat it as such. Generally, then, two different judges, one with a reason conception and the other a rule conception, will, if not obsessed, end up deciding the same issues in the same way.

Even so, there is still much to choose between if one is considering whether it is better for a judge to hold a rule or a reason conception.

5. THE "REASON" AND THE "RULE" ALTERNATIVES: SOME COMPARISONS

Given that the notion of law as a reasoned resolution qualifies as a possible working conception, the further question arises: Is the reason alternative better than the more widely held rule notion? I will, in this section, compare these alternatives on two grounds: serviceability, and normative "side effects."

A. Comparative Serviceability

It is not possible here to compare exhaustively the efficacy of the two main alternatives. I will treat efficacy for judges, and then only in relation to what I conceive to be three primary functions of a working conception. At this exploratory stage, my conclusions can be only tentative.

One primary function of any working conception is to facilitate the identification of relevant pre-existing normative phenomena (justificatory resources) of the law. It may be that the notion of law as reason can fulfill this function better than the rule idea. It caters for *more varieties* of pre-existing law than does the rule conception. In general, reason figures prominently in the law, including the content of pre-existing rules. It follows that when a judge seeks to determine relevant forms of pre-existing law he may safely assume these to be phenomena in which reason somehow significantly figures, except when fiat necessarily holds sway, or when predecessors have simply failed to bring reason to bear at all (and this is rare). These latter two exceptional varieties of law for which a reason conception does not cater in the processes by which judges determine relevant pre-existing law must be compared with varieties for which a rules notion does not cater. These latter varieties include: (1) law governing exercises of discretion in accord with substantive criteria not reducible to rule; (2) law in the form of "equities" between the parties in the particular case – equities themselves not specifiable in rules; (3) law in the form merely of case law "holdings" with accompanying reasons (not readily reducible to rule). Even if the rule notion is one that also incorporates the reasons behind the rules, it is not at all evident that it would then cater for the foregoing important varieties of "non-rule" law. In sum, the rule notion ranges over far less of the normative phenomena of the law than the reason conception.

Moreover, I believe that the reason notion "takes hold" in a *higher proportion of the total instances* of law identification than does the rule notion. To put this another way, the proportion of instances in which the pre-existing law to be identified consists of fiat (necessarily) or of failed reason is far smaller than the proportion of instances in which pre-existing law does not consist of rules.

A second primary function of a working conception is to facilitate the sound interpretation of relevant pre-existing law once identified. Much pre-existing law requires interpretation. Yet there are basic alternative approaches to interpretation – the literal and the rationale-oriented.[15] Though I cannot go into this here, the latter is vastly superior. Thus a working conception that tends to put judges on to the rationale-oriented approach is, in my view, the more serviceable. I think the notion of law as a reasoned reconciliation of conflicting considerations does just this. It more or less naturally calls for a rationale-oriented approach, for the law itself is conceived mainly in such terms. A conception of law as rules, on the other hand, is *at best* more or less neutral as between the literal and the rationale-oriented, and a case can be made that the rule notion and the literal are far more congenial than the rule notion and the rationale-oriented. This is, I think, certainly true if the rule conception is one that does not also incorporate reasons behind the rules. And even if it does, some differences on this score may still remain.

A third primary function of a working conception is to facilitate the identification and resolution of issues calling for creation of new law. The rule conception presupposes that the law takes the form of a pre-existing rule. Thus when new legal needs arise, a judge must immediately turn away from this conception (except for such sustenance as it may provide by analogy). On the other hand, a judge who holds a reason conception will find that it, as such, stands him in good stead when new legal needs arise. It recognizes that much of the law is not "pre-existing" but must be made up in light of reason as we go along. The law is not something that simply "is the case" – a hard chunk of reality. Rather "the law" must often be argued for. Gaps in the law present themselves. Authorities come into conflict. Mistakes and misjudgments occur

---

15 There is a vast legal literature on these two approaches.

(as in the doctrine of *Butterfield* v. *Forrester*). Change brings new needs and renders old law obsolete. Interpretation itself imposes creative demands. Thus numerous issues of varying types arise for which pre-existing rules provide no, or only an inadequate, solution, and to which reason must be applied afresh. The superiority of a reason conception is evident, too, when it is recalled that frequently a sharp line cannot be drawn between pre-existing law and new law anyway. The rule conception requires that such a line be drawn.[16]

I should concede at this point that *for the ablest judges* it may be that neither alternative working conception is any more, or less, serviceable than the other in any of the foregoing three ways. These judges will be relatively less dependent on working conceptions, and may on their own readily identify relevant law, adopt preferred interpretational method, and come to grips with problems of making new law from scratch. (It may also be true that the ablest, and perhaps even the abler, judges will only rarely become obsessed with a working conception. On this, more later.)

B. "Normative" Side Effects

Pursuit of each basic alternative working idea has subtle normative implications for judges generally. The most general norm "implied" for other judges who learn that a judge is following a rule idea might be formulated: "Generally do things by well-made rule." Similarly, the norm "implied" by the reason notion would be: "Generally do things by sound reason." We may assume that the side effects of the former would include an increase in the proportion of well-formed rules within the system, and the side effects of the latter, more soundly reasoned resolutions than otherwise.

In moral and political terms, what might be the general comparative value of the two types of side effects, assuming that they

---

[16] See further Robert S. Summers, 'Professor Fuller's Jurisprudence and America's Dominant Philosophy of Law', *Harvard Law Review* 92 (1978/9): 433–449.

turn out to be roughly equivalent quantitatively? (This is a large assumption, but empirical study of relative quantity would be exceedingly difficult if not impossible.) I will begin by trying to put the case for the importance of rules as strongly as I can.

In a variety of ways it could be valuable for a given society to have more rules (and better formed ones) than it actually has.[17] Rules can restrict scope for official arbitrariness, secure that like cases (as marked out by the law) are treated alike, bring regularity and predictability, and facilitate "followability" of the law and "self-regulation."

Relatedly, rules are among the things that enable us to have confidence in officials. When citizens know that officials must follow known rules this diminishes an important source of insecurity. Citizens "know where they stand." And they also know it is at least harder for officials discriminatorily to victimize an individual under a régime of known rules, for rules apply to *all* who fall within their terms.

A requirement that officials proceed by known rule (where appropriate) may exert pressure for sound substantive content. At least demands for justification will be heard more often and with more focus under a régime of known rules than under a régime in which officials proceed *ad hoc.* Moreover, if officials address themselves only to particulars of the case at hand, they will not do as well at weeding out irrelevancy as they would if forced to formulate and follow general rules.

Further, procedural rules define features of legal processes required for the regular realization of "process values," e.g., fairness and participation.[18] Without a sufficient number of well-formed rules, this form of value realization would significantly diminish.

---

[17] For a recent book devoted in major part to this theme, see Kenneth C. Davis, *Discretionary Justice: A Preliminary Inquiry* (Urbana, Ill.: University of Illinois Press, 1971).

[18] See Robert S. Summers, 'Evaluating and Improving Legal Processes – A Plea for "Process Values",' *Cornell Law Review* 60 (1974/5): 1–52.

Rules also serve as *required* means, more or less, to substantive ends. A full articulation of how this is so would take us far afield. It is enough for my purposes to cite examples. Without known rules, a value of such importance as liberty would be far harder to secure, for rules demarcate boundaries with distinctive efficacy and thus enable citizens to plan and choose on their own within these boundaries. Without rules, the welfare state as we know it would be impossible, for it would be impossible to set up and run an effective system of taxation. Without rules, dispute settlement by adjudication (with its distinctive "process" and other values) would also be far less effective. Rules structure adjudicative processes to provide fair participation, and also establish standards for defining the issues and determining what is relevant.

Corporations, trusts, and other "legal inventions" are creatures of rules and thus could not exist without them. Indeed, centralized government itself would probably be impossible in a complex society without rules defining roles in the required division of legal labor. This is not only because in a sizeable society any such division must be elaborate and complex. It is also because the officialdom could not command legitimacy, for there would simply be no sufficiently *defined* governmental *set-up* to serve as the *object* of this legitimacy.

Rules also distinctively facilitate private ordering of affairs without official intervention. They can guide and induce private parties not to interfere with others, and enable private parties to coordinate their activities. Without firm and known rules, there would be far more interference with each other's plans, and far less effective social coordination. Elemental rules of the criminal law and basic rules of the road are aptly illustrative.

In sum, rules can help bring many values to social life. Resort to them is to be encouraged, as appropriate. When judges harbor and publicly act upon a working conception of law as pre-existing rule, they presumably encourage each other generally to resort to rules – and doubtless we end up with more (and presumably better formed) rules than we otherwise would have.

What of sound reason in matters legal? Well-formed rules may even be evil in content. And sound content is widely called for in the law, not just in those provinces governable by rules. Except when reason peters out and fiat is necessarily called for, soundly reasoned content is always possible in law, too. Yet in a significant proportion of cases the content of American law, at least, is not sound. The "rule" of *Butterfield* v. *Forrester* that contributory negligence of a plaintiff is a complete bar to any recovery, though extreme, is only one of many examples (though it is now being overhauled).

If more judges were to adopt and publicly act upon a working conception of the law as a reasoned reconciliation of conflicting considerations, what would be the likely side effects? The corollary norm for legal actors that this behavioral shift would "imply" is: "Generally do things by sound reason." The side effects of thus promoting this norm would presumably include more soundly reasoned content than would otherwise exist.

It is not to me evident that the normative side effects of a working notion of law as reason would necessarily be less important to individuals and society than the normative side effects of a law as rules notion. Indeed, some theorists have even argued that a *system* of law would not be possible without a certain "minimal" core of soundly reasoned content.[19] To the extent that the normative side effects of a reason conception contribute to maintenance of this core of content, such effects would be of the most profound significance.

Rule proponents might argue that officials simply need more encouragement to make rules than they do to act by reason. Hence the likely normative side effects of following a rule conception are of greater value, and the case for this notion correspondingly stronger. Doubtless officials have often failed to make rules when they could and should have. But substantive content contrary to reason has been all too familiar in law, too. Indeed, in this century, as never before, laws of the most heinous kind have been operative within some societies for extended periods. Of

[19] See H. L. A. Hart, *The Concept of Law*, chapter 9.

course, pre-existing levels could make a difference. A particular society might, for example, be greatly deficient in rules. In that event, the normative side effects of adopting and publicly acting upon a rule conception would be all the more desirable, for a time.

Thus far in this exploratory venture, I tentatively conclude: (1) that in terms of their comparative efficacy in serving the primary functions of a working conception, there is more to be said for "the law as reason" than for "the law as rules"; and (2) that in terms of the comparative value of their likely normative side effects, any claim that the rule conception has an edge is at best inconclusive.

6. THE "REASON" AND THE "RULE" ALTERNATIVES: CONSEQUENCES WHEN OFFICIALS BECOME PREOCCUPIED

Judges not merely hold and act on working notions of law in desirable ways; they also become obsessed with them, and this factor contributes to unwise decisions. It may be that one of the two basic alternatives is preferable on the ground that general preoccupation with it has less objectionable consequences. To map out such likely consequences would be no simple task. What I offer here must also be less ambitious.[20]

I will first review how judicial obsession may show itself in particular cases, and identify its main causes. A judge obsessed with a working conception will not abandon it when that is the wise course, but a judge who is not obsessed will readily turn to other phenomena of the law, as appropriate. For example, a judge preoccupied with a working notion of the law as pre-existing rule will be more inclined to tolerate even an exceedingly harsh rule (*Butterfield* v. *Forrester*) than he will be to overrule or modify that rule. This judge will also be less inclined to recognize a

---

[20] It might be that one of the two alternatives is preferable on the ground that those who hold it will simply be less likely to become obsessed with it in the first place. I cannot go into this here.

genuine case of first impression for what it is and instead will tend to cling even to a remote pre-existing rule "by analogy." Such a judge will want to "distinguish" conflicting precedent rather than confront the real choice at hand. Similarly, he will be disinclined to create exceptions (for this will not appear "law-like"). Further, a judge preoccupied merely with the idea that law consists of pre-existing rules will, in my view, be more likely to read statutes and case-law precepts literally rather than in light of their rationales, for he will think of the latter as somehow unfaithful to the wording of the real law. And our obsessed judge will be inclined to read case-law precepts and even statutes governing private consensual arrangements as if they always ousted general equitable principles that come into play in the particular case.

Similarly, a judge may become obsessed with a conception of law as the reasoned reconciliation of conflicting considerations. This might lead him, for example, to refuse to give a pre-existing rule its appropriate due, or to make new law without sufficient regard to how it harmonizes with existing law.

The foregoing examples are not exhaustive, but in each the judge fails to see that a working conception, however useful generally, has limits of its own. For a working notion of law is only a "partial" schematization of the law's justificatory resources that may have rational bearing. Thus there is more to phenomena of the law than rules: equities in the particular case, appropriate discretionary judgment, general ideas of justice and the common good, reason as such, and more. Moreover, pre-existing rules may simply not apply, and are thus limited in this way, too. Yet in relevant instances of prejudicial preoccupation, the judge "plays by the conception" – sticks to the idea of a pre-existing rule – even when that is quite inappropriate because the particular rule is inapplicable, or other facets of "the law" come into play (or both of these).

At the same time, there is also more to phenomena of the law than the reasoned reconciliation of conflicting considerations. Thus there are rules (with the reasons for them). There is even fiat. And more.

Why do some judges become obsessed with their working notions of law? First, if a given notion generally stands judges in good stead, this may lead them to over-use it. In such instances, judges fail to recognize that the conception, like any such idea, has its limits. Second, a few judges may mechanically substitute their working conception for close analysis of particulars. It thus becomes a crutch, and an anodyne for the pains of reasoning. Third, the *normative* influences of an adopted working conception may be direct, too, and not confined merely to side effects. That is, some judges may unconsciously take the conception directly as a standard for what "the law" always *ought* to be, e.g., a pre-existing rule, or some ideal of reason. Fourth, the working conception a judge has may lead him to lapse into a more or less habitual predisposition that influences his decisions without rising to the level of a normative influence.

Let us turn, then, to what a legal system as a whole would presumably look like if it were to go awry and if this were attributable to widespread preoccupation with one or the other of the two basic alternatives. I will take up the probable state of affairs under a pre-existing rule conception first. Again, I offer rationalistic speculation:

(1) "The law" would generally be "nailed down" in rules in advance, even when discretion or other forms of open-endedness would be more appropriate. This would bring more predictability and equality before the law.

(2) The general quality of the substantive content of the rules would decline, for predictability of outcomes under rules would be the primary qualitative concern. It would generally be thought more important to have predictable outcomes than to have rules otherwise good. Also, there would be a tendency to think that more issues are truly matters of fiat than would be so under a régime of "reason legality."

(3) There would be general unresponsiveness to desires for changes in existing rules, and the burden of proof would be heavily on advocates for change. As a result the rules would change relatively little, even when initially bad or later quite outmoded.

(4) Only in the most obvious cases would pre-existing common law rules be superseded by "equities arising in the particular circumstances," and such equities would almost never displace explicit statutory language, even when it deals with private consensual arrangements.

(5) Except for issues plainly political or ideological, few more or less wholly *new* rules would be introduced. Thus it would be widely assumed that novel cases of first impression and new statutory needs are rare. (After all, it would be thought in the very nature of law that it is something that pre-exists.)

(6) At least those judges who leave the reasons for the rules out of their working conceptions would generally interpret and apply law in accord with "plain meaning" and other literal methods rather than in accord with rationale-oriented methods, for it would be assumed that only the former are faithful to the true rules (especially their wording).

The foregoing might be called an "excess of rule legality." There might even today be legal systems that approximate the one I have sketched. And widespread preoccupation with a working idea of "the law" as pre-existing rule may significantly account for such a system.

What might a legal system look like that has gone seriously awry in circumstances in which this is significantly attributable to widespread preoccupation with a notion of the law as a reasoned reconciliation of conflicting considerations? My account here must be even more speculative, for, to my knowledge, nothing approximating such a system has existed, at least not in recent times. We do, however, know what it is like for a particular judge to be obsessed with a reason conception, and it is possible to extrapolate from this. In offering the account below of an "excess of reason legality," I will be *striving* evenhandedly to characterize an opposite polarity that is roughly the same "distance from mid point" as the polarity of excessive rule legality I have already characterized.

(1) Formulations of "the law" in terms of rules would generally be left to the future, "for then we would know more." Hence, less law would be "nailed down" in advance of specific occasions

for applying it, inasmuch as there would be a general desire to leave scope for the free play of reason, and what is rationally relevant (as well as its force) can be fully determined only in light of the details of actual cases as they arise.

(2) The quality of the substantive content of rules and other forms of law would be the primary concern in lawmaking, and predictability of outcome secondary. Thus, the general quality of the content of law would improve, but there would be some loss of predictability, and of evenhandedness.

(3) The existing law would tend to change more with mere changes in personnel. For example, new judges would stand ready to remake the law even though their notions of reason might not differ much from those of predecessors. Predictability would decline, and costly resources would be expended as well. Also, there would be losses in terms of evenhandedness – of equality before the law.

(4) There would be ready responsiveness to demands for changes in the law, especially demands rooted in new developments requiring that new ideas of reason be brought to bear. This, too, would generate some loss of predictability and would likewise entail investment of more resources in lawmaking. It would diminish official evenhandedness over time, too.

(5) In the application of law, any significant equities between the parties arising in the particular case would triumph over pre-existing rule far more often than under a régime of rule legality.

(6) Rationale-oriented modes of interpretation would generally be brought to bear when applying the law, and in the guise of these, judges and others would also sometimes bring in their own merely personal notions of reason to interpret the law.

The foregoing excesses of "reason legality" are (in my view) the main risks of widespread preoccupation with a working notion of law as the reasoned reconciliation of conflicting considerations. Are these *more serious* than the corresponding risks of widespread preoccupation with a working notion of law as pre-existing rules? I cannot here consider this issue at length. The biggest losses under the "régime of reason" appear to be losses in predictability, in evenhandedness, in excessive diversion of resources into lawmaking activities, and in, perhaps, undue substitution by some judges of their own merely personal notions of reason. These strike me as, on the whole, less serious than the widespread losses likely over time under a "régime of rules," in terms of quality of substantive content.

I, for one, would rather live under a régime run by officials obsessed with reason than under a régime run by officials obsessed with rules. Of course, we need not choose between such extremes. I merely suggest that if called upon to live under one or the other, the reason régime seems less objectionable. The same would be true, *mutatis mutandis*, even if, as is far more likely, the society involved falls somewhere between the two extremes. Thus it will not do to say that if *some* preoccupation with a working conception is inevitable, it is better that this be with a rule rather than a reason conception. Again, the starting point could, however, make a difference. A particular society might be greatly deficient in rules, for example. In that event, widespread resort to a rule conception might be more desirable (for a time), even with the excesses of rule legality that the inevitable preoccupations of some judges would bring.

Given that many judges appear to hold a rule conception of "the law," and given that some more or less inevitably become obsessed with the law as pre-existing rule, this factor may well be one important explanation for the refusal of the court in *Maki* v. *Frelk* to overrule the harshest doctrine of the common law. In any event, it is almost certain that preoccupation with a reason conception would not have led the judges to their decision.

7. CONCLUSION

After hundreds of years in which a working conception of law as pre-existing rule seems to have held sway, might it not be time for judges generally to try reason as an alternative – for a few years anyway? In my view, the serviceability of this alternative as a working conception is superior. Also, the argument for a rule conception based on allegedly preferable normative effects is at best inconclusive. Further, I believe the consequences of any obsession with a reason conception would generally be less untoward.

But working conceptions are not like hats of the wrong fit. They have to be unlearned, not merely removed. This kind of learning runs deep and becomes second nature. After a while, it may not be unlearnable without resort to methods that would not be acceptable. Thus the change I propose, even if desirable, is probably long off.

Cornell Law School

J. L. MACKIE

RULES AND REASON

1.

It is somewhat embarrassing to have to reply to Professor Summers' very interesting and challenging paper, for I have a great deal of sympathy with his line of thought. However, I think there is room for some further clarification of his suggestions, and perhaps for some reconsideration too.

Summers seems to be putting forward the following four theses:

(1) What he explains a working conception of the law to be is a pragmatic necessity for most judges.

(2) Such a conception is necessarily incomplete, and therefore should be used rationally; judges should not become obsessed with it.

(3) Among working conceptions used rationally, that of 'reasoned reconciliation of conflicting considerations' is better than that of 'pre-existing rules'.

(4) If judges are going to become obsessed with their working conception, it is better to be obsessed with 'reasoned reconciliation' than with 'pre-existing rules'.

However, in the course of his third Section Summers notes a complication: the conception of pre-existing rules may 'incorporate the reason or reasons for the rules'. But he seems to be saying, in theses 3 and 4, that the 'reasoned reconciliation' conception is superior even to that of 'pre-existing rules with reasons'.

2.

To illustrate his theses, Summers uses the case of *Butterfield* v. *Forrester* and the rule drawn from it, that a plaintiff's contributory negligence is a complete bar to his recovering any compensation

M. A. Stewart (ed.), Law, Morality and Rights, 31–42.

from a defendant whose negligence also contributed to the plaintiff's loss. I want to discuss this example, and his use of it, before considering Summers' theses in a more general way.

First, as Professor Hart and Professor Honoré have made very plain,[1] there are many different ways in which causes (whether they are negligent acts or omissions or anything else) may loosely be said to contribute to the bringing about of some result, so that it is not likely that any rule so simple as that contributory negligence is a complete bar to compensation would be appropriate in every kind of case. Secondly, it is clear from the opinions of the judges in *Butterfield* v. *Forrester*, which Summers quotes, that they construed the situation as one in which, although the defendant had wrongfully obstructed part of the road, it was the plaintiff's own riding without ordinary care that caused the accident, which therefore happened 'entirely from his own fault'. It is also clear from the reported evidence that this is at least a possible way of interpreting the causal situation in that particular case. The decision in that case, therefore, gives no justification for the development from it of the 'complete bar' rule for all cases of contributory negligence, where the causal situation may well be of some very different form. Summers himself suggests that it was 'not without some license' that the rule was extracted from this precedent. Thirdly, therefore, the moral that should be drawn from this example is not that there is anything wrong with a rule conception of the law, but rather that precedents which in themselves are quite good should not be misused, that care should be taken in deriving rules from them, and that very simple rules should be regarded with some suspicion. But, fourthly, as Summers recognizes, this rule has by now been abandoned, in one way or another, in many of the jurisdictions where it was formerly accepted. Is it not, then, prejudicial and unfair of him to use as his one example a bad, excessively simple, old, and largely abandoned

---

[1] H. L. A. Hart and A. M. Honoré, *Causation in the Law* (Oxford: Clarendon Press, 1959), chapter 8.

rule to show the demerits of a rule conception of the law in general?

3.

I turn now to Summers' main theses. I find some obscurity in his notion of the working conception which most judges will need. Is it a conception of the legal system as a whole, or a conception of the job of a court of law? Much of what he says suggests that what he has in mind is a conception of the law as a whole; but to speak of pre-existing rules, as he does with one of his conceptions, is to look at things from the point of view of a particular court: it is to think of rules which exist already before *this* court works on *this* case. This distinction matters little, perhaps, where the pre-existing rules view is concerned. For if one has a conception of the law as a whole as a system of rules which change relatively seldom, or only slowly, then one will naturally also see the job of a court as being nearly always to discover the relevant pre-existing rule and apply it. But our distinction matters much more when the reasoned reconciliation conception is under discussion. For it is one thing to see the law as a whole as being largely concerned with the reasoned reconciliation of conflicting considerations, but quite another thing to see this as the best description of the job of each court in each particular case. It might well be held that the legal system as a whole, including legislative procedures, aims at the reasoned reconciliation of conflicting considerations and to some extent achieves this, but that the way in which it achieves it is by developing rules and, where it becomes necessary, changing these either through legislation or through decisions of the highest courts of appeal, so that the job of most courts in most cases is simply to find the appropriate pre-existing rule and apply it. What this means is that if we are thinking of working conceptions of the law as a whole, the two that Summers contrasts, that of reasoned reconciliation and that of rules, are not in conflict with one another and are hardly even alternatives, since these two notions can go very neatly together as parts of a single working conception.

They are rivals only if we are thinking of conceptions of the job of each particular court in each particular case, so that the reasoned reconciliation of considerations, if this notion is employed, is seen as coming directly into the work of ordinary courts, and is not regarded as being admittedly the overall function of the legal system, but something that is adequately looked after elsewhere, so that particular courts contribute to it indirectly, without trying to achieve it explicitly and directly.

4.

Remembering that a working conception, as Summers explains it, is a very much oversimplified picture, I am not persuaded of the correctness of what I have called his first thesis, that a working conception of the law is a pragmatic necessity for most judges, *if he means a conception of the legal system as a whole.* Summers gives in his third Section a short list of recurrent phenomena of the law. Is there any reason why all judges should not be aware of all these recurrent phenomena, and indeed of a considerably expanded description of each of the items on this highly-condensed list? I am sure that Summers has a much better knowledge than I have of the typical range of judicial intelligence, but I find it hard to believe that even a judge who came near the bottom of that range could not understand that all these recurrent phenomena play a part in the legal system as a whole. If so, why would he also need a much simplified picture which left out many of these and brought only one or two of them into focus? Surely what he may need a working conception of is, rather, his own work.

5.

From Section 3, therefore, I conclude that the conflict of conceptions with which Summers is most concerned arises only if these are conceptions of the job of each particular court in each particular case, and from Section 4 I conclude that it is only of this matter that judges need a working conception. So a charitable interpretation, which would make the best sense in both these respects of what Summers says, is that what he is speaking of is working conceptions of the job of each particular court and hence of the judge's own work. However, this interpretation is too charitable to fit the text. For example, when Summers says in his fourth Section that 'the scope and potential bearing of the notion of law as reason is sufficient. Indeed, it may be the most wide-ranging of candidates', he must be thinking of this as a conception of the law as a whole, not of the judge's work, and the same is true of his remarks under the heading 'Comparative Serviceability'. In fact, his different arguments seem to me to require different interpretations: sometimes that the working conception should be simply of the job of each particular court or judge, sometimes that it should be of the law as a whole. So I hope that he will tell us which of the two he really intends, and then, how he meets the difficulties which seem to me to tell against this interpretation. If he opts for the law as a whole, then the conflict with the rules view is spurious, and most judges do *not* need such a working conception. But if he opts for the job of each particular court, then he cannot support the reason conception on the grounds of its range and scope. However, let me leave this problem of interpretation and discuss other questions as well as I can despite this uncertainty.

6.

On comparative serviceability, Summers makes three points in favour of reason as against rules: the first, that much of the pre-existing law does not consist of rules; the second, that pre-existing law requires interpretation, and the reason view will encourage a 'rationale-oriented' approach whereas the rule view will be at best neutral between this and the (inferior) literal approach; the third, that often there is no relevant pre-existing law, that the law 'must be made up in light of reason as we go along'.

The second of these points is easily disposed of. I would agree in favouring a rationale-oriented method of interpretation. But if the rule conception in question is, as Summers allows that it may be, that of rules with reasons, then this is clearly not neutral between the two approaches to interpretation, but favours the rationale-oriented one just as much as does the reason conception.

The other two points seem incompatible with one another. Once we recognize that pre-existing law need not consist wholly of rules, we shall be much less willing to admit that there are many cases where there is no relevant pre-existing law. I would refer here to the view of Professor Ronald Dworkin, that the law should be seen as a body of principles rather than of rules. From this assumption Dworkin draws the conclusion that in any reasonably rich and well-developed system of law, like that of England or that of the United States, there will in practically every case be a 'right answer', an already determinate and in principle discoverable correct decision, even though this may be controversial, not 'settled'. Now I have my own reason for questioning Dworkin's view, which I have stated elsewhere.[2] But the possibility of such a view seriously undermines Summers' attempt to use *both* his first *and* his third points together against the rules conception.

What is more serious is that something like Dworkin's view would provide another competitor for the rôle of a working conception, different both from the reason view and from the rules view. It differs from the reason view because it sees the law as almost wholly pre-existing: it presents the judge's task as always being that of finding what the law already requires, or which of the two parties has, in advance, a right to a decision in his favour. It differs also, though this is a subtler and indeed controversial point, in severely restricting the scope of what Summers calls 'goal reasons' (in particular appeals to utilitarian considerations of the general interest). But Dworkin's view also differs from the rules view just in so far as principles differ from rules: they are more flexible and often more general; reasoning in terms of principles allows parts of the law remote from that with which the present case is concerned to have some bearing upon it; and they therefore

---

[2] See J. L. Mackie, 'The Third Theory of Law', *Philosophy and Public Affairs* 7 (1977/8): 3–16.

provide a reserve of relevant material that will help to answer a question which is not answered, or not satisfactorily answered, by any directly relevant rule. The grounds on which Summers dismisses several other alternative working conceptions will plainly not suffice to eliminate the 'principles' or 'rights' view as Dworkin explains it, and while this third candidate is in the field we could not take whatever defects the rule view may have as grounds for recommending the reason conception as an alternative to it.

7.

What Summers classifies as '"Normative" Side Effects' seem to me to call for a grander description. Indeed his subordinating of these considerations to what he calls 'Comparative Serviceability' puts the cart before the horse. Prior to the question 'What working conception will be best for the judges to have?' is the question 'What sort of a legal system do we want to have? Do we want one in which particular courts mainly apply pre-existing rules, or one in which they work out the consequences of a body of pre-existing principles, or one in which they frequently aim explicitly at a reasoned reconciliation of conflicting considerations, not all of which are previously incorporated in the law?' What Summers downgrades into normative side effects are essentially the relevant features of these contrasting sorts of legal systems. When the question of what sort of legal system we want to have is thus explicitly raised, the points which Summers correctly sets out in favour of rules remain very much in force. These are good reasons for preferring a system in which there are clearly recognized rules and in which courts proceed mainly by applying them. The points Summers makes under this heading are plainly right and I hope well known, so I shall not repeat them. But has he a case also for the opposing side? One argument he uses is that some existing rules are bad: but that is an argument for changing the bad rules, by legislation or perhaps by decision of the highest courts, not for reducing the extent to which the law consists of rules. And ironically the one explicit example he gives of a bad rule is, as he admits, now being overhauled. Otherwise, all that he says here in favour of the reason view is that law needs a core of soundly reasoned content, and that there would presumably be more soundly reasoned content if judges were to shift to the reason conception. But this is a *non sequitur* made plausible only by Summers' failure to use the distinction on which I insisted earlier between the law as a whole and the job of each particular court. It is not even *prima facie* plausible to suppose that the best way to get reasoned content into the law as a whole is to encourage particular courts to work mainly by explicitly trying to reconcile conflicting considerations for themselves. It seems to me, therefore, that on what is really the prior question, whether we want the law to consist largely of fairly stable rules or largely of *ad hoc* reasoned reconciliations by particular courts, the arguments so far presented strongly favour the former. There is, I believe, more of a case for Dworkin's proposal that the law should operate rather as a body of principles, though as between this and the rules view the considerations on either side are more evenly balanced. Let me quote what I have said elsewhere about this:

> This is why I am tempted to speak of Professor Dworkin playing fast and loose with the law.[3] The alleged determinacy of the law in hard cases is a myth, and the practical effect of the acceptance of this myth would be to give, in three ways, a larger scope for what is in reality judicial legislation. First, it would shift the boundary between the settled and the unsettled law, it would make what on another view would be easy cases into hard ones. Secondly, this approach would encourage a holistic treatment of the law, letting very general principles and remote parts of the law bear upon each specific issue. Thirdly, it would encourage judges, in this holistic treatment, to rely upon their necessarily subjective views about a supposedly objective morality.
>
> The third theory of law is thus a plea for a more speculative and enterprising handling by judges of their traditional materials and data. Like the natural law doctrine, this theory allows the consciences and the speculations of judges to intervene more significantly between what the legislative and

---

[3] Cf. *Oxford English Dictionary*: 'Fast and loose: A cheating game played with a stick and a belt or string, so arranged that a spectator would think he could make the latter fast by placing a stick through its intricate folds, whereas the operator could detach it at once.'

executive branches try to do – or, for whatever reason, leave undone – and the law as it actually operates. We know well that people's prejudices, training, and social position – the movements in which they are caught up and the ideologies linked with these – strongly influence their consciences and their speculations. Whether we consider this a merit or a demerit depends upon our judgment of the judges, and particularly upon comparative judgments we make between them, the legislators, and the holders of executive office. Which of these three, with their characteristic methods and the influences to which they are exposed or from which they are sheltered, are the more to be trusted with the opportunity for partly independent decision in the making and remaking of the law? Should we give up some certainty and determinacy about what the law is, and some freedom for legislators to decide what it shall be, in order to give greater weight to what judges will see as people's rights or just claims? I do not know what answer to give, but I want it to be clear that this is the choice.[4]

8.

There is little that I would want to add to or correct in what Summers says in his sixth Section about what is likely to go wrong if judges become obsessed with one or other of the conceptions he is considering. But he still seems to be ascribing to the rules conception in general features which it would not have in the 'rules with reasons' form. Even a judge who is 'preoccupied' with the notion that the law consists of rules along with the reasons for those rules is not likely to read statutes and case-law precepts literally, and the phrase 'at least' should be deleted from Summers' supposition that 'At least those judges who leave the reasons for the rules out of their working conceptions would generally interpret and apply law in accord with "plain meaning" and other literal methods.' The consequence he fears is probable *only* if judges leave out the reasons for the rules. But of course it would be better to ensure, as far as possible, that judges do not become obsessed with any working conception, than to speculate about

---

[4] 'The Third Theory of Law', pp. 15–16. Copyright © 1977 by Princeton University Press; reprinted by permission. Note 3 above is a part of the original quotation.

which conception, if they do become obsessed with it, will do less harm.

9.

I am afraid that much of what I have said is merely negative or destructive criticism, though it is in part a plea for further clarification. In conclusion, let me say something a bit more constructive.

I suggest that we should see the legal system as a whole as having the function of protecting and reconciling rights – primarily the rights of individuals, but derivatively also of corporate bodies or institutions. This is not exclusively the function of the law, for it is also the function of a large part of morality (what I have called elsewhere[5] 'morality in the narrow sense'). But the law contributes in a distinctive way to the fulfilling of this function. But what are these rights and where do they come from? I suggest that we need a distinction between basic rights and derived or resultant rights. Let us think of persons as having a fundamental right to make what they can of their lives, and hence progressively to choose how they shall live – by 'progressively' I mean in an indefinite sequence of choices throughout their lives, not just once and for all – that is, something like Jefferson's rights to life, liberty, and the pursuit of happiness. But this fundamental right is, of course, very vague, and also one person's exercise of such a right will often conflict with another's. So we must think of them only as *prima facie* rights, which will need to be specified and made determinate and also adjusted to and reconciled with the potentially conflicting rights of others. Such determination and reconciliation is necessarily a historical process, that takes place in general quite gradually, by the introduction of both moral and legal norms, by interplay between these, and by changes in both through pressure of changes either in socio-economic conditions or in ideas, as well as through explicit legislation. So the determinate,

---

[5] Cf. *Ethics: Inventing Right and Wrong* (Harmondsworth: Penguin Books, 1977), pp. 106 ff.

resultant rights that people have at any time are partly determined by the positive law that is then in force; nevertheless, this positive law is in principle open to moral criticism, ultimately in terms of the question whether it does not achieve a reasonable reconciliation of what I have called the fundamental *prima facie* rights of all persons. However, since the opportunity progressively to choose how one shall live presupposes a fairly stable background of expectations in relation to which long-term choices can be made, such criticism, if it takes account of all the relevant considerations based on fundamental rights, will seldom justify very rapid changes in the main structure of a society or its legal system: there is always a presumption in favour of stability or only gradual change.

With these background assumptions, we can see the merits of both the working conceptions which Summers has stressed and contrasted. The overall working of the legal system is indeed concerned with the reasoned reconciliation of conflicting considerations, namely people's fundamental *prima facie* rights, but the need for a historical determination of resultant rights and with it the need for a fairly stable and knowable background in relation to which choices, including long-term choices, can be made, entail that the law at any time should consist largely of rules which, from the point of view of any particular court considering a particular case, already exist and need merely to be discovered, applied, and enforced.

However, let us bring in here the distinction that Dworkin stresses between the settled law and 'hard cases'. Most cases will be decided by the settled law, and in them decisions can well be seen as consequences of pre-existing rules. But there will also be some hard or controversial cases, cases where learned, intelligent, and reasonable judges may well disagree about what the law requires. These may be of several kinds: first, cases of first impression; secondly, cases where conditions and circumstances have changed so greatly that it is doubtful whether an old law still applies to them; thirdly, cases where relevant precedents or statutes seem to conflict with one another; and fourthly, cases where what seems to be the settled law is blatantly unjust, or radically at variance with principles well established elsewhere in the law, or very much against the public interest. We might suggest that the appropriate way of dealing with hard cases of the first three kinds is essentially that which Dworkin recommends, appeal to and reliance on principles to be found elsewhere in the legal system. There may be more dispute about the best way of dealing with hard cases of the fourth kind. Here it seems that a change in the so-far settled law is called for, but the crucial question is what body or institution should perform this legislative task – courts of law in general, or some small number of the highest courts of appeal, or Parliament (Congress, etc.), aided perhaps by expert commissions charged with thorough consideration of proposed changes in the law? As I have said, this is a highly controversial question, and I would not attempt to settle it out of hand.

I suggest that this is a very rough outline of what we want a legal system to be like. In itself, this will not produce a just society, but it will go some way towards maintaining a decent society, and it may be most appropriate to ensure, as far as possible, that we achieve and go on achieving this more modest goal. (I owe this thought, that we should aim first at the attainable goal of a decent society rather than simply at a just one, to Avishai Margalit.) Now, assuming that this is the function and very general structure of the sort of legal system we want to have, we may come back to the question of a working conception of the law: I see no reason why judges should not have something like this overall view of the legal system, and see the work of their own courts, at whatever level they operate, as contributing to a system of this sort. What more do they need of a working conception than this?

University College Oxford

TONY HONORÉ

THE ROLE OF THE JUDGE

1.

Mackie summarizes Summers' theses in four points which can be used as a starting point for discussion:

(1) A working conception of the law, as explained by Summers, is a pragmatic necessity for most judges.

(2) Such a conception is necessarily incomplete, and therefore should be used rationally; judges should not become obsessed by it.

(3) Among working conceptions used rationally, that of 'reasoned reconciliation of conflicting considerations' is better than that of 'pre-existing rules'.

(4) If judges are going to become obsessed with their working conception, it is better to be obsessed with 'reasoned reconciliation' than with 'pre-existing rules'. However, the conception of pre-existing rules may 'incorporate the reason or reasons for the rules'.

A subsidiary theme is that the interpretation by the Illinois court in *Maki* v. *Frelk* in 1968 of the contributory negligence rule laid down in 1809 in *Butterfield* v. *Forrester* is a good example of a mistake made by a court which adopted the pre-existing rule approach to its rôle.

Mackie disagrees with or challenges the Summers theses in a number of respects:

(1) He says that Summers is not consistent in his conception of what the judge's working conception is a conception of. Is it, as the phrase 'working conceptions of "the law"' would suggest, a conception of the legal system as a whole, of what that system is trying to achieve, or is it a conception of the judge's rôle in trying a given case? Summers oscillates, he thinks, between the two.

M. A. Stewart (ed.), Law, Morality and Rights, 43–50.

(2) If the former, Mackie doubts whether a working conception (of the legal system as a whole) is a pragmatic necessity for most judges, but he concedes that it is as regards the judge's own rôle in a given case.

(3) Taking the object of the working conception to be the judge's own rôle, Mackie prefers the rule-applying conception on the score of comparative serviceability, but points out that there is a third competitor in the field – the Dworkinian idea of the judge as giving effect to rights derived from pre-existing principles in accordance with a procedure which requires an overall, holistic view of the political system of the society in question.

(4) On the question of 'normative side effects', i.e. whether the rule-applying approach or the reasoned-reconciliation approach will lead to a better society, Mackie holds that there are good reasons (of a well-known sort) for preferring a system in which there are clearly recognized rules and in which courts proceed mainly by applying them, while Summers concludes that in this respect 'any claim that the rule conception has an edge is at best inconclusive'. Both agree that judges should not become preoccupied to the point of obsession with their chosen working conception.

(5) Finally Mackie returns to the question of what conception we should have of the legal system as a whole and argues that we (including, presumably, the judge) should think of it as having the function of progressively protecting and reconciling rights. The basic right to be protected is the right of everyone to make what they can of their lives. Morals, law and other social processes refine this over a long period and reconcile one person's right with another's. But Mackie does not think, as noted above, that this or any other conception of the legal system as a whole is a pragmatic necessity for the judge trying a given case.

Despite the points of dissent, Mackie professes to have a great deal of sympathy with Summers' line of thought. It is not altogether clear what part of Summers' paper (except for the obsession point) he agrees with. But there are some common assumptions in the papers. Instead of dealing directly with the points of conflict between Summers and Mackie, I should like to say a little by way of introduction about two assumptions which I think they share and which I believe to be mistaken, and then about two further assumptions, also in my view mistaken, which they make separately.

2.

Summers and Mackie discuss the merits of the alternative approaches to the judge's conception of his own rôle on two assumptions which I believe to be mistaken: (i) that the judge is free to choose his rôle for himself, and (ii) that the rôle is the same in all areas of jurisdiction. The judge is treated in their papers as if he were a free agent, allowed to decide for himself how to go about his job. But is this correct? Is not the position rather that the proper working conception for a judge is a matter of the job specification? What is a judge employed or appointed to do? That must depend on his terms of appointment. What jurisdiction is he given? How is he to exercise it? What principles bind him in the exercise of his functions? The answers to these questions have to be drawn from statutes, conventions, decisions and practices which bear on the point to be decided. The judge has to decide these before he decides anything else. The answer clearly varies according to the society in which he is a judge, its relative sophistication and the expectations of its members. In modern industrial societies a judge administering the civil law (from which Summers' example is drawn) is appointed to do justice according to law, i.e. to hand down a reasonable solution, if he can, which is consistent with rules which bind him. These rules and principles are taken to be pre-existing, at least in most instances, and the doing of justice is subordinated, at least in this sort of society and this area, to respect for existing rules. If anyone is inclined to dispute this, let him consider whether he himself would be willing to pay taxes in order that, in disputes affecting his civil rights, e.g. the tenure of his employment or the mortgage on his house, an official should reach a decision by a reconciliation of conflicting interests contrary to accepted rules. If, as a professor, my contract of employment gives me tenure until the age of 67, and my university wishes to dismiss me before that age, I want the judge who hears my case to apply the terms of the contract and not to reconcile them with the national interest, which may call for early retirement, or with the interests of my discipline, which require a younger man to take my chair, or the interests of my university, which call for the money invested in my field to be redeployed into molecular science. These national, cultural and institutional interests ought indeed to be taken into account by and reconciled by someone (the government, the Department of Education, the UGC, the Vice Chancellor), but not by judges. For a judge is appointed and expected, at least in this society and this area of civil law, to do a specialized rule-applying job and not to conduct a far-ranging inquiry into competing interests.

The job of a doctor is a parallel. A doctor is employed to cure his patient. If he were to conceive his rôle as that of taking into account the conflicting considerations bearing on the health of the patient, the pressure of population, the proportion of elderly people in the society in question, the social utility of the patient and the burden which he presents to his family and friends, and in the light of that to reach a decision for or against curing, his profession would be a very different one, and people would be much less inclined to appoint, pay and trust him. So with a judge. But there are three qualifications to be made.

(i) The job specification varies from area to area of jurisdiction. In sentencing, for example, the job consists in fixing a sentence which takes account of all the relevant social and moral considerations and is rule-guided only to the extent that an informal tariff operates. When a judge has to fix a sentence, therefore, it would be correct to suggest that the approach 'What is a reasonable reconciliation of competing interests?' is the correct and (in this context) virtually the exclusive one; though even here, there will in the end be the question which he should put to himself, 'Is my conclusion – a fine of a hundred pounds – very much out of line with the general practice in a case of this type?'. There are intermediate types of cases. A case on the adjustment of matrimonial property rights on divorce falls somewhere between one on contract law and one on sentencing, the weight to be given to the rules of property law on the one hand and the various considerations of fairness between the parties, interests of the children, social considerations etc. on the other, being about equal.

(ii) Even if the job specification enjoins a rule-applying rôle, there will be instances in which the judge is entitled to and, in some instances, has a duty to change the rules or make an exception to them. I shall say a word about this in a moment.

(iii) Even if the job specification enjoins a rule-applying rôle on the judge, he is entitled, as a dialectical method, to begin by asking himself 'What result would I regard as reasonable on the facts of this case?', and then to go on to the question 'Do the existing rules permit me to reach this reasonable conclusion?'. Other judges, of course, will prefer to put the questions in the opposite order. They will begin with the question 'What conclusions do the rules enjoin on these facts?' and then go on to 'Is there any need to depart from or change the rules in this instance?'.

But, supposing that the first dialectical procedure is adopted, the judge is none the less playing a rule-applying rôle. His feeling for what would be a reasonable result will often be largely, if perhaps unconsciously, rule-governed. But in any case his decision will either be determined by the rules, or fall within a limited area of freedom to depart from them. I have the impression that part of what Summers is trying to do is to describe this difference in dialectical approach between different types of judge with differing temperaments.

3.

If I am right in thinking that the proper rôle of the judge is a function of the expectations of the society in which he lives and the terms, express or implied, of his appointment, then it seems to me that Summers must be wrong in thinking that he can leave on one side, in discussing the Illinois decision, the constitutional question whether the supreme court of that state had the power to change a long-standing course of precedent or, on the contrary, were bound to leave the matter to the legislature. Since the Florida and California courts have taken a different view, while England and some other jurisdictions have agreed with the Illinois view, about the authority to change the law of contributory negligence as a complete bar, the answer is doubtful. Summers may be right in thinking that the Illinois court had the power to make the change. But the question whether it had this power cannot be divorced from the question of what the judge's working conception of his rôle should be in a given case (unless we give that question the limited, dialectical interpretation which I think may be a possible one). The area of jurisdiction with which the Illinois court was concerned was one which can in general be described as an area for the application of rules; but of course, that this is so does not imply that the existing rules are to be applied, come what may, in every case which comes before the courts. If that were so there would be no room for adapting the law to changing conditions, or at least very little.

The judge, or anyone else who must apply rules, does not have to do so blindly. The legal and moral doctrine of necessity recognizes this. The judge should ask himself what purpose will be served by observing the existing rules, and whether perhaps, as a result of changed social conditions, they have become pointless or absurd. But, unlike in the case of the motorist, he must take account of the possibility that their mere existence may have caused people, including the litigants in the case before him, to rely on their continuing to be observed in the future. And there are some changes in rules which a court cannot make; it cannot overrule statutes – though in the US it may declare them unconstitutional.

I think, therefore, that Summers was wrong to suppose that one can separate the question of the constitutional competence of the judges to overrule precedents of long standing without recourse to the legislature from the general notion of the proper rôle of the judge in an individual case. The constitutional position of the judge is an important factor in determining what his conception of his rôle should be. It may follow from this that the issue between Summers and Mackie has to be answered somewhat differently as regards a US and an English or Scottish judge.

4.

Finally, I believe Mackie to be mistaken in the following respect. He thinks that we should see the legal system as a whole as having the function of protecting and reconciling rights, the primary right being that of each person to make what he wishes of his life by a series of choices. Though he does not say so explicitly, I think we can take it that he thinks that the judge should have this view in mind when he is not concerned simply to apply existing rules. In a case in which the rules do not unequivocally apply, one which is new in principle or markedly different from those that have been decided before, to what should the judge have recourse in reaching a decision?

It seems to me that the answer must depend on two matters. The first, to which Dworkin attaches, I think, excessive importance, is the general principles and notions already prevailing in the legal system. Often, these will point to the best result, for example by providing an analogy with some existing rule. But to confine himself to these would make the judge overly conservative and the system introspectively self-perpetuating. The judge must also have recourse, I think, to the values current in the society at large of which he is the servant. If this happens to be a liberal democracy, then indeed it will be appropriate for him to postulate the sort of rôle for the law which Mackie has in mind. So, if all Mackie means is that he personally would prefer to live in such a society, I have no quarrel with him. I would too. But it is another matter to put this rôle forward as a guide for judges *in general* in cases in which they are not bound by rules and have a relatively free choice. A judge must surely have regard to the values which are current in his own society, which he is implicitly bound to uphold as a condition of his appointment. If he is living in a Marxist society, where the interests of the collectivity and of the state are intended, as a matter of principle, to prevail over those of the individual, he must seek to achieve that predominance when he comes to decide the doubtful case not covered by a clear rule. If he is living in an authoritarian society in which discipline and self-control is a principal virtue, it would be very inappropriate to act as if Mackie's aim was a suitable one to adopt. If he is a judge in South Africa, he must accept that separate racial development is a fundamental value in the society in which he is judging and he must pay regard to that.

Of course this may be a good reason for not accepting a judicial appointment in the Soviet Union or the Republic of South Africa. And it is true that, to the extent that the rule of law operates in any society, however oppressive, freedom and equality are necessarily to some extent promoted, simply because the clear definition of what is permitted and what forbidden, if the definitions are relatively stable and infringements sanctioned, tends to create areas of freedom, while on the other hand the generality of legal rules tends to promote a certain form of equality, namely equality before the law. But judges are officials of particular states and societies. Their rôle depends on what the societies in which they judge want them to do. They are not on the bench to apply some sort of liberal natural law.

All Souls College Oxford

ROBERT S. SUMMERS

CONCLUDING COMMENTS

I.

I thank Mr John Mackie for his helpful comments. In general, I accept his summary of my main theses at the beginning of his comments. I will take up his criticism point by point. In this response, the Arabic numerals correspond to the same sections in Mr Mackie's comments.

2. I cited the cases of *Butterfield* v. *Forrester* and *Maki* v. *Frelk* to illustrate a point. I noted that the court in the second case – the Illinois Supreme Court in 1968 – followed the so-called rule of *Butterfield* v. *Forrester* that contributory negligence is a complete bar, even though the latter rule may well be the harshest doctrine known to the common law. I suggested that one likely explanation for the Illinois court's adherence to this doctrine was that some of the judges of the Illinois court may have harbored a working conception of the law as pre-existing rule and have become obsessed with this notion. Mr Mackie does not deny this possibility, yet it was the main point of my illustrative use of these cases.

I was not, at this point, using the illustration to show the possible "demerits of a rule conception of law *in general.*" Of course, it is partly by assembling such particular instances that one might show such "demerits in general." Mr Mackie says that it is "prejudicial and unfair of [me] to use as [my] one example a bad, excessively simple, old, and largely abandoned rule." I agree that the rule is bad, but this in fact supports me, for it indicates that something of importance is at stake. I agree that the rule is excessively simple, but we have many such simple rule formulations in the books, a state of affairs attributable in part, I believe, to an excessive rule-mindedness – to over-reliance upon a "rules" working conception. I concede that the so-called rule of *Butterfield* v. *Forrester* is largely abandoned today. Its abandonment by any

M. A. Stewart (ed), Law, Morality and Rights, 51–63.

form of legal action has been exceedingly slow, however. Only four American states abandoned it by judicial action (and no English court did so). It remains very much alive in some American states. Yet it has been said that we are talking here of the harshest doctrine known to the common law.

3. Mr Mackie says that he finds some obscurity in my notion of a working conception. He asks: "Is it a conception of the legal system as a whole, or a conception of the job of a court of law?"

A working conception as I conceive it is neither a conception of the legal system as a whole nor a full conception of the job of a court of law. It is a conception a judge holds of some "recurrent normative phenomena of the law." I repeat the list of features (all of which may recur in cases for decision) I gave in my paper:

(a) pre-existing rules,
(b) actual reasons for those rules,
(c) equities between the parties outside any relevant rules,
(d) discretionary judgment (including that involved in the overruling or modification of precedent),
(e) the bearing of ideas of justice and the common good characteristically found in some forms of law,
(f) the general dictates of reason, including "goal" reasons and "rightness" reasons, relevant to the justification of judicial decisions, and
(g) fiat.

I have singled out a rule conception as a viable judicial working conception. (It derives partly from the rules feature.) I have singled out a reason conception in this way, too. I do not claim that there is a corresponding viable working conception for all features on this list, however. Note that all phenomena on the list may be classed as justificatory resources – resources by reference to which a judge may, as appropriate, decide a case. (Note, too, that I am not saying that a judge who holds a "rules" working conception must believe that the whole of the law consists of a fixed body of pre-existing rules.)

Mr Mackie also refers to a working conception as "the best description of the job of each court in each particular case." But this, too, is not my characterization. The best description of the total job of a judge would include taking into account (appropriately) all recurrent general phenomena of the law – all justificatory resources – that bear on the case. In my scheme of thought, a working conception is a conception of one type of such phenomena considered in some appropriate sense to be primary.

Mr Mackie suggests that a conflict between working conceptions cannot arise if the rival conceptions are of the legal system as a whole. In my view, however, a conflict is possible even if the conceptions are of the legal system as a whole. It will not do (as Mr Mackie seems to try to do) to legislate away any possibility of conflict between working conceptions of the law *as a whole* by hypothesizing a system in which the only function of courts is to apply rules made by a legislature duly concerned with reason. I did not, however, pursue this in my original paper, for there I address rival working conceptions of general features of legal phenomena that recur in cases and bear on the decisional and justificatory tasks of judges.

4. Contrary to one of my theses, Mr Mackie says that a working conception with its narrow focus on some recurrent general feature of legal phenomena is not a pragmatic necessity for most judges. He says judges can and should be aware of *all* recurrent general phenomena of the law when deciding cases. Now, I do not deny that a judge can and should be *aware* of all the various types of justificatory legal resources that the case involves. I do not support my pragmatic necessity thesis on the ground that a judge cannot be aware of all such phenomena. Nor do I (any longer, at least for now) try to support that thesis on the ground that a judge can cope with only one kind of recurrent general feature of the phenomena at a time. (It may be that he could simply take each feature as it comes, so to speak.)

I will now briefly try to support the pragmatic necessity thesis with something new, though I confess that I cannot myself get hold of it very well, and in the end it may not do. There is more to the story than the illustrative list of recurrent general features of legal phenomena I have set forth. There is also a problem of the relation between these phenomena. I believe the adoption of a working conception signifies an assignment of primacy to the feature involved in light of such factors as its authoritative place within the system, its intrinsic justificatory significance, the regularity of its recurrence, and so on. It is not for nothing that a judge has a working conception. Such a conception enables him to cope far more readily (and more efficiently) with the complexity of the relations between instances of legal phenomena that recur in the cases. It provides a kind of tentative "fix" or ordering of those relations which he may bring to each case. Thus if he harbors a rule conception this signifies that he accords a kind of provisional primacy to rules as justificatory resources compared to the other recurrent general phenomena of law. He assumes that this fix or ordering serves him well. It may even seem to "decide" a high proportion of cases for him. A judge without any such (rule or other) working conception is left to work out this matter of primacy *ad hoc* in each case. Of course, for the above-average or unusually gifted judge, this may not prove a difficult matter. But for many judges it may not be too much to say that a working conception is, on the foregoing ground, a pragmatic necessity. This is all I now have to offer to support the pragmatic necessity thesis, and I agree that the matter calls for further exploration.

But let us suppose I am wrong that a working conception is a pragmatic necessity for most judges. If my interpretation of the evidence is correct, it nonetheless remains true that many judges do in fact approach the decision of cases with a working conception in mind. If this be so, then it remains important to inquire into the nature of these conceptions and into whether there are grounds for preferring any one possibility (including ones I have not considered here).

Note that judicial reliance on working conceptions might be *explained* on a variety of bases: the simple truth that certain types of justificatory legal phenomena tend to be more recurrent than others; the normative predominance of some phenomena over others; deep psychological leanings, e.g., the desire for the certainty that rules seem to bring, etc. Note that Mr Mackie assumes that on my account of the matter only one feature of relevant legal phenomena is *ever* brought into focus – that embodied in the working conception. But I stated in my paper that this is not so. The feature that the working conception brings into focus may be dispositive of the case, but then it may not be, too. And the judge may end up focusing on other justificatory phenomena. Thus I am not saying we must ultimately choose between a *system* of rules and a *system* of reason. I am saying there are different possible working conceptions and that one may be preferable to others.

5. Mr Mackie thinks that if I opt for his proposed interpretation of my allegedly ambiguous claims, namely, that a working conception must be addressed not to the legal system as a whole but to a feature of recurrent legal phenomena from the point of view of a particular court, then this interpretation will fail, as he puts it, to fit other parts of my text. His proposed interpretation is in fact the one I intend. And my text is not inconsistent.

In another part of my text I contended that a working conception of the law as reasoned reconciliation of conflicting considerations meets one of the criteria for a viable working conception, namely that its scope and potential applicability to particular cases is sufficient. I went on to say that this conception may even be the most wide-ranging of candidates. But I fail to see how this is inconsistent with construing my working conception as addressed to a feature of recurrent legal phenomena from the point of view of a court in particular cases. On the contrary, if some degree of reasoned reconciliation were not a sufficiently common feature of the materials that judges confront from case to case, it could hardly serve as a viable working conception. Thus when I say that the reason conception is wide-ranging, I do not mean that *it* is actually a conception of the system as a whole. I am, for one thing, saying that it ranges over – is applicable in some way to – other recurrent features of legal phenomena relevant in cases for decision. For example, it figures in rules and exceptions thereto. It figures in exercises of discretion. It figures in the formulation and application of equitable ideas, and so on.

A reason conception is wide-ranging in a further yet related way without being what Mr Mackie calls a conception of the system as a whole. Unforeseen considerations are always cropping up in particular cases. On the reason conception, the judge is a kind of sentry whose duty it is to "be there" to take appropriate account of such considerations.

A reason conception is wide-ranging in the still further sense that it ranges over highly varied institutional, processual, and other sociological structures of the law. This, too, is not to be equated with a conception of the system as a whole.

Finally, a reason conception is wide-ranging in the sense that it is not confined to the law's experience with any narrow class of social relations.

6. Under the heading of "Comparative Serviceability," I argued in favor of a reason over a rule *working* conception on the ground that the reason conception is more congenial to a rationale-oriented method of interpreting legal materials. I do not stop to go into the complexities of interpretation, but Mr Mackie, unlike a great many English and American judges of the past, agrees with me that a reason conception is more congenial in this way. But he says *if* I allow that a rule conception may also include the reasons for the rules then there is really no ground here for choosing the reason conception over this (more sophisticated) rule conception, and he notes that I acknowledge that one rival in the field is in fact a "rule with reasons" working conception.

To this I have two responses. First, I believe that a significant proportion of judges who appear to harbor a rules working conception simply do not incorporate into their conception the actual reasons for the rules as well. Thus, in regard to such judges, the difference between the two conceptions, and my ground for preferring the reason conception, remain real.

Second, it is not clear to me that if a rule conception also incorporates the actual reasons for those rules, then the reason conception and the rule conception must necessarily collapse into one another (in this respect). For example, a judge who works with a "rule with its reasons" conception may believe that, if the evidence as to reasons is ambivalent (as it not uncommonly is), he may either fall back on the merely literal import of the language of the materials or may regard himself free simply to substitute his own personal views. On the other hand, neither of these possibilities follows from harboring a reason conception as such.

Moreover, there is, beyond ambivalence of actual reasons, a further matter. A rule plus its actual reasons even when not ambivalent is still not to be equated with a reason conception. The possible available reasons may go beyond or be different from those embodied in the rule or "attached" thereto. On the reason conception, the judge would be more readily led to these and thus be more inclined to discard the rule (rather than adhere to it, as in *Maki* v. *Frelk*). Or there might be new and better reasons for the rule than its original ones. On a reason conception, the judge would more readily resort to these (as he should). Not only would this be likely to lead him to uphold the rule; it might also enable him to interpret and apply it better, in light of these new and better reasons.

I argued in my original paper in favor of a working conception of the law as a reasoned reconciliation of conflicting considerations on two further grounds: (1) much pre-existing law does not consist of rules; and (2) often there is no relevant pre-existing law so that it must be made up in light of reason as we go along. Now, Mr Mackie says that these two grounds "seem incompatible." He seems to assume that if I allow for any general type of pre-existing non-rule law, this may somehow commit me to the proposition that *all* the law pre-exists for all possible cases, and that therefore there cannot be any genuinely new issues, any actual "cases of first impression" (as lawyers say), or the like.

But I do not see why this should be so. Let me take merely one type of example familiar to lawyers. Case law as well as statute law sometimes confers broad discretion to be exercised by judges on a case-by-case basis in light of criteria at least partially specified. I call this non-rule law, although specific rules may over time emerge from some of the exercises of discretion. Yet even within the fields that such non-rule law addresses, relatively novel issues may arise for which, in my view, this non-rule law provides no determinate solutions. But for my point to hold, it is enough that such issues may arise outside these fields, too.

I think I know what influences Mr Mackie here. A contemporary legal philosopher known to him (and to me) has ably contended that there are forms of non-rule law that "occupy the whole" and thus predetermine (and uniquely so) very nearly all questions. But it is enough for my purposes to note that there are various forms of non-rule law, some of which are not of this allegedly all-encompassing character.

The contemporary legal philosopher to whom Mr Mackie alludes sees the law as almost wholly pre-existing (and uniquely determinative at that). Mr Mackie takes me to task for not addressing this view as a possible working conception. In defense, let me say this. My own topic grew out of my work with judges in "continuing judicial education seminars," as they are called in America. At no time, in a substantial number of those seminars, did I ever encounter a judge who appeared to hold as a working conception the view that for almost every issue that arises there is almost always controlling pre-existing law, and law that provides a single right answer at that. At the same time, it is a rare judge who holds that judges do not and ought not to make any law. Even the most conservative judges readily recognize that they sometimes must and do *make* law; for law may have to be remade because originally in error or now obsolete, law may be conflicting and thus call for choice, issues of first impression arise, and so on. On the other hand, I have in those seminars met many judges who, it seemed to me, hold one or the other of the two basic working conceptions I address in my paper. Of course, I concede that the best working conception for the usual judge might be something different from either of these. I really only wanted to consider these two widely held ones (if I am right on my facts). I suspect, too, that the contemporary legal philosopher to whom Mr Mackie alludes would not be happy to have his stimulating and instructive theory downgraded to the status of a mere working conception.

(I add, for the record, that my conception of "goal reasons" is not to be equated with "public policy reasons" and thus my "goal reasons" are not severely restricted in their scope in the way "policy reasons" may be.)

7. Under the head of "normative side effects" I set out to explore what some of the side effects of harboring one working conception rather than another might be, and to consider whether one is preferable to the other on this score. I suggested that rule-minded judges will tend to go in for rules as such and that reason-minded judges will tend to go in for reason as such. I tried to put the general case for the importance of rules as strongly as I could and I tried to do the same for the importance of reason.

Mr Mackie says that in this part of my paper I put the cart before the horse. He says that "Prior to the question 'What working conception will be best for the judges to have?' is the question 'What sort of a legal system do we want to have?'" Now I am not sure what, if anything, is at stake here. I agree with Mr Mackie on the priority question. But I do not see how it would follow from this that I have put the cart before the horse. My topic is working conceptions of "the law," and *in the course of* treating it, I have (partially) addressed Mr Mackie's prior question.

Now we turn to more substantive matters, but still under the heading of the comparative value of the rule conception and the reason conception in light of what I call normative side effects.

First, there is a point of some importance on which Mr Mackie appears to have misunderstood me, though this may be my fault. He suggests that I advocate a system in which the law consists largely of *ad hoc* reasoned reconciliations by particular courts with few or no rules. But I do not say this. What I do say is that *if* judges generally harbor a reason conception, this is likely to bring more reason into the law's content than would be the case if judges generally harbor a rule conception. Judges working with a reason conception would, among other things, be constantly looking for opportunities to bring substantive reasons to bear both within and beyond the province of pre-existing rules. This would be one general ground for preferring a reason conception. But in saying this I am not committed to favoring a *system* of law that consists solely of *ad hoc* reasoned reconciliations of particular courts. Nor does it follow that a reason conception carried to its logical end would give us a system of law consisting solely of *ad hoc* single-instance reconciliations. It just is the reasonable thing, for example, to have some rules, and reason will show us that too.

Second, there is a further and related point of some importance on which Mr Mackie seems to have misunderstood me, though again this may be my fault. He suggests that I think "the best way to get reasoned content into the law as a whole is to encourage particular courts to work mainly by explicitly trying to reconcile conflicting considerations for themselves." Again, I did not say this. I said we are likely to get more substantive reason out of a reason conception than out of a rule conception as such. I speak here only of *working* conceptions. A working conception (used rationally) leaves a place for *all the phenomena* of the law, including rules.

Third, let me say straightaway, however, that if I were faced with the false choice between what Mr Mackie calls a *system* consisting "largely of fairly stable rules" on the one hand, and a system consisting "largely of *ad hoc* reasoned reconciliation by particular courts" on the other hand, I would, *without knowing more*, be inclined to opt for the latter. Fairly stable rules may be utterly devoid of rightness and goodness. It is, I think, somewhat more implausible to suppose that *ad hoc* reasoned reconciliations by particular courts may be similarly devoid of rightness and goodness. Let us not assume that everyone is morally haywire. Let us take Anglo-American societies. One (but not the only) argument for my position here would be that, in such a society with a legal system consisting of *ad hoc* reasoned resolutions, each decision would have to be publicly justified on its own terms. Comparable problems governed by rule would all be settled in advance in one relatively short rule-creative moment. Such "rule" law would thus not be continuously tested case after case. Yet we know that, among other things, law becomes obsolete as social conditions change. Processes of *ad hoc* reasoned reconciliation stand ready to take account of such factors. Furthermore, a bad *ad hoc* decision is confined in its effect to the parties at hand; not so, a rule. But of course, as I have said before, no choice is required between a system obsessed with rules and one obsessed with reason. I have pursued this merely because Mr Mackie seems quite certain that, as between the two, a "rule" system would be preferable.

Fourth, I suspect Mr Mackie and I do differ in our perceptions of the need to improve the quality of substantive law through the injection of reason (by whatever means). He suggests I would be hard pressed to find very many examples of bad law (whether in rule form or other). He notes twice in his comments that I cite only one example of bad law and notes that I admit that even that one is now being overhauled. Without undertaking the tedious task of citing chapter and verse, let me assure him that at least in America the law is not so well off as all that. This is not to say that very much of it is now evil (though that, too, was so only a very few years ago). It is to say that, through reason, there is considerable scope, in America at least, for the improvement of the substantive law.

8. Mr Mackie says it would "be better to ensure, as far as possible, that judges do not become obsessed with any working conception, than to speculate about which conception, if they do become obsessed with it, will do less harm." With this much I agree. But it does not follow that it is of no importance so to speculate. If I am right, judges do become obsessed with their working conceptions (I note that philosophers write about rule worship). It is not evident to me that the consequences of these obsessions may not vary significantly, depending on the conception involved. I know of no way to prevent obsessions, but it may be possible to induce judges to opt for the working conception that causes the least havoc when it is known that some proportion of judges will become preoccupied with whatever working conception they happen to hold.

In conclusion, I want to address briefly an important assumption I find running through Mr Mackie's comments. The theme is that in the best justified division of legal labor in a modern system of law, rules are to be made and changed largely by the legislature and only occasionally (and then only "perhaps") by the highest courts. If this be assumed, then what Mr Mackie says against my position in his Section 7 may be somewhat more plausible. But again I am not ready to grant Mr Mackie his assumption about the best division of legal labor. First, there is always genuine scope for common law. (Where, incidentally, did it come from?) Many lawyers, liberal and conservative, would even agree that some kinds of matters are better left to judges than to legislatures. It strikes me as far from obvious that the work of legislatures is generally well reasoned and defensible, or even that it is regularly better in quality than law made by judges. Moreover, I do not see why all judge-made law must be viewed as undemocratic. Second, I have always found it difficult to understand why in recent times there should have been, in the English system, such unwillingness to overrule precedent. The common law is not always sound when made. I do not think *Butterfield* v. *Forrester* was rightly decided at the time. Moreover, change takes its toll even on common law which was sound when made. Why should not the courts have responsibility for some – perhaps most – genuine common law renovation that does not pose controversial issues on which political parties divide (and that would otherwise be appropriate)? And would the House of Lords be able to do a better job in such cases if it had before it arguments pro and con from the courts below? Of course, there are many complexities here, and I have been able to touch on only a few of them.

II.

I turn now to Professor Honoré's comments.

First, Professor Honoré says that I (and also Mackie) assume "(i) that the judge is free to choose his role for himself and (ii) that the role is the same in all areas of jurisdiction." These are not, in fact, my assumptions. Nor does Professor Honoré cite evidence or construct argument that would support attributing these assumptions to me. My view is that a judge in a civil law case may be constrained by law. Obviously, he cannot overrule a statute. In common law matters, however, he may have considerable freedom to modify, depart from, or even overrule precedent. In discussing *Butterfield* v. *Forrester*, I did not ignore the question whether the Illinois Supreme Court had the freedom to change a long-standing precedent. Indeed, I explicitly noted that one explanation for the court's decision might have been that "the judges believed (what in my view would be mistaken) that only the Illinois legislature had power to modify the complete bar rule." Nor did I divorce the question of the appropriate division of legal labor between court and legislature from the question of what is the appropriate conception of "the law" for judges to have. Indeed, I stated that the relevant phenomena of the law encompass "discretionary judgment (including the overruling or modification of precedent)." Such judgment is not, in my view, wholly free or unfettered. Its exercise is governed by norms and criteria. A judge who does not become preoccupied with his working conception will take these into account. And this he ought to do.

Second, I agree that the resolution of the question I explored in my paper would vary to some extent depending on the society involved, and therefore my question is one of jurisprudence rather than of pure legal philosophy. But let us assume the existence of a statute – one that says, for the society involved, that judges may never overrule precedent. Would it follow that, in such a society, there would be no room for my concern to compare a working conception of the law as reason with a working conception of the law as pre-existing rule? Not at all. Among other things, a reason conception can come into play other than through the overruling or modification of precedent, and this would give considerable point to my exercise.

Cornell Law School

PART II

JUSTIFICATION AND PRECEDENT

MARSHA HANEN

JUSTIFICATION AS COHERENCE

I suppose it is fair to say that any contemporary discussion of legal methodology must in some way take account of the theory of the justification of judicial decisions that is partly explicit, partly implicit, in the Rights Theory of Ronald Dworkin.[1] In this paper I focus on that theory by examining in some detail the relation between judicial justification in Dworkin's characterization and justification in two other areas – in science and in literary criticism. Both are comparisons Dworkin explicitly makes, and I want to challenge some of what he says both about justification in each of these areas and about the relations among them, thereby, I hope, throwing some light on the nature of both judicial and scientific reasoning.

Dworkin's theory of justification is, of course, complex, and I cannot hope to summarize it adequately here. But fortunately it is also well known, so I need but recall a few aspects of what he thinks is involved in coming to decisions in hard cases at law. He distinguishes, you remember, between arguments of principle and arguments of policy,[2] and only the former, which justify decisions in terms of individual or group *rights* (rather than in terms of some collective goal of the community), may be used in the justification of precedent. This is how he provides a connection between his rights thesis and the doctrine of judicial justification. He also invents a philosophical judge of "superhuman skill, learning, patience

[1] Ronald Dworkin, *Taking Rights Seriously* (Cambridge, Mass.: Harvard University Press, 1977) (hereinafter *TRS*), especially chapter 4.

[2] This distinction appears in Dworkin's earlier papers, such as 'The Model of Rules', which appeared in 1967 and is reprinted as chapter 2 of *TRS*. But it was somewhat modified in 'Hard Cases', which first appeared in 1975, and is chapter 4 of *TRS*.

M. A. Stewart (ed.), Law, Morality and Rights, 67–92.

and acumen"[3] whom he calls Hercules and who constructs a scheme of principles that best justifies the precedents. Hercules

> must discover principles that fit, not only the particular precedent to which some litigant directs his attention, but all other judicial decisions within his general jurisdiction and, indeed, statutes as well, so far as these must be seen to be generated by principle rather than policy.[4]

There are two problems that Hercules will face. The first is to decide what weight to give the actual arguments the judges used in deciding the precedent-cases. Here Dworkin is quite forthright. If a principle other than the one the judge cited both justifies the case in question and also provides a smoother fit with the arguments taken to justify other related cases, then this new principle should be adopted. Dworkin cites Brandeis and Warren's famous argument about the right to privacy:

> they argued that this right was not unknown to the law but was, on the contrary, demonstrated by a wide variety of decisions, in spite of the fact that the judges who decided these cases mentioned no such right.[5]

The theory of justification is thus directed not merely to the descriptive question of what justification was actually offered for a particular decision: it also addresses the normative question of what would be the best justification, in some sense of 'best' yet to be explained.

The second problem faced by Hercules is that the requirement of consistency with all previous decisions is clearly too strong. No set of principles can reconcile all standing statutes and precedents. Some part of 'settled' law will have to be re-interpreted as mistaken, but this must be a principled re-interpretation, else the consistency requirement has no real force. The details of how this is done need not concern us: it is the general technique that is important. What Hercules must do is to engage in what might be described as inference to the best theory, in the sense that his justification is stronger than any alternative that fails to recognize

---

[3] *TRS*, p. 105.
[4] *ibid.*, p. 116.
[5] *ibid.*, p. 119.

any mistakes or that recognizes a different set of mistakes. He may, for example, find on balance that he must reach a decision that opposes popular morality on some issue – say, abortion. Here he judges that the community's morality is inconsistent, and he must opt for the decision that coheres with whatever general theory does the least violence to the whole system, including some reasonably coherent notion of what morality requires. What this amounts to in particular cases is, of course, highly controversial. But Dworkin insists that the fact that well-informed and responsible judges disagree about what the right answer is goes no way at all toward showing that there is no right answer. Indeed, he holds that in every civil case there is some particular truth of the matter, and one of the parties has a *right* to win, even though the decision may be controversial, and seriously underdetermined by the black-letter rules.

So we have the outlines of a coherence theory of judicial justification. Of course, no merely human judge could be expected to make decisions in this way, but Dworkin clearly believes his characterization can serve at least as a model to which judges can and ought to achieve some more-or-less close degree of approximation.

Theories of justification that are, broadly speaking, coherence theories, are, of course, common in many areas of philosophy. The Rawlsian notion of reflective equilibrium as a method for developing a theory of justice provides one such theory:

> By going back and forth, sometimes altering the conditions of the contractual circumstances, at others withdrawing our judgments and conforming them to principle, I assume that eventually we shall find a description of the initial situation that both expresses reasonable conditions and yields principles which match our considered judgments duly pruned and adjusted.[6]

---

[6] John Rawls, *A Theory of Justice* (Cambridge, Mass.: Harvard University Press, 1971) (hereinafter *ATOJ*), p. 20n. Rawls actually distinguishes between wide and narrow reflective equilibrium in a later paper, 'The Independence of Moral Theory', *Proceedings and Addresses of the American Philosophical Association* 48 (1974/5): 5–22, but this distinction is not important for our purposes.

Rawls tells us further that the "process of mutual adjustment of principles and considered judgments is not peculiar to moral philosophy".[7] In this connection he refers us to Nelson Goodman's discussion of the justification of principles of inductive and deductive inference. The classic formulation of the sort of principle Rawls has in mind occurs in this passage from Goodman's *Fact, Fiction and Forecast:*

> The point is that rules and particular inferences alike are justified by being brought into agreement with each other. ***A rule is amended if it yields an inference we are unwilling to accept; an inference is rejected if it violates a rule we are unwilling to amend.*** The process of justification is the delicate one of making mutual adjustments between rules and accepted inferences...[8]

More to the point of the present topic, Joel Feinberg has compared this general sort of characterization of philosophical method with the kind of reasoning that goes on in courts of law:

> General principles arise in the course of deliberations over particular problems, especially in the efforts to defend one's judgments by showing that they are consistent with what has gone before. If a principle commits one to an antecedently unacceptable judgment, then one has to modify or supplement the principle in a way that does the least damage to the harmony of one's particular and general opinions taken as a group. On the other hand, when a solid, well-entrenched principle entails a change in a particular judgment, the overriding claims of consistency may require that the judgment be adjusted. This sort of dialectic is similar to the reasonings that are prevalent in law courts. When similar cases are decided in opposite ways, it is incumbent on the court to distinguish them in some respect that will reconcile the separate decisions with each other and with the common rule applied to each. Every effort is made to render current decisions consistent with past ones unless the precedents seem so disruptive of the overall harmony of the law that they must, reluctantly, be revised or abandoned.[9]

Now, according to Rawls, moral philosophy and "the study of

---

[7] *ATOJ*, p. 20.

[8] Nelson Goodman, *Fact, Fiction and Forecast*, 3rd ed. (Indianapolis: Bobbs-Merrill, 1973), p. 64, italics original.

[9] Joel Feinberg, *Social Philosophy* (Englewood Cliffs, N.J.: Prentice-Hall, 1973), p. 34.

other philosophical principles such as those of induction and scientific method"[10] provide but a few examples of a widespread phenomenon. The same sort of method is evident in linguistics when we try to describe the "sense of grammaticalness that we have for the sentences of our native language":[11] our linguistic theory can be expected to affect to some degree that sense of grammaticalness, even if it can hardly be expected to effect "a substantial revision of our sense of correct grammar".[12] So there is only a difference of degree between the sort of method appropriate in moral philosophy and what is suitable for theoretical linguistics. But when it comes to the natural sciences we find a rather sharp contrast. Thus, to take what Rawls refers to as an extreme case,

> if we have an accurate account of the motions of the heavenly bodies that we do not find appealing, we cannot alter these motions to conform to a more attractive theory. It is simply good fortune that the principles of celestial mechanics have their intellectual beauty.[13]

The suggestion seems to be that in the moral sphere we *can* alter whatever the analogues of the motions of the heavenly bodies are, in the interests of a better theory. And this implies that Rawls believes there is an important difference between the sort of methodology appropriate in philosophical theorizing, even when that theorizing is about science, and scientific theorizing itself.

The view that there is this difference is espoused also by Dworkin in his discussion[14] of Rawls' method in 'Justice and Rights'. Dworkin describes two general models – the natural model and the constructive model – that define the kind of coherence meant to be achieved by the technique of reflective equilibrium, and gives reasons for saying that the Rawlsian account requires the constructive model and, indeed, is incompatible with the natural one.

---

10 *ATOJ*, p. 49.
11 *ibid.*, p. 47.
12 *ibid.*, p. 49.
13 *ibid.*, p. 49.
14 This paper appears as chapter 6 of *TRS*, though it was first published in 1973.

Pretty clearly he means these observations to apply to his own 'Rights Thesis' as well, and thus to be central in the correct account of the justification of judicial decision. Yet some of the ways in which Dworkin elaborates his thesis suggest a close analogy with science itself. Thus he says:

> I oppose the popular theory that judges have discretion to decide hard cases. I concede that principles of law are sometimes so well balanced that those favoring a decision for the plaintiff will seem stronger, taken together, to some lawyers but weaker to others. I argue that even so it makes perfect sense for each party to claim that it is entitled to win, and therefore each to deny that the judge has a discretion to find for the other.... I do not claim (indeed I deny) that the process of decision will always yield the same decision in the hands of different judges. Nevertheless I insist that *the process, even in hard cases, can sensibly be said to be aimed at discovering, rather than inventing, the rights of the parties concerned*...[15]

There is something noble at stake in this conception, according to Dworkin, and it has to do with our overall view of the political process. He says:

> Citizens are encouraged to suppose that each has rights and duties against other citizens, and against their common government, even though these rights and duties are not all set out in black-letter codes. They are therefore *encouraged to frame and test hypotheses about what these rights are*, and to treat one another, and demand to be treated by the state, under the beneficial and unifying assumption that justice is always relevant to their claims even when it is unclear what justice requires.[16]

This basic theme that rights are to be discovered rather than invented and that this is to be done by some form of hypothesis-testing is both characteristic of Dworkin's recent work and analogous to a very common conception of scientific methodology. In trying to clarify his views in response to various criticisms, Dworkin tells us that we have all (including even Hart) had a mistaken notion of what law is, for we have thought of the expression

---

15 *TRS*, pp. 279–80, emphasis added.

16 Ronald Dworkin, 'Seven Critics', *Georgia Law Review* **11** (1977), p. 1249, emphasis added.

'existing law' as referring to some sort of independent entity. In contrast, he hopes

> to persuade lawyers to lay the entire picture of existing law aside in favor of a theory of law that takes questions about legal rights as special questions about political rights, so that one may think a plaintiff has a certain legal right without supposing that any rule or principle that already 'exists' provides that right. In place of the misleading question, whether judges find rules in the 'existing law' or make up rules not to be found there, we must ask whether judges try to enforce the rights they think parties have, or whether they create what they take to be new rights to serve social goals.[17]

Now, from the point of view of the ontology, as it were, of the situation, one is at first led to wonder what difference there can be between believing that there is existing law and believing that there are rights which can be discovered. The picture sounds very like the one implicit in Dworkin's idea of the natural model of reflective equilibrium wherein theories of justice (and presumably theories of rights?) "describe an objective moral reality; they are not, that is, created by men or societies but are rather discovered by them, as they discover laws of physics."[18] But it soon becomes clear that the discovering of principles in the law, as opposed to creating them, is not meant by Dworkin in the scientific sense. Legal principles do not mirror some independent reality in the way that scientific laws do, he might say, for whereas scientific laws are descriptive, legal ones are fundamentally prescriptive. Legal reasoning, instead, can be captured in the other – the constructive – model. This second model, he says,

> treats intuitions of justice not as clues to the existence of independent principles, but rather as stipulated features of a general theory to be constructed, as if a sculptor set himself to carve the animal that best fits a pile of bones he happened to find together. This 'constructive' model does not assume, as the natural model does, that principles of justice have some fixed, objective existence, so that descriptions of these principles must be true or false in some standard way. It does not assume that the animal it matches to the bones actually exists.[19]

---

[17] *ibid.*, pp. 1202–3.
[18] *TRS*, p. 160.
[19] *ibid.*, p. 160.

It is instructive that Dworkin pictures a sculptor here rather than, say, an archaeologist. An archaeologist might make the same carving as the sculptor, but perhaps with something else in mind. What becomes clear as one thinks about the analogy is the centrality of the notion of 'best fit'. A sculptor might be satisfied with just an interesting or beautiful animal-like shape, whereas the archaeologist will insist on an outcome at least consistent with what else we know about animals that existed at the relevant time and place. She will, in short, construct a figure that provides the best fit not only with these bones, but with other things we know: she may even decide that some of the bones that belong with these are missing, or, on the other hand, that some we have here belong elsewhere. But what the archaeologist does fits the natural model on Dworkin's view, rather than the constructive. On the natural model "[m]oral reasoning or philosophy is a process of reconstructing the fundamental principles by assembling concrete judgments in the right order, as a natural historian reconstructs the shape of the whole animal from the fragments of its bones that he has found."[20]

On the constructive model, Dworkin seems to be saying, we seek 'best fit' in the sense of consistency. But the theory thus constructed does not have the additional constraint he takes to be imposed on theories in science – of a tie somewhere to objective reality, either in the form of observation sentences, or predictions or some such thing. So there is an important difference between the two models, for Dworkin, which can be summed up in the remark that on the scientific model observation, or its moral analogue, intuition, is primary,[21] whereas on the constructive model the theory is primary. Suppose a judge finds that he has some intui-

---

[20] *ibid*., p. 160.

[21] The moral analogue of observations is, for Dworkin, moral intuitions, produced by a moral faculty that is the instrument for discovering an objective moral reality. "These intuitions are clues to the nature and existence of more abstract and fundamental moral principles, as physical observations are clues to the existence and nature of fundamental physical laws." See *TRS*, p. 160.

tion – one of Dworkin's examples is the intuition that a particular minority is entitled to special protection – that he cannot by any consistent set of principles reconcile with his other intuitions, for example, the view that distinctions based on race are inherently unfair to individuals. This latter view apparently is intended by Dworkin to represent the judge's considered moral theory. Faced with this dilemma, Dworkin thinks the scientifically-minded judge will follow "the troublesome intuition... submerging the apparent contradiction, in the faith that a more sophisticated set of principles, which reconciles that intuition does in fact exist though it has not been discovered."[22] This analysis emerges from an analogy between moral intuitions and observational data, and the latter, Dworkin supposes, must always hold sway in science.

The constructive model, on the other hand, requires that the theory be regarded as primary in the sense that intuitions that just won't fit the theory must be compromised. The coherence requirement is an independent requirement of political morality rather than a requirement that flows from the assumption that moral convictions are accurate observations of some actual state of affairs.

There is thus, for Dworkin, a sharp line to be drawn between his two models. He would grant, I think, that in science there might be different explanations of the same data, that our theories are underdetermined by the evidence, and so there is more than one way of 'saving the phenomena'. But, he maintains, this

> is not a picture of the procedure of equilibrium, because this procedure argues not simply that alternative structures of principle are available to explain the same phenomena, but that some of the phenomena, in the form of moral convictions, may simply be ignored the better to serve some particular theory.[23]

This is too starkly put, I suspect, from two standpoints. In the first place, I don't think we really *do* simply *disregard* evidence that won't fit our moral or legal theory. Dworkin's example here is that we might be utilitarians and yet think that slavery is unjust,

---

[22] *TRS*, p. 161.
[23] *ibid.*, p. 165.

even if it leads to greater utility. If even on reconsideration we still hold both views and cannot reconcile them, the constructive model authorizes us to ignore the slavery intuition in order to maintain equilibrium. I think what really happens in a case like this is that we continue the effort at reconciliation, seeking either to modify the theory to accommodate the intuition or modify the intuition, perhaps by finding reasons that it shouldn't be given such great weight. It is at least unlikely that we will simply grant that slavery is, after all, acceptable; instead, we will surely make some other adjustment such as trying to show that slavery is really different from what we had supposed, or perhaps even, in an extreme case, continuing to maintain incompatible beliefs, recognizing them to be in conflict, having no means for resolving them, but believing that some resolution will present itself eventually. Further, the example is particularly unfortunate in being inapt for Dworkin's purposes, for utilitarianism does claim to accommodate the slavery intuition by showing that slavery has long-term bad consequences, so that this is not even a case where we are seriously tempted to think we may have to relinquish the uncomfortable intuition.

In the second place, if historians of science are to be believed, then it is not true that the natural model is so insistent on the primacy of observation. Sometimes we say the test-tubes were dirty, or we make adjustments elsewhere in the system without giving up the theory, and sometimes we even do what Dworkin says only the constructive model allows: we say the theory *must* be right and either something's gone wrong with the observation or we'll soon find a way to accommodate it, though that way eludes us for the moment. It is true that we don't *simply* ignore the recalcitrant observation in science, but neither do we *simply* forget about the discordant moral intuition or legal decision: we regard ourselves as bound to explain the discrepancy.

A plausible analogy is the inductive process of curve-fitting. If there is a point in the data that falls some distance from the best curve, however measured, there are surely circumstances in which we may be entitled to disregard it. Furthermore, the curve that best fits settled law may have to change as more law becomes settled. Theories that would best justify decisions before and after *Brown* v. *Board of Education*[24] are presumably different in some important respects. We might even go so far as to say there are occasional 'conceptual revolutions' (in Kuhn's sense) in law, as with the introduction of accident compensation schemes not based on fault.[25] As a matter of fact, Kuhn is, I suppose, our most obvious source of the view that we do not reject theories in science on the basis of falsifying instances. And yet, one consults Kuhn in vain for specific examples of situations in which scientists have straightforwardly ignored or even rejected observational data in favor of a well-entrenched theory; what he gives us are examples in which anomalies and even crises in the prevailing scientific theory failed to occasion its abandonment until a plausible alternative was available. But the offending observations were rarely just ignored.[26]

There are, however, some interesting examples of what appears to be just glossing over recalcitrant observations in the history of science. One occurs in Turbayne's account of how Isaac Barrow dealt with a problem he encountered in optics, involving the question of where an object seen through converging lenses and mirrors should appear. Barrow argued from the accepted geometrical theory of optics that the object should appear " 'extremely remote' because diverging rays mean near, less diverging rays mean less near, parallel rays mean far, therefore converging rays mean very

---

[24] *Brown* v. *Board of Education of Topeka, Shawnee County, Kansas*, 347 US 483, 74 S.Ct. 686, 98 L.Ed. 873 (1954).

[25] See, for example, Robert E. Keeton and Jeffrey O'Connell, *Basic Protection for the Traffic Victim: A blueprint for Reforming Automobile Insurance* (Toronto: Little, Brown, 1965).

[26] See T. S. Kuhn, *The Structure of Scientific Revolutions*, 2nd ed. (Chicago: University of Chicago Press, 1970), especially chapters 6–8.

far."[27] But when he looked, he found "that the facts were directly opposite to what they ought to have been." Turbayne comments:

> Barrow's observation report was good. Although he was completely nonplussed by this turn of events, he remained undismayed. Having found the facts 'repugnant' to the theory which, he said, "I know to be manifestly agreeable to reason", he refused to renounce the theory.[28]

Barrow was sure there was something that needed explaining, but admitted that he was unable to solve the problem. Nonetheless, the existence of the recalcitrant observation apparently didn't move him in the least to abandon the theory, nor did he even suppose that the ultimate solution to the problem would involve a modification of the theory.[29]

An even more interesting example of this sort of phenomenon is discussed at some length by Michael Polanyi. He writes of the way in which the Michelson-Morley experiment of 1887 has been treated in the textbooks as the crucial evidence which compelled Einstein to formulate his theory of relativity. The problem is that, although Einstein mentions the experiment in support of his theory, it actually did not give the result required by relativity. Polanyi describes how the positive effect present in the observations of

---

[27] Colin M. Turbayne, *The Myth of Metaphor* (New Haven: Yale University Press, 1962), p. 174. Turbayne, of course, wants to claim that the anomaly of the Barrovian case can be resolved by shifting from the geometrical theory to the linguistic theory that he takes Berkeley to have been advancing in *An Essay Towards A New Theory of Vision*.

[28] *ibid*., p. 175.

[29] Paul Feyerabend, in his *Against Method* (London: New Left Books, 1975), p. 60, has this to say about the example of Barrow: "Barrow *mentions* the qualitative difficulties, and he *says* that he will retain the theory nevertheless. This is not the usual procedure. The usual procedure is to forget the difficulties, never to talk about them, and to proceed as if the theory were without fault. This attitude is very common today."

Feyerabend's book is in part an extended argument, using Galileo as a case study, that precisely the kind of ignoring of data that Rawls and Dworkin countenance only for moral theory does and should go on in science. I argue that these views are exaggerated, though they do provide a useful antidote to a too rigid conception of methodology.

Michelson and Morley, first pointed out by W. M. Hicks in 1902, was later reproduced by D. C. Miller and his colleagues many thousands of times during the next 24 years, using new and more accurate apparatus.

The layman, taught to revere scientists for their absolute respect for the observed facts, and for the judiciously detached and purely provisional manner in which they hold scientific theories (always ready to abandon a theory at the sight of any contradictory evidence), might well have thought that, at Miller's announcement of this overwhelming evidence of a 'positive effect' in his presidential address to the American Physical Society on December 29th, 1925, his audience would have instantly abandoned the theory of relativity. Or, at the very least, that scientists – wont to look down from the pinnacle of their intellectual humility upon the rest of dogmatic mankind – might suspend judgment in this matter until Miller's results could be accounted for without impairing the theory of relativity. But no: by that time they had so well closed their minds to any suggestion which threatened the new rationality achieved by Einstein's world-picture, that it was almost impossible for them to think again in different terms. Little attention was paid to the experiments, the evidence being set aside in the hope that it would one day turn out to be wrong.[30]

---

[30] Michael Polanyi, *Personal Knowledge* (Chicago: University of Chicago Press, corrected edition, 1962), pp. 12–13. Actually there is good reason to think that Polanyi's account is an oversimplification, for the adherents of Special Relativity apparently did not simply ignore negative evidence; rather they "surmised… that the conditions under which Miller obtained his results were different from what he had supposed them to be." For a thorough and helpful discussion of this issue see A. Grünbaum, *Philosophical Problems of Space and Time*, 2nd enlarged edition (Dordrecht and Boston: Reidel, 1973), pp. 379–386. What we seem to have here is another instance of the kind of theorizing I have suggested goes on in science *and* morals, where anomalies are supposed to have some explanation, even if we can't at the moment see just what it is. This example is discussed at greater length in my 'Legal Science and Legal Justification', in *Science, Pseudo-Science and Society*, edited by Marsha P. Hanen *et al.* (Waterloo, Ontario: Wilfred Laurier University Press, 1980).

There is, in science, a related phenomenon that also does not fit Dworkin's account. This is the phenomenon that scientific theories are sometimes replaced by successor theories, generally thought to be better than their predecessors; and yet the successor theories cannot explain certain facts that *were* explained by their predecessors. For interesting examples of this phe-

So, at least according to this account, it would appear that there are cases in science in which the data are disregarded, though this is probably rare. But it is equally rare in the moral/legal sphere, as I have argued.

Another difficulty with the natural model is said by Dworkin to be this. The equilibrium technique is relativistic in two ways: in that (1) it selects the best theory from a small finite list; and (2) the results are relative to an area of initial agreement. The first species of relativism is said to be a problem because if we think only that we have the best theory from a small list, and that further work will yield a better one, then we have very little reason to suppose that the principles we have arrived at at a given stage are an accurate description of moral reality. Now I think this begins to point to what has gone wrong with the models: it is the supposition that the natural model requires that we believe our observations put us in touch with transcendent reality and so the moral version must imply that moral intuitions put us in touch with a transcendent moral reality. But all of this is surely questionable. For, even if we think of science as ultimately directed toward discovering the truth, it surely does not follow that we have attained that truth at any particular stage, or that there is a clear and unassailable correspondence between our observations and certain features of an external reality, as Dworkin apparently believes.

Indeed, it seems patent that Dworkin accepts some fairly naive version of scientific realism. He refers to an

> astronomer who has clear observational data that he is as yet unable to reconcile in any coherent account, for example, of the origin of the solar system. He continues to accept and employ his observational data, placing his faith in the idea that some reconciling explanation does exist though it has not been, and for all he knows may never be, discovered by men.[31]

What this means when applied to the moral or legal sphere is that

---

nomenon, see L. Laudan, 'Two Dogmas of Methodology', *Philosophy of Science* 43 (1976): 585–597. Related points are made by P. Feyerabend, *op. cit.*, and by A. Grünbaum in 'Can a Theory Answer More Questions than One of its Rivals?', *British Journal for the Philosophy of Science* 27 (1976): 1–23.

we are stuck with the data – for example, the intuition that slavery is wrong. Considered moral judgments – intuitions or convictions – are analogous to direct perception reports which are in some important way privileged and immune from revision. But very little of science is built on this sort of foundation, and so from this point of view the constructive model is really a better model for science than is the natural one. However, even this way of putting it gives too much to Dworkin's characterization, for I want rather to claim that the contrast he draws between the two models is too sharp. Insofar as the natural model fits scientific theorizing, it equally well fits the Herculean judicial enterprise; and insofar as the constructive model fits the latter, it equally well fits science. Perhaps it would be more accurate to say that a better picture of the scientific enterprise is a kind of composite of the natural and constructive models. If there are existence assumptions in science they are much weaker than the ones Dworkin attributes to the natural model; and the adjustment between theory and intuition can come out either way, though most often we cling to our theory if it has been carefully thought through and tested – at least until the anomalies pile up, or some better theory comes into view.

As a matter of fact, the first species of relativism that Dworkin attributes to the equilibrium technique – that of selecting the best theory from a small finite list – is characteristic also of scientific inference conceived in a certain way. This conception trades on a fact that has gradually become clear over the period since the heyday of positivist philosophy of science – that we do

---

[31] *TRS*, p. 161. I do not mean to claim here, of course, that there is no tie to observation in science, or that anything goes. Rather, it is that the observational tie is complex, and may not be different in principle from the moral sphere, where we have ties to the realities of human nature and social organization.

Scientific realism has come to the forefront of debate in philosophy of science in recent years. Perhaps the most interesting and cogent anti-realist position is advanced by Bas C. van Fraassen in his book *The Scientific Image* (Oxford: Clarendon Press, 1980).

not have any formal way of providing necessary and sufficient conditions for theory acceptance in science. High probabilities are not sufficient, as the lottery paradox shows us,[32] and probably not necessary either, and no other formal or quantitative criterion seems to do the job any better. Instead, it appears plausible to regard scientific inference as inference to the best explanation or theory – a form of eliminative inference, where the eliminations are made from a small finite list of hypotheses or theories.[33] Our theories are always open to revision, and the most we can say of those we now accept is that they are the best we can do for the moment. As to the second form of relativism – that results are relative to an area of initial agreement – it is widely accepted that, in science *and* philosophy, justification *always* rests on initial commitments.[34] One must start somewhere, though this does not mean the initial commitments are immune from criticism or revision, or that objectivity cannot be achieved.

Thus, I think that most of what Dworkin wants to say about the nature of judicial reasoning is at least consistent with a scientific model, properly construed. Legal propositions such as "Plaintiff is entitled to damages" are either true or false, he would insist, though we may not know which. He says:

> A proposition of law may be asserted as true if it is more consistent with the theory of law that best justifies settled law than the contrary proposition of law. It may be denied as false if it is less consistent with that theory of law than the contrary.[35]

---

[32] For a discussion of the lottery paradox (first formulated by H. Kyburg) and its significance for acceptance theory see Marsha Hanen, 'Confirmation, Explanation and Acceptance', in *Analysis and Metaphysics*, edited by Keith Lehrer (Dordrecht and Boston: Reidel, 1975).

[33] *Ibid*. See also Gilbert Harman, *Thought* (Princeton, N.J.: Princeton University Press, 1973); Bas C. van Fraassen, 'The Pragmatics of Explanation', *American Philosophical Quarterly* 14 (1977): 143–150; and Paul R. Thagard, 'The Best Explanation: Criteria for Theory Choice', *Journal of Philosophy* 75 (1978): 76–92.

[34] See Israel Scheffler, 'On Justification and Commitment', *Journal of Philosophy* 51 (1954): 180–190.

[35] *TRS*, p. 283.

But we might still want to insist, both in law and in science, that to be justified in asserting a proposition as true is not to have shown that it *is* true. Furthermore, it is not clear, despite Dworkin's insistence on the point, that there is a *single* theory that best justifies settled law. Some accepted decisions will have to be ignored, and there may well be different ways to do this that yield equally acceptable theories from the coherence point of view. Similarly with the scientific case: here too there may at a particular time be equally acceptable explanations of what we take to be the facts.

One reason, of course, that we are inclined to say this is that we are always operating with some measure of ignorance and uncertainty, and equally rational, sincere, well-trained and intelligent lawyers, or scientists, often disagree. This fact, and the fact that in the law we do not and cannot have rules to cover explicitly every conceivable case, has led jurisprudents such as Hart to say that, in hard cases where the rules run out, judges have discretion to decide as they see fit: there is no single right answer. If what we mean by a "right answer in the law" is one that expresses a true proposition of law – perhaps something like "Jones is liable for Smith's injuries" – then, according to Dworkin, the underlying thesis of the "no single right answer" view must be that if a proposition is true it is demonstrable as true, presumably on the basis of the facts at our disposal.[36] This is, as one might expect, a thesis that Dworkin wishes to deny, and to do this he asks us to consider yet another analogy. We are to imagine a group of Dickens scholars engaged in a kind of literary game in which they discuss David Copperfield as though he were a real person. They might play this game with different sets of ground rules which will, naturally, lead to different results.

Consider, for example, a rather ascetic set of ground rules:

(1) Any proposition about David may be asserted as 'true' if Dickens said

---

[36] Ronald Dworkin, 'No Right Answer?' in *Law, Morality and Society*, edited by P. M. S. Hacker and J. Raz (Oxford: Clarendon Press, 1977), p. 73.

it, or said something else such that it would have been inconsistent had Dickens denied it.

(2) Any proposition may be denied as 'false' if Dickens denied it, or said something else such that it would have been inconsistent had Dickens said it.[37]

Now with these ground rules, there will be many propositions about David that are neither assertable nor deniable. For example, as Dworkin tells us,

Dickens never said that David had a homosexual affair with Steerforth, and it would not have been inconsistent with anything he did say if he had denied it. But he did not deny it, and it would not have been inconsistent with anything he said if he had asserted it. So the participants can neither assert nor deny the proposition, not because they lack sufficient information, but because they have sufficient information to be certain that, under their rules, the proposition is neither true nor false.[38]

But clearly there can be far less ascetic ground rules, some of which, Dworkin thinks, define a game very like the actual practice of literary criticism. In this game,

a further proposition about David is assertable as true (or deniable as false) if that further proposition provides a better (or worse) fit than its negation with propositions already established, because it explains in a more satisfactory way why David was what he was, or said what he said, or did what he did, according to those already established propositions.[39]

In this game it is very likely that all or almost all questions about David will have a right answer. Those that won't will be trivial, such as the question whether David had freckles on his toes. And of course it is clear that Dworkin similarly imagines that, although there can be different forms of the *legal* enterprise, with more or less strict ground rules, the form we should have and do have to some extent is the form that corresponds with the 'best fit' version of the literary exercise.

Now, what is interesting, I think, is Dworkin's willingness to

---

[37] *ibid.*, p. 73.
[38] *ibid.*, pp. 73–74.
[39] *ibid.*, p. 75.

buy this analogy when he was unwilling to accept the scientific one. This is because, although he thinks both the literary and the legal enterprise depend upon certain facts, these are not the 'hard facts' upon which the scientific enterprise depends. Instead they are, in the literary case, what might be called 'aesthetic facts', such as facts of narrative consistency which are, however, not even in principle demonstrable by ordinary scientific methods. But surely these facts of narrative consistency are to at least some extent parasitic on facts and generalizations about the behavior of ordinary people, which Dworkin acknowledges to be 'hard' facts. For example, we will decide what behavior David might have engaged in partly on the basis of how people we know, similar to David in some respects, behave in like actual situations, which is to say, partly on the basis of psychological facts. Thus it is not so clear that in the literary case we lack any tie to the external world, even though this tie may be extremely tenuous in some literary works. But further, the problem of reconciling the judicial precedents is much more complex than the David Copperfield game, not only because we must consider myriads of cases decided by different judges over long periods of time, but even often in situations where, on the face of it, the issues appear to be fairly circumscribed. Consider, as an example, a torts problem that has recently been before the Supreme Court of Canada, concerning the standard of care required of police officers in apprehending a suspected criminal, and, in particular, the extent to which police officers are justified in using force in effecting an arrest. If the courts are prepared to give clear direction in these cases this will presumably act as an incentive to police officers to behave in particular ways, so the potential social importance of these cases is considerable.

The two cases to be considered are *Priestman* v. *Colangelo, Shynall and Smythson,* and *Beim* v. *Goyer.*[40] The 'facts' are suc-

---

[40] *Priestman* v. *Colangelo, Shynall and Smythson*, [1959] S.C.R. 615, 30 C.R. 209, 124 C.C.C. 1, 19 D.L.R. (2d) 1; *Beim* v. *Goyer*, [1965] S.C.R. 638, 57 D.L.R. (2d).

cintly summarized by Paul Weiler as follows:

There was a marked similarity in the events. ... Smythson, a 17-year-old in Toronto, and Beim, a 14-year-old in Montreal, each stole new cars, apparently to take 'joy rides'. Each was spotted by police officers in their vehicles, Smythson by Priestman and Beim by Goyer. When the boys refused to stop, the police gave chase at dangerous speeds along city streets. There the situations diverge. Priestman aimed his gun at the tire of Smythson's car as he was reaching a busy intersection, in order to stop him. Just as he fired, his arm was bumped and the bullet accidentally struck Smythson in the neck, rendering him unconscious. The car went out of control, ran up on the sidewalk and killed Columbo Colangelo and Josephine Shynall who were talking quietly while waiting for a bus. By contrast, Beim, the driver of the stolen car in the other case, collided with a parked vehicle and thus stopped himself. He hopped out of his own car and fled across a deserted, snowy and rocky field. Goyer gave chase with his gun in his hand. He fired two warning shots in the air and he also fell twice while crossing the field. Unfortunately, when he tripped and fell a third time, the gun went off and the bullet hit Beim in the neck, paralyzing him.[41]

Consider the four possible pairs of outcomes in these cases.

(1) Both policemen are negligent.
(2) Neither policeman is negligent.
(3) Priestman is negligent; Goyer is not.
(4) Goyer is negligent; Priestman is not.

Now on the face of it, one might suppose that the important features of the cases are sufficiently similar as to dictate either (1) or (2) as the result. But there are differences:

Priestman *intentionally* fired his gun in a crowded city area and as a result injured two completely innocent bystanders. Goyer's gun went off *accidentally* while he was running across a deserted field and as a result injured the escaping offender.[42]

This points to (3) as the proper result. On the other hand Beim was not posing any additional threat of injury to members of the community when the mishap occurred, whereas Smythson was

---

[41] Paul Weiler, *In the Last Resort* (Toronto: Carswell/Methuen, 1974), p. 75.
[42] *ibid.*

driving recklessly, so one might say it was less important that Beim be stopped; and Goyer had already fallen during the foot chase, so it was perhaps negligent for him to go on running with gun in hand. These features suggest that the result should be (4), as it in fact was. But the question is whether any *principled* rationale can be given for this outcome – a rationale that makes it clear why (4) should be preferred to the alternatives.

Both opinions make reference to section 25(4) of the Canadian Criminal Code which reads:

> A peace officer who is proceeding lawfully to arrest ... any person for an offence ... is justified, if the person to be arrested takes flight to avoid arrest, in using as much force as is necessary to prevent the escape by flight, unless the escape can be prevented by reasonable means in a less violent manner.

Now, however much this provision may relieve both Priestman and Goyer of criminal liability, it certainly does not settle the matter of civil liability. On that point Mr Justice Locke argued in the *Priestman* case as follows:

> The performance of the duty imposed upon police officers to arrest offenders who have committed a crime and are fleeing to avoid arrest may, at times and of necessity, involve risk of injury to other members of the community. Such risk, in the absence of a negligent or unreasonable exercise of such duty, is imposed by the statute. ... Police officers in this country are furnished with firearms and these may, in my opinion, be used when, in the circumstances of the particular case, it is reasonably necessary to do so to prevent the escape of a criminal whose actions, as in the present case, constitute a menace to other members of the public.[43]

The conclusion, of course, was that Priestman was not liable. Neither the argument that shooting should be considered a last resort, nor that in this case more harm than good was likely to result from trying to stop Smythson, especially given the relative lack of seriousness of his crime, moved the Court. But these matters *were* relied upon in a vigorous and convincing dissent.

Nevertheless, given the *Priestman* decision, it seems clear that either (a) Goyer should also have been exonerated from liability,

---

[43] *Priestman* v. *Colangelo*, [1959] S.C.R. 615 at 623, 624–25.

or (b) the Court should have overruled *Priestman* in reaching the contrary result in *Beim*. Instead, the Court in the latter case held that there was evidence on which the jury could reasonably base its finding that Goyer "was at fault in failing to exercise proper care in the use of firearms when pursuing the appellant."[44] In addition, it said: "Each of the decided cases dealing with the use of fire-arms by peace officers... turns largely on its own facts."[45] Thus the Court suggested that the traditional ploy of distinguishing cases on the facts was appropriate in this situation where it desired to uphold the finding that Goyer was liable, even though Priestman, in what appeared to be similar circumstances, was not liable.

But there is a difficulty, for the decision in *Beim* seems to be a reversal of that in *Priestman*, and yet both decisions stand. It is hard to see how this state of affairs can be thought to provide any reasonable guidance in similar situations either to the police, to injured citizens, or to the courts, for although distinguishing cases on the facts is a common judicial technique, it is just not clear that the factual differences in these two cases are *relevant* factual differences sufficient to justify different outcomes. At the very least, we need to be given more reason to think that the facts in the two cases are relevantly different; and without such reason one could hardly be blamed for thinking the differences to be unimportant from the standpoint of attempting to construct a coherent legal theory. If this is so, then on Dworkin's theory and many other theories of adjudication, we have a situation in which at least one of the precedents should be viewed as mistaken, and the one that stands should be the one that coheres best with the rest of settled law. Which result actually does this I am not prepared to say, though I think strong reasons of principle and policy can be given for holding the policemen liable in both cases. No doubt this way of putting the matter would be too explicitly result-oriented for Dworkin; and in addition the stumbling block of the Canadian Supreme Court's reluctance to overrule itself shouldn't be underestimated. But at least for it to have done so on this mat-

[44] *Beim* v. *Goyer*, [1965] 57 D.L.R. (2d) at 255.
[45] *ibid.*

ter seems compatible both with our ordinary sense of fairness about this kind of case and with Dworkin's theory, so far as its abstractions can be made to apply to such a concrete situation. And if the theory does apply to this kind of case and, as well, to the David Copperfield case, it is no less apropos, I submit, for a typical example of small-scale scientific theorizing.

Another problem with the law–science separation is that Dworkin's use of 'truth' and 'fact' in both the literary and the legal realm is somewhat peculiar, for these terms used in these contexts do not have the meanings he apparently supposes them to have in science. Truth in law and literature is wholly a matter of coherence, on his view, whereas truth in science also involves correspondence with reality. It is difficult, then, not to suspect Dworkin of embracing paradox for its own sake, and it is equally difficult not to wonder what is the point of the talk about 'discovery' and 'truth' and 'right answers in the law', since on his account it would seem to bear little relation to such talk elsewhere. My own view, which I do not have space to develop here, is that the notions of discovery and fact and even truth in science are more metaphorical than Dworkin's picture allows,[46] so the sense of paradox his use of these concepts generates is more apparent than real. This, of course, is just an extension of my earlier argument that Dworkin's contrast between the natural and constructive models of equilibrium is overdrawn.

But I shouldn't want to convey the impression that I think there is nothing to Dworkin's insistence on a separation between the legal and scientific models of reasoning. In a recent Massachusetts case[47] the Supreme Judicial Court decided that, in a will

---

[46] For a thoroughly radical view about the correspondence between the world and our pictures and descriptions of it, see Nelson Goodman, *Ways of Worldmaking* (Indianapolis: Hackett, 1978). For a much earlier argument for the view that facts are constructed rather than discovered, see Ludwik Fleck, *Genesis and Development of a Scientific Fact* (Chicago and London: University of Chicago Press, 1979). This is an English translation of Fleck's 1935 German work.

[47] *Ebitz* v. *Pioneer National Bank*, Mass. 361 N.E. (2d) 225 (1977).

which directed the establishment of a scholarship fund "to aid and assist worthy and ambitious young men to acquire a legal education," the phrase 'young men' must be construed in its generic sense which includes women. In justification of this construction, the Court cited the following facts, among others: (1) the fund was to be the Richard W. and Florence B. Irwin Scholarship Fund; (2) it was suggested that the trustee use the educational program of the Knights Templar as a model, and this program provides financial assistance to students without regard to their sex; (3) the testator wanted to help "as many students as possible" and limiting the applicant pool is inconsistent with this objective. The Court concluded that the testator had no wish to confine his bounty to young men, and hence that its interpretation allowing women to receive scholarships from the fund was consistent with his wishes. This seems little short of preposterous, but one can see that the Court thought that the law clearly favors giving effect to the intent of the testator, and saw no other unproblematic way to reach the desired result. On its face this appears to be a case in which the most reasonable theory to be extracted from settled law would yield a decision rule restricting these scholarships to males. But it might be that a more candid court could have justified the decision actually reached partly on the basis of social and legal changes that have taken place since the will was drafted in 1963; it might, that is, have tried to claim that this is an area in which the law is in flux, and that the theory that best justifies that law is changing from what it would have been a decade or two ago.

On the other hand, it might be that there is no way ultimately to justify the decision without making a *moral* case for the underlying duties being presupposed. It is this moral appeal that is not required in justification in science and Dworkin obviously thinks this is a difference that *makes* a difference. Clearly he wants to insist on the different roles played by coherence in the legal and scientific models: in law coherence is fundamentally a moral requirement of equality or justice, whereas in science it is a more purely intellectual demand. But this, I suspect, is really to say that the differences between the two have more to do with content than with form, and that view I find quite acceptable.

Dworkin's theory has been referred to as the "Third theory of law"[48] in that it is meant as an alternative both to legal positivism and to natural-law doctrines. What makes his work particularly slippery is that it contains elements of both those positions, and they are hard to reconcile. It is like a natural-law theory in that legal propositions are true or false and rights are pre-existing; but it is like a positivist theory in that these rights do not represent transcendent realities but are rather constructed from the fabric of legal decisions. The underlying assumptions appear to include somewhat simple versions of scientific realism, moral objectivism, and the doctrine that rights can at least in principle be balanced in some objective way, perhaps even along a linear scale. Much of this is unexceptionable. My quarrel with him is not about his claim that judicial decision rests on a coherence theory of justification, for I think he is right about that, at least as a piece of idealized legal methodology. Where I think he is mistaken is about the appropriate notion of coherence, both for the law and for science. By insisting that the former is theory-centred and the latter fact-centred he perpetuates a false dichotomy that has informed most thinking about science until very recently. This is the idea that scientific facts have some sort of independent existence in a world in which they simply await discovery, and once we have collected enough of them we can develop some sort of theory. But this picture is both false for science and out of step with Dworkin's own conception of coherence. A better picture would, I suggest, be a modification of his constructive model to achieve a greater balance between the demands of fact or moral intuition on the one hand and theory on the other, with no *a priori* pronouncement about which wins when there is a conflict. Such a view would allow us to see the deep similarities between justification in the two realms without obscuring the difference that stems from the ineradicable presence of a moral dimension in legal theorizing.

University of Calgary

---

[48] See J. L. Mackie, 'The Third Theory of Law', *Philosophy and Public Affairs* 7 (1977): 3–16.

ACKNOWLEDGEMENT

The author is greatly indebted to the Calgary Institute for the Humanities and Wilfred Laurier University Press for permission to use material from her paper 'Legal Science and Legal Justification', which appeared in *Science, Pseudo-Science and Society*, edited by Marsha P. Hanen, Margaret J. Osler and Robert G. Weyant (Waterloo, Ont.: Wilfred Laurier University Press, 1980).

ROGER A. SHINER

PRECEDENT, DISCRETION AND FAIRNESS

I.

The notions of a court being *bound* by precedent to take a certain decision, of earlier cases being *authorities* for the case in question, are notions fundamental to the practice of law in common-law jurisdictions. Yet, like any other fact in the world, the existence of the practice of *stare decisis* provokes speculation as to its underlying nature and justification. The purpose of this paper is to offer an account of what it is for a court to be bound by precedent, an account which is broadly speaking Positivist in orientation but which is rooted more deeply than existing accounts in philosophical, rather than merely jurisprudential, understanding of concepts like those of "rule" and "practice". As will emerge in the paper, the tendency is for jurisprudential discussion about binding precedent to introduce baldly terms like 'rule', 'practice', 'necessity', 'choice' and so forth as if there was an antecendently existing and accepted meaning for those terms – so that we know exactly what is being said when binding precedent is said to be a matter of judicial practice, for example. But to the philosopher the meaning of those terms is itself also a matter of dispute. A genuinely deep understanding of binding precedent will therefore only come when those terms themselves are subjected to some discussion and the results of that discussion applied back to binding precedent itself. To reach such understanding is the goal of this paper.

Some important preliminary distinctions must first be made. Firstly, the courts standardly distinguish between "authoritative" or "binding" precedent and "persuasive" precedent. Whatever the term 'bound' means, as things now stand the English Court of Appeal is "bound" by decisions of the House of Lords, whereas it is not "bound" by decisions of the Australian High Court, or

M. A. Stewart (ed.), Law, Morality and Rights, 93–136.

the Supreme Court of Canada. It may consider and take what it will from decisions of courts of another jurisdiction, but it cannot be "required" to follow those decisions. In this paper, I am concerned only with this notion of being "bound", with "authoritative" or "binding" precedent. Secondly, it has been well emphasized by Joseph Raz[1] that for the Court of Appeal, for example, to be in *Broome* v. *Cassell*[2] "bound" by the House of Lords' decision in *Rookes* v. *Barnard,*[3] as the House of Lords vociferously insisted that it was,[4] is not tantamount to saying that the Court of Appeal must decide *Broome* as *Rookes* was decided *simpliciter.* Rather, the Court of Appeal's being "bound" amounts to the more complex idea that it must *either* decide *Broome* in the same way as *Rookes*, *or* else *distinguish Broome* from *Rookes.* Distinguishing an instant case from a precedent authority is an important function of common-law tribunals. Distinguishing is not to be regarded as something opposed to binding precedent but rather as part of that practice.

Thirdly, I want to distinguish myself between what I shall call the *formal* and the *material* aspects of binding precedent. Two quite different jurisprudential questions arise about precedent – (i) What is meant by the idea that a lower court is bound to follow the decision of a higher court without the full hearing of argument on legal issues characteristic of appellate courts?; (ii) What is it about some specific case, say *Ross* v. *Caunters*,[5] which means

---

[1] Joseph Raz, 'Law and Value in Adjudication', in his *The Authority of the Law* (Oxford: Clarendon Press, 1979), p. 185.

[2] *Broome* v. *Cassell & Co. Ltd. and another*, [1971] 2 QB 354.

[3] *Rookes* v. *Barnard*, [1964] AC 1129.

[4] *Cassell & Co. Ltd.* v. *Broome and another*, [1972] 1 All E.R. 801. The House of Lords nonetheless affirmed the Court of Appeal's decision, though on what the reporter coyly calls "different grounds" (804). Julius Stone refers to this decision as "what may well be the most hostile affirmation of a Court of Appeal decision in our history" ('On the Liberation of Appellate Judges: How Not to Do It!', *Modern Law Review* 35 (1972): 449–77, p. 451).

[5] *Ross* v. *Caunters (a firm)*, [1979] 3 All E.R. 580; cf. esp. pp. 593–6.

that, given *Donoghue* v. *Stevenson*[6] and *Sharp*[7] as authorities for that case, decision must be given in favour of the plaintiff Ross? The former question is about binding precedent as a formal procedure; the latter question is about the material way in which a decision in an instant case is derived from the formal authorities for that case. It is important to keep these two different questions apart; if one does not, then it is difficult to appreciate why legal philosophers get so exercised about binding precedent. The problematic nature of binding precedent only emerges when one acknowledges that its primary role is as a formal procedure. Lord Scarman failed to keep the two questions distinct in the recent *Duport Steel* case.[8] He wished to criticize the Court of Appeal for finding in favour of Duport Steel when, in his view, they were bound by *McShane*[9] to find in favour of the respondent union. He remarks that the Court of Appeal "failed to do justice according to law" (551). Does he mean that they simply committed the formal error of refusing to acknowledge that they were bound by precedent, or does he mean that the Court of Appeal's attempt to distinguish *Duport Steel* from *McShane* is founded on a mistaken view of the material content of the law? He seems to want to bring the first criticism, but his argument is largely about the second. The point is that binding precedent as a formal procedure raises difficulties precisely because it seems to operate independently of legal substance, and therefore independently of the demands of justice. It is a commonplace that to follow precedent mechanically can produce unfairness and injustice.[10] This is not to deny that

---

6 *Donoghue (or McAlister)* v. *Stevenson*, [1932] AC 562.

7 *Ministry of Housing and Local Government* v. *Sharp and another*, [1970] 1 All E.R. 1009.

8 *Duport Steel Ltd. and others* v. *Sirs and others*, [1980] 1 All E.R. 529; the Queen's Bench, Court of Appeal and House of Lords hearings are all at this reference.

9 *Express Newspapers Ltd.* v. *McShane*, [1980] 1 All E.R. 65.

10 Cf. remarks of Scarman L. J. (*Farrell* v. *Alexander*, [1976] 1 All E.R. 129, p. 147), and the discomfiture of Goff L. J. in *Davis* v. *Johnson* ([1978] 1 All E.R. 841, p. 870).

there are arguably other values that are represented by *stare decisis* – one recent article has listed "guidance, predictability, efficiency, uniformity and impersonality".[11] But by 'binding precedent' we do not *mean* 'being part of a system of law that represents certain values'. Legal philosophers know very well what the role of binding precedent is in relation to those values; they still feel the need to ask the first of my two questions. Let us therefore proceed to consider that question, and try to find a satisfactory answer.

II.

One possible answer is easily disposed of – that by 'must' in a statement like "the court must decide for the plaintiff" one means the 'must' of logical necessity. Philosophers, legal theorists and judges have all despaired of shedding light on binding precedent by appealing to the notion of logical necessity. The reason is not hard to find. Logical rigour transports one with infallible directness from point *A* to point *B*. But in courts of law, the most interesting questions are as to whether one is at point *A* in the first place, or whether point *B* is the point at which one wishes to arrive. Thus, if it is true that pheasants are livestock if and only if they are kept and bred for the production of food,[12] and if it is true that given pheasants were not kept and bred for the production of food, then those pheasants are not livestock. But logic alone will not settle whether the antecedents are true, and the truth-value of the antecedents, not propositional logic, will be dispositive of the case. The matter is elegantly put by Lord Diplock:[13]

---

[11] James Hardisty, 'Reflections on *Stare Decisis*', *Indiana Law Journal* 55 (1979/80): 41–69, p. 55. See also R. L. Brilmayer, 'Judicial Review, Justiciability and the Limits of the Common Law Method', *Boston University Law Review* 57 (1977): 807–31. Her defence of the U.S. Supreme Court's practice of using common-law methods to decide issues of justiciability amounts to an extolling of the virtues of those methods *per se*.

[12] *Earl of Normanton* v. *Giles*, [1980] 1 All E.R. 106.

[13] *R.* v. *Knuller (Publishing, Printing & Promoting) Ltd.*, [1973] AC 435, p. 470.

My major criticism of the reasoning of the majority of this House in *Shaw's* case [*Shaw* v. *D.P.P.*, [1962] AC 220] does not depend upon the charge having been one of conspiracy. That reasoning can be reduced to a single syllogism.

Every agreement to do any act which tends to corrupt public morals is a crime at common law. *Shaw's* act of publishing advertisements for prostitutes soliciting fornication tended to corrupt public morals. Therefore *Shaw's* agreement to do that act was a crime at common law.

In English law it is for the judge alone to determine whether the major premise in such a syllogism is true. The truth of the minor premise is a question for the jury, if there is any material upon which a rational being could hold it to be true. I do not criticise the jury's verdict in the instant case upon the minor premise. I deny the conclusion only because I am convinced that the major premise is false.

If the following of a precedent case is to be represented as a logical derivation, then the instant case and the precedent case must have identical legally relevant properties. The determination of the identity of this relevance must occur *prior to* determining the validity of the derivation. The derivation as such is therefore useless.

The rejection of logical necessity characteristically produces the extreme reaction of rule-scepticism, that if the determination of relevant similarity comes first, then the idea of one court being bound to follow the decision of another makes no sense. C. K. Allen has put this view well. He[14] remarks that the judge is bound, not in the sense that the superior court imposes fetters on him; rather, he places the fetters in his own hand. "The humblest judicial official has to decide for himself whether he is or is not bound, in the particular circumstances, by any given decision of the House of Lords" (290). Likewise, Winston has recently remarked[15] that any litigant can always raise the question of whether his case is an exception to a given rule. This response is inadequate because it blurs significant differences between cases. I shall mention three different cases where it might seem plausible to talk of a

---

[14] C. K. Allen, *Law in the Making*, 7th edn. (Oxford: Clarendon Press, 1964).
[15] K. I. Winston, 'On Treating Like Cases Alike', *California Law Review* 62 (1974): 1–39, p. 31.

court's "deciding for itself" or "placing the fetters in its own hand". It will be seen that even if we suppose that this talk *is* plausible in these cases, they are very specialized cases; in this manner one will throw into relief the ordinary instances of courts using authorities so that the implausibility of describing those ordinary cases in Allen's terms is manifest.

Consider first of all the position of Bristow J. in the original High Court hearing of *Miliangos*.[16] He was faced with, on the one hand, the House of Lords decision in *Havana Railways*[17] that a judgment providing remedy for breach of contract must always be in sterling, and, on the other hand, the Court of Appeal's decision in *Schorsch Meier*[18] that judgment should be given in the creditor's currency. Bristow J. considered himself (492) bound to follow the House of Lords ruling independently of the merits of the case. But it could be argued, and indeed was by Lord Denning (502), that Bristow J. was also bound by the Court of Appeal's decision, his court being lower in the hierarchy than the Court of Appeal. In so far as this thought is valid, then it can be said that Bristow J. decided for himself to fetter himself to the House of Lords and not the Court of Appeal.

The difficulty with this example is that one could argue that the House of Lords and the Court of Appeal are not coordinate, even though the High Court is bound by both. This feature vanishes in the position of State Supreme Courts in Australia in the late 1970's. The Privy Council (Appeals from the High Court) Act

[16] *Miliangos* v. *George Frank (Textiles) Ltd.*, [1975] 1 QB 487.

[17] *Re United Railways of the Havana & Regla Warehouses Ltd.*, [1960] 2 All E.R. 332.

[18] *Schorsch Meier GmbH* v. *Hennin*, [1975] 1 QB 416. The Court of Appeal's decision was upheld by the House of Lords, the House being impressed by Lord Denning's substantial, rather than his procedural argument, that the economic times had changed and that the law must change with them. They did not however accept this kind of argument when Denning attempted in *Federal Commercial & Navigation Co. Ltd.* v. *Tradax Export S.A. (The Maratha Envoy)*, [1977] 2 All E.R. 41, to overturn the House's recent decision in *E. L. Oldendorff & Co. GmbH* v. *Tradax Export S.A. (The Johanna Oldendorff)*, [1974] AC 479, on similar grounds; see [1978] AC 1.

1975 banned further appeals from the High Court to the Privy Council, and in *Viro*[19] the High Court declared itself not bound by decisions of the Privy Council. The question then arose of the position of State Supreme Courts if faced with a decision of the High Court conflicting with a decision of the Privy Council.[20] The High Court themselves in *Viro* were not of one mind (see headnote, 257–8), but there was a strong tendency to say that the decision of the High Court should be preferred. But a distinction must be drawn between the competence of the High Court to make this kind of announcement with respect to matters of federal law and with respect to matters of state law. In the latter case, it was doubtful whether the High Court could pronounce with authority. This created a situation in which, in theory, there could be conflicting decisions of two coordinate courts, the High Court and the Privy Council, and no greater formal authority vested in one than in the other. A case before a State Supreme Court would then seem to require a choice; the court would decide for itself by which decision to be bound, if indeed (cf. Blackshield 65) one could speak of being "bound" at all. When, as has happened in the case of New South Wales,[21] a State Supreme Court declares that

---

19 *Viro* v. *R.*, [1978] 18 ALR 257.

20 The issue is discussed briefly by Gordon Bale, 'Casting off the Mooring Ropes of Binding Precedent', *Canadian Bar Review* 58 (1980): 255–79, pp. 265–71. I should like to thank Prof. Bale for letting me see the typescript of this paper before publication, and indeed before the Conference. The issue is explored with relentless thoroughness by A. R. Blackshield in his monograph *The Abolition of Privy Council Appeals: Judicial Responsibility and "The Law for Australia"*, Adelaide Law Review Research paper No. 1 (Melbourne: Law Book Co., 1978).

21 In refusing leave to appeal to the Privy Council in *National Employers' Mutual General Association Ltd.* v. *Waind & Hill No. 2*, [1978] 1 NSWLR 466, Moffitt P. for the Court remarks (474) that "since the High Court and the Privy Council are equal, States must make their own decision on the matter". In the Supreme Court of South Australia, likewise refusing leave, in *Australian Government Workers' Association* v. *Armstrong*, [1980] 25 SASR 441, Mitchell J. quotes with approval Moffitt's argument in *Waind*. The Privy Council themselves seem prepared to cooperate. Giving judgment for

it will as a matter of principle consider itself bound by High Court decisions and not Privy Council decisions, the initial appropriateness of Allen's characterization is evident. But, again, one only has to consider how exotic these cases are to realize that a State Supreme Court, faced with a case raising the issue of excessive force in self-defence, is straightforwardly now bound by *Viro* in a way which cannot be appropriately described by Allen's characterization.

My third example is again from Australia. Quite soon after *Viro*, the High Court heard *Atlas Tiles Ltd.* v. *Briers*,[22] a case which raised the issue of whether an award of damages for personal injury or wrongful dismissal should take into account the liability of the plaintiff to income tax on the lost income. The controlling case to that point had been the House of Lords' decision in *Gourley*,[23] according to which liability to taxation is to be taken into account. The High Court in *Atlas Tiles* took the opposite view. However, two years later, in *Cullen*,[24] the issue was re-heard by the full Court, and this time the rule in *Gourley* was upheld. Given the fact that the High Court in *Cullen* was bound neither by *Gourley* nor by *Atlas Tiles*, it having the power to overrule its own decisions, and given that either the rule in *Gourley* would be upheld or it would not, then again we seem to have a case

---

the Council in *Max Cooper & Sons Pty. Ltd.* v. *Sydney City Council*, [1980] 29 ALR 77, Lord Diplock states: "In an area of law in which the High Court and their Lordships' Board now have concurrent final appellate jurisdiction, their Lordships consider that in the interests of legal certainty, they should give to decisions of the High Court the same respect as they give to previous decisions of this Board itself, and, although not strictly bound by those decisions, they ought to follow them unless they are convinced beyond a doubt they are wrong." (p. 83) Accordingly, the High Court's decision in *T. C. Wintle Pty. Ltd.* v. *T. & G. Mutual Life Society Ltd.*, [1977] 18 ALR 431 is applied with very little discussion of the merits.

22 *Atlas Tiles Ltd.* v. *Briers*, [1978] 21 ALR 129.

23 *British Transport Commission* v. *Gourley*, [1955] 3 All E.R. 796. The Supreme Court of Canada quietly rejected *Gourley* some time ago; see *R. (in right of Ontario)* v. *Jennings*, [1966] 57 DLR (2d) 644.

24 *Cullen* v. *Trappell*, [1980] 29 ALR 1.

where the Court could decide for itself which precedent to follow. As the highest appellate court, it would not be appropriate to speak of fetters. Again, if we do wish to speak in these terms of the High Court's position in *Cullen*, this only serves to make clearer the way in which it would not be appropriate to speak in those terms of the normal case of Allen's "humblest judicial official", or even for that matter the frequent position of a less humble official such as the Master of the Rolls.

I do not wish the thrust of my argument against Allen to be misunderstood. I am simply offering a phenomenological description of the differences between cases. I am not claiming outright that Allen's description is straightforwardly true of the three cases cited, but not of other cases. I am simply claiming that the cases are different, and leaving alone the matter of the most philosophically perspicuous way to represent the differences. Pre-philosophical intuitions of differences are the data for philosophy. Nonetheless, I shall now go on and claim that even in the three cases cited it is possible to overemphasize the freedom to choose, and that rule-scepticism does this. Raz (185) contrasts what he calls a "tame" view of distinguishing from a stronger view. According to the tame view, a court distinguishes a precedent case simply when it determines that its *ratio* does not apply to the instant case. According to the stronger view, some further conditions must be satisfied than simply a determination of non-applicability; these conditions are formal in character. Even taking into account what Raz rightly refers to as the "special revisability" of judge-made law (195), Raz's point is well taken, that not just any old refusal to follow counts as distinguishing within the notion of binding precedent. That being so, the sense of 'deciding for oneself' applicable to courts faced with precedents is weak. Moreover, even though one can and should differentiate between distinguishing and overruling, the latter being the prerogative of highest appellate tribunals,[25] overruling no more than distinguishing is done in a vacuum.

---

[25] *Pace* Lord Denning and his view that the Court of Appeal should be allowed to overrule its own past decisions; see pp. 116–17 below.

The House of Lords in its original Practice Statement[26] indicated that it would use the freedom to overrule sparingly, giving good reasons why this should be so, and indeed they have so used it. In considering whether to overrule, the House of Lords does not exactly consider precedents; in fact, it would be incoherent to suppose it did. But it does consider existing law and the principles instinct in such law. So, once again, one has to be very careful with what one builds into the idea of the House "deciding for itself".

I conclude therefore that it will not do either to try to represent the 'must' of binding precedent as the 'must' of logical necessity, or to move from the reasons for rejecting that thought to eschewing talk of courts' being "bound" altogether. There are three further explanations of binding precedent that have been favoured by theorists. Dworkin[27] argues that the bindingness of precedent is ultimately a moral bindingness. By merging law and morality into one homogeneous system, he devises a coherentist and deductivist view of legal argument in general and of arguments from precedents as a special case. A second view is that the bindingness of precedent is simply, in the words of Lord Scarman in *Duport Steel*, a "self-denying ordinance", "a judicially imposed limitation" (551). That is, the officials of common-law legal systems have simply decided to operate the system that way, and there is nothing else to be said about it. This view has been expressed academically by Dias[28] and Glanville Williams,[29] and also from the bench by Lord Denning.[30] On this view, the philosophical view to take is that there is no philosophical view to take. This view is not the same as Allen's, for it does not deny the existence of systematic rules of precedent; it simply offers a certain account of those systematic rules. The

---

26 [1966] 1 WLR 1234.

27 R. M. Dworkin, *Taking Rights Seriously*, 2nd edn. (Cambridge, Mass.: Harvard University Press, 1978) (henceforth *TRS*).

28 R. W. M. Dias, *Jurisprudence*, 4th edn. (London: Butterworth, 1976).

29 Letter to *The Times*, March 16th, 1978.

30 *Davis* v. *Johnson*, 853–7.

third view is Hart's,[31] who represents argument from precedent as partly like deductive argument and partly not much like argument at all. I shall say something about each of these theories in turn; my own positive remarks will grow out of the discussion of Hart.

III.

Dworkin's "rights thesis", that judicial decisions enforce existing political rights (*TRS* 87), is a complex, sophisticated and unified theory of law. I shall be trying here to isolate and discuss but one element of it, his doctrine of precedent. Judges are, for Dworkin, political officials. Any political official, and *a fortiori* any judge, must, to be responsible, bring any particular decision in any instant case "within some comprehensive theory of general principles and policies that is consistent with other decisions also thought right" (*TRS* 87). His decision must, in other words, be defensible by a sound argument of principle (cf. *TRS* 82). The ultimate touchstone for any argument of principle is the total theory of background political morality worked out by Dworkin's ideal judge Hercules (cf. *TRS* 105ff.). Dworkin's position on precedent is that the rights thesis, as embodied in the activities of Hercules, "provides a more satisfactory explanation of how judges use precedent in hard cases than the explanation provided by any theory that gives a more prominent place to policy" (*TRS* 87). In general terms, we should construe the use of precedent as a matter of proceeding to an adjudicative conclusion by principled arguments from background political morality. Dworkin thus appreciates that argument from precedent cannot be represented as formal deduction from premisses wholly within positive law. He wants us instead to view arguments from precedent as justified if and only if they are fragments of a deductive argument from background political morality. Let us look at his account in more detail.

---

[31] H. L. A. Hart, *The Concept of Law* (Oxford: Clarendon Press, 1961) (henceforth *CL*).

Dworkin begins by asking why arguments from precedent "are ever, even in principle, sound" (*TRS* 110). He then makes (*TRS* 111) a valuable distinction between the "enactment force" and the "gravitational force" of a precedent. The former is supposedly when Hercules "does find, in an earlier case, a canonical form of words" (*ibid.*), and then treats himself as bound by that form of words much as he would be bound by the language of a statute.[32] The latter, gravitational force, is exerted by a precedent when it is held to be dispositive of the instant case in spite of the fact that no *language* used in the statement of the earlier case directly dictates its applicability to the later case.

For Dworkin, the key to understanding precedent is understanding gravitational force. Here, Dworkin appeals to the principle (*P*), "Treat like cases alike", which he refers to as a principle of fairness (*TRS* 113). The sense of 'fairness' here is given by this remark (*ibid.*), that Hercules "must limit the gravitational force of earlier decisions to the extension of the arguments of principle necessary to justify those decisions", or, more briefly, that "Hercules, when he defines the gravitational force of a particular precedent, must take into account only the arguments of principle that justify that precedent" (*TRS* 115). In this way, Hercules is not free to do whatever he wants with precedent, so some "bindingness" is preserved.[33] The conclusion Dworkin

---

[32] Unlike a statute, there is no canonical form of words in a *ratio decidendi* appropriate for interpretation. Cf. R. C. Cross, *Precedent in English Law*, 3rd edn. (Oxford: Clarendon Press, 1977) (henceforth *PEL*), ch.2. Note also Lord Hailsham's warning in *Cassell* v. *Broome* that in a case (e.g. *Rookes* v. *Barnard*) when the judgment of an undivided court is delivered by a single voice, "the result may be an unduly fundamentalist approach to the language employed". Likewise Lord Reid (at 836) refers to it being found difficult in these circumstances "to avoid treating sentences and phrases in a single speech as if they were provisions of an Act of Parliament". Cf. also Lord Diplock at 873.

[33] J. L. Mackie ('The Third Theory of Law', *Philosophy and Public Affairs* 7 (1977/8): 3–16) has recently argued that, despite his disclaimers, precisely such licence is entailed by Dworkin's view. I will not adjudicate *that* hard case

goes on to draw from the existence of gravitational force so understood is that

> Since judicial practice in [Hercules'] community assumes that earlier cases have a ***general*** gravitational force, then he can justify that judicial practice only by supposing that the rights thesis holds in his community. ... He now sees that the familiar concept used by judges to explain their reasoning from precedent, the concept of certain principles that underlie or are embedded in the common law, is itself only a metaphorical statement of the rights thesis. (*TRS* 115–6; his italics)

> If precedents have gravitational force, and if this must be justified on the ground that fairness requires consistency, then it follows that these precedents must be supposed to have been generated by arguments of principle, as the rights thesis stipulates. (*TRS* 319)

In other words, once we have accepted that precedents work by having gravitational force, then we are committed to accepting Dworkin's rights thesis, for gravitational force can be adequately explained only if the rights thesis is assumed to be true. Dworkin thus hangs on to the goal of "mechanical jurisprudence", a decision dictated by superior general principle; but he achieves this only by going outside positive law for his general principles.[34]

---

here. But I will say that Dworkin's account seems to me to face analogous problems to those facing theorists such as A. L. Goodhart who wish to define *ratio decidendi* in terms of "material fact". Cf. Cross, *PEL* 66ff.

[34] Cf. Hart's description of Dworkin as "the noblest dreamer of them all", *Georgia Law Review* 11 (1977), p. 982. Dworkin does say (*TRS* 81) that it is no part of his theory "that any mechanical procedure exists for demonstrating what the rights of parties are in hard cases". Nonetheless, he does think that there is no reason to deny that every legal question has one right answer (cf. *TRS* ch.13 and *New York University Law Review* 53 (1978): 1–32). He also favours a coherentist model of justification akin to Rawls' notion of "reflective equilibrium" (cf. *TRS* 115–8, 159–68; J. Rawls, *A Theory of Justice* (Cambridge, Mass.: Harvard University Press, 1971), pp. 19–21, 46–53, 577–80). This approach is incompatible with an "intuitionistic" approach that does not seek to organize principles and particular judgments into one complete whole (cf. Rawls, p. 34). I think therefore that my treatment of Dworkin is strategically legitimate. Subsequent to the original Conference, my attention was drawn to Raz's review of *TRS* ('Professor Dworkin's Theory

Because Dworkin's account of precedent is part of his total theory, it is difficult to prove the account as taken in isolation to be false. I shall instead try to show how this account of precedent does not independently argue for, but rather presupposes, the soundness of the total theory and of the rights thesis. I shall show that a pre-analytic consideration of actual decisions does not force us into accepting Dworkin's view; the use of precedent in these decisions can be adequately explained by a weaker theory.

Take firstly the notion of fairness. We can distinguish here three senses in which a decision based on precedent can be fair. The first is that such a decision is fair only because the system of *stare decisis* is a fair way to administer justice. Dworkin seems to have this sense in mind when he talks (*TRS* 116) about fairness being the general justification of the practice of precedent. However, it would seem[35] that it is a complex (and open) question which system of *stare decisis*, a system as it operates in Britain, or a less rigorous practice as that in France, produces greater fairness in actual decisions. This sense of 'fairness' is not relevant to our present discussion. The second sense of 'fairness' requires taking a closer look at principle *P*. On a minimal interpretation, *P* simply states a need for internal consistency within positive law itself, without any demand that positive law be consistent with abstract general principles of justice. This is a weak sense of 'fairness'. It is one that Positivism embraces. It allows for unjust and unfair decisions and rules, if they are not inconsistent with the system of positive law. Positivism (cf. Hart *CL* 204–7) does not want the issue of the moral quality of a rule or a decision tangled up with

---

of Rights', *Political Studies* 26 (1978): 123–37). On pp. 135–6, Raz criticizes Dworkin in much the same terms as I do, although his motivation is different. I have argued that Dworkin's coherentist approach gets him into severe difficulties in 'The Metaphysics of Taking Rights Seriously', *Philosophia* 12 (1982). See also Marsha Hanen's paper in this volume.

[35] Cf. A. L. Goodhart, 'Precedent in English and Continental Law', *Law Quarterly Review* 50 (1934): 40–65; Lyndel V. Prott, 'Judicial Reasoning in the Common Law and Code Law Systems', *Archiv für Rechts- und Sozialphilosophie* 44 (1978): 417–35.

the issue of their validity or legality as such. The third sense of 'fairness' is a strong sense, and the one that Dworkin is advocating. Here, a decision based on precedent is fair just in case it is consistent not merely with settled law but also, and more importantly, with independent substantial principles of fairness that are part of background political morality.[36]

My claim will be that, even if one grants that to explain precedent one needs to explain gravitational force, and that to explain gravitational force one needs to refer to fairness, nonetheless all this can be cashed out well enough in terms of the weaker, or Positivistic, sense of 'fairness'; we are not forced, as Dworkin thinks, to appeal to the stronger sense. The issue can be presented in terms of two cases, one mentioned by Dworkin as illustrating his position (*TRS* 83, 111–5), *Spartan Steel*,[37] and a more recent case in the same area of liability in tort for economic loss, the *Caltex* case.[38] As is well known, the law in this area is in a state of flux. The widespread opinion that liability in the tort of negligence did not as a matter of rule extend to purely economic loss[39] seemed

---

[36] This is an oversimplication. Dworkin realizes that, given facts of institutional history, perfect coherence may not be available. This is why Hercules has to have a theory of *mistakes*; cf. *TRS* 119–22. However, this complication does not affect my present argument.

[37] *Spartan Steel & Alloys Ltd.* v. *Martin & Co. (Contractors) Ltd.*, [1972] 3 All E.R. 557.

[38] *Caltex Oil (Aust.) Pty. Ltd.* v. *The Dredge "Willemstad"*, [1976] 11 ALR 227.

[39] Cf. P. S. Atiyah, 'Negligence and Economic Loss', *Law Quarterly Review* 83 (1967): 248–76; C. Harvey, 'Economic Losses and Negligence: The Search for a Just Solution', *Canadian Bar Review* 50 (1972): 580–621; L. L. Stevens, 'Negligent Acts Causing Pure Financial Loss: Policy Factors at Work', *University of Toronto Law Journal* 23 (1973): 431–67; J. C. Smith, 'Clarification of Duty-Remoteness Problems Through a New Physiology of Negligence: Economic Loss, a Test Case', *U.B.C. Law Review* 9 (1974): 213–43; P. P. Craig, 'Negligent Misstatements, Negligent Acts and Economic Loss', *Law Quarterly Review* 92 (1976): 213–41. The Canadian case *Seaway Hotels Ltd.* v. *Gragg (Canada) Ltd.* ([1959] 17 DLR (2d) 292) seems to be a straightforward case of damages for purely economic loss; but the case seems scarcely to have been noticed as a precedent. This may well be in part because the

to be refuted by *Hedley Byrne.*[40] But no clear theory of the positive law on this matter has emerged to take its place. Ultimate control is exercised by various fundamental notions, duty to take care, reasonable foreseeability of damage, proximity of cause, the spectre of unlimited liability. On the other hand, powerful intuitions operate in cases such as *Caltex, Rivtow Marine,*[41] *Oppen,*[42] or *Ross* that in justice there is a party who should pay for its negligence. This state of affairs presents sharply just what it is for courts to be bound by precedent, and what the relationship is between precedent and substantial justice.

Note, first, that there is one short way of dealing with all of this; it is, not surprisingly, Lord Denning's. In *Spartan Steel*, he proposes (561, 563–4)[43] that one should decide each such case on the basis of *ad hoc* judgments of policy, and should not continue to tinker around with the concepts of duty and remoteness. This same approach, though there rooted in economic theory, is

---

Court's justification for its opinion is minimal, and the Court does not even seem to notice that it is breaking new ground. The decision refers straightforwardly to the concepts of foreseeability and remoteness. In particular, there is no mention of the doctrine of "parasitic damages" for which Rogers, discussing *Caltex*, praises the case (W. V. Horton Rogers, 'Economic Loss in the High Court of Australia', *Cambridge Law Journal* 34 (1978): 27–30).

[40] *Hedley Byrne & Co. Ltd.* v. *Heller & Partners Ltd.*, [1963] 2 All E.R. 575.

[41] *Rivtow Marine Ltd.* v. *Washington Iron Works et al.*, [1974] 40 DLR (3d) 530.

[42] *Union Oil Company et al.* v. *James J. Oppen et al.*, 501 F. 2d 558 (1974). In *Adams* v. *Southern Pacific Transportation Company*, [1975] 50 Cal. App. 3d 37, the prohibition on recovery of economic loss is reaffirmed; *Oppen* is regarded as some sort of surd exception.

[43] Cf. also his strenuous defence of the same approach in *Dutton* v. *Bognor Regis United Building Co. Ltd.*, [1972] 1 All E.R. 462, at 475 and 480, an approach repeated in a very recent case, *Lamb and another* v. *London Borough of Camden and another*, [1981] 2 All E.R. 408, pp. 412–14. On the other hand, Denning is not averse to employing the traditional concepts of duty, causation and remoteness where it suits his intuitions to do so – see *Compania Financiera Soleada S.A. and others* v. *Hamoor Tanker Corp. Inc. (The Borag)*, [1981] 1 All E.R. 856, p. 861.

followed by the U.S. 9th Circuit Court of Appeal in *Oppen.*[44] I shall not consider this approach; Dworkin is quite right to claim that such an approach makes a mockery of the doctrine of *stare decisis.*[45] The interesting questions concern the extent to which hard cases such as these, and a study of the way in which judges form their opinions in relation to positive law, force upon us a Dworkinian moralistic account of precedent. I shall argue that no such account is forced on us.

In respect of *Spartan Steel*, the stage seems set for the entrance of a Dworkinian theory in that Denning, as remarked, opts for a policy approach, while Edmund-Davies L. J. talks about "principle" (566) and Lawton L. J. says policy has no place in a court of law (573). However, we must be careful. Parallel to the distinction between two senses of 'fairness' is one between two senses of 'principle'. In a weak sense, which again a Positivist could acknowledge,[46] a principle is any expeditious summing up of the import of a set of materials in positive law. The stronger, Dworkinian, sense is that of a maxim not merely in that way summary but also coherent with background political morality. Dworkin wants us to construe statements of gravitational force as principles in this strong sense; but this is not necessary. Edmund-Davies finds for Spartan Steel while Lawton allows the defendant Martin's appeal on the issue of damages for economic loss. Both take themselves to be arguing from principle and from precedent. Edmund-Davies says that (569):

> Having considered the intrinsic nature of the problem presented in this appeal, and having consulted the relevant authorities, my conclusion, as

[44] Cf. 568–71, and also the Comment on this case, *Iowa Law Review* 60 (1974): 315–27. For Dworkin's view on the economic approach, see *TRS* 96–100.

[45] A fact which has not eluded Denning's critics – see the massive academic attack mounted in *Justice, Lord Denning and the Constitution*, edited by P. Robson and P. Watchman (Aldershot: Gower, 1981), and the quotations in that book from members of the Bench.

[46] See Joseph Raz, 'Legal Principles and the Limits of Law', *Yale Law Journal* 81 (1972): 823–54, *passim*.

already indicated, is that an action lies in negligence for damages in respect of purely economic loss, provided that it was a reasonably foreseeable and direct consequence of failure in a duty of care.

Lawton refers simply to the rule laid down by Blackburn J. in *Cattle*,[47] and claims that that is still the law. So both judges argue that the precedents are in their favour, on the ground that the standard notions of the law of torts, as standardly understood by the courts, apply to the case. In so far as the facts in *Spartan Steel* are not quite the same as in *Cattle*, or *Hedley Byrne*, or *Greystoke Castle*,[48] or *SCM* v. *Whittall,*[49] one wants of course to agree that gravitational force and not enactment force affects *Spartan Steel*. But the force comes entirely from within positive law. No winds of change blow from background political morality.

The carefully argued *Caltex* case makes the point still clearer.[50] The (simplified) facts are as follows. An underwater pipeline owned by Australian Oil Refining Pty. Ltd. carried petroleum products from AOR's refinery across Botany Bay to a Caltex terminal. The pipeline was negligently broken by the dredge "Willemstad". Cal-

---

[47] *Cattle* v. *Stockton Waterworks Co*., [1875] LR 10 QB 453.

[48] *Morrison Steamship Co. Ltd.* v. *Steamship "Greystoke Castle"*, [1946] 2 All E.R. 696.

[49] *SCM (United Kingdom) Ltd.* v. *W. J. Whittall & Sons Ltd*, [1970] 3 All E.R. 245.

[50] At the time when the original Conference version of this paper was written, little academic comment on *Caltex* had appeared. Since then, apart from the paper by Rogers mentioned in footnote 39, there have appeared the following discussions: H. H. Glass, 'Duty to Avoid Economic Loss', *Australian Law Journal* 51 (1977): 372–85, pp. 383–5; Peter F. Cane, 'Recovery in the High Court of Purely Economic Loss Caused by Negligent Acts', *Western Australian Law Review* 13 (1977): 243–61; G. R. Walker, 'Negligent Acts – Recovery for Economic Loss', *New Zealand Law Journal* (1978): 46–8; David Partlett, 'Recovery of Economic Loss for Negligence in Australia', *Sydney Law Review* 9 (1980): 121–61. Partlett's discussion is extremely thorough and valuable. However, I should like to say that none of this material has led me to believe that my original comments on the case were mistaken, and this part of the paper remains essentially unrevised from the Conference presentation.

tex brought action against the dredge for damages, these being the costs of arranging alternative means of transporting petroleum products until the pipeline was repaired – i.e., for purely economic loss. This action succeeded in the High Court of Australia with no dissent. Of the five judges, Murphy J. did little more than press his button in favour; Mason J. and Jacobs J. presented what look like arguments of principle; Gibbs J. and Stephen J. proceed in a more complex manner which invites special attention. Dworkin lays down two conditions, conceived of as severally necessary and jointly sufficient, for the soundness of a judicial decision from precedent in a hard case – (i) that the method of justification must be coherentist (cf. *TRS* 115–8), and (ii) that the justification must proceed ultimately from background political morality. We shall see from *Caltex* that neither of these conditions is in fact necessary.

The essential problem for the court in an economic loss case such as *Caltex* is well put by Mason (273–4):

> The problem is to yield compensation to the individual who suffers financial loss not necessarily consequential upon damage to his property when that loss is closely connected with the failure to take care and yet at the same time to deny compensation "in an indeterminate amount ... to an indeterminate class", in particular to a large class of persons whose loss arises because their use of a public utility or facility has been interrupted.

Both he and Jacobs attempt to solve the problem by laying down a more refined general principle than has hitherto operated in this area. Jacobs (284) deploys the notion of "physical propinquity" and Mason that of duty to a specific individual (274).[51] They take

---

[51] In *Yumerovski et al.* v. *Dani*, [1978] 4 CCLT 223, the references of Gibbs and Mason in *Caltex* to the role of the notion of a specific individual are quoted by McCart Co. Ct. J. (231), and are an essential part of his opinion. The plaintiffs purchased return charter flight tickets from Toronto to Yugoslavia for themselves and their families through a travel agency of which the defendant was Vice-President. The defendant agreed to drive some of the family to the airport. *En route* the defendant was involved in an accident which resulted in the death of one of the family members. As a consequence, none of the family members boarded the flight. The plaintiffs were unable

these concepts from the existing positive law, and argue that the adoption of such a principle would make the award to Caltex Oil cohere with the existing authorities and concepts. Thus they seem implicitly to accept Dworkin's condition (i). But Gibbs and Stephen do not. While looking at the problem in the same substantial terms, Gibbs explicitly rejects a coherentist approach (245):

In my opinion it is still right to say that as a general rule damages are not recoverable for economic loss which is not consequential upon injury to the plaintiff's person or property.... However, there are exceptional cases.... It is not necessary, and would not be wise, to attempt to formulate a principle that would cover all cases in which such a duty is owed. ...

Stephen initially calls for (258)

some principle of law which will operate as a sufficient restraint upon excessively wide liability without calling in aid as a control mechanism the quite random incidence of damage resulting from a particular act of carelessness.

But he shortly displays commendable *sang-froid* at his lack of success in finding such a principle.[52] He remarks (260–1):

But in the general realm of negligent conduct it may be that no more specific proposition can be formulated than a need for insistence upon sufficient proximity between tortious act and compensable detriment. The articulation, through the cases, of circumstances which denote sufficient proximity will provide a body of precedent productive of the necessary certainty; the gradual accumulation of decided cases and the impact of evolving policy considerations will reflect "the court's assessment of the demands of society for protection from the carelessness of others". ...

As the body of precedent accumulates some general area of demarcation between what is and is not a sufficient degree of proximity in any particular

---

otherwise to recover the cost of the tickets, and their action against the defendant for these economic losses was unsuccessful. To my untrained nose, it seems excessive to regard baldly this case as controlled by *Caltex*. The causal nexus seems different. If the *Caltex* "individual" principle is applied as unthinkingly as this, no short solution to the problems in this area lies in it.

[52] This point is missed by Cane in 'Recovery...'; he conflates (252) Stephen's approach here with that of Edmund-Davies in *Spartan Steel*, whereas this aspect of Stephen's decision marks an important difference on the matter of "principle".

class of case of economic loss will no doubt emerge; but its emergence neither can be, nor should it be, other than as a reflection of piecemeal conclusions arrived at in precedent cases. The present case contains a number of salient features which will no doubt ultimately be recognised as characteristic of one particular class of case among the generality of cases involving economic loss. This will be typical of the development of the common law. ...

He then goes on to enumerate five such features, the details of which do not concern us, prefacing the list with the remark that "the existence of these features leaves no doubt in my mind that there exists in this case sufficient proximity to entitle the plaintiff to recover its reasonably foreseeable economic loss" (261). Stephen therefore, like Gibbs, thinks that the award to Caltex Oil is justified by an argument which examines in detail particular features of the instant case and other cases, and makes no attempt to construct a grand Herculean coherentist justification. The point, and I shall say more on this later (see section VI, below), is that Gibbs and Stephen are quite right. In theory, the method of justification they employ leads to as sound an argument from precedent as does the coherentist method of Mason and Jacobs. The introduction of unifying principles makes no difference.

With regard to Dworkin's second condition, Gibbs, Mason and Jacobs contrast with Stephen. The former trio draw for their opinions entirely on the standard notions of the law of torts, as they are held to be instantiated in the standard range of authorities. By contrast, Stephen sounds more "Dworkinian". He inveighs against the Denning-style *ad hoc* policy approach as adopted in *Oppen* (254). While he acknowledges the relevance of policy considerations, he continues (254–5), in language strongly evocative of Dworkin's policy/principle distinction:[53]

That process [sc. of policy considerations] should, however, result in some definition of rights and duties, which can then be applied to the case in hand, and to subsequent cases, with relative certainty. To apply generalized policy considerations directly, in each case, instead of formulating principles derived from policy and applying those principles, derived from policy, to the case in

---

[53] Cf. *TRS* 22–3, 87–100, 294–327.

hand, is, in my view, to invite uncertainty and judicial diversity. This suggests a need for some more positive guidance as to the entitlement, if any, to recover in negligence for solely economic loss than is provided by judicial policy making based upon a case-by-case consideration of whatever factors the particular court may deem relevant.

There are passing references to "justice and morality" (257) and "the demands of society" (261). But these are both picking up *dicta* of other judges. Otherwise, Stephen is, for all his talk of principles and entitlement, as concerned strictly with the resources of positive law as are his fellow judges.

It follows, therefore, that Dworkin's second condition is not necessary either. Certainly, to speak of "gravitational force" is to use a vivid metaphor for illuminating the working of precedent. It is even appropriate to cash out gravitational force in terms of the idea of "principle". However, not only is a reference to principle not necessary for interpreting "gravitational force"; also, if one is to use the notion of "principle", it can be perfectly well cashed out in terms of concepts instinct in positive law, concepts whose relation to background political morality remains properly unconsidered. I conclude, therefore, that Dworkin has failed to prove that we must interpret the binding force of precedent in terms of the bindingness of obligations drawn from background political morality, and failed to show that the justification of a decision based on precedent must take a coherentist form.

Another way of putting this criticism of Dworkin is to say that he is simply conflating the formal and the material questions about precedent which I distinguished in section I. As has been forcibly argued by David Pannick in another recent critique of Dworkin's theory of precedent,[54] the whole idea of a court's being bound by rules of precedent to decide a case in a certain way is meant to exclude the possibility that the court decides the issue on the merits as such. In itself, this point is well taken, but one must state more carefully than Pannick does how it cuts into

---

[54] David Pannick, 'A Note on Dworkin and Precedent', *Modern Law Review* 43 (1980): 36–44.

Dworkin's position. From where Hercules stands, the two questions about precedent are *not* distinct. The lower nodes in his ideal structure will be points at which what justice demands and what precedent demands are identical. That is the whole point of his ideal justificatory theory of law. But of course mundane judges are not Hercules; so for them there will be conflicts arising from discrepancies between their conceptions of what the law demands and Hercules' conception. In so far as Dworkin takes himself to be describing how, for example, the English system of binding precedent actually operates, then to give an account which presupposes that the Lords Justice have Herculean insight is inappropriate. It does not, however, follow from this, as Pannick claims (e.g. 37), that binding precedent cannot be reconciled with the rights thesis. Pannick is insensitive to the Fullerian[55] resonances of Dworkin's position. The values which a system of binding precedent promotes (see p. 96 above) could in principle be represented as abstract, background rights (cf. *TRS* 93). Consequently, a litigant could claim an entitlement to a certain decision based on rules of binding precedent,[56] and that is a claim that the courts have the competence to consider. But even to look at precedent this way is not to shed light on what it is in a formal sense for a court to be bound by a precedent, and to try to do precisely that is my concern here.

IV.

I turn now to the claim that the rules of precedent must simply be accepted as brute assumptions of the legal system as an idiosyncratic institution. If that is so, then the force of the notion of "binding" precedent, though certainly not weakened in the short run, is weakened in the long run. If this view is right, then at any

---

[55] See L. L. Fuller, *The Morality of Law*, 2nd edn. (New Haven: Yale University Press, 1969), ch.2.

[56] This is in fact done in cases such as *Miliangos, Davis* and *Ross*, where defendants submitted that, as the authorities stood, a decision in their favour was dictated by precedent.

moment it is possible for the participants in the institution to vary the constitutive rules of the institution. In what sense therefore could there be a system of *binding* precedent? The system is quite autonomous, and not subject to the heteronymy of morality or logic.

Although, as I have said, this approach is not the same thing as rule-scepticism,[57] it seems to me open to the same kind of objection, that is, that it does not fit the cases. As is well known, for several years[58] Lord Denning has been attempting (so far, unsuccessfully) to persuade his fellow judges in the Court of Appeal to lay aside the rule adopted in *Young*'s case[59] that the Court would consider itself, with limited exceptions, to be bound by its own previous decisions. In *Davis*, Denning produces the following argument (853–7). He characterizes the pre-*Young* situation as one where the Court held to rules of precedent as a matter of judicial comity. The Court in *Young*'s case purported to make the matter one of the rule of law, not mere comity. The 1966 Practice Statement in the House of Lords shows that this distinction in untenable:

> That shows conclusively that a rule as to precedent (which any court lays down for itself) is not a rule of law at all. It is simply a practice or usage laid down by the court itself for its own guidance; and, as such, the successors of that court can alter that practice or amend it or set up other guidelines, just as the House of Lords did in 1966.

Therefore, Denning concludes, the Court is in 1978 no more bound by the rule in *Young* than it was in 1944 by judicial comity.

This argument is highly ingenious, but philosophically confused. To appreciate this, consider the response of the House of Lords to Denning's activities. In tone, it began with strident accusations of

---

[57] Though at 195–6 Dias does seem to espouse such scepticism.

[58] Cf. 856–7 of Lord Denning's opinion in *Davis* (footnote 10 *supra*) for detailed references. Bale approves of Denning's argument in *Davis*, and thus commits himself to the same unsatisfactory appeal to the concept of judicial comity (pp. 273–5).

[59] *Young* v. *Bristol Aeroplane Co. Ltd.*, [1944] 2 All E.R. 293.

disloyalty[60] and has by now modulated through affectionate despair to reluctant but sincere admiration.[61] Two aspects of this response are significant. Firstly, there is the use of modal concepts. Lord Hailsham (*Cassell*, at 809) talks of the "necessity" for courts to observe the rules of precedent. Cross[62] glosses this as "essential to the workings of a judicial system like the English". In *Davis*, Lord Dilhorne uses 'conclusively' (1146), and Lord Salmon 'must' (1153). How is the use of these modal notions to be explained? We have a clear intuitive sense of their appropriateness for explaining binding precedent, and yet we have also seen that it is difficult to regard them as the modalities of deductive logic.[63] There is some difference between a matter of rule and a matter of mere comity, and the use of modal notions does much to bring out that difference. The other aspect worth remarking is the reference to disloyalty. This is a moral notion, and invites the Dworkinian moralistic approach to binding precedent which I have criticized. Again, talk of disloyalty, for all that the bindingness of precedent is not purely moral obligation, does seem a proper way of registering the distinction between rule and mere comity. The ties of comity are too weak to support allegations of disloyalty, and there is a dimension other than the strictly logical involved here.

---

[60] Cf. Lord Diplock (*Cassell & Co. Ltd.* v. *Broome*, p. 874) with respect to the attempt in *Broome* v. *Cassell* to depart from *Rookes* v. *Barnard*; Lord Simon of Glaisdale (*Miliangos*, p. 822), with respect to the attempts in *Miliangos* and *Schorsch Meier* to depart from *Havana Railways*.

[61] Compare Lord Diplock in *Davis* v. *Johnson*, pp. 1137, 1139; Lord Scarman, *Duport Steel*, p. 551.

[62] R. C. Cross, 'The House of Lords and the Rules of Precedent', in *Law, Morality and Society*, edited by P. M. S. Hacker and J. Raz (Oxford: Clarendon Press, 1977), p. 147.

[63] C. E. F. Rickett, 'Precedent in the Court of Appeal', *Modern Law Review* 43 (1980): 136–58, is an example of a theorist who apparently thinks that the bald introduction by themselves of modal notions explains binding precedent; see pp. 141–2. Nonetheless, Rickett ends his paper with a valuable discussion of the policy justification for a rule binding the Court of Appeal to follow its own previous decisions.

I conclude therefore that the strategy of trying to understand a system of binding precedent as an idiosyncratic autonomous institution is mistaken. Courts in discussing problems of the operation of precedent naturally use terms which embody comparison between precedent and other functioning institutions, namely, morality and logic. Such comparisons must be taken seriously, even though to regard precedent as simply a sub-institution of those institutions is equally mistaken. It is not sufficient simply to avoid the issue, as this approach does, of explaining the naturalness of these terms.

V.

The direction the discussion must now take has already been hinted at. Implicitly, I have been saying that precedent is properly thought of as a system of *rules*. Mention of the notion of "rule" in a jurisprudential context leads by familiar association to mention of Hart. The details of Hart's "social rule" theory of law are by now well known. There are two dimensions to the view of precedent embodied in it. Firstly, what one may call the formal rules of precedent (e.g., the rule laid down in *Young*) are, in Hart's theory, secondary rules founded on the social practice among officials to accept from the internal point of view these rules as binding upon themselves (*CL* 85, 229). The talk of "disloyalty" is easily interpretable as reference to the internal aspect of rules, for, on Hart's view (*CL* 55–6), that aspect is manifested in criticism of oneself and others.[64] However, there seems to be no room in the social-rule theory for any account of the modal qualities, if we may call them that, of a system of binding precedent. By 'necessary' we do not mean 'regarded by officials as necessary'. The internal aspect gives us a concept of normative standards. Rules

---

[64] As Cross deliciously points out in 'The House of Lords...', p. 149, the Court of Appeal had "no truck" with Bristow J.'s decision to ignore their rules in *Schorsch Meier* – "the antics of the biter bit are inevitably of interest in any context".

of logic are normative standards; but it would be a fallacy to conclude that therefore the internal aspect gave us the logical modalities. The problem raised by the Denning position discussed above remains. Consider remarks such as that by Lord Scarman (*Duport Steel* 552) that "the Court of Appeal in this case ... strayed beyond the limits set by judicial precedent". If the Court of Appeal is bound by the rule in *Young* just in case *it* has the internal point of view (cf. *CL* 86–8) towards the rule in *Young*, what reason is there to claim that the Court of Appeal would still be so bound *even if it no longer* had the internal point of view towards the rule in *Young*, but this internal point of view was confined to the House of Lords?[65] It is at this stage that appeal to the logical modalities is made (cf. p. 117 above), and it is here that more is needed than merely the assertion that legal rules are social rules.

Hart's doctrine is also ultimately inadequate when one turns to the other dimension of precedent, the dimension in which Dworkin's "gravitational force" operates, that which I call the material dimension. If we are interested in what it is about just those precedents considered in *Caltex* which generated just that decision, it is not enough to state formally that the precedents were authoritative. The material content of the precedents is what concerns us. Hart's general theory analogous to Dworkin's gravitational force is twofold. He rejects (*CL* 135) the rule-sceptic's argument that open-texturedness implies no bindingness at all. If a case falls clearly under a valid rule, then it is simply an error to argue that, because the rule is fuzzy at the penumbra, the court is not determinately bound in a core case. Elsewhere,[66] he expresses the moral of his doctrine of the penumbra as "man cannot live by deduction alone" – which suggests that that is how man does live at the core

---

65 Blackshield (68) has shrewdly commented that the House of Lords' position does not seem to be to deny that courts can be creative; rather it is to insist on having a monopoly on creativity!

66 'Positivism and the Separation of Law and Morals', reprinted in *Law and Philosophy*, edited by E. A. Kent (New York: Appleton-Century-Crofts, 1970), p. 575.

(cf. also how he deals with syllogistic at *CL* 124). Hart's account here seems to amount to no more than Dworkin's "enactment force". The *ratio* of the precedent case is formulable in certain language; that language applies to the instant case; therefore the appropriate disposition of the instant case follows by logic alone. Consider the way in which Megarry V-C. argues that he is bound by *Sharp* to decide for the plaintiff in *Ross* (596). Expressed formally, Megarry's argument goes: the *ratio* of *Sharp* is of the form "If F_1, F_2, F_3, F_4, F_5, then V_p; *Ross* has features $F_1, \ldots, F_5$, therefore in *Ross* the verdict should be V_p".

Even if this style of analysis will work for the established core, it will not of course work for the rest of the material dimension of precedent. *Ex hypothesi* when a case is a hard case, a penumbral case, there exists nothing which "binds" in the sense of "yielding a decision by mechanical deduction". Hart's account of adjudication in hard cases, as is well known, is that such decisions are *discretionary*, that courts, as Dworkin puts it, are "simply *not bound* by standards set by the authority in question" (*TRS* 32; my italics). Hart talks of "choices" (*CL* 124, 126, 127), a "rule-producing function" (*CL* 132), "legislative" or "creative" activity (*CL* 132, 142), a "law-creating power" (*CL* 141), the exercise of "a creative function" (*CL* 144). One must certainly note his disclaimers (e.g., *CL* 132) that much of the daily operation of the law is *not* like this. Nonetheless, this element of the law is the source of its ability to suit the human predicament (*CL* 124), and is therefore of paramount importance. One must note also Hart's disclaimer that this talk of discretion does not mean that adjudication in penumbral cases is arbitrary. A judge exercising discretion

> chooses to add to a line of cases a new case because of resemblances which can reasonably be defended as both legally relevant and sufficiently close. In the case of legal rules, the criteria of relevance and closeness of resemblance depend on many complex factors running through the legal system and on the aims or purpose which may be attributed to the rule. (*CL* 124)

> Neither in interpreting statutes nor precedents are judges confined to the alternatives of blind, arbitrary choice, or 'mechanical' deduction from rules

with predetermined meaning. ... [Judges] often display characteristic judicial virtues ... [including] a concern to deploy some acceptable general principle as a reasoned basis for decision. No doubt because a plurality of such principles is always possible it cannot be *demonstrated* that a decision is uniquely correct: but it may be made acceptable as the reasoned product of informed impartial choice. (*CL* 200; Hart's italics)

Nonetheless, Hart must think that *something* significant about penumbral adjudication is brought out by the use of terms like 'discretion', 'choice', 'creation', etc. I can only interpret this as a denial of any constraint, bindingness or obligation with respect to the *particular* gravitational force ultimately deemed dispositive. I.e., on Hart's terms, there was no sense in which Lawton was *bound* in *Spartan Steel* to see the resemblance between *Cattle* and *Spartan Steel* as decisive. He exercised discretionary choice in doing so. Perhaps he *was bound* to choose impartially, judiciously, with due attention to alternative possibilities. But he *was not bound* to decide for the defendants; that he *chose* to do.

Hart thus seems to accept for hard cases an Allen-type "rule-scepticism". This is not the pure rule-scepticism of the game of "scorer's discretion" or of uncertainty in the rule of recognition (cf. *CL* 138–50), but it is still some form of scepticism about the genuineness of gravitational force. Moreover, if one adopts the plausible view that the rules of precedent in a common-law system are part of the rule of recognition for that system,[67] then as soon as a would-be reformer like Lord Denning generates some legitimate support for his view, we *do* have uncertainty in the rule of recognition, and therefore in Hart's view we do have a situation correctly described by pure rule-scepticism. This view will not be perceived as adequate by the House of Lords and its supporters, and thus Hart's view indicates and does not resolve the root philosophical problem of binding precedent.

---

[67] A view expressed by Rickett (144). He, however, thinks that an appeal to Hart's theory is sufficient to explain the tug-of-war between the Court of Appeal and the House of Lords on this matter.

The use by Hart of the label 'discretion' and his emphasis on 'choice' indicates that he has not freed himself from the grip of mechanical jurisprudence as much as he thinks he has. Certainly his positivism leads him to regard as horrific the construction of an axiomatic structure linking law and morality (cf. *CL* 200). Also the emphasis on open texture is a valuable rejection of mechanical jurisprudence within the limits of settled law as determined by the rule of recognition. But how else to construe the idea that what faces a judge in a hard case is *genuinely a choice*, except in terms of the idea that demonstration is impossible (cf. the quote from *CL* 200, above)? If this is right, then there is something odd about the notion of "reasoned choice". For if 'reasoning' means 'deductive reasoning', what seems to be given with 'reasoned' is taken away from us with 'choice'. One might say at this point that "reasoned choice" is simply one of those illuminating paradoxes in philosophy, that the deep nature of penumbral adjudication can only be brought about by such a juxtaposition of clashing ideas. In an important way, as will be seen, this is absolutely right. However, tactical questions arise about the stage in the discussion of these problems at which the deployment of the paradox will be most effective. The argument of the remainder of this paper may be taken as an argument that Hart deploys it too soon. His talk of discretion and choice has caused disquiet among opponents which his disclaimers have not removed. The reason is that his understanding of the nature of logic and of the notion of rule is too shallowly rooted in background metaphysical understanding of these matters.[68] If we can deepen our grasp of the metaphysical background, then the notion of "choice" will be purged of its troublesome connotations, and the paradox can do its therapeutic work.

---

[68] Hart acknowledges that Wittgenstein has had valuable things to say about rules; cf. *CL* 249, also 'Definition and Theory in Jurisprudence', *Proceedings of the Aristotelian Society*, Suppl. 29 (1955), p. 258. But he does not develop any of this in relation to accounts of legal argument from precedent.

VI.

The notion I would like to pick up on is contained in the 1966 declaration on precedent by the House of Lords. This reads in part, "[Their Lordships] propose therefore to modify their present *practice* and, while treating decisions of this House as normally binding, to depart from a previous decision where it appears right to do so" (my italics). The notion of the system of precedent as a *practice* is the way into the remarks I want to make.[69] I will show how, in Wittgenstein, the notions of "rule" and "practice" are given a metaphysical depth which helps to put the notion in law of a practice of binding precedent in its proper perspective.

Hard cases have the following characteristic which leads to the difficulty in understanding how the notion of "binding precedent" applies to them. They are contexts where the question at issue remains open after all the relevant facts have been ascertained and all mechanical inferences from accepted principles have been made. John Wisdom[70] has claimed that argument in these contexts proceeds, not by deduction or induction, but by argument from parallel cases. He claims also that argument from parallel cases is a perfectly valid form of argument in itself. He points to the reasoning characteristic of courts of law as a palmary case of argument from parallel cases. Legal theorists have remarked on Wisdom's claims, but they have not on the whole felt them to shed a great

---

[69] Cf. also "By 'binding status' is meant the status of a rule which is such that for a judge to reject it would be a gross departure from the practice of the courts", D. H. Hodgson, *Consequences of Utilitarianism* (Oxford: Clarendon Press, 1967), p. 111. Likewise Cross remarks, "Can there be any doubt that it [sc. the 1966 Declaration] owes its validity to the inherent power of any court to regulate its own practice?", 'The House of Lords...', p. 157.

[70] Cf., e.g., 'Gods', in *Philosophy and Psychoanalysis* (Oxford: Blackwell, 1953). The fullest account is in the as yet unpublished lectures on 'Proof and Explanation'; these lectures are discussed in D. C. Yalden-Thomson, 'The Virginia Lectures', in *Wisdom: Twelve Essays*, ed. Renford Bambrough (Oxford: Blackwell, 1974). Wisdom also in that work argues the further claim that case-by-case reasoning is the fundamental form of reasoning. I shall not pursue that issue here. Note that this too is hinted at in Wittgenstein; cf. *RFM* V. 24.

deal of light on legal reasoning.[71] This is because the philosophical background to Wisdom's claims has not been considered. It does seem a boring truism that legal reasoning proceeds by the examination of particular cases. To make it more than a boring truism, one has to see it as linked to Wittgenstein's account of rules, and *that* as a proper model for understanding how a system of binding precedent functions. The task here, that is, is to turn Wisdom on his head, and use what he and Wittgenstein have said, directly or indirectly, about argument from parallel cases to illuminate the nature of a system of binding precedent.

There are three essential elements to Wittgenstein's account of rules – (1) that the concept of a rule is not inconsistent with the concept of a practice; a rule is neither an untouchable piece of language nor a mere agreement in opinion; (2) a rule is still a rule, even though it is not the case that all its future applications are determined by the language in which it is phrased; (3) even given this account of a rule, a concept of necessity is available. I shall deal with these in turn.

1. *Rule and Practice*

"Obeying a rule" Wittgenstein says (*PI* 202)[72] *is a practice*. "A rule stands there like a signpost. Does the signpost leave no doubt open about the way I have to go?" (*PI* 85). "A person goes by a

---

[71] Cf. A. G. Guest, 'Logic in the Law', *Oxford Essays in Jurisprudence*, Vol. 1, ed. A. G. Guest (Oxford: Clarendon Press, 1961), p. 183; Cross, *PEL* 194ff. (he distinguishes Wisdom's idea from reasoning by analogy; the former is used in cases of first impression and the latter in "normal" cases: Cross does however suggest that this distinction is but one of degree); P. Weiler, 'Two Models of Judicial Decision-Making', *Canadian Bar Review* 46 (1968), p. 435. Weiler associates Wisdom's view with Polanyi's, and glosses it as "intersubjective acceptability". This is wrong as a picture of what Wisdom intends; the knowledge of particular cases is in principle as objective as any other kind of knowledge.

[72] References to Wittgenstein's works are to *Remarks on the Foundations of Mathematics* (*RFM*) (Oxford: Blacwell, 1956), *Philosophical Investigations* (*PI*), 2nd edn. (Oxford: Blackwell, 1958), and *On Certainty* (*OC*) (Oxford: Blackwell, 1969). References to these works are given by *paragraph number*.

signpost only in so far as there exists a regular use of signposts, a custom" (*PI* 198). Wittgenstein is asking us to reflect here on what really constitutes behaviour according to a rule. It is not simply that the rule says, "Do *X*" and *A* does *X*. My following the signpost to Lancaster is not a matter of the signpost pointing to the right and reading 'Lancaster' together with my turning to the right. I must recognize that *this* is a signpost, and that *that* is the way the signpost is telling me to go. Those things are not given by the existence of the signpost and my right turn. They are a matter of my taking the signpost in a certain way. But what is the foundation of *that*? It is no kind of idiosyncratic decision on my part (cf. *PI* 199). Nor is it that the signpost itself tells me (*PI* 85). Rather, this is just the way that signposts function in our society. It is part of our form of life; it is a practice, a custom for us to behave that way. "It is not a kind of *seeing* on our part; it is our *acting* which lies at the bottom of the language-game" (*OC* 204; Wittgenstein's italics). He expresses the same idea in a fundamentally important distinction made at *PI* 241–2 between "agreement in opinion" and "agreement in judgment", the latter glossed as "agreement in form of life". The conscious deliberation and discussion of a jury will result in agreement in opinion. But our normal application of language to the world is not like that. We do not normally deliberate before calling red things red, cars cars, and courageous acts courageous. We learn as children to apply these terms naturally, and what we all naturally learn by this process is *how things are. This* agreement is an agreement in judgment. Our *judgments* are attuned to one another by natural development, by inheriting a language and a form of life; it is not that our opinions become attuned to one another by deliberation.[73]

2. *Rule and Determination*

Given that rules are practices, based on agreement in judgments,

[73] I have discussed Wittgenstein's idea of action as the basis for knowledge more fully elsewhere; cf. 'Wittgenstein and the Foundations of Knowledge', *Proceedings of the Aristotelian Society* 78 (1977/78): 103–24.

how then do rules determine their applications? It is tempting to think that a rule determines in advance how it is to be applied – that this is precisely what is meant by there being *a rule* about some matter. Without this antecedent determination, how can there be a rule? We have already noted that many of the problems both in understanding the bindingness of precedent as the bindingness of a rule and in interpreting the principle *P* "Treat like cases alike" stem from the need to make a separate determination of whether the instant case is, in the appropriate sense, "like" the precedent. Wittgenstein accepts this need. "The use of the word 'rule' and the use of the word 'same' are", says Wittgenstein, "interwoven" (*PI* 225). That is, we do not understand a rule unless we understand what the rule will countenance as identical actions performed according to it. However, Wittgenstein also warns (*PI* 215–6) against the philosophical (and, I would add, practical) uselessness of using the identity of a thing with itself as a paradigm of sameness. This is to put at a more general metaphysical level the inadequate idea, born of the hopeless quest for perfectly justified decisions, that a case is only a genuinely binding precedent for another case *exactly* like it. In this context of uncertainty, the determination of what counts as "the same case" for the purposes of a given rule comes about only from a *practice* of taking the rule that way. But this means that the rule *is* that practice. The rule *qua* piece of language does not determine what counts as the same thing; only the rule *qua* practice does that.

3. *Rule and Necessity*

One might feel inclined now to say the following. Wittgenstein may be right in the above two points about fuzzy-edged social rules such as the rules of etiquette or of morality. But the hard-edged rules of logic and mathematics are different. Why should not law as a rigorous discipline aspire to be like the latter? And if it does, then will not the above two points be irrelevant?

Notoriously, Wittgenstein gives this same account of mathematical rules – "But then what does the peculiar inexorability of mathematics consist in?. ... It is usable, and, above all, *it is used*"

(*RFM* I.4; his italics). Later he writes:

> We now draw attention to the fact that the word "inexorable" is used in a variety of ways. There correspond to our laws of logic very general facts of daily experience. They are the ones that make it possible for us to keep on demonstrating those laws in a very simple way (with ink on paper for example). They are to be compared with the facts that make measurement with a yardstick easy and useful. This suggests the use of precisely these laws of inference, and now it is *we* that are inexorable in applying these laws. Because we '*measure*'; and it is part of measuring for everybody to have the same measures. Besides this, however, inexorable, i.e., *unambiguous* rules of inference can be distinguished from ones that are not unambiguous, I mean from such as leave an alternative open for us. (*RFM* I.118; his italics)

There are various images that the notion of "binding" can be used to express, as there are various cases of inexorability. In one sense, a law binds only when it is unambiguous. We have seen how Hart's use of 'discretion' and 'choice' seems to presuppose such a sense. But that notion of binding does not illustrate anything deep about the operation of precedent, any more than taking deductive inference as the paradigm of inexorability reveals anything deep about the inexorability of mathematics.[74]

Wittgenstein's account of mathematics and logical necessity depends on relating it to fundamental human practices such as counting and so-called natural deduction. The point of this is *not* to defend rule-scepticism in mathematics and logic. Rather, it is to show in what the character of being governed by inexorable rules consists. He does it by the well-known device of considering what could be said about one who wishes to continue the series 996, 998, 1000, ... by 1004, 1008, ... (cf. e.g. *PI* 183ff., *RFM* I *passim*), and how such a one may be said to be ignoring a valid rule. This account of what it is to follow mathematical and logical rules makes following such rules a *special case* of what it is to follow *any* rule. What is being marked by talk of "inexorability"

---

[74] Wittgenstein makes some more remarks about law in *RFM* I.116–8. But these sound like nothing so much as an Austinian command theory, law as command backed by coercive threats. I can only make the obvious remark that Wittgenstein does not have a developed theory of law.

is simply the peculiar relation of mathematical and logical rules to social practice and to "very general facts of daily experience" (*RFM* I. 118). In the world we live in, calculating in the way we count is *the* way to calculate, to use numbers as they should be used. In a world suitably different, where very general facts of nature were different, this would not be so. But we are not in, and cannot conceive of, such a world.

We must now apply these doctrines to a philosophical consideration of binding precedent. I shall discuss first the formal aspect of precedent and then the material aspect. I have two points to make about the formal aspect. Firstly, what is the purpose of introducing Wittgenstein's remarks about mathematics? It is this. Theorists considering binding precedent are pulled in different directions by conflicting intuitions. On the one hand, they sense the appropriateness of using modal language to characterize the requirements of *stare decisis*. On the other hand, they see clearly that legal rules are not like and do not function like the rules of mathematics or logic with respect to clarity and immutability, and moreover they see that legal inference, unlike mathematical or logical inference, is not "inexorable". In these circumstances, the second intuition generally wins the tug-of-war, and the modal language is either regarded as a naively optimistic projection or else the modalities are given a weak explanation in terms of "necessary to the English legal system", along the lines referred to earlier. The point of introducing Wittgenstein's philosophy of mathematics and logic is to show that in fact there is *no* deep metaphysical conflict between these intuitions. It is perfectly possible for modal language to be entirely appropriate even though there is also something important about a human activity brought out by calling it a practice. Only because a false picture of the inexorability of mathematics holds theorists captive are they tempted either to search for similar perfection in law or else to adopt various drastic strategies for coping with its absence.

Secondly, Wittgenstein's general account of rules shows that there really is no conflict either between something's being a matter of rule and a matter of practice. Yet frequently theorists discussing precedent do proceed as though these notions are incompatible. Again, this is because of too abstract and idealized a picture of rules. This is quite explicit in some recent discussion,[75] but it also turns up in more subtle ways. Brian Simpson, for instance, stages a lengthy attack on the idea of the common law as a system of rules.[76] I will mention two points where the wrong picture of rules influences him. He remarks (86) that it is misleading to speak of "judicial legislation". Part of his point here is very well taken – that when judges develop the common law in new ways they do not do so by conferring privileged status on a form of words, whereas that is the way that legislatures develop the law. However, he then goes on to regard this fact as a reason for denying that the common law is a system of rules. Statute law is the nearest that law ever comes to being like logic or mathematics (and that is not *very* near!). The assumption underlying the thought that common law *rationes* are not like statutes, and therefore not rules, can only be that the rules of mathematics and logic are the ideal paradigms for what it is to be a rule. But that assumption is false, and so this reason for regarding the common law as a system of rules falls away. Shortly afterwards (87), Simpson derides the thought that the 1966 Practice Statement is a rule of precedent by saying "one moment the House of Lords or the Court of Criminal Appeal is absolutely bound by its own decisions, the next moment it is not". Of course, the Practice Statement is absurd, if looked at in that way. However, events leading up to the Practice Statement are an essential part of the evolution of *stare decisis*, as are also events after it. The "black and white" aspect of the application of a rule is characteristic of the rules of mathematics and logic, and it is silly to imagine that legal rules have that

---

[75] See, for example, Rickett, pp. 144–6; Laurence Goldstein, 'Four Alleged Paradoxes in Legal Reasoning', *Cambridge Law Journal* 38 (1979): 373–91, pp. 388–9.

[76] A. W. B. Simpson, 'The Common Law and Legal Theory', in *Oxford Essays in Jurisprudence*, Vol. 2, edited by A. W. B. Simpson (Oxford: Clarendon Press, 1973), pp. 77–99.

characteristic also. But that is no reason to deny that they are rules; again, only bewitchment by the picture of logical and mathematical rules leads Simpson to think that it is. Consider also the more subtle influence of this picture in remarks like the following. I have mentioned already (in section III above) Stephen J.'s emphasis in *Caltex* on a gradualistic development of the law on economic loss. One academic commentator, Rogers, has caustically labelled this a rejection of the system of settling disputes according to law (29). But where is it laid down that, unless disputes are settled by deduction from prior premisses, then there is no settlement according to law? One could think that it was so laid down only if one was seduced by a certain picture of rules. Lord Edmund-Davies is no better when in *Duport Steel* (548) he remarks that *McShane* is "in reality, though not in strict law, also binding on this House". Presumably, what he means is that, having uttered the Practice Statement, the House of Lords could, if it wanted to, overrule *McShane* and accept the arguments of the Court of Appeal in *Duport Steel*; however, for various good reasons it would be inappropriate to do so. But to make this point, sound in itself, by distinguishing "reality" and "strict law" is again to fail to see that the Practice Statement, as a legal rule, is just that, a statement of a practice. Therefore, there is no need to consider the view that *McShane* is binding as something which "strict law" could not countenance.

Another variation on this theme is to say that the rules of precedent are not rules, but customs or matters of comity. This way of talking finds favour with Simpson; he says explicitly that the concept of "custom" is better than that of "rule" for understanding the common law, and that the common law is customary law – the practices and ideas of a judicial caste (91, 94). Rickett has also approved of Lord Denning's referring to the rule in *Young* as a matter of comity (146). If there is any subtle difference between the concept of "custom" and the concept of "practice", it would seem to be that things one does by custom are even less binding on one than things one makes a practice of doing. "Comity" would seem weaker still. As one proceeds along this gradient, one is passing from the domain of "agreement in judgments" to "agreement in opinion", and in so doing in my view passes into theoretical misdescription. As the story of Lord Denning illustrates, the practice and rules of precedent have a more powerful inertia than can be made to deviate by one voice. It is not simply that other judges hold different opinions from Lord Denning; it is rather that the weight of the rules and the practice lie against him. They have a life independently of given particular judges, because of the values and goals the judges agree in judging them to represent.

I turn now to the material aspect of precedent. I shall submit that the Wittgensteinian account I am offering is the best way of accounting for a striking feature of the way cases actually function as precedents. The feature in question is alluded to by Lord Wilberforce in *Anns*[77] when he remarks (503) that the relevance of *Donoghue* v. *Stevenson* to statutory bodies only became clear in *Dorset Yacht.*[78] (I feel like amending this to "it only became clear in *Anns* that it was clear in *Dorset Yacht*", but that is by the way.) The feature remarked on is that the precise law for which a particular case is authority will standardly only become clear after a line of subsequent cases has been decided. With great decisions, such as *Donoghue*, the process continues and continues; Megarry V-C. in *Ross* derives the defendant's liability, even though it is a matter of a misstatement, directly from *Donoghue* without any detour through *Hedley Byrne*. It is in this same spirit that Peter Cane, in a very recent article,[79] remarks that "there have been enough cases since *Hedley Byrne* to make worthwhile a review of the present state of what might be termed the '*Hedley Byrne* principle', that is the principle that a plaintiff may recover in tort for economic loss resulting from negligent words" (862). If we assume that 'rule' and 'practice' are complementary, this fact

---

77 *Anns and others* v. *London Borough of Merton*, [1977] 2 All E.R. 492.

78 *Home Office* v. *Dorset Yacht Co. Ltd.*, [1970] 2 All E.R. 294.

79 'The Metes and Bounds of *Hedley Byrne*', *Australian Law Journal* 55 (1981): 862–75. Cf. also Cross, *PEL* 77.

about great precedents is easy to understand and accept – for it is a direct manifestation of that complementarity. If we do not accept this view, then we get into unnecessary tangles. For instance, it is certainly true that, after *Hedley Byrne*, there was no absolute prohibition against recovery in tort for economic loss not consequent upon physical damage. But, given the wrong picture of rules, spurious questions come thick and fast. Does *Hedley Byrne* constitute simply a narrow exception to the so-called exclusory rule, or does it show that there is no such rule (Megarry in *Ross* (593), although he does not wish to answer the question)? If the rule no longer exists, was it *Hedley Byrne* that put paid to it (Lord Salmon [*Sharp* 1027]), or *Sharp* (as Megarry seems to think [*Ross* 594ff.]), or *Caltex* (Partlett 122)?[80] Despite the grist that these questions would seem to provide for the academic mill, they are questions which it is impossible and unnecessary to answer. The rule concerning recovery for economic loss is not reducible to any *ratio* in any one case, but is an organic practice which is still growing. Recognition of this fact does not require one to think therefore that speaking of rules here is a bad joke; rather, it requires sensitivity to the kind of rule we are dealing with.

VII.

As Simpson has rightly emphasized (90), another signal characteristic of the common law, one that involves both the formal and the material aspects of precedent, is its great cohesion. Moreover, as Simpson also rightly emphasizes, this cohesion predates the historical developments in the last part of the nineteenth century which founded the modern system of *stare decisis*. But again, this

---

[80] Partlett compounds the confusion by saying that four of the judges all "found the exclusory rule not to be law in Australia" (p. 140); this form of words implies that *prior to Caltex* the law in Australia really was as the High Court subsequently declared it to be. This is the old declaratory theory of law in full colours.

is no reason to discard the conception of the common law as a system of rules. Simpson takes the fact of this predating to imply that the cohesion cannot be the result of agreement. That is true, only if we have in mind agreement in opinions; but it is quite compatible, and indeed probative of, a fundamental agreement in judgments. Simpson refers to rule-like formulations of the common law as being like the rules in which grammarians formulate grammatical practice. This is indeed a significant analogy, but its significance is to bring out that common-law rules are not mere descriptions of customs. For what grammarians are describing are not mere customs or comity; grammarians are describing not merely the way we speak, but the way we live and act, and the world in which we do those things. The common-law rules which express, and, in the sense described, are the practices of the common law are equally descriptions of our legal world, the cohesiveness of our society.

The bindingness of precedent can certainly be called "institutional" if one wants to distinguish it from the bindingness of logical necessity, of moral obligations, or of pure coercive threat. One uses such a notion to indicate that the bindingness of precedent depends upon the *practice* of the officials of a legal system. However, the deeper metaphysical significance of the concept of a practice must be realized. In the end *any* rule is applied only according to a practice; in the end the argument from parallel cases which is employed in the application of open-textured rules is ultimately as fundamental a form of reasoning as are inexorable deductions from non-open-textured rules. Thus we have no need to read into the notion of "institutionally binding" any implications that accounts of the functioning of precedent must be given entirely from within the law itself, and that comparison of legal reasoning with non-legal reasoning has nothing illuminating to reveal.

There is a deeper unity yet behind the ideas of principles of fairness, rules of a social institution such as a system of *stare decisis*, and laws of logic and mathematics. Hart has hinted at this with his doctrine (*CL* ch. 9) of the minimum content of law and morality. Such a thesis must again be seen as making a point not intrinsic to those areas of human life, but about *any* part of the scaffolding of human existence.

I use the term 'scaffolding' deliberately, to remind us of its use in Wittgenstein's *Tractatus*[81] as a metaphor for the status of the propositions of logic. This metaphor is repeated in *On Certainty* (211), to apply now also to fundamental assumptions about how the world works which are not necessarily truths of pure logic.[82] Philosophy has the task of showing us the scaffolding of the human language-game (cf. *OC* 554) from within it. Philosophy makes remarks about the natural history of human beings (*PI* 415, *RFM* I.141), but it does so in a special way. It is not the same as natural science, for the truths of philosophy are truths of the dependence of grammar on natural history (*PI* p. 230e). Thus philosophy is concerned with the exhibition of *natural laws*. It is a natural law that our inferring follows the principle that the future will be like the past (*OC* 135). Our knowledge depends on a natural law of taking for true, rather than a fundamental epistemic principle (*OC* 172). It is a fact of natural history that one goes through a given proof in mathematics or logic and is convinced by it (*RFM* I.63). Rules which can be read off from practice are like natural laws governing the play (*PI* 54).

Hart links the principle *P* "Treat like cases alike" to the citizens' "right to mutual forbearance from certain kinds of harmful conduct", and talks also here of "a structure of reciprocal rights and obligations" (*CL* 160). Later, in chapter 9 of *CL*, he refers to "the necessity for a system of mutual forbearance and compromise" as a part of the minimum content of natural law. Consider the use Wittgenstein makes of the notion of "natural law", as a term to characterize fundamental structural features of human practices of whatever kind. The implication of this is that *both* the principle *P*, even in the vastly more elaborate institutional form it takes in a

---

[81] *Tractatus Logico-Philosophicus* (London: Routledge & Kegan Paul, 1961), 3.42, 4.023, 6.124.

[82] Cf. pp. 107–12 of my paper referred to in footnote 73.

developed system of *stare decisis, and* the open-textured legal rules which generate the determination of relevant likenesses, even in the vastly more elaborate institutional form of a complex legal system, have their metaphysical roots in the natural history of human beings.[83]

Certainly the specific details of any given system of *stare decisis* will contain many provisions which can be assessed externally and descriptively as simply specific features of that system. But the philosopher's question of what it is for a court to be bound by precedent ultimately transcends any such external description of specific features. This feature of metaphysical depth is obscured by standard attempts to answer it from within the legal system.[84] Theories that this bond is some idiosyncratic institutional bond are in a sense *right*, for there are many specific features peculiar to such systems. But they are also wrong, in that such systems are at bottom instances of the genus "social practice". If *that* is realized, then it can be seen how the other two responses discussed also mislead. Both Dworkin and Hart share the idea that the gravitational force of precedents cannot be explained by any notion of "bindingness" which trades on the idea of logical bindingness. Dworkin rightly sees that there is bindingness, and therefore concludes, because of the fact that law and morality do have some links, that the bindingness must be moral bindingness. Hart rightly sees that this claim over-assimilates law to morality, and therefore denies that there is ultimately any bindingness at all.

"Social practice", however, is a genus which includes logic and mathematics as well as law, morality, etiquette, game-playing, and

---

[83] Cf. Alan Gewirth, 'Obligation: Political, Legal, Moral', in *Political and Legal Obligation*, edited by J. R. Pennock and J. W. Chapman (New York: Atherton, 1970), esp. pp. 74–6; also my 'Towards a Descriptive Theory of Legal Obligation', *Proceedings of the IVR World Congress*, Basel, 1979.

[84] Dworkin's criticisms (*TRS* 1–3) of the limitations of a narrowly analytic approach to deep problems of jurisprudence do seem to me justified, although, as is clear, the remedy he offers is not one that I accept.

so on. In all cases, we have rules that are obeyed, to constitute the practice. The rules are obeyed from within.[85] The most fundamental rules we can only *show* from within.[86] A philosopher wishing to characterize the metaphysical nature of precedent can only in the end *show* it by comparing it and contrasting it with other social practices, and by discussing the attempts of others to draw such comparisons. I have tried to use the work of Wittgenstein and Wisdom on rules and arguments from parallel cases to go against the tendency mentioned at the beginning of the paper to deprecate analogies between arguments from precedent and logical argument. I have tried to argue that, when *both* parts of this analogy are understood as social practices, we can arrive at a rewardingly deeper view of the relations between Precedent, Discretion and Fairness.[87]

University of Alberta

---

[85] Cf. the comparison of law and mathematics at *RFM* II.65. Wittgenstein suggests that neither mathematical propositions nor what is in a statute book are purely anthropological propositions; at any rate, the judge, he says, does not use the statute book as an anthropological textbook.

[86] On p. 98 of *CL*, Hart says of the rule of recognition of a legal system, that it is not stated, but "its existence is *shown* in the way in which particular rules are identified, either by courts or other officials or private persons or their advisors" (his italics). This remark resonates with Tractarian implications; but there is no indication that I see that Hart intends the notion that way.

[87] I am grateful for helpful comments on earlier versions of this paper to Jerry Bickenbach, Joel Feinberg, Marsha Hanen, Kai Nielsen, Iain Ramsay, Bob Rieter, and an anonymous referee for the RIP Conference. I must also thank Prof. T. D. Campbell for his comments at the Conference itself. The time-lag between the Conference and the publication deadline for this volume has contained evolution in the law as well as in my thinking about these matters. I am deeply grateful to Sandy Stewart for permitting not inconsiderable revision.

PART III

RIGHTS AND CLAIMS

ALAN R. WHITE

RIGHTS AND CLAIMS

Philosophers frequently, and jurisprudents almost invariably, assert a necessary connection between rights and claims. Such an assertion, however, takes several different forms. Many philosophers equate a right with either a claim[1] or, at least, a justified or recognised claim,[2] and a common jurisprudential definition of a right is that it is a legally enforceable claim;[3] while some philos-

[1] Catholics as quoted by H. J. McCloskey, 'Rights', *Philosophical Quarterly* 15 (1965), p. 115; R. A. Wasserstrom, 'Rights, Human Rights and Racial Discrimination', *Journal of Philosophy* 61 (1964), p. 630; A. I. Melden, *Rights and Persons* (Oxford: Blackwell, 1977), pp. 10, 57; D. D. Raphael, 'Human Rights', *Proceedings of the Aristotelian Society*, Suppl. 39 (1965), pp. 210–11; B. Mayo, *ibid.*, pp. 231 f. The *OED* gives as one definition of 'claim', 'a right or title to'.

[2] Adam Smith, *The Theory of Moral Sentiments* (1759), 'What he had a right to and could justly demand from others ...'; D. G. Ritchie, *Natural Rights*, 3rd edition (London: Allen & Unwin, 1916), p. 78; W. D. Ross, *The Right and the Good* (Oxford: Clarendon Press, 1930), p. 50; A. S. Kaufman, 'A Sketch of a Liberal Theory of Fundamental Human Rights', *Monist* 52 (1968), p. 605; J. Feinberg, 'Wasserstrom on Human Rights', *Journal of Philosophy* 61 (1964), p. 642; 'Duties, Rights and Claims', *American Philosophical Quarterly* 3 (1966), p. 142, and 'The Nature and Value of Rights', *Journal of Value Inquiry* 4 (1970), pp. 253 f. Feinberg's 1966 and 1970 papers are reprinted in his *Rights, Justice and the Bounds of Liberty* (Princeton: Princeton University Press, 1980).

[3] Cp. A. Kocourek, *Jural Relations* (Indianapolis: Bobbs-Merrill, 1927), p. 3 ('capability to claim an act from another'); R. Pound, *Jurisprudence*, Volume 4 (St. Paul, Minn.: West, 1959), pp. 69–71; J. Stone, *The Province and Function of Law* (London: Stevens, 1947), p. 489; W. N. Hohfeld, *Fundamental Legal Conceptions* (New Haven: Yale University Press, 1919), pp. 38 f., and American and early British cases quoted by him at pp. 36–38; P. G. Vinogradoff, *Collected Papers*, Volume 2 (Oxford: Clarendon Press, 1928), pp. 367 f.; H. L. A. Hart, 'Bentham', *Proceedings of the British Academy* 48 (1962), p. 315.

M. A. Stewart (ed.), Law, Morality and Rights, 139–160.

ophers and jurists equate a claim only with one – though that the fundamental – kind of right or sense of the word 'right'.[4] Other philosophers contend merely that a right implies a claim or that a right implies a right to claim.[5]

A prerequisite to any evaluation of these different assertions is an examination of the diverse ways in which the notion of a claim is ordinarily used.

1. CLAIMS

The basic idea of a claim is a call (Latin *clamare*) for the acceptability of something admittedly contestable, whether it is, e.g., my right to *X*, my ownership of *Y*, that so and so *is* such and such, or that so and so *be* such and such. This idea takes three different forms, which are, however, not due to, nor do they imply, different senses[6] of the word 'claim', but syntactically different constructions which explain different implications and different characteristics. These I shall dub the 'indicative' use, the 'subjunctive' use, and the 'possessive' use.[7]

1.1 *The Indicative Use*

An indicative claim is a call for acceptability of the supposed fact that so and so *is* the case, just as an allegation is a dubitable assertion that it is, or a suggestion a tentative proposal that it is. And to make such a claim, that is, to claim, is to assert in this fashion that so and so is the case, just as to make an allegation or to allege, and to make a suggestion or to suggest, is to assert in these other fashions.

---

[4] This is one formulation of Hohfeld's thesis, *op. cit.*

[5] 'Implies a claim': cp. M. P. Golding, 'Towards a Theory of Human Rights', *Monist* 52 (1968), pp. 530–2. 'Implies a right to claim': cp. H. D. Aiken, 'Rights, Human and Otherwise', *ibid.*, p. 508; J. Feinberg, 'Duties, Rights and Claims', p. 143.

[6] *Pace* Feinberg, 'The Nature and Value of Rights', pp. 251–2.

[7] These are quite different distinctions from those of Feinberg, 'The Nature and Value of Rights', which I did not come across until I had finished my paper. I have added footnotes to show where I disagree with his analysis.

An indicative claim *that* so and so *is* the case can sometimes also be advanced either by claiming (making a claim) *to V* or claiming (making a claim to) *X*, where '*V*' stands for a verb and '*X*' for a noun phrase,[8] just as to expect or hope *that* someone *will depart* is to expect or hope for him *to depart*, or to expect or hope for *his departure*; and to promise or arrange *that* you *will return* is to promise or arrange *to return*, or to promise or arrange *your return*. Thus, to claim, or a claim, to use a pint of oil per 100 miles, to have climbed Mount Everest, to be heir to the estate, to be or have been victimised, to know the names of the Kings of England, or to be full of remorse for one's deeds, is to claim, or a claim, that these things are so. Similarly, to claim, or a claim to, an ability, a power, some knowledge or complete ignorance of the matter, several advantages for one's invention, 80% accuracy in one's forecasting, a hit or other success, is to claim, or a claim, that this is the case. To disclaim any of these is to deny them. But though any indicative claim *to V* can grammatically be expressed as a claim *that* so and so *does V*, the converse is not necessarily true. There is no simple infinitival variant for the claim that someone has stolen my car or that Bacon wrote Shakespeare's plays. The indicative is replaceable by the infinitive usually only when the subjects of the main clause and of the subordinate clause are the same. In this respect the verb 'claim' is exactly like a host of other verbs, such as 'hope', 'promise', 'expect', 'arrange', 'intend', 'agree', or 'plan'.

Indicative claims, whether made or not,[9] can be weak or strong, wide or limited, dubious or plausible, clear or confused, wise or rash, examined or tested and, most importantly, they can be true or false, proved or disproved, confirmed or unconfirmed, supported or unsupported by evidence.

---

[8] Feinberg, *art. cit.*, p. 250, separates 'making claim to' from 'claiming that' because he wrongly confines the former to legal claiming and to making claim to something as a right. But one can make (some, any, no) claim to originality, perfection or infallibility or to be original, perfect or infallible.

[9] *Pace* A. I. Melden, *Rights and Right Conduct* (Oxford: Blackwell, 1959), p. 13. Unmade claims can be examined as easily as, e.g., unmade allegations or suggestions.

1.2 *The Subjunctive Use*

A subjunctive claim is a call for acceptability of the proposal that something *(should) be* the case; it is a call *for* it, a request or demand[10] for it. Such a claim can – in ways parallel to an indicative claim – sometimes also be expressed either as a claim *to V* or to *be Ved* or a claim *to X* or *for X*, just as a request or demand is a request or demand to *V*, to be *V*ed or for *X*. And to make such a claim is to claim to *V* or to be *V*ed or to claim *X*, just as to make such a request or demand is to request or demand to *V* or be *V*ed or to request or demand *X*. Thus, a claim to take 50% of the profits or to go first, to be fed properly or to be told what happened, to protection, immunity, a fair hearing, one's attention or compassion, is a claim, request or demand, for these things to be, or that they should be, the case. Similarly, a claim *for* expenses or a new carpet, *on* someone's time or on the family estate, is a claim that one (should) have these things. Conversely, one can disclaim what has been left to one in a will.

Subjunctive claims, unlike indicative claims, are not true or false; they are not confirmed or unconfirmed, proved or disproved, made out or not made out. Nor are they supported or refuted by evidence. They are just or unjust, legitimate or illegitimate. They are supported by reasons. They are granted, turned down or refused. One can subjunctively, but not indicatively, claim something *as* a reward or a recompense, as one's due or as a favour, as damages or expenses, as a privilege or a right. Subjunctive, but not indicative, claims can be made against others; such a claim can be the first, or a prior, claim on something or somebody. Commonly, we claim, indicatively, to have what we think we have – whether it be knowledge, an advantage or success – but subjunctively, to have or be given what we think we do not already have – whether it be protection, attention or fair treatment – just as we commonly assert what we think to be so, but ask for what we think we do not have. We can, however, claim indicatively that we will have

[10] E.g., Adam Smith.

what we know we do not yet have and subjunctively that we should have what we know we already have, if the legitimacy of our possession of it is being contested.

When either indicative or subjunctive claims are expressed grammatically as claims to *V*, or be *V*ed, and as claims to some *X*, often only the context or the nature of what is claimed will make it clear which claim is being made. Thus, a claim to know what happened could be either a claim that one does know, or a claim that one should be allowed to know; a claim to be fed only bread and water is likely to be a claim that one is being fed only these, whereas a claim to be fed decently is likely to be a claim that we should be fed decently. To claim a share in the work that made the company successful is probably to claim that one did have such a share, whereas to claim a share in the profits is more likely to claim that one should have such a share. To claim immunity from prosecution, exemption from tax, or the privilege of bringing in a measure, could be either to claim that this is the case or that it should be the case.

It is worth remarking that this contrast between what I have called the 'indicative' and the 'subjunctive' use of a concept, and also the syntactical ambiguity to which it gives rise, occurs with other philosophically important concepts. Take *ought*, *must* and *reason*. There is an ambiguity in the remark that the teachers *ought* to get a rise in salary, between the reasonable prediction that this will happen, since it has been agreed by Parliament, and the reasonable prescription that it should happen, since they have such a demanding job. There is a similar ambiguity in the remark that the Opposition *must* be bold, between the suggestion that this is the only explanation of their success in having stopped a measure and the advice that this is their only way to stop it. Similarly, a *reason* for disliking something can be either a reason why one does dislike it or a reason why one should dislike it.

1.3 *The Possessive Use*

This is not a kind of claim or a kind of claiming additional to the indicative and subjunctive. It is a peculiarity about the notion of 'having a claim', whether the claim is indicative or subjunctive, or ambiguous between the two. The peculiarity is that, though indicative claims can be either true or false, and subjunctive claims can be either justified or unjustified, the phrase 'to have a claim' – as well as 'to have some, a slight, a good, a certain claim' – seems to imply that the claim is either true or justified. Though someone can *make* a false or unjustified claim, he cannot *have* a false or unjustified claim.[11] To admit that he *has* a claim, whether indicatively to be the first man to have climbed Mount Everest or to a longer acquaintance with the President than any other man, or subjunctively to be given preferential treatment or to mercy, or ambiguously to a share in the money, is to admit at least some truth or justice in his claim. In a similar way, to say that he *can* claim so and so is to say that he can fairly, properly, rightly claim it. In this respect 'to have a claim' is like 'to have a point, an argument, a case'. Though one can 'put' a point, an argument or a case which is invalid, one cannot 'have' a point, an argument or a case unless there is at least something in it. Furthermore, one can 'have' a claim only *to V*, not a claim *that* oneself, much less another person or anything, *does* or *should V*.

Though, as we shall see, philosophers and jurists who conceptually link claims and rights move around confusingly and confusedly between the indicative and subjunctive and the possessive and non-possessive use of 'claim', the possessive use is the most relevant. It is, therefore, important to show that the existence or the making of either an indicative or a subjunctive claim neither implies nor is implied by the having of a claim.

I do not have to have a claim in order to make one; nor do I have to make one in order to have one. One can claim either that so and so *is* the case, as when one claims to be innocent or to have been assaulted, or claims a certain skill or some experience,

---

11 Feinberg's denial of this (*art. cit.*, p. 253) on the ground that 'if it is not redundant to pronounce another's claim valid, there must be such a thing as having a claim that is not valid' confuses the correct '*A*'s claim is invalid' and the incorrect '*A* has an invalid claim'.

or that so and so *should be* the case, as when one claims to be heard or claims shelter; but if the former claim is false or the latter unjustified, then one has no claim to any of these things. Only a small number of those who make competing claims on someone's time may have any claim to that time. Indeed, often when one makes a claim, true or false, to something, e.g., to ache all over or to be full of remorse, it is not clear what sense it would have to ask whether one has a claim to this; and one can, of course, claim, truly or falsely, that one has a claim. Conversely, one can have a claim, whether it is a claim to be the discoverer of a new process or to be treated honourably or a claim to fame or to fair treatment, which, for various reasons,[12] neither he nor anyone else has ever made on his behalf. Because there is no necessary connection between making a claim of any kind and having one, the inarticulate, the ignorant or the unconfident are, in this respect, at no disadvantage compared to the more advanced. Children and animals can have claims to possess qualities and to receive treatment despite their inability to make any such claims.

This is not to deny that if the claim one makes is true or justified, then – provided this makes sense – one has a claim; and, conversely, if one has a claim to something, then any claim to it which one were to make would be true or justified. But, of course, this truism is no different from a host of others which have nothing to do with claims. Thus, if the point one makes, the explanation one gives, the solution one suggests, the argument one advances or the case one argues is valid, then one has a point, an explanation, a solution, an argument or a case; and conversely, if one has a point, an explanation, a solution, an argument or a case, then any such which one were to advance would be valid. Furthermore, just as one can put forward an objection, an explanation, a solution, a point, a case or an argument without 'having' one, because to put forward any of these is to put forward something

---

[12] Cp. cases quoted by R. W. M. Dias, *Jurisprudence*, 3rd edition (London: Butterworth, 1970), p. 243, Note 1; Golding, *art. cit.*, pp. 530, 544, 549; Melden, *Rights and Right Conduct*, pp. 13–15.

as one, which it, unfortunately, may not be, so to put forward a claim is to put forward something *as* a claim, which one can do without 'having' any claim. And just as what someone puts forward in these other instances is called 'his' objection, explanation, case, etc., so the claim he makes is his claim. Hence, paradoxically, so and so can be 'someone's' claim, though he 'has' no claim, just as such and such can be 'someone's' explanation, solution, point or case though he 'has' no explanation, solution, point or case.

The notion of a claim is used in the law in exactly the three ways in which, I have suggested, it occurs in everyday thought and language. First, the landlord who claims that he had given the tenant notice,[13] the woman graduate who claims that she is entitled to vote,[14] Parliament which claims jurisdiction over all that happens in the House, a body which claims that a power has been conferred on it by law, the trader who claims for breach of contract, the employee who claims wrongful dismissal, a spouse who claims that the furniture in the matrimonial home is hers,[15] and the plaintiff who claims that he is the owner of the goods, are all claiming indicatively that so and so is the case. Secondly, to claim or disclaim a gift in a will,[16] to claim a patent for an invention,[17] to claim something under an insurance policy,[18] to claim to levy taxation without consent of Parliament, to claim a special prerogative and, more obviously, to claim that one's husband pay one a

---

[13] For relevant circumstances, cp. *Woodfall on Landlord and Tenant*, 26th edition, Volume 1 (London: Sweet & Maxwell, 1960), Chapter 18 §7.

[14] *Nairn* v. *University of St Andrews* [1909] AC 147.

[15] Cole (A bankrupt), *Re, Ex parte The Trustee* v. *Cole* [1963] 3 All E.R. 433, and cases given in P. R. H. Webb and H. K. Bevan, *Source Book of Family Law* (London: Butterworth, 1964), Chapter 16.

[16] W. J. Williams, *The Law Relating to Wills*, 3rd edition (London: Butterworth 1967), Chapter 37.

[17] T. A. Blanco White, *Patents for Inventions and the Protection of Industrial Designs*, 4th edition (London: Stevens, 1974), Chapter 2.

[18] Cp. *MacGillivray and Parkington on Insurance Law*, 7th edition (London: Sweet & Maxwell, 1981).

sum of money or that others not interfere with one's business, is to claim subjunctively that one should have what one claims. All such claims, whether indicative or subjunctive, can be stated, made, entered, advanced, proved, made good, satisfied, met, maintained, enforced, registered, disputed, rejected, fail. One can in these ways be entitled or have a right to claim, e.g., a writ of delivery, or, conversely, claim to be entitled or to have a right, e.g., to compensation, to a car, or to judgment in a case. Finally, to hold that a claim to a patent is valid, that a claim to the whole of a debt has been established, that an insured has proved his claim, or that a subject has maintained his claim against the Crown for compensation, is to allow in all these cases that the plaintiff has a claim.

2. CLAIMS AND RIGHTS

Having sketched out the various uses of the notion of a claim, I want now to examine their relations to rights. And this in two ways. First, to show briefly that though rights are something which can be claimed, either indicatively or subjunctively, possessively or not possessively, they are claimed in exactly the same way as any of the countless other things which we have seen can be the subject of claims. Secondly, to investigate how the idea of a right to something is related to the idea of a claim to the same thing.

2.1 *The Claiming of Rights*

One can indicatively claim possession of a right to something, whether by claiming that one has the right to it, or that it is one's right, or by claiming the right to it. Thus, the House of Lords may claim to have the right to hold up legislation which is not popularly supported; a Head of a Department might claim that to have one secretary for every ten members of his Department is his right, and the management may claim the right to refuse admission to whomever it pleases. Claiming possession of a right is, however, no different from claiming possession of anything else, whether it is knowledge, experience or an umbrella, by claiming that one has it or that it is one's own or simply by claiming it. And just as neither claiming to have anything else implies that one does have it nor does having it imply making any claim to have it, so claiming to have a right neither implies, nor is implied by, having a right. It is just as mistaken to say 'that a right should exist, it must be *claimed* ... in other words the subject must assert something as his right'[19] as to assume – as philosophers who make the conviction that one knows a necessary condition of knowing sometimes seem to do – that 'for knowledge to exist, it must be claimed ... in other words the subject must assert something as his knowledge'. The former would be too quick a way to deprive children and – as does Ross[20] – animals of their possible rights, just as the latter would be too quick a denial of knowledge to the unconfident. It is even misleading to suggest that 'there cannot be a right where there is no possible, or potential claimant, no one [whether the possessor or another on his behalf] who might assert the right in question'.[21] For this is as much true or false of anything whatsoever which cannot exist without an owner. Of course, if the claim to a right were true, it would imply that the claimant had the right, and, conversely, if the claimant had a certain right, then any claim he made to it would be true. But, as we saw, this holds for a claim to possession of anything whatsoever. Further, since the fact that someone who had something would be undoubtedly right in claiming that he had it does not in general provide any reason for supposing that

---

[19] Vinogradoff, *op. cit.*, pp. 367–8; cp. M. Cranston, *What are Human Rights?* (London: Bodley Head, 1973), p. 81; Melden, *op. cit.*, p. 14. Feinberg's 1970 view that a claim is an 'assertion of right' would allow no sense to 'having a claim' – to which he rightly does allow sense – since this would then be the senseless 'having an assertion of right'.

[20] Ross, *loc. cit.*; cp. J. Narveson, 'Animal Rights', *Canadian Journal of Philosophy* 7 (1977): 161–178. J. Feinberg, 'Can Animals have Rights?', in *Animal Rights and Human Obligations*, edited by T. Regan and P. Singer (Englewood Cliffs: Prentice-Hall, 1976), pp. 190–6, allows that animals can have rights because others can make claims on their behalf; on this, cp. McCloskey, *art. cit.*

[21] Aiken, *art. cit.*, p. 508.

he would have a right to claim that he had it, it is difficult to see why 'for every right, there is a further right to claim, in appropriate circumstances, that one has that right'.[22] *Rightly* claiming to have what one does have is not the same as *rightfully* claiming to have what one does have.

Similarly one can subjunctively claim that one should have a right to something, whether by claiming it as a right or by claiming a right to it. Thus, one may claim certain goods as a right, in contrast to claiming them as a reward, as expenses, or as one's due; one may claim for one's self the rights of any citizen or those of a husband; one may claim the right to something, whether to property or protection, to go or to be accepted, to know or to feel annoyed, or one may simply claim one's rights as one might claim one's wages. Once again, however, a claim that one should have or be given a certain right is no different in kind from a claim that one should have anything else. Certainly, to claim the right to protection, a fair hearing, damages, one's audience's attention, or the right to be treated properly or be fed decently, is to claim something different from what one claims when one claims protection, damages, to be fed properly, etc., themselves, just as to vote, to fight or to die for the right to freedom, money or a change of party is to vote, fight or die for something different from freedom, money or a change of party themselves. But claims for different kinds of things are no more different kinds of claims than votes or fights for different kinds of things are different kinds of votes or fights.

Nor is there any closer logical connection between a subjunctive claim that one should possess a particular right and the actual possession of that right than between an indicative claim that one does have it and the actual possession of it. Not only can a claim that one should have a right as easily – though on different kinds of grounds – be disallowed as a claim that one does have it can be disproved; we saw that sincerely to claim that one should have something, whether a right or anything else, often suggests, though

---

[22] Feinberg, 'Duties, Rights and Claims', p. 143.

it does not imply, that one thinks that one does not already have it. In short, it is simply a fallacy to assimilate, as many jurists[23] seem to do, a 'right' and a 'claim of right'.

One source of the fallacy that a right is a claim may be that in *saying* 'I have a right to *V*' I am making a claim. But equally in *saying* 'I know that *p*' or 'I own *X*' I am making a claim; yet neither knowledge nor ownership is a claim. What we claim, that is the thing claimed, in making a claim to a right, is not itself a claim, any more than what we claim in making a claim to knowledge or ownership is itself a claim.[24]

Finally in this section, we should note that the syntactical ambiguity in the remark that someone is claiming something, e.g., an exemption or privilege or to be fed, as between claiming that one does have and that one should have this, infects claims to rights. Though the manager who claims the right to refuse admission to a drunk is probably claiming that he does have this right, and the parent who claims the right to send his children to a school of his choice is probably claiming that he should have this right, a chairman who claims the right to veto and the political group who claim the right to picket may be making either an indicative or a subjunctive claim. Claims to legal rights are usually indicative, though claims to, e.g., possession of a child may be subjunctive. Claims to political rights, as contrasted with political declarations of rights, are usually subjunctive.

2.2 *The Question of Logical Relation*

The second important question about the relations of rights to

---

[23] E.g., Wasserstrom, *art. cit.*, p. 630; R. M. Dworkin, *Taking Rights Seriously* (London: Duckworth, 1977), pp. 146, 199, 269. A 'claim of right' as a term of art, e.g., in the Larceny Act 1916, is really an honest claim (or belief) that one has a right; cp. G. L. Williams, *Criminal Law: The General Part*, 2nd edition (London: Stevens, 1961), §§107–117; *R.* v. *Bernhard* [1938] 2 KB 264.

[24] Feinberg, 'The Nature and Value of Rights', p. 251, argues that claiming is 'essential to the very notion of right'; but equally plausibly or implausibly we might argue that claiming is essential to the notion of ownership.

claims is whether either the making, the existence or the possession of a claim, whether indicative or subjunctive, to something implies, is implied by, or is equivalent to, the having of a right to that same thing.

Clearly, there is no logical connection between making a claim, whether indicative or subjunctive, and having a right to that which is claimed. For first, one may have a right to something which one has not claimed, either indicatively or subjunctively, at all. I may have a right to some money or a right to know a name, though I don't indicatively claim the money or to know the name, either because I don't think I have the money or the knowledge or because I know I haven't. Or I may have a right to be given something, whether money, protection or freedom, for which I make no subjunctive claim because I have no desire for it. Secondly, one may claim something, either indicatively or subjunctively, to which one has no right. Thus, I may claim to have some money, to be surprised at something or to attack people, though I have no right to the money, to be so surprised or to attack such people. Or I may claim that I should be given some protection, immunity or goods which I have no right to have. Indeed, my claim that I have or do so and so may be proved and my claim that I should have or be given such and such may be granted, without its being proved or granted that I have or be given rights in respect to so and so and such and such. To uphold my claim to be the long-lost heir to the estate is to admit that I am the heir, not that I have a right to be the heir, even though being the heir gives me a right to the estate. To admit my claim to the authorship of the document is not to admit any supposed right to be the author. And granting my claim, like granting my request or demand, to be given protection or immunity is granting that I should be given them, not that I should be given a right to them. Not even rightly claiming, much less merely claiming, something gives one a right to it. Hence, taken at their face value, common philosophical and juristic analyses of *rights* as 'legally enforceable claims', as 'recognised' (Ritchie), 'inviolable' (Catholic writers quoted by McCloskey), 'strong' (Wasserstrom) or 'valid' (Feinberg) claims, are confusions between 'rightly claiming' something and 'having a right' to it. It is simply a mistake to assert that 'we mean by a right something that can be justly claimed'.[25] Thirdly, not only is it often false to say that that which I claim I have a right to or that which I have a right to I claim; but, in indicative claims at least, it sometimes does not even make sense to talk of having a right to some of the things which one can claim, for one can claim almost anything. Thus, I can claim – even rightly claim – but not have a right, to be able to do so and so, to need such and such, to intend this or that, to ache all over or to be full of remorse, to be of such and such a size, age, colour, etc.

This shows itself also in the syntactical feature of English that, whereas a claim to *V* or be *V*ed is, when the claim is indicative, a claim that one does *V* or is *V*ed, a right to *V* or be *V*ed cannot be a right that one *does V* or *is Ved*, but only a right that one *V* or *be Ved* (or that one *should V* or *be Ved*). That is, the infinitive construction with the word 'right' – both when it occurs in 'having a right to *V*' and in the quite different 'being right to *V*' – as with the word 'claim' in subjunctive claims, is a grammatical alternative only for a subjunctive construction and not also for an indicative construction. This syntactical relation between the infinitive and what grammarians sometimes call the 'putative *should*' or the subjunctive is, of course, very common,[26] as in 'essential, necessary, natural, possible, important, desirable, advisable, unbelievable, unforgivable, an idea, the plan, his ambition, for *X to V* or that *X (should) V*'.

It might be, however, that philosophical and juristic analyses of rights in terms of claims are intended to equate 'having a right' not with 'rightly claiming', but with 'having a claim',[27] that is, with what I have called the 'possessive' use of the notion of a claim. Let

---

[25] Ross, *loc. cit.*; cp. 'justly demand' (Adam Smith).

[26] R. Quirk and others, *A Grammar of Contemporary English* (London: Longman, 1972), §§11.21, 11.22, 11.72; P. and C. Kiparsky, 'Fact', in *Semantics*, edited by D. D. Steinberg and L. A. Jakobovits (Cambridge: Cambridge University Press, 1971), pp. 345–69, esp. §7.

[27] E.g., Wasserstrom, Feinberg (1964, 1966), etc.

us, therefore, conclude with an examination of the relations between having a right to something and having a claim to it.

It is, independently, clear that having an indicative claim to something neither implies nor is implied by having a right to it. The former does not imply the latter, since one may have, e.g., some claim to fame as a philatelist or to be the inventor of such and such a process without our being able to say, either truly or sensibly, that he has a right to fame as a philatelist or a right to be the inventor of such and such a process. Nor is having a claim implied by having a right, since one can have various rights, e.g., to laugh when one likes or to assume certain premises, without its even making sense to talk of having an indicative claim to do these.

It is also clear that having a subjunctive claim, e.g., to special consideration or to be treated decently, does not imply having a right to them, for one's possession of a claim may be based on other considerations, such as the justice of such treatment. To suppose otherwise is to confuse what it is only right for one to have – or right that one (should) have – with what one has a right to have – or a right that one (should) have. It may be (only) right for me to sacrifice myself for another without its being my right to make such a sacrifice, while the fact that I have a right to chastise my son may not make it right for me to do so. One can ask whether someone has a rightful claim to such attention, or by what right he claims such authority. The question can arise whether, e.g., one immigrant has a stronger claim than another to entry to this country, even though neither has a right of entry. Nor, conversely, is having a subjunctive claim to something implied by having a right to it, as when someone has a right to special consideration, to be treated decently, to go where he wishes. Having a right to something is usually a, though not the only kind of, reason for possession of one's claim to it or to something else.[28] Furthermore, many of the things one can have a right to are things to which it makes rather dubious sense to speak of having a claim. We can certainly have a right to, but rather dubiously have a claim to, do or

---

28 Melden, *Rights and Right Conduct*, p. 17.

say what we like, to inspect and make copies of certain documents, to make, in California, a right turn against a red light, to drink moderately, to marry – or to advise, disagree, beg, begin, kill, choose, conclude, laugh, promise, prevent, etc. – to assume so and so or to expect such and such, or to feel certain things, e.g., to feel badly done by or indignant or jealous; or a right to a second chance, or one's own opinion.

It is significant that analyses of rights in terms of claims[29] usually go hand in hand with an emphasis either on rights to property or, as jurisprudents unidiomatically phrase it, on rights 'against' people, both of which are rights to have something done to one, rather than a right to do anything, and therefore exist in areas where the idea of a claim to something, like the idea of a request or demand for it, is appropriate. Thus, Kocourek says[30] that a right 'in the strict sense' is a 'capability to claim an act from another', whether this be *in personam* or *in rem*. Such a view is fostered by the assumption that where one person has a right, someone else has a duty whose performance one can demand or claim and to which one has a claim. Hence, followers of Hohfeld call some rights 'claim-rights';[31] Hohfeld himself suggested 'claim' as one sense, the strict sense, of 'right' and quoted some early American and Scottish court *obiter dicta* in support of this suggestion.[32] Where there is no correlative duty and, hence, no claim

---

[29] Cp. Feinberg, 'Duties, Rights and Claims', pp. 137 f.; 'Wasserstrom on Human Rights', p. 642; D. Lyons, 'Rights, Claimants, and Beneficiaries', *American Philosophical Quarterly* 6 (1969), p. 174.

[30] Kocourek, *op. cit.*, p. 3; Pound, pp. 56, 69–71.

[31] See, e.g., D. N. MacCormick, 'Rights in Legislation', in *Law, Morality and Society*, edited by P. M. S. Hacker and J. Raz (Oxford: Clarendon Press, 1977), p. 193. Professor MacCormick points out to me that the widespread attribution of the term 'claim-rights' to Hohfeld himself is a mistake of glossators who wish to retain a 'sense' of 'right' which is the correlative of 'duty', and who conflate Hohfeld's thesis that this is the 'strict sense' of 'right' with his identification of rights in this sense with claims.

[32] E.g., as cited by Hohfeld, *United States* v. *Patrick* (1893) 54 Fed. Rep., 338, 348 *per* Jackson J.; *Lonas* v. *State* (1871) 3 Heisk. (Tenn.), 287, 306–7 *per*

against another, he thought, wrongly in my opinion,[33] that the so-called 'right' was really a 'privilege' or 'liberty'. Similarly, philosophers sometimes introduce two senses of 'right', namely that in the 'right to act' and that in the 'right to receive'; the latter of which is then analysed as a 'claim on another'.[34] At other times, even the right to act is analysed as a claim on others, e.g., as a claim to their non-interference.[35] But, apart from its own implausibility, a division of two senses of 'right' leaves unexplained such rights as the right to assume or expect that *p*, the right to feel pleased with oneself or the right to feel indignant, which are rights neither to act nor to receive. Sometimes, the further step is taken of denying that there is, strictly speaking, such a thing at all as a right *to act*; there is, it is said, strictly speaking a 'liberty' to act.[36]

It is, therefore, important in this context to examine the assumption common among philosophers[37] and jurists,[38] that

---

Sneed J.; *Mellinger* v. *City of Houston* (1887), 68 Tex., 45, 3 SW, 249, 253 *per* Stayton J.; *Studd* v. *Cook* (1883) 8 App. Cas., at 597 *per* Lord Watson.

[33] As I have argued in 'Privilege', *Modern Law Review* 41 (1978): 299–311.

[34] D. D. Raphael, 'Obligations and Rights in Hobbes', *Philosophy* 37 (1962), p. 348; 'The Rights of Man and the Rights of the Citizen', in *Political Theory and the Rights of Man*, edited by D. D. Raphael (London: Macmillan, 1967), pp. 102–5. Cp. R. S. Downie, 'The Right to Criticise', *Philosophy* 44 (1969): 116–26; C. Arnold, 'Analyses of Right', in *Human Rights*, edited by E. Kamenka and A. E. Tay (London: Arnold, 1978), p. 77.

[35] E.g., F. Pollock, *Jurisprudence and Legal Essays*, edited by A. L. Goodhart (London: Macmillan, 1961), pp. 33, 46–7; W. D. Lamont, *The Principles of Moral Judgement* (Oxford: Clarendon Press, 1946), Ch. 3; Ross *op. cit.*, pp. 48 f.

[36] Raphael and Downie (see Footnote 34 above); Kocourek, *loc. cit.*; G. L. Williams, 'The Concept of Legal Liberty', *Columbia Law Review* 56 (1956): 1129–1150. Mayo, *art. cit.*, p. 225, holds that the so-called 'right to act' means only 'it is right to act', while Raphael and Downie say it means 'it is not wrong to act'.

[37] E.g., Lamont, *loc. cit.*; S. I. Benn and R. S. Peters, *Social Principles and the Democratic State* (London: Allen & Unwin, 1959), Chapter 4; Melden, *Rights and Persons, passim*; Feinberg, 'The Nature and Value of Rights', p. 253, who allows rights without duties only in a limited and special sense. Raphael, in common with some jurisprudents (e.g., T. E. Holland, *The*

rights, either in general or of a specific kind, imply duties and claims that these duties be exercised.

Certainly, one person's right may involve another's duty, as when an employer has a duty to protect his employees because they have a right to protection, or a husband has a duty to support his wife who has a right to be supported. But, first, it is at most the *kind* of right which dictates whether there is an accompanying duty, not the *nature* of a right. At most, we have different kinds of rights, not different concepts of right. Thus, though both *B*'s right to repayment and *A*'s duty to repay him may arise from *A*'s debt to *B*, the existence of *A*'s duty is no part of the notion of *B*'s having a right, just as it is no part of the notion of *A*'s having a father that there should be a *B* who has an uncle, though if *A* and *B* are first cousins, then when *A* has a father *B* will necessarily have an uncle.[39] It is because of the nature of a gift or a treatment that one person's right to be given something, e.g., to be protected, to be repaid, to be told the truth or to safe working conditions, involves a duty on someone else to give it; and it is because of the nature of the exercise of an ability that one person's right to act, e.g., to walk in the park, to raise an objection or to work where he wishes, may possibly involve a duty in others not to interfere.[40] So a contract between *A* and *B* will give rise both to rights in *B* and to duties in *A*.[41]

Contrariwise, what might be called different *kinds* of rights in one person give rise to no duties in others and, hence, to no claims

---

Elements of Jurisprudence, 13th edition (Oxford: Clarendon Press, 1924), p. 87) even says that '*A* has a right against *B*' and '*B* has a duty to *A*' say the same thing; cp. Arnold, *art. cit.*, p. 76. It is on the ground that rights imply duties and that we have no duties to animals that some philosophers, e.g. Joseph Rickaby and D. G. Ritchie, quoted in Regan and Singer, *op. cit.*, pp. 179–84, deny rights to animals.

38 E.g., Bentham, Austin, Salmond, Keeton, Kelsen, Allen, Hart.

39 Cp. D. Lyons, 'The Correlativity of Rights and Duties', *Noûs* 4 (1970): 46–9.

40 Cp. Lamont and Ross (note 35 above).

41 Cp. K. Olivecrona, *Law as Fact*, 2nd edition (London: Stevens, 1971), pp. 137 f.

by the former that such duties be exercised by the latter. Thus, my right to treat people in certain ways, e.g., to teach them, heal them, protect or punish them, does not impose on them a duty to be treated or to allow themselves to be treated in these ways by me. No one has a duty corresponding to my right to assume, expect, hope for or resent something. The right of a chairman to a casting vote or of a university to refuse admission to an intending student does not involve a duty in others. It is ridiculous to suppose[42] that *A*'s right to criticise *B* implies that *B* has a duty to be criticised or to listen, for *A* may criticise *B* in the latter's absence or even long after he is dead. Nor is my right to pick up a stray pound note lying on the road a right against anyone and, therefore, it does not involve a duty on anyone to allow me to do this.

In the law, there are, on the one hand, frequent *obiter dicta* that 'right' and 'duty' are correlative terms, as in *Quinn* v. *Leathem*,[43] *Attorney-General* v. *Adelaide Steamship Co.*,[44] *Howley Park Coal, etc., Co.* v. *N.W. Ry.*,[45] *Lake Shore & M.S.R. Co.* v. *Kurtz*,[46] all quoted in Hohfeld. And the court in *Broome* v. *D.P.P.*[47] used the argument that Parliament could not have meant to impose a duty on anyone to stop and listen to a picket in order to prove that it had therefore not given any right to stop anyone and make him listen, but only to try to persuade him to stop.[48]

On the other hand, not only might we ask by parity of reasoning what duty Parliament has, or could have, imposed on *B* when it gave *A* a right to try to persuade *B* to stop,[49] but it has often

---

42 E.g., Downie, *art. cit.*, p. 123.
43 [1901] AC 495, 534, *per* Lindley L. J.
44 [1913] AC 781, 793, *per* Lord Parker of Waddington.
45 [1913] AC 11, 25.
46 (1894) 10 Ind. App. 60; 37 NE 303, 304.
47 [1974] AC 587.
48 See the objections to this principle by G. S. Goodwin-Gill, 'Judicial Reasoning and the "Right" to Picket', *Law Quarterly Review* 91 (1975): 173–9.
49 Cp. Hart's interpretation of Bentham's rights which result from an

been decided that a particular right involves no duty. Thus, in *Piddington* v. *Bates*[50] the right to picket implied only a *prima facie* correlative duty on others not to interfere, which could cease to exist if a policeman thought a breach of the peace could possibly occur. Nor is there any warrant for Hohfeld's[51] and Dias's[52] criticism that the courts' argument in trade competition cases must, wrongly, assume that the right of *A* to pursue his business implies a duty of *B* not to interfere, when they ought, according to them, only to suppose that what *A* and *B* have are privileges or, according to Glanville Williams,[53] liberties. *Quinn* v. *Leathem*,[54] *Allen* v. *Flood*,[55] *Mogul S.S. Co.* v. *McGregor, Gow & Co.*,[56] and *Sorrell* v. *Smith*[57] make it clear that the right of *A* to pursue his business interests does not imply a duty of *B* to refrain from interference, but only a duty to refrain from unlawful interference, such as interference for the purpose of injuring *A* or with malice or in a conspiracy. Such cases – as well as those between employer and employee, e.g., *Crofter Hand Woven Harris Tweed Co. Ltd.* v. *Veitch*[58] and *Rookes* v. *Barnard & Others*[59] – show that there is no

---

absence of legal obligation rather than from any correlation with obligations or duties, in 'Bentham on Legal Rights' in *Oxford Essays in Jurisprudence*, edited by A. W. B. Simpson (Oxford: Clarendon Press, 1973), pp. 171–201; cp. R. Pound, *op. cit.*, pp. 43–53.

[50] [1960] 3 All E.R. 660.

[51] *Op. cit.*, pp. 42 f. Cp. T. D. Perry, 'A paradigm of philosophy: Hohfeld on Legal Rights', *American Philosophical Quarterly* 14 (1977): 41–50.

[52] 3rd ed., p. 256 and Note 3.

[53] G. L. Williams, *art. cit.*

[54] [1901] AC 495.

[55] [1898] AC 1.

[56] (1889) 23 QBD 598.

[57] [1925] AC 700, particularly Lord Dunedin at 728 and Lord Sumner at 733.

[58] [1942] AC 435; [1942] 1 All E.R. 142, *per* Lord Wright at 462–6, 158–160.

[59] [1962] 2 All E.R. 579.

logical difficulty, as Hohfeld supposes, in the notion of conflicting rights.

Even where my right is what the law often calls a 'right against someone', his duty, and, hence, my claim to the exercise of his duty, is not so much a logical consequence of my right as a legal protection for it.[60] In many cases it would be pointless, though not logically impossible, to give a right to *A* without laying a correlative duty on *B*. This is why jurists often suggest that *A*'s possession of a right must involve a duty on others not to interfere with his exercise of it, and suppose that a right is distinguished from a liberty by the presence of the duty of others not to interfere.[61] It is, therefore, at most a legal, not a logical, truth that having a right involves having a claim to that to which one has the right, in that the law allows the claim of him who has the right.

Furthermore, it is, at best, misleading and, at worst, mistaken to suppose that there are even different *kinds* of right, some of which involve, and others of which do not, either duties or claims to the exercise of duties. For what distinguishes these rights from each other is not the nature of the rights, but the nature of that to which they are rights. It is the nature of a debt, a gift, a contract, a treatment – one might even say of the passive voice – that its existence hints at or involves a correlative person to whom, when appropriate, claims, demands, requests, etc., may be made. The right to various kinds of things no more implies various kinds of rights – much less different senses of the word 'right' or different concepts of *right* – than being free to do different kinds of things, taking pleasure in different kinds of things, or having abilities to do different kinds of things, imply different kinds of liberties, pleasure or abilities. Most importantly, whether or not we call these different kinds of rights, liberties, pleasures, etc., it is what

---

[60] Cp. Lamont, *op. cit.*, pp. 71–3, who seems to deduce the former from the latter; Hart, 'Bentham on Legal Rights', pp. 179 f.; and Pound, *op. cit.* pp. 47–53.

[61] E.g., J. F. Salmond, *Jurisprudence*, 7th edition (London: Sweet & Maxwell, 1924), pp. 237 f.

these are rights, liberties, pleasures, etc., to or in, which dictates what different kinds of consequences they will have.

But even if having a right to something and having a claim to it were mutually implicative – which I have argued they are not – they would not necessarily be the same notion. Much less are rights and claims themselves – even true or justified claims – the same. As we have seen, rights, but not claims, can be given, conferred, taken away, earned, enjoyed or exercised; while claims, but not rights, can be made, advanced, laid, made out, settled, allowed, met or rejected.

University of Hull

NEIL MacCORMICK

RIGHTS, CLAIMS AND REMEDIES

1.

Professor White's paper starts with claims and then moves on to rights. Let mine follow the reverse order and start with rights.[1] My question is whether there are, as Professor White implies, any common features shared by all that we call 'rights'. My answer is: several.

First, rights belong within normative orders. They do not belong in the world of brute facts. That somebody has a right, if true, is a proposition which belongs to the class of 'institutional facts',[2] presupposing some body of norms relevant to human conduct. Thus there can be legal rights and moral rights; there can be rights in common courtesy, like my right to expect an answer when I ask a friend a question;[3] there can be rights, by the rules of football, like the right to a penalty kick if an opponent other than the goalkeeper handles the ball in his own penalty area, and so on. That rights can obtain within such diverse orders is not evidence that the rights involved are conceptually different. (No more than

---

[1] The argument in this section is based on positions put more extensively in other papers of mine. See 'Children's Rights: A Test-Case for Theories of Right', *Archiv für Rechts- und Sozialphilosophie* 62 (1976): 305–317; 'Rights in Legislation', in *Law, Morality and Society*, edited by P. M. S. Hacker and J. Raz (Oxford: Clarendon Press, 1977), pp. 189–209; 'Dworkin as Pre-Benthamite', *Philosophical Review* 87 (1978): 585–607; 'The Obligation of Reparation', *Proceedings of the Aristotelian Society* 78 (1977/8): 175–93.

[2] See D. N. MacCormick, 'Law as Institutional Fact', *Law Quarterly Review* 90 (1974): 102–129.

[3] Professor White refers, in his concluding section, to 'a right ... to assume so and so or to expect such and such'.

M. A. Stewart (ed.), Law, Morality and Rights, 161–181.

a football 'penalty' instantiates a different concept from that which occurs in the case of a legal 'penalty'.)

Secondly, rights vest in individuals – not necessarily individual human beings; whatever counts as an individual within a given normative order (human being, company, trade union, club, football team, etc.) can have a right ascribed to it.

Thirdly, ascription of rights to individuals, or vesting of rights in individuals, depends on rules or principles which are logically universal in tenor (or 'general', as we are more apt to say in loose everyday discourse). But these rules or principles deal with individuals severally, in the sense that whoever qualifies by virtue of certain generic characteristics, or because of the occurrence of generically specified events, has such and such a right. Each has his/her/its own right.

Fourthly, having a right relates to something which in normal circumstances is deemed to be a good for individuals, or at least, for individuals of the class in question. And the good in question is one which is susceptible of enjoyment by individuals severally, as against diffuse common advantages or goods. Of course, not all the rights each individual has are actually beneficial to each particular individual in all circumstances. But the point of rights is that they concern or relate to individual goods, in the sense of 'things' which are normally considered good for normal individuals.

Fifthly, not everything which is good for any individual is his/hers/its by right. There are many things which it would be advantageous to me to have, but to which I have no right. Only those goods actually secured to me under some rule or principle of a relevant normative order are mine by right. How then can 'goods' be secured to me? Again, my answer is: in several ways.

(i) The most basic concept of any normative order is of that which it is wrong to do, or to omit to do. If it is not wrong to do (or omit) x, then it is all right to do (or omit) x. One is normatively at liberty to do (or omit) x, whether or not in a given case one wishes to, or indeed is physically able to, do so.

Obviously, it is in principle and in general a good to be free in this way. But free from what, precisely? The answer depends on our understanding of what a normative order is, namely an order of norms accepted by somebody or some group and implemented both as a guide to conduct and as a ground of judgment of people's actings. Hence, the acknowledgement of a norm against doing *y* involves one in a standing attitude of disapprobation of whoever does *y*. I do not say that people in this case disapprove of doing *y* in order to induce people to conform, though they may indeed adopt means of expressing disapproval which are aimed at inducing conformity. Whether or not they do, it remains in general somewhat disagreeable to be the object of disapprobation for having done *y*.

That which one is free from when one avoids doing acts which are wrongs under a given normative order is, therefore, *justified* disapprobation, criticism and, indeed, punishment (or whatever other modes of expressing disapprobation there may be). It is only justified to treat as wrongs of a given order deeds and omissions which actually are wrongs of that order.

For this freedom from justified disapprobation to be in any degree secured as a standing freedom, it is necessary that there be some reasonably clear and constant definition or understanding of what kinds of actings and omissions are wrongful. This feature of reasonable clarity and constancy is written into the very idea of a normative *order* as I would conceive such. That 'the Rule of Law' is treated as a significant value and *nulla poena sine lege* is deemed an important principle shows the importance we attach to laws being in this sense orders of norms, not congeries of the kind of arbitrary decisions and judgments which appear to have been features of Amin's Uganda and of Stalin's Soviet Union as depicted by Solzhenitsyn.

That there are legal rights to do things appears then to depend at the minimum on there being reasonable clarity and constancy in the legal order about wrongs and offences. That there is a realm of *secured* normative liberty is what is essential to there being *rights* to act or refrain from acting. Analogous moral rights depend on the same basic idea – contentious as moral norms may be, we at least postulate some kind of a standing moral order if we employ the notion that people have moral rights to do as they please in certain matters (which notion, of course, does not preclude *disliking* what is done, or disapproving it aesthetically, or thinking that it evinces a lack of wisdom or of some other virtue). A belief that there are such moral rights is often also a ground for advocating the recognition of at least coextensive legal rights. Hence the *moral* dimension of *nulla poena sine lege*, etc.

Some confirmation of what I have just been saying is found in the fact that one characteristic use of such expressions as 'I have every right to do what I am doing' is as a response to criticism or accusations or disputes over the matter whether we are, in doing x, doing wrong. Appeals to one's rights, and to others to recognise one's rights, are normally necessary only when one's rights are being contested or overridden, or when demands to desist or accusations are in the air. If well founded, the appeal to one's rights is a mode of rejecting criticism etc. as unjustified within the normative order in question.

In at least some legal systems there are formal methods for obtaining an authoritative determination whether such an appeal to one's rights is well-founded. Courts have power to grant declaratory judgments in disputed matters of right.[4] For example, the Ministry holds that a certain quarrying operation is unlawful under the Town and Country Planning legislation, and is threatening to serve an enforcement notice. The quarrying company obtains a declaration of its right at law to continue with the quarrying operations, on the grounds that the statute does not prohibit these operations.[5] But of course, such a remedy is only available in matters of disputed *legal* right. If one medical practitioner is attacking another for practising in breach of medical ethics, a

---

[4] See, e.g., F. H. Lawson, *Remedies of English Law*, 2nd edition (London: Butterworth, 1980), Chapter 16; D. M. Walker, *The Law of Civil Remedies in Scotland* (Edinburgh: Green, 1974), Chapter 8.

[5] See *Pyx Granite Ltd.* v. *Ministry of Housing* [1960] AC 260; [1959] 3 All E.R. 1.

declaration that the latter is *legally* entitled to go on with his practice would not be material to the real issue in dispute.[6]

(ii) That I have a right to do something implies at least that doing it is not wrong. But it may also be that in doing it I exercise a 'normative power'. Binding oneself to do something by making a promise is the obvious and hackneyed example of this in the moral sphere (though there are others), and the law is of course full of examples – contracts, transfers of property, agency, establishment of trusts, making rules of law, giving judicial decisions, issuing governmental orders, and so on. The rules of most institutions and organizations provide yet further examples, such as the ones alluded to by Professor White when he speaks of 'the right of a chairman to a casting vote or of a university to refuse admission to an intending student'.

To take these two cases, what we must note is that the 'rights' in question involve the exercise of normative power.[7] The chairman's casting vote, if he does have the right to it, *counts* as a valid vote, and indeed when cast determines the Committee's decision one way or the other. The University, if it does have the right in question, makes a decision which takes effect as precluding the applicant from validly matriculating as a student (or, in other cases, as enabling students validly to matriculate). In both cases the decision is necessarily admitted as 'counting', as having valid effect, even by those who think the wrong decision was made, if they also accept the relevant body of norms and cannot discover or point to any invalidity arising from the mode of exercise of the power in the particular case.

What the normative order secures to an individual in such cases is that his/her/its decision is to be recognised and respected (whether or not agreed with or approved for its wisdom or moral

---

6 See *Cox* v. *Green* [1966] 1 All E.R. 268.

7 See D. N. MacCormick and J. Raz, Symposium on 'Voluntary Obligations and Normative Powers', *Proceedings of the Aristotelian Society*, Suppl. 46 (1972): 59–102; J. Raz, *Practical Reason and Norms* (London: Hutchinson, 1975), pp. 98–106, on the concept of 'normative power'.

propriety). The institution of normative powers secures for individuals spheres of competence, spheres of decision-making, within which it is their decision that counts. And although the justification of norms conferring powers is or may be in terms of the ulterior general goods which they promote, it is, as it were, an immediate good for the power-bearer that his judgment or decision, being authoritative within the system, is recognised to be such, not flouted or defied.

In such cases again the remedy by way of a declaratory judgment is available at law, to determine whether a given purported exercise of power is in fact 'within the rights' of the individual concerned. For example, a Minister has made an instrument by way of delegated legislation – was he within his rights? Is the instrument valid as law as against this or that person or class of persons who are contesting it?[8] Equally, the party adversely affected by the purported exercise of a private power may contest the validity of its exercise, e.g., on equitable grounds, as when a highland chief, whose ancestral lands had been heavily mortgaged, while serving on the Western front in the 1914–18 War, failed to pay a sum of interest due until seven days after the contractual date; the lenders thereupon *inter alia* sought a 'declarator that [they] were entitled to call up and demand payment of the principal sums contained in the ... bonds and dispositions in security [*anglice* mortgage deeds]'.[9]

Maclaine of Lochbuie advanced an argument on equitable grounds that the lenders were debarred by their own conduct from insisting on the strict terms of the bond. But he lost. 'I confess I think the case a hard one,' said Lord Dunedin, 'but I think the pursuers *are within their rights*'; 'I do not think ...' said Lord Atkinson, 'that the conduct of Sir Stephen Gatty is very com-

[8] See *McEldowney* v. *Forde* [1969] 2 All E.R. 1039; [1971] AC 632; *Hotel & Catering Industry Training Board* v. *Automobile Pty. Ltd.* [1969] 2 All E.R. 582: both discussed in D. N. MacCormick, 'Delegated Legislation and Civil Liberty', *Law Quarterly Review* 86 (1970): 171–80.

[9] Quoted from *Gatty* v. *Maclaine* 1920 SC 441 at 442.

mendable, but at all events *he cannot be deprived of his rights* ...' (italics added in both cases).[10]

This notion that people can be, or can be acting, 'within their rights', as Lord Dunedin put it, draws attention to the way in which spheres of action, judgment and decision can be secured or assigned to individuals (a) in those areas where, under a given normative order, their actings are not wrongs of that order; and (b) in those instances in which the individual's decisions and acts are deemed valid exercises of normative power. That fidelity to the normative order requires in one case recognition of the non-wrongful character of actings, and, in the other case, recognition of their validity in effecting normative change, and requires such recognition even or especially by those who dislike or (from other points of view) disapprove of what has been done, clarifies the notion that the acting individual is protected in enjoyment of a 'good'. Broadly, the good in question is the being treated as an individual possessed of discretion and judgment, able to take his/her/its own decisions about what to do and what normative changes to bring about, and entitled to have these decisions tolerated or respected. (Here we are thinking, of course, of 'discretion' as a valued personal attribute, but in a context which enables us to see the more-than-etymological connection with 'discretion' in the other sense – judicial discretion, the discretionary powers of tribunals, etc.[11])

(iii) That aspect of rights which yields the notion of 'acting within one's rights' is an aspect under which they can be contested, flouted, not respected, rendered nugatory, etc. The remedy of a declaratory judgment at law affords, as we saw, an institutional protection against such contestation, flouting, etc. But it is in relation to rights in another aspect that we can and do speak of

---

[10] *Gatty* v. *Maclaine* 1921 SC (H.L.) 1 at pp. 10, 11 respectively.

[11] A not dissimilar point is made by my colleagues Z. K. Bankowski and D. Nelken in their 'Discretion as a Social Problem', in *Discretion and Welfare*, edited by M. Adler and S. Asquith (London: Heinemann, 1981), pp. 247–268.

rights being 'infringed'. My right of free speech on a certain matter is contested by someone who raises an action against me for libel or prosecutes me for blasphemy. It is infringed by a mob who turn up at a meeting to shout me down.[12]

I have other rights which can be infringed, of course; libels infringe my right to an unsullied reputation, assaults my right to bodily security, breaches of contract my right to the agreed performance and so forth. Such infringements are wrongs; but not wrongs at large, like breaches of the peace or publications of grossly obscene articles, rather wrongs *to me*. The first level of normative protection in such cases is, of course, the existence of norms against infringement of the rights; norms whereby it is a duty not to assault, not to defame, not to break contracts made. The second level of protection is the existence of norms whereby wrongdoers in such cases are required to desist from further infringement and to make reparation for harm already done. The third level of protection in legal and other institutionalised systems is that courts etc. are empowered to order desistence by interdicts or injunctions and to order reparation in cash or kind. Characteristically, by positive law such orders are *enforceable*, either by self-help or by official action.

In this so to say 'passive' aspect of rights, it seems obvious that what constitutes the securing of goods to individuals, or their protection in enjoyment of them, is the subjection of people to duties to refrain from injuring interests of others. Yet axiologically, it would appear that the guiding concept here is that of interests – 'goods' – which-ought-to-be-protected; that there should be a right, should be security in this good, is the reason for imposing or accepting the duty-norm. And to that extent the 'right' has primacy over the duty, though without the duty it is, as an older school of thinkers used to say, an 'imperfect right'.[13]

---

[12] It does not necessarily follow that *this* infringement is legally actionable as a civil wrong; it is however apt to be punishable as a breach of the peace.

[13] See, e.g., Francis Hutcheson, *An Inquiry Concerning Moral Good and Evil* VII.vi, in *British Moralists 1650–1800*, edited by D. D. Raphael, Volume 1 (Oxford: Clarendon Press, 1969), p. 298.

But there is great importance morally in this idea of an imperfect right, or aspirational right. To perceive that education is a good for human beings which ought to be secured to them is not a reason for concluding that someone is now in direct breach of duty to the uneducated. It is a reason for seeking the establishment of public or other institutions whose functionaries shall be charged with the duty to provide universal education, and to be answerable for failures. Recognition of such rights requires us to seek means of implementing them; and while failure to implement a right in such cases is wrong, it is not to be conflated with infringement of a perfect right.

Even in law, we find instances of rights which are secured by provision of means for their implementation rather than by the direct imposition of 'correlative' duties. I have elsewhere[14] given as an example of this certain rights of intestate succession in Scots law which vest in the beneficiaries prior to the identification of any duty bearer charged with implementing the already vested rights to be put in possession of property. And here legal measures of implementation exist to the extent that a beneficiary or someone acting on his/her behalf is enabled to take steps to procure, by court order, confirmation of an executor who is charged with the duty of winding up the estate according to the statutory scheme.

(iv) Finally, it needs but little reflection to reveal that the three preceding aspects of the securing of goods to individuals may be more than a little precarious. Normative protection depends on norms, and norms can change or be changed – at least those of institutionalised orders, such as legal systems, can be deliberately changed. Hence the security of rights depends at least as a matter of degree on restricting the ability of all or most individuals unilaterally to change the norms under which rights are constituted. Hence restrictions on normative powers, up to the very point of formal constitutional entrenchment of fundamental rights, is an important element in that securing of goods to individ-

[14] 'Rights in Legislation' (Footnote 1 above).

uals which has been proposed here as the very gist of 'rights' as such.

To the extent that a person's position is immune from change, the 'rights' secured under all or any of the preceding three aspects are the more firmly secured. And without some durability in time, we should barely think of them as rights at all.[15] This point need not be laboured further.

2.

The foregoing brief account suggests that there are common features shared by all that we call 'rights': normative orders can afford to individuals security in the enjoyment of what are normally goods for individuals; that someone has a right to *x* (a) implies that either *x* or freedom or discretion in relation to *x* is a good, and (b) is true if in one mode or another the individual fulfils the conditions for having some appropriate form of normative security over *x* or freedom or discretion in relation to *x*.

But within this characterization of the concept 'a right' we find that there are different ways in which such 'normative security' is achieved. Our first instance, in which having a right to do *x* depends on being normatively at liberty to do *x*, further depends on an implied normative permission[16] to do whatever it is not (within a given normative order) wrong to do. Our second instance depends on having power to bring about *x*, and thus on the existence of norms which confer powers. Our third depends either on there being already duties *vis-à-vis* other individuals not to infringe their enjoyment of certain goods or on provisions for implementation of their enjoyment, and hence is dependent on the actual or possible existence of norms imposing duties. Our fourth instance depends on the existence of more or less stringent and well-defined limitations on powers to change the permissions or norms under

---

[15] See A. M. Honoré, 'Rights of Exclusion and Immunities against Divesting', *Tulane Law Review* 34 (1959/60): 453–68.

[16] See J. Raz, *Practical Reason and Norms*, pp. 85–97, on 'permissions'.

which in the other three ways goods are secured to individuals.

From the point of view of a general theory of legal systems or of other normative orders, these differences are important, since they show how the admittedly unitary concept of 'a right' is related to or presupposes different kinds of norms. Certainly, as Professor White says, it is 'the nature of that to which [one has] rights' which determines what mode of normative security is relevant. A concern with maximising the right to free speech will manifest itself mainly in a programme of abolishing or restricting norms which make various forms of speech offences or wrongs. A concern to secure more fully the right to one's reputation will manifest itself contrariwise in further restrictions on the written, spoken and broadcast word. And so on.

But it seems to me, with respect, to be unduly squeamish of Professor White to take the line that

> it is, at best, misleading and, at worst, mistaken to suppose that there are even different *kinds* of right, some of which involve, and others do not, either duties or claims to the exercise of duties. For what distinguishes these rights from each other is not the nature of the rights, but the nature of that to which they are rights.

As we have seen, 'the nature of that to which they are rights' is significant in determining the appropriate mode of normative security. But precisely because there are different modes thereof, there is good reason to distinguish different kinds of rights. Within the genus 'rights' there is perfectly good reason to distinguish the right to speak one's mind, the right not to be defamed, the right to foreclose a mortgage, and the right not to be subjected to taxation without Parliamentary authority.

That is just what Hohfeld and other jurists and philosophers[17]

---

[17] See W. N. Hohfeld, *Fundamental Legal Conceptions* (New Haven: Yale University Press, 1919). Notice how Hohfeld remarks at p. 38: 'Recognizing, as we must, the very broad and indiscriminate use of the term "right," what clue do we find, in ordinary legal discourse, toward limiting the word in question to a definite and appropriate meaning?' Similar remarks occur throughout the text. Hohfeld conceives himself to be *improving* on ordinary legal dis-

criticised by Professor White sought to do – to clarify the different kinds of 'legal relations' which in ordinary usage can be lumped together, sometimes confusingly, under the general rubric of 'rights'. Hohfeld, as it were, tells us to call the right to speak one's mind 'a privilege', the right not to be defamed 'a right *stricto sensu*' or 'a claim', the right to foreclose a mortgage 'a power', the right not to be subject to unauthorised taxation 'an immunity', and so on. As an exercise in stipulation for clarity's sake, this is surely unobjectionable in itself; though Hohfeld certainly errs in claiming that he is really only clarifying what is already the best or the proper usage.[18]

A more significant error, in my view, lies in Hohfeld's judgment that these 'relations' have nothing in common sufficient to justify the ordinary usage whereby they are *all* 'rights' or species of 'right'. And a further, related, error stems from the view that all are essentially relational in the sense of being relations between paired individuals (a view which yields, notoriously, the rather absurd conclusion that for every 'privilege' that I have, there is some other individual who has a 'no-right'). This leads to an entire ineptitude in the treatment of complex 'institutional' rights like property and other 'rights *in rem*' as though these were just names for an aggregation of infinitely numerous atomic legal relations.[19] The truth, as I have elsewhere pointed out,[20] is that 'institution' concepts of that sort have the function of enabling us to organise

---

course, not merely analysing it. Is this *necessarily* a misconceived activity? For a useful discussion and résumé of attempts further to refine Hohfeld's proposals, see W. J. Kamba, 'Legal Theory and Hohfeld's Analysis of a Legal Right', *Juridical Review* (1974): 249–62. Among philosophers criticised by White, at least D. D. Raphael has in several cases made clear that he is *stipulating* a special meaning for 'claim' etc. See, e.g., 'Justice and Liberty', *Proceedings of the Aristotelian Society* 51 (1950/51): 167–196, esp. at p. 172 in relation to 'claims'.

18 Hohfeld, *op. cit.*, numerous passages. See, e.g., pp. 38–40.

19 *Op. cit.*, pp. 71–4.

20 See my 'Law as Institutional Fact' and 'Rights in Legislation' (Footnotes 1 and 2 above).

and make comprehensible considerable bodies of legal or other norms which secure a variety of modes of normative protection to individual 'right-holders'. We can exhibit the various aspects or incidents (to use A. M. Honoré's term[21]) of such institutions, involving as they do many possible variations in different systems and at different times, the variations being dependent on differences of legal politics and ideology as well as on mere chance. Not all rights are either instances of the simple Hohfeldian categories, or reducible without residue to aggregations thereof.

Even ostensibly simple, but politically contested, rights like the 'right to work', 'the right to picket',[22] 'the right to privacy',[23] may have more than one aspect, involving more than one mode of normative security. How much, if any, security one should have at law in one's job and job opportunities, one's picketing, and one's private life, are matters for political decision, not for conceptual analysis. Only once the political decisions have been taken about what, if any, restrictions there are to be on one's working and one's picketing or on one's personal conduct of one's affairs, and what, if any, duties others are to be subjected to in favour of workers, pickets, or personal privacy, can the task of analysis commence *for that legal system* in order to determine what various aspects these complex rights have.

Hence, while agreeing with Professor White that the concept of 'right' does have a basic unity, I disagree with his doubt that there really are different kinds of rights. I see more virtue than he sees in the Hohfeldian enterprise, whose admitted defects I diagnose differently from Professor White.

---

[21] A. M. Honoré, 'Ownership', in *Oxford Essays in Jurisprudence*, edited by A. G. Guest (Oxford: Clarendon Press, 1961), pp. 107–47.

[22] See, e.g., *Piddington* v. *Bates* [1960] 3 All E.R. 660, *Broome* v. *D.P.P.* [1974] AC 587, discussed by Professor White in the final section of his paper.

[23] See D. N. MacCormick, 'Privacy: A Problem of Definition?', *British Journal of Law and Society* 1 (1974): 75–8.

3.

I turn now to the topic of claims. Here I find myself in direct disagreement with Professor White. What I said in my first section lays the ground for the view I shall here put.

I do not, by and large, dispute Professor White's ingenious elucidation of 'indicative', 'subjunctive' and 'possessive' claims. Nor do I dispute the relatively loose character of the connection which he asserts to hold even as between subjunctive claims and rights. (As to subjunctive claims, I do disagree with White that these have no truth-value. Normative statements can be true or false relative to particular normative orders[24] – e.g., it is true for all legal systems which allow for contracts of sale that a buyer of goods who has accepted goods delivered under the contract should pay the seller the price. Such statements can, as in the example given, be framed in the subjunctive mood. Hence the claim that all buyers, or that this buyer, should pay the price for goods delivered and accepted under a contract of sale, is also capable of being, and is normally, true.)

What I principally dispute is whether Professor White has given a complete analysis of 'claiming'. There are indeed claims expressible indicatively – 'I am the best boy in the class at writing'. There are indeed claims expressible subjunctively – 'I should be given a prize for my good writing'. But there are also claims expressible as imperatives – 'Give me the £100 you owe me'.

There is a clear difference between claiming (demanding) £100 allegedly owed by another person, and either claiming (alleging) that £100 *is* owed by another person or claiming (contending) that £100 *should be* paid over by another person. Certainly, he who claims £100 from another impliedly represents both that he believes (contends) that there is some general ground on which £100 should be paid and that he believes (alleges) that particular facts obtain as between the two parties which make that general

---

[24] See J. Raz, *Practical Reason and Norms*, pp. 154f., 170–7, on 'normative statements'.

ground operative. But these implied representations follow from what J. L. Austin called the 'sincerity conditions'[25] apposite to this particular 'speech act'. The utterance of a claim and the claim uttered are not to be confused with the conditions required for it to be a sincere utterance or a justified one.

To say 'Treat me in a civilized fashion', given an appropriate context, is to claim, or make a claim for, civilized treatment. The 'explicit performative' version is 'I claim civilized treatment', or 'I claim to be treated in a civilized fashion'. Such claims are, to all intents and purposes, a species of demands. (Compare: 'I demand civilized treatment'; 'I demand to be treated in a civilized fashion'.)

But apart even from the point that demanding is perhaps a bit stronger or more forceful than claiming, there is one key difference between imperative claims and demands. Bank robbers, blackmailers, extortionists and kidnappers as well as creditors and tax collectors can and do issue demands for money, even 'final demands'. As that suggests, demands do not as such presuppose legitimate entitlements. Demands can be founded on might as well as on right. Not so claims.

He who claims the reward for finding your dog impliedly represents himself as being entitled to the reward. Of course, he may do so mistakenly (it's not your dog) or fraudulently (it wasn't he who found it) or jestingly (the pretence will in due course be dropped and everyone will laugh consumedly). But since a sincere and justified claim requires both a belief in an entitlement to the reward and an actual entitlement to the reward, and since mistaken claimants believe they have a genuine entitlement while fraudulent or jesting claimants purport to have a genuine entitlement though they know they have no such thing, anyone who makes an imperative claim does impliedly represent himself as being entitled to that which is claimed – aside from the special case of a claim explicitly made on behalf of someone else, in which case what is represented is a belief in that other party's

---

[25] See J. L. Austin, *How to do Things with Words*, 2nd edition (Oxford: Clarendon Press, 1975), Lecture IV.

entitlement to the thing claimed. Claims of this sort overlap with demands; to wit, with those demands which purport to be founded on some entitlement rather than on considerations of force.

As a matter of 'felicitousness'[26] at least there is no ground for making an imperative claim to that which you already have or which no one is actually denying you or threatening to deny you or otherwise putting in dispute. It can even be fraudulent to make a claim in such a case, as if I claim from you £5 lent, knowing that you have already repaid but hoping you have forgotten. (And it is at least rude to claim what I know you are on the point of repaying unprompted.)

It is not at all surprising that imperative claims have a special position in the law. This comes out most clearly in the English system of civil pleading and procedure, where a plaintiff sets an action in motion (after issuance of the original writ of summons) by serving on his opponent a 'Statement of Claim'.[27] A statement of claim comprises a numbered list of allegations of the material facts which the plaintiff means to put in issue, and of the claim for a remedy which he makes in the light of these allegations of fact and of some presupposed but undisclosed legal ground for the remedy. There is a set formula for the concluding sentence of a statement of claim, viz., 'And the plaintiff claims [damages/a money sum/an injunction restraining the defendant from further wrong-doing/specific performance of some duty by the defendant/a declaration of the plaintiff's rights or of the lawfulness of his actings or of the unlawfulness of the defendant's].' (Of course, more than one such remedy may well be claimed in a given action.)

In the light of what has been said about imperative claims, this legal usage is entirely in order. To claim an appropriate remedy is an entirely fitting act on behalf of one whose rights have been

---

26 Austin, *op. cit.*, Lectures II and III.

27 See, e.g., W. B. Odgers, *Principles of Pleading and Practice in Civil Actions in the High Court of Justice*, 21st edition, edited by D. B. Casson and I. H. Dennis (London: Stevens, 1975), Chapter 12 and Appendix 2 (for precedents of Statements of Claim).

allegedly infringed or flouted or put in serious dispute by another. As we saw, a justified claim is one based on an entitlement of the claimant. Legal claims are based on legal rights, at least on what the claimant contends are his legal rights. Raising legal actions by making 'statements of claim' and all the rest of it is however appropriate only where another party has refused to acknowledge and make good one's alleged right voluntarily and extra-judicially.

What remedy it is relevant and appropriate to claim depends on the kind of right which is in dispute, or the aspect(s) of one's rights which is/are in dispute. To claim damages and/or an injunction or specific performance is appropriate to those cases in which a right of the plaintiff's has been infringed, the defendant being in breach of some duty owed. For such a claim to be raised judicially, it would at least be normal practice[28] to have already claimed formally but extra-judicially of the defendant that he make reparation for damage done and desist from injurious activity. It is rejection of such a claim by the defendant which makes necessary the raising of an action, and the reiteration of the claim, this time as a claim that the court order the appropriate remedy.

As we saw in Part 1, when what is in issue is a contest whether the plaintiff has any right to do this or that, or whether he can within his rights validly bring about some legal change, or whether indeed some purported exercise of power has valid effect in changing or restricting the plaintiff's rights – in all these instances it may be appropriate to claim a declaration of one's rights (or of the legal position as it affects one's rights) from a court. Again, it is in cases where one's extra-judicial claim or demand that one's rights be recognised and the rightfulness of one's actings acknowledged has been rejected or ignored that the conditions for raising an action at law are satisfied.

---

[28] In Scotland, it is common practice to make a formal claim of one's opponent, and to aver its rejection, in pleading an action. In France, it is a technical requirement (sometimes rendered more or less fictitious) to have made such a claim, as the basis on which a civil action may be raised. As it happens, the Scottish form of pleading does not use the performative 'claim' as does the English. But claims are certainly made in our pleadings.

Although the action at law requires the specific institutions of the legal system, it is not a peculiarity of law that one can justifiedly claim recognition of the rightfulness of one's actings (and/or validity of one's actings, and/or invalidity of another's actings). To take any normative order seriously is to be committed to avoiding treating as offenders against that order those who have not in fact done wrong. 'Do not treat me as a wrongdoer; I have done no wrong', 'Accept the validity of my act', are imperative claims which can be made in any normative order. The peculiarity of legal orders is that there are institutionalised agencies competent to grant declaratory judgments when such claims are rejected, if they are unjustifiedly rejected.

Because Professor White has overlooked imperative claims, as distinct from indicative and subjunctive ones, he has, I submit, erred in denying that rights have a specific relationship to claims. To have a right is to have the basis for a justified imperative claim: (a) against people who infringe, reject, ignore, flout, dispute, or fail in appropriate cases to implement, that right; and (b) against courts and suchlike institutions, that they award an appropriate remedy where a claim of the former sort is rejected or ignored.

Others have made the same or a similar point before now. Dr Haksar in a recent essay[29] introduces what he calls a 'demand theory' of rights with this suggestion:

> When a person is not given what he has a right to have, he has been wronged. And he (or someone acting on his behalf) is entitled to complain and censure the guilty party or parties ... Moreover he can (validly) demand that he should be given what he has a right to have.

With this, I agree. But it seems that it fails as a distinguishing mark of rights 'in the stronger sense' (which excludes 'mere liberties' and 'mere privileges'), as Dr Haksar puts it. For although rights

---

[29] Vinit Haksar, 'The Nature of Rights', *Archiv für Rechts- und Sozialphilosophie* 64 (1978): 183–204, at p. 183. Compare also his remark *(ibid.)* that 'talk of rights is linked with demands, or claims, or complaints, that can validly be made by the person who has the right, or by those who speak on his behalf'.

may be of different kinds or manifest different aspects, as was shown in Parts 1 and 2 of the present paper, all may give rise to justified claims for appropriate remedies in certain circumstances, whether such claims be made by or be made on behalf of the individual concerned.

Dr Haksar's theory is offered in opposition *inter alia* to the kind of 'benefit' theory of rights which I adumbrated at the beginning of this paper. It should now be clear that the 'theories' are not opposed, but rather advert to different aspects of the same truth. Since normative orders which confer rights do so by normatively securing individuals in the enjoyment of various 'goods', it is not surprising that remedial action is called for when that enjoyment is disturbed or contested, or that those who are so disturbed are justified in claiming (imperatively) an appropriate remedy.

This is perhaps a variant on the old theme that every description of right is hedged with 'claim rights'; but at least it *is* a variant thereon. What is being stressed is that primary rights require remedial rights, and remedial rights are characteristically ones which do have corresponding duties – the duty to afford the remedial action. That a claim for a justified remedy is itself a justified claim gets on for being a tautology.

Could it be an objection to this that, in some legal systems (e.g., the English but not the Scottish), certain judicial remedies such as declarations, injunctions and orders for specific performance are said to be discretionary remedies? I do not think so. The discretion in question arises only on the ground that a number of factors have to be weighed in order to decide whether the remedy sought is appropriate to the given case and whether it ought, all things considered, to be granted. But once these questions are answered affirmatively, it is mere mumbo-jumbo to say that there is any discretion left.[30]

My conclusion that having rights entails having justified claims, which claims are however appropriately issuable only given infringement etc. of a right, is different from Professor White's. The

---

[30] See Lawson, *op. cit.*, pp. 235–8; and contrast Walker, *loc. cit.*

difference between us seems to turn on my identification of a type of claim not acknowledged by him, and I wonder whether he accepts my addition to the list. We are at least at one in holding the view that no rights are themselves claims in any ordinary sense of the latter term. That does not of itself rule out stipulatively redefining the term 'claim', but the usefulness of the term in its ordinary meaning in this particular context seems to me a strong ground for neither making nor accepting such a stipulation.

4.

Finally, as a brief coda, I should like to make two methodological points.

Firstly, the kind of analysis here offered both by Professor White and, less expertly, by myself, depends heavily on careful attention to linguistic usage for the purpose of conceptual clarification. This type of work is sometimes dismissed as an arid exercise in intellectual pedantry. Yet at a time at which legal and political philosophy – see for example the work of Dworkin and Nozick – is concentrating heavily on rights and the requirements for taking them seriously, there is all the more reason for also taking 'rights' seriously. Of course there is a place for normative as well as for analytical philosophising, but if based on insufficient analysis of key terms such as 'right', or on stipulative departures from what are ordinarily held to be rights, the former slithers into a morass of ambiguity and mere assertion.

Secondly, it can be and has been urged, from the point of view of a pure Kelsenian science of law,[31] that: (a) rights-talk always presupposes an ideological orientation towards some variety of individualism; (b) as such it does not belong within legal science at all; and (c) rights are in any event secondary elements of legal orders whose primary element by way of norms authorising the

---

[31] See R. H. S. Tur, 'The Leaves on the Trees', *Juridical Review* (1976): 139–55, and 'The Notion of a Legal Right: A Test Case for Legal Science', *Juridical Review* (1976): 177–88.

imposition of sanctions reveals in pure form the essence of all legal orders. To this the short reply is that (a) may well be true, but understanding of the general ideological orientation in question as manifested in many legal orders is a worthwhile objective which positively *requires*, not stipulation, but careful analysis of the rights-talk itself. As to point (b), therefore, analysis of rights-talk as distinct from advocacy of its use thus does belong to 'legal science'. And as to point (c), not till the analysis is done can it be held as proven that any particular Kelsenian or other analysis of legal norms has the desired universality which would enable it adequately to depict those legal orders which do exhibit such an ideological orientation. All this without prejudice to the further question whether Kelsenian 'legal science' has the primacy its exponents (subjunctively) claim for it.

University of Edinburgh

SAM COVAL

RIGHTS AND JUSTIFIED CLAIMS

Professor White reminds us that the fact that a claim has been made does not imply the truth of the proposition which is its content; nor, conversely, does the truth of a proposition imply the occurrence of the relevant claim. These denials of inferrability, from the fact of a claim to a proposition and *vice versa*, will hold even when the propositional content of the claim concerns rights. The topic of the proposition is irrelevant to the fact that inferrability in either direction does not exist between the occurrence of a claim and its proposition. The source of the independence of an occurrent claim from its propositional content is that each has different criteria for its truth-values. Claims have occurred, if some act was performed which constituted such an event as a claim, while the propositional content clearly, but perhaps unfortunately, has truth criteria other than that.

There is, however, the case of "having a claim", which is what White calls the "possessive" use, to be considered. When one "has a claim" then the propositional content is true whether or not one has actually made the claim. Connors has a claim to being the No. 3 tennis player in the world whether or not he or anyone else has actually so claimed for (or against) him. Consequently, White is prepared to consider what the relationship between a true or proven or granted or justified, *although perhaps unmade*, claim and a right might be. What then if I uphold his claim to be the heir to an estate? That admits "that I am the heir, not that I have a right to be the heir," says White, "even though being the heir gives me a right to the estate," he adds. Similarly, "to admit my claim to authorship ... is not to admit any supposed right to be the author", even though being the author gives me a right to put my name to it or a right to royalties.

I have some trouble with this. Consider that he is the heir:

M. A. Stewart (ed.), Law, Morality and Rights, 183–187.

he has therefore a right to inherit the estate; but if he does not have a right to be the heir then he does not have a right to the right to inherit the estate. Expectedly, this can be taken several ways.

1. "No right to the right" can mean, simply, that he does not have the right to inherit. This would deny a given implication of the main premise that he was admitted to be the heir. We had, then, better not take the phrase in this reductive way if White's thesis is to stand.

2. Perhaps, however, "having rights to rights" is a solecism. If it is, then that is evidence that the right to be the heir, insofar as it may be distinguished from justifiedly being the heir, is non-existent. To be the justified heir is to be the justified holder of certain rights, and no further distinction of any use such as whether or not he has the right to be the justified holder of certain rights remains to be made. This possibility cannot satisfy White either since he insists (must insist) that rights are not implied by justified claims.

3. Suppose we take the position that a distinction can be made between the right to be the heir and justifiedly being the heir. Then we should have to account for two embarrassing things. First, out of what are we to fashion the distinction? *Ex hypothesi*, no reasons or justifications remain since the most relevant claim is supposed already to be fully justified: "rightly claimed", "granted", "proved" and "justly claimed". Remember that it is being denied that such a totally just and right claim is even a necessary condition of a right. White seems to have forgotten this. He argues at this point only that, "Not even rightly claiming, much less merely claiming, something gives one a right to it." This is at the most only to show us that rightly claiming is neither a sufficient condition for, nor equivalent to, rights. If, however, the most relevant of the justified claims of agents are not even a necessary condition for rights it is difficult to see what could be a condition. It begins to look as if, on this view, the phrase "rights are justifiable" is often false.

This takes us to the second embarrassment which occurs if we accept, as White's thesis implies, that a distinction exists between justifiedly being the heir and having the right to be the heir, and furthermore that the former is not even a necessary condition of the latter. Then we must admit, as White does, that we may have no right to matters to which we do have a right and a right to matters to which we do not have rights. The first case is the one in which he does not have the right to be the heir but has the right to inherit the estate, and the second is when he has a right to be the heir but not one to inherit the estate.

This means that in White's view rights are logically independent not only of even the most relevant and justified claims but of other rights as well. Consider the case where I have the right to be the heir but have not the right to inherit (since I am not the heir). If I were the heir or had a justified claim to being so I would of course have the right to inherit. The fact that a certain status such as being an heir can imply a right but that a right to the identical status cannot imply the consequent right is an indication that on this view rights are established in a *fiat* fashion rather than by any pattern of justification or inference. Remember that not even the justice of *x* would imply a right to *x* according to White. That would explain why rights are not inferrable from claims and *vice versa.* It appears that, on White's account, rights can be created only by the invocation of a certain rule of recognition or by *fiat* – only this logical position seems to remain for rights. Only that would keep them independent of even the most justified claims of agents and therefore of all conceivable relevant practical reasons. But this overly-positivistic position has its well-known problems.

There is evidence however that White does not quite believe this position himself. He says: "Having a right to something is usually a, though not the only kind of, reason for possession of one's claim [having a justified claim] to it [the right]." This means that rights do imply justified claims although other things do as well. The last clause is irrelevant. White, we recall, wants to establish that rights neither imply nor are implied by even justifiably claiming to have a right. So apparently rights do imply justified claims. The only point of adding the irrelevant clause would be to show that the implication is not mutual, but White's hypothesis is that the implication is not even unilateral.

There is one final piece of evidence that White himself does not quite believe his own position. He says: "the fact that I have a right to chastise my son may not make it right for me to do so." This is meant to show again that having a right to do so does not imply that he has a justified claim – does not make it right – for him to do so. But if I have a right to do so then surely I have the right to do so, only *ceteris paribus*. The "*ceteris paribus*" tells us when it is right to exercise our right. The "*ceteris paribus*" rider to the exercise of rights sets them into a system of justification such that their exercise is meant to be coincident with – is limited to – doing the right thing. Without such a "*ceteris paribus*" rider as a necessary condition to their exercise (it is not the case that one can exercise his right unless it is right to do so), rights would be outside the economy of relevant justified considerations. Since the support of such a right so unconnected would be without any idea, even in principle, as to when it is right to do so, or when it is exercisable, we may assume that rights must imply that they will fit themselves into the system of truths or justified claims. Suppose then, if you have a right to do *x*, that *x* is do-able or exercisable. Whatever is do-able will be the right thing to do under certain conditions or *ceteris paribus*. This is the corollary to the more recognizable idea that whatever is do-able will be the wrong thing to do under certain conditions. Therefore, if you have a right to do *x* then it will be the right thing to do – under certain conditions. The fact that he has a right to chastise his own son makes it right for him to do so under these conditions. This is to say that if he has a right then it is right for him to do so when it is justified. I am sure that some proponents of a logical relation between rights and claims must be willing to hold this; for the sake of the argument, I hope White is not, or – better still – was not, but now is.

It is not clear what Professor MacCormick's view is with regard to the logical relation between a claim and a right. He does say, near the end of his paper, that "To have a right is to have the basis for a justified imperative claim…". This means presumably that a right implies an imperative claim. He also says, however, earlier in Part 3, that "anyone who makes an imperative claim does impliedly represent himself as being entitled to that which is claimed." This could mean that a right is implied by an imperative claim. I am going to assume that Professor MacCormick holds the view which I quoted first, since it occurs most frequently.

His objection to Professor White's position is that imperative claims, a type of claim he thinks not noted by Professor White, are implied by rights. It will probably be arguable by Professor White that imperative claims are subsumable under subjunctive ones, but there is a more direct line of argument available to him. Professor MacCormick's idea that to have a right is to have the basis for (to imply) a justified imperative claim can be treated by Professor White exactly as he has treated the purported connection between rights and other forms of claim. There is no feature of justified hortatory claims – is that a redundancy? – which will relevantly differentiate them from ordinary justifiable claims. Consequently Professor MacCormick's argument must stand or fall on whether Professor White's existing arguments against any logical connection between rights and claims are supportable.

I have argued that they are not supportable; and invite Professor MacCormick to join in that enterprise if he believes claims of any sort to be implicated by rights.

University of British Columbia

ALAN R. WHITE

CONCLUDING COMMENTS

I.

Professor MacCormick raises at least three objections to my general thesis of the independence of a right to *V* and a claim to *V*, and one to my specific minor point that what I called 'subjunctive' claims are neither true nor false. The three objections to my main thesis are, first, that in fact 'having rights entails having justified claims'; secondly, that there is a kind of claim, namely 'claims expressible as imperatives', whose neglect by me is the cause of my failure to see the validity of the first objection; thirdly, that, contrary to my view, a right to different kinds of things does imply either a different kind of right or, though I don't think MacCormick, despite his plea for Hohfeld, would go as far as this, different senses of the word 'right'. The first objection can be found at the end of his section 3, the second in that section *passim*; the third is found in section 2.

1. A preliminary difficulty with MacCormick's view that 'having rights entails having justified claims' is that it wavers between the view that having a right to *V* entails having a claim to *V* and the view that having a right to *V* entails having a claim to *F*, where *F* is the claim to a remedy for the infringement of the right to *V*. The second reading is supported by his explicit remarks on page 178 (para. 2) and page 179 (para. 4) and his variation on Haksar. The first reading is supported by his discussion on page 175 (paras. 1–3) of his 'imperative claims', by his agreement on page 178 (para. 3) with the quotation from Haksar, by his contention, page 179 (para. 2), that 'primary rights require remedial rights' which imply claims to remedies, and by his explicit assertions on page 174 (para. 1) and page 179 (para. 4) that he is in direct disagreement with me, who was arguing that a right to *V* neither implies nor is implied by a claim to *V*.

M. A. Stewart (ed.), Law, Morality and Rights, 189–198.

(a) The difficulty with the view in its first reading is that, first, it cannot be true of all rights, since 'having a claim to so and so' – or, similarly, 'claiming or making a claim to' – whether it is what I call an indicative or a subjunctive claim or what MacCormick calls an imperative claim, often makes no sense, though having a right to the same thing does. I illustrated this on pages 153–4 of my original paper. Thus, I can have a right to assume so and so, to marry whom I please or to feel indignant, without its being either true or perhaps even sensible to say that I have (or make) a claim of any kind to any of these.

Secondly, this objection is assimilated to or confused with another of MacCormick's arguments leading to the different conclusion that 'to have a right is to have *the basis for* a justified imperative claim' (page 178, my italics). Moreover, this second version of the objection meets the same difficulty as the first, namely that there are things to which one could have a right which either are not or could not be things for which we have or could have any kind of claim, and therefore, *a fortiori*, for which we could have a basis for such a claim. In addition, it has the difficulty that if to have a right *is* to have a basis for a claim, then to have a right must not only imply but be implied by having such a basis. But this cannot be correct, since to claim (or have a claim to) something as a reward, recompense, favour, due, expenses, privilege, etc., is to have a basis for the claim which does not imply having a right.

(b) The difficulty with MacCormick's thesis in its second reading is also that it cannot be true of all rights, for there are some, e.g., the right to expect or assume so and so or to feel such and such, where the idea of invasion or infringement of a right and remedy for such hardly makes sense, and others, e.g., rights in trade competition, which don't entail claims for remedies against all such interference.

2. MacCormick's second objection depends on the introduction of a third type of claim, which he calls a 'claim expressed by an imperative', additional to my 'indicative' and 'subjunctive' claims. My answer, as the chairman of the session predicted, is that there

is no such third type of claim. First, it cannot be substantiated by MacCormick's alleged 'clear difference' between 'claim' followed by a noun (his examples are £100, civilised treatment, reward, £5, damages, a money sum, an injunction, specific performance, a declaration, a remedy) and 'claim' followed by an indicative clause or 'claim' followed by a subjunctive clause. For (a) both the indicative claims and the subjunctive claims can, as I showed, be expressed by 'claim' followed by a noun, e.g., claiming an ability, advantages, ignorance, or claiming protection, immunity, a fair hearing. The use of a noun form for the subjunctive is, indeed, common with many other verbs than 'claim'. Thus, one can demand or require £100 or that one be given £100; one can advise a return to work or that there be a return to work. (b) MacCormick himself often lapses (e.g., page 177) into the subjunctive construction to express his 'imperative' claims, e.g., 'that he make reparation', 'that the court order be the appropriate remedy', 'that one's rights be recognised'. (c) MacCormick also expresses his 'imperative' claims in the infinitive form, e.g. 'to be treated in a civilised manner' (page 175), which I had shown (page 152) to be a variant on the subjunctive.

Secondly, MacCormick suggests that a proof of the existence of his 'imperative' claim in law can be drawn from the official way in which a plaintiff sets an action in motion by serving on his opponent a 'Statement of Claim'. MacCormick himself explains that such a Statement consists of a list of allegations of the material facts and a claim for a remedy. But the former of these are, as I have exemplified on page 146, our familiar indicative claims, e.g., the landlord's claim that he had given the tenant notice or the employee's claim that he was wrongfully dismissed. And the latter, which in the words of MacCormick's 'set formula' are expressed by 'claim' followed by a noun, e.g., 'claim damages, an injunction or a declaration', are, I submit, subjunctive claims that the plaintiff should be given these.

Thirdly, as I have already hinted, there is no more difference between a claim expressed in the imperative and one expressed in the infinitive or the subjunctive than between a host of other things, such as warning, advice, requests, demands, etc., expressed in each of the three. We can advise caution, advise someone to be cautious or that he be cautious, just as we can warn him against haste, not to be hasty or that he should not be hasty.

Fourthly, my original characterisation of subjunctive claims as like a 'call for, request or demand' had already anticipated MacCormick's suggestion that his 'imperative' claims are 'a species of demand'.

3. MacCormick's third objection is that I am 'unduly squeamish' in not allowing that rights to different kinds of things are different kinds of rights. The difference between us here is not substantial, yet it is more than merely terminological enough to warrant a few comments. First, it is clear it is not great since MacCormick admits that it is 'the nature of that to which things are rights which is significant in determining the appropriate mode of normative security'. Secondly, at the beginning of his paper MacCormick rightly argued that the difference between a legal penalty and a football penalty does not imply different concepts of *penalty*. Thirdly, MacCormick seems to assume (page 171) that the mere existence of rights to different kinds of things and the different consequences which follow from these differences – whose existence I do not of course deny – is sufficient to show that these are different kinds of rights. But this is akin to arguing – what would to me seem 'at best misleading, and, at worst, mistaken' – that since being immune from taxation is being immune from a different kind of thing from being immune from criticism, it is, therefore, a different kind of immunity, or that since being in charge of Scotland is being in charge of a different kind of thing from being in charge of a Scotch terrier, therefore, it is a different kind of being-in-charge. It is the fallacy of supposing that because '*ab*' implies something different from that which '*ac*' implies, therefore the difference must be due to different kinds of *a* or even different senses of '*a*'. Though I can understand a harmless sense in which being able to do or taking pleasure in doing different kinds of things could be said to be different kinds of abilities or pleasures, I think that it can also lead to conceptual confusion.

Fourthly, MacCormick is led to just such confusion in his partial defence of Hohfeld. For Hohfeld did not just insist that different implications could follow from rights to different kinds of things; he talked, as MacCormick himself says, of 'different kinds of "legal relations" which in ordinary usage can be lumped together, sometimes confusingly, under the general rubric of "rights" '. And Hohfeld went on to allege that in one sense 'right' really meant a claim, in another a privilege, in another a power, in another an immunity, and so on. But this is exactly what I want to deny. I want, first, to stress – what would need several other papers to develop – that what we ordinarily, either within or without the law, call 'a right' to be exempt from taxation does *not* just mean an immunity, that 'a right' to have the first dance is *not* the same as the privilege of having it, that 'a right' to foreclose on a mortgage is *not* simply a power to foreclose.

My reason for dwelling on what might seem at first sight to be a small disagreement between us is that I believe the consequence of supposing, as is commonly done, that the differences between a right to *V* and a right to *F* are due to differences in the right and not in that to which there is the right is that, instead of facing up to the difficulties of discovering an analysis of *right* which will account for these differences, one avoids them by pretending that some of them are not really rights at all, but, e.g., privileges, powers, claims, immunities, etc., for which, therefore, separate solutions can be given.

4. MacCormick objects to my assertion that subjunctive claims can be neither true nor false. I think, however, that his objection rests on a confusion between the view, which I did not propose, that subjunctive *statements* – or statements containing the modal 'ought' – can be neither true nor false, and the view, which I did and do hold, that subjunctive *claims* are neither true nor false. The difference between these two views and, I hope, the validity of the second can be seen by comparing them with the difference between holding, correctly in my opinion, that, e.g., warnings, advice, promises, threats, can be neither true nor false and holding, wrongly in my opinion, that any statement one makes in giving a

warning or advice or in making a promise or a threat can be neither true nor false.

II.

I turn now to three positive theses which MacCormick puts forward in his reply, all of which I shall briefly argue are mistaken. These are, first, 'that someone has a right to *X* implies that *X* ... is a good' (page 170; cp. page 162); secondly, 'That I have a right to do something implies at least that doing it is not wrong' (page 165; cp. page 164); thirdly, that the 'ascription of rights to individuals ... depends on rules or principles which are logically universal in tenor' (page 162).

1. As MacCormick admits, the first thesis is akin to Bentham's well-known 'benefit' theory of rights. Though MacCormick has hedged (page 162) his version around with several caveats, including that what one has a right to need only be something which is 'normally considered good for normal individuals' – which in fairness to MacCormick would require more space to consider – I think it is still open to the well-known objections to Bentham. Here I will only briefly comment, first, that there are many things, e.g., to enter a burning building, to eat poisoned food, to go to Hell in one's own way, to which one can have a right, though these things are not good. Secondly, one of the hoary problems of the philosophy of religion is raised by the at least apparent fact that man's possession of free will was given to him so that he could exercise a right to do things which his Maker knew to be evil. Thirdly, history shows that men have often in fact had a right to things which are not good, even if – which is often doubtful – they were thought to be good at the time, e.g., owning slaves or killing those one does own. Fourthly, sometimes (e.g., page 167) MacCormick seems to shift from the view that what someone has a right to do is necessarily good to the view that it is good to have a right to something. But this latter view would, like the former, depend entirely on what it is one has a right to. Is having the right to kill necessarily a good thing?

2. MacCormick's second thesis, namely that to have a right to

do something implies at least that doing it is not wrong, derives its plausibility, I suggest, from an assimilation of having a right to *V* to either being right to *V* or being right in *V*ing, since the last of these does imply, or is possibly equivalent to, not being wrong in *V*ing. But such an assimilation is mistaken. First, it may be right for someone to waive his right to *V*. Secondly, someone can have a right to do what is in fact wrong, whether it is a right to assume a mistaken premise or to deprive someone of his livelihood; and, conversely, it may be right to do something, such as helping the needy, which the helper has no right to do, even if others have. Indeed, the rightness of something can be the same whether done by someone who has a right to do it or by someone who has no right to do it. Thirdly, the arguments and evidence relevant to proving or disproving whether it is right to *V* and proving or disproving whether someone has a right to *V* are quite different. Fourthly, the difference between being right to *V* and having a right to *V* comes out in that between what one rightly does and what one rightfully does. One can rightly object without rightfully objecting and rightfully take a place at a table without rightly taking it. Fifthly, the false assimilation of what it is right to do and what one has a right to do is parallel to the fallacy of supposing that what one has a reason to believe is what is true and *vice versa.*

Contrary to MacCormick, a basic difference, I believe, between having a right to *V* and being right (or not wrong) to *V* or in *V*ing is that, whereas the latter depends on the nature and the consequences of *V*ing, the former depends on something prior to *V*ing, such as the position, circumstances, experience, etc. of the agent or of others.

3. MacCormick's claim that the ascription or vesting of rights depends on universal rules or principles seems to me, first, to confuse the view that *A* can only have a right to *V* *if* there is a universal rule to the effect that *A*'s as such (*A*'s in such circumstances, with such and such characteristics, etc.) have that right with the view that *right* is 'supervenient', that is, that if *A* with such and such characteristics has a right, then anything else with exactly the

same characteristics has that right. Secondly, though rights can be conferred by, and depend on the existence of, rules, they need not be. By what rule have I a right to feel hurt when a friend forgets my birthday, to smile when I like, to assume that the majority of readers of this discussion will be lawyers or philosophers, or to stick to my own opinion?

III.

I turn now to the Chairman's remarks. Though Professor Coval agrees with Professor MacCormick that my arguments against various purported logical connections between rights and claims are not supportable, he does so only because of his objections to one of these connections, namely that between having a claim and having a right. He does not disagree that the making of a claim is independent of the having of a claim and, *a fortiori*, on his view, of the having of a right. Nor does he have any more sympathy for MacCormick's 'imperative claims' than I do.

Coval's worries centre on my contention that having a (justified) claim to be the heir to an estate or the author of a book neither implies nor is implied by my having a right to be the heir or the author, even though having a (justified) claim to be the heir or the author implies, since these are both indicative claims, that I am the heir or the author and have, therefore, any rights which these positions carry. His first worry seems to be with the conclusion that someone who has a (justified) claim to be the heir and is therefore the heir, and hence has a right to the estate, nevertheless, in my view, does not have a right to be the heir and, therefore, not a right to a right to the estate. Put symbolically, he is worried by my conclusion that having a claim to be *X* does not imply having a right to be *X*, even though having a claim to be *X* implies having a right to *Y*, where being *X* implies having a right to *Y*. That his worries here, however, are self-made appears from his struggles with the phrase 'a right to a right' which he thinks must either be a pleonasm for 'a right' or be a solecism or lead to an absurdity. Clearly it is neither a pleonasm nor a solecism, since someone could have a set of rights, e.g. as President, which he had no right to have because he had no right to the position of President.

Coval's attempt to show that the distinction between having a (justified) claim to be and, therefore, being an *X* and having a right to be an *X* leads to an absurdity is, first, based on his unnoticed slip from 'having a justified claim to be an *X* (e.g. the heir)' and, therefore, being an *X* (e.g. the heir) to the curious 'justifiably being an *X* (the heir)'. Second, Coval's first absurdity – or 'embarrassment' as he calls it – that, in my view, 'the most relevant of the justified claims ... are not even a necessary condition for rights' arises from his confusing the relation between a justified claim to be the heir and a right to the estate – which I am not discussing – and that between a justified claim to be the heir and a right to be the heir (or if you like, a right to a right to the estate) – between which I am denying any implication either way. Thirdly, his second embarrassment that in my view 'we may have no right to matters to which we do have a right and a right to matters to which we do not have rights' arises from the same confusion. There is nothing embarrassing about the conclusion that one does not have a right to be something, e.g. an heir, which one undoubtedly is and, therefore, no right to have those rights, namely those of an heir, which one undoubtedly has; nor, as Coval (centre page 185) seems to admit, about the conclusion that one has a right to be something, e.g. an heir, which unfortunately one is not, and therefore lacks the right, e.g. to the estate, which one would have if one were the heir and which is a right which one has a right to have. Throughout his paper Coval moves about disconcertingly between arguments over relations between specified rights and those over relations between unspecified rights; so that his attribution to me of the view that 'a certain status such as being an heir can imply a right but that a right to this identical status cannot imply the consequent right' does not differentiate between the view which I argue for, namely that being an heir implies having a right to the estate but that having a right to be the heir does not imply having a right to the estate, and a view which I do not discuss and need not dispute, namely that having a right to be the heir implies having a right to have the right to the estate, though, because one is not the heir, one does not have a right to the estate. I do not say, *pace* Coval (page 185), that rights 'can be created only by the invocation of a certain rule of recognition or by *fiat*' and that 'rights are not inferrable from claims and *vice versa*', but only that the right to *X* and the claim to *X* are not mutually inferrable.

Coval alleges on pages 185–6, for two reasons that I don't quite accept, my own position that a right to *X* and a claim to *X* are not mutually implicative. But his first reason rests on misinterpreting me. He quotes me as saying on page 153 that 'having a right to something is usually a, though not the only kind of, reason for possession of one's claim [having a justified claim] to it [the right]'. But the words in brackets are his. I do not say in the quotation that having a right to *X* is a reason for having a claim to the right to *X*, but that having a right to *X* is a reason for having a claim to *X*, where the claim is of the 'subjunctive' kind, e.g. to protection, money, etc. I do, of course, admit that where it makes sense – as it does not always do – to have a (justified) indicative claim to *Y*, then if one has a *Y*, one has a justified claim to *Y*; and hence, if one has a *Y*, where *Y* is a right to *X*, then one has a justified claim to *Y*, that is a right to *X*. His second reason seems to be – though I am uncertain of Coval's argument here – that I must surely agree, despite my insistence that having a right to *V* does not make it right for me to *V*, that if I have a right to *V*, then it is right for me to *V* under certain conditions or *ceteris paribus*, e.g. 'when it is justified'. My answer would be that to hold this is hardly to hold a logical relation between to have a right and to be the right, let alone between to have a right and to have a claim, since surely it is right for someone to do *anything whatsoever* under certain conditions or *ceteris paribus*, or when it is justified *sans phrase*, and not merely if one has a right to do it. Indeed, Coval admits this when he says 'Whatever is do-able will be the right thing to do under certain conditions or *ceteris paribus*'. But then 'if he has a right to do it' is otiose.

I cannot, therefore, see that Coval has produced any proof that my arguments against any logical connection of the kinds I specified between rights and claims are not supportable.

University of Hull

PART IV

OBSCENITY

A. D. WOOZLEY

THE TENDENCY TO DEPRAVE AND CORRUPT

1.

It is hardly a matter for dispute that the Obscene Publications Acts 1959 and 1964[1] are unsatisfactory. (For convenience, they are hereafter jointly referred to as 'the Act'.) There has to be something wrong with an Act when the DPP's deputy concedes that it gives no help at all to a judge in deciding how to direct a jury on the question which is central to the issue in a trial under s. 2(1) for publishing obscene material.[2] It is true that the Act represented a considerable improvement over the previous position, chiefly because it gave authors and publishers a measure of protection which they had not enjoyed when publication of an obscene libel remained a common law misdemeanour. Under that, the test for obscenity had been the famous one laid down in 1868 by Cockburn, C. J. in *Hicklin*:[3]

> I think the test of obscenity is this, whether the tendency of the matter charged as obscenity is to deprave and corrupt those whose minds are open to such immoral influences, and into whose hands a publication of this sort may fall.

At least the statutory formulation in the Act prevented courts from ignoring the Cockburn test, and from instead simply presuming a tendency to deprave and corrupt if the material was obscene in some ordinary sense of being filthy or disgusting. It required the work to be judged as a whole (s. 1(1)), rather than to be found obscene if individual parts of it were found to be obscene. The reference class of persons was narrowed down from those into

---

1 8 *Halsbury's Statutes* (3rd edition) 479 and 524.

2 *R.* v. *Calder & Boyars Ltd.* [1968] 3 All E.R. 644, 646.

3 (1868) L.R. 3 QB 360, 371.

M. A. Stewart (ed.), Law, Morality and Rights, 201–222.

whose hands the publication might fall to those "who are likely, having regard to all relevant circumstances, to read see or hear the matter". And it allowed the defence that "publication of the article in question is justified as being for the public good on the ground that it is in the interests of science, literature, art or learning, or of other objects of general concern" (s.4(1)). In the first prosecution brought under the Act, *R.* v. *Penguin Books*,[4] the parade of literary and other luminaries who passed through the witness box to testify to the literary and moral virtues of D. H. Lawrence's *Lady Chatterley's Lover* was long enough to fill the pages of a subsequent Penguin Special.[5] An unfortunate consequence of the cloak of silence which enshrouds the deliberations of an English jury (so unlike their gabbling American cousins) was that the acquittal in that case left everybody in the dark whether *Lady Chatterley* had been found not to be obscene, or whether its obscenity had been purged by its literary and other contributions to the public good.

Basically what is unsatisfactory about the Act (given that the law should concern itself with obscenity at all) are (i) the unclarity of its characterisation of obscenity, and (ii) the awkwardness, even the illogicality, of its structure, which requires the question whether an article is obscene to be settled before the issue of literary, artistic, scientific, etc. merits can even be raised. Intrinsically related to those two defects is (iii) a failure to make any distinction, which is surely essential to the whole enterprise, between obscenity and pornography. (Parenthetically, the guidelines suggested in the USA by the Model Penal Code,[6] and largely followed in American practice, avoid defect (ii): testimony to a publication's literary or other merits is admissible as evidence that the work is not obscene, rather than as a counterweight to its

---

[4] *R.* v. *Penguin Books* [1961] Crim. L.R. 176.

[5] C. H. Rolph, *The Trial of Lady Chatterley* (Harmondsworth: Penguin Books, 1961).

[6] American Law Institute, *Model Penal Code, Proposed Official Draft* (1962) §251.4.

obscenity.[7] As to (i), their characterisation of obscenity is different, at least partly because of dissatisfaction with the English formulation,[8] but theirs is not obviously a great improvement. And any serious attempt (iii) to distinguish between obscenity and pornography is frustrated by the timidity of their courts, from the US Supreme Court downwards, in the face of the overblown First Amendment right of free expression.)

In its 100-year history the phrase 'tend to deprave and corrupt' has had a bewildering number and variety of meanings found for it (some of which simply cannot, except by stipulation, be accepted as meanings), and has shown a tenacity in hanging on to life which some have deplored. The Herbert Committee's private bill of February 1955 dropped it, included no definition of obscenity, and recommended instead making the state of mind of the accused person an essential element in the offence, shifting the emphasis to intention. But the government put it back in its own substitute bill of the same month, and there it still is in the Act. As an example of the intellectual slackness shown towards the phrase, one may cite the *Lady Chatterley* case. In his opening address for the prosecution, Mr Griffith Jones asserted that to say that something tends to deprave and corrupt is to say that "it may, it might deprave and corrupt".[9] Surprisingly perhaps, the judge did not intervene, and Mr Gardiner, in his closing speech for the defence, contributed his mite towards confusing the jury by referring to Mr Griffith Jones's remark and then misquoting it as having been that an obscene article is one which may tend or might tend to deprave and corrupt.[10] And of the words 'deprave and corrupt' themselves Mr Griffith Jones said that they meant (and that judges have regarded them over the years as meaning) "raising impure thoughts in the minds of those who read the book".[11] He may

---

[7] *ibid.*, § 251.4(4)(c).

[8] American Law Institute, *Model Penal Code, Tentative Draft No. 6* (1955) § 207.10(2), Comments, p. 10.

[9] n. 5 above at 12.

[10] n. 5 above at 202.

[11] n. 5 above at 210.

have been right about the practice, or rather one of the practices, of courts under the common law, but it would be astonishing if now the courts were to take him seriously. What percentage of everyday advertising, especially pictorial advertising, is aimed at attracting attention to itself by raising impure thoughts in the minds of its readers I do not know, but it is surely high; it is scattered all over the pages of supposedly respectable newspapers and magazines – young jocks coming on strong in cigarette advertisements, girls in minimal bikinis in travel advertisements, and all the rest of that whole world of what is known concisely in the trade as tit and bum. Fortunately, in a more recent case the trial judge was held to have misdirected the jury for having characterised obscenity to them in that kind of way.[12] Lord Wilberforce has properly complained that the "illogical and unscientific character of the Act has forced justices into intolerable positions",[13] because it offers no definition of 'deprave and corrupt', nor even guidelines to assist judges, with the consequence that courts have said that no definition can be provided, and that judges/juries must decide on their own the question whether the article has a tendency to deprave and corrupt as a question of fact, on which no expert advice (except in the case of children) is admissible.[14] After ploughing through the cases one must have some sympathy with the trial judge in *Calder & Boyars* who directed the jury as follows: "those vital words 'tend to deprave and corrupt' really mean just what they say. You have heard several efforts to define them. 'Tend' obviously means 'have a tendency to...'."[15] That is a robust, no-nonsense way with words – synonymy is all – but we should either do better, or find some other quite different way of characterising what we are talking about. I think we can do better with those actual words. I am going to argue that what the law should be after is not obscenity at all, but pornography, that there

---

12 *R.* v. *Anderson* [1971] 3 All E.R. 1152, 1161.
13 *D.P.P.* v. *Whyte* [1972] 3 All E.R. 12, 18–19.
14 n.13 above at 19.
15 n.2 above at 647.

is a sense in which pornography does tend to deprave and corrupt, that it tends to deprave and corrupt a much wider class than those contemplated in the present Act, and that the tendency is *neither a definition nor a test* of pornography (in the past it has been referred to indifferently as either, as though there were no difference between them), but it is a definitional property of it.

Whatever 'deprave and corrupt' is going to mean where it is alleged that an article tends to deprave and corrupt persons likely to read it (I say 'read', because I am going to use written work as my example), it has to mean that the article tends to *do* something to the persons concerned, i.e., it is a causal expression. There is therefore the question of the meaning of the causal expression, *what* effect the article allegedly has; and there is the question of empirical evidence, what evidence there is that the article does have such an effect. Even without the first question, the second question would be hard enough, because it is notorious that causal statements about the effects on people of what they are exposed to are, most of all when the effects are not physically or physiologically measurable, extremely difficult to verify. Establishing that a diet with a high cholesterol content is a major factor in causing heart disease is child's play compared with establishing what are the effects on the minds and morals of TV viewers of sex, violence or whatever in their programmes. Sociological pronouncements are therefore as cheap to make as they are expensive to confirm, and preconceptions, being without empirical confirmation, are reasonably secure from empirical refutation. Only a kangaroo court could have found no difficulty in pronouncing Socrates guilty of corrupting youth – not of tending to corrupt it, but actually corrupting it. Occasionally a defence has tried a short way with the expression by arguing that, whatever it may be to corrupt, the article in the case could not be held obscene because the persons likely to read it were incorruptible. That defence succeeded in one case, where the only persons who had seen the material (and there was no evidence of its publication, or likelihood of its publication, to others) were two police officers who gave acceptable testimony that they had long been handling such material in the course of their duties and were not susceptible to depravity and corruption.[16] Jury members, presumably, either are to be supposed to be similarly immune or must accept the risk of corruption in the performance of their duty of reading the material complained of. The defence failed in another case, where it was claimed that the likely readers of the article in question were incorruptible because they, from their earlier reading, already were in a state of depravity and corruption.[17]

Whether the depravity and corruption which the obscene material allegedly tends to produce is internal or external makes very little difference, because in either case the commonsense judgment of an intelligent and unbiased jury simply cannot have the information on which to base its causal hypothesis, affirmative or negative, and hence its verdict. The Model Penal Code's criticism of the English rule was simply that there was no evidence that the people who indulged in reading the material complained of engaged in consequence in conduct different from what they would have engaged in anyway. So, if the test were simply that of depraving and corrupting those likely to read the material (i.e., omitting for the present the notion of tending), and if the depravity and corruption were to consist in their subsequent (and consequent) conduct being different from, and worse than, it would otherwise have been, no convictions could properly be expected. At least *some* known cases of people whose conduct had been made worse by exposure to such material would need to be produced, to confer any plausibility on the charge that some likely readers of the material complained of would find their conduct changed. Alternatively, if, as courts have held,[18] it is not necessary that conduct should be different and worse, only that the person's inner life should be, a similar problem arises. If people, as a result of reading the material, are going to have lascivious thoughts or desires or sexual fantasies which otherwise they might

---

16 *R.* v. *Clayton & Halsey* [1962] 3 All E.R. 500, 502.

17 n.13 above at 19–20.

18 Norman St. John-Stevas, *Obscenity and the Law* (London: Secker & Warburg, 1956), p. 127.

not have had, then perhaps that should count as corruption and should be charged to the responsibility of the publishers of the material; but, unless those inner changes manifested themselves in external conduct, how could it be more than conjectural that the condition set out in the 'if' clause had been fulfilled? And conjecture should not be the basis for a criminal conviction.

What difference does it make when we reintroduce the notion of tending? Given that depravity and corruption is the effect which the law is concerned to prevent from being produced on the character and conduct of those (or a significant number of them) likely to read the article, and given that there is the difficulty about establishing that such an effect has been, or will be, produced, is that problem eased by characterising obscene material as what tends to deprave and corrupt likely readers? Does that somehow cautiously stop short of saying that it actually does deprave and corrupt them? Basically, no – if we are thinking still of depravity and corruption as a condition produced as an effect in people. The introduction of 'tend' does stop short of saying that the material will deprave and corrupt those likely to read it, but it does not stop short of saying that it is of a kind that does deprave and corrupt its (or some portion of its) readers. To say of something that it tends to *f* can mean that usually it *f*'s, with the implication that sometimes it does not; more often than not, it does. Americans tend to be coffee-drinkers, university students tend to wear jeans, my car tends to stall in cold weather – those are examples of statements that can be taken to be of the "most" or "usually" kind: most Americans are coffee-drinkers, most students are jeans-wearers, my car usually stalls in cold weather. 'Tend' in this use is stronger than 'is liable to', exactly as 'is inclined to' is stronger than 'has an/some inclination to'; the weaker expression indicates a risk, but possibly quite a small risk, of such-and-such happening or being the case. If my car occasionally, but not often, stalls in cold weather, it would be correct for me, in lending it to a friend unfamiliar with its ways, to tell him that by saying that it is liable to stall, whereas, if I tell them that it tends to stall, I am telling him that that often happens.

In that sense 'tend' is a frequency word, where the frequency is at least more than ½. And, if the word is being used in *that* sense in the Act's characterisation of obscenity, then none of the difficulties previously mentioned about what effect depravity and corruption is, and what the evidence is that such an effect occurs, are removed. For the obscenity claim would be that the material was of a kind which usually depraves and corrupts. All that the insertion of 'tend' into the expression does is to allow for depravity and corruption being an effect which is produced with something less than a frequency of 1.

In another, different but related, sense, the word says that the effect is likely to be produced. A likelihood statement is not a frequency statement, although it may be (but need not be) an extrapolation from it. In this sense, an event or substance might tend to produce a certain effect, even although it seldom does, even although perhaps it *never* has, because, e.g., effective counteractive measures are usually, or have always been, taken. Examples are plentiful in a pharmacopoeia: the pharmaceutical manufacturer may warn doctors of the likely side-effects which a new drug will have (*unless* it is administered in a certain way, or in combination with another drug), not because trials on human patients show that it does have such side-effects, but because of its chemical similarity to another drug which does have them.

If 'tend' in 'tend to deprave and corrupt' were being used in this second way, meaning that the material claimed to be obscene was likely to deprave and corrupt those likely to read it, then the phrase would not be directly open to the previous objection. For there is no logical incompatibility between material being of a kind that is likely to deprave and corrupt and its being of a kind that never actually has depraved and corrupted anybody. For it could be the case that in all instances hitherto of people's exposure to the material, sufficiently strong counteractive factors have been at work or measures taken – parental or other influence, cold baths at school, or whatever. Not a very plausible hypothesis perhaps, but not logically impossible. So, within the wording of the Act, material *could* tend to deprave and corrupt likely readers, even although none had ever been depraved and corrupted by such material. But difficulty could arise over evidence for the material's being obscene. There is no analogy with the drug case, where it can legitimately be claimed that the drug is likely (unless precautions are taken) to have a certain effect, even although (precautions having been taken) it never has had it, because of its close similarity to another drug which has had such an effect. It is not remotely plausible to claim that certain material which, because of counteractive factors or measures, never has had a depraving or corrupting effect, is likely to have such an effect, because of its similarity to other material which has had the depraving and corrupting effect. It is not plausible, because the only other material available for comparison, and from which inferences might be drawn, will be material which resembles the first in being supposedly obscene. It will be, say, pictorial, e.g., photographs, paintings, drawings or movies. If a movie of a certain kind were known to deprave and corrupt, it would be evidence that a novel of a closely similar kind would be likely to corrupt; but then we would be back with the original difficulty, that of knowing that such a movie had actually had its corrupting effects. If movie and novel are closely similar in both being in the same way supposedly obscene, i.e., if it is claimed that each in its different mode is likely to deprave and corrupt, then, unless material of a similar kind has been established as having the depraving and corrupting effect, no reason is being offered in support of the claim that the material, although it never has depraved and corrupted, is likely to do so. (All this apart from the question whether the counteractive factors or measures which supposedly have prevented the occurrence of the depraving and corrupting effects are likely to continue operating.) It is no easier to see in this likelihood sense of 'tend' than in the previous frequency sense that it is reasonable to ask a jury to pronounce on the question of an article's obscenity. And it is no answer to that to say that, fortunately for society, morality and justice, juries are people of common sense, not logic-chopping philosophers. Much of the trouble and inequity of obscenity adjudication in the past has been due to its being decided by unguided common sense, and frequently by that of a single magistrate rather than that of a jury; even now, if proceedings for forfeiture are taken under s. 3 of the Act, rather than on indictment under s. 2, the author or publisher of a book can be deprived of the right of a jury trial.

I conclude that if 'tend to deprave and corrupt' is taken in a causal way – and, given that the objects of the tendency are the persons who are likely to read the article, it is hard to see what other way there could be of taking it – it is a highly unsatisfactory way of characterising anything on which a jury is to be asked to pronounce. There is another way in which it can be maintained that much of the material at which the Act is aimed does tend to deprave and corrupt, but I can come to that only after dealing with the other two defects of the present state of the law.

The first lies in the unsatisfactory structure of the Act, separating in the way it does the test of obscenity from the offence of publishing (or of having for publication) an obscene article and from the permitted defences, particularly the defence of public good. Thus, s. 2 specifies the details of prosecution on indictment, and provides for a defence that the accused had no reasonable cause to believe that the article was obscene. Then later, in s. 4, there comes the defence of public good which I quoted in my first paragraph.[19] Consequently, a jury can come to the conclusion both that an article is obscene and that, even so, its publication is justified; it really would be interesting to know whether or not that was their conclusion in the case of *Lady Chatterley*. With, so far as I know, the single exception of one judge dissenting from a decision in the House of Lords,[20] the courts have consistently throughout the twenty years since the passing of the Act taken the view that a jury must first address itself to the question of obscenity, and only after it has found the article obscene go on to consider whether its publication could be justified under the terms of s. 4. I know of only one reported case in which the court suggested

---

[19] n. 1 above at 485.

[20] *D.P.P.* v. *Jordan* [1976] 3 All E.R. 775, 784.

that there might be something wrong with this particular two-step procedure;[21] and even there the court seems to have made a wrong diagnosis of what was wrong.

Byrne, J., in the *Lady Chatterley* case:

> if ... you are satisfied that the book is an obscene book, then you must go on to consider the further question ... have the defendants established the probability that the merits of the book as a novel are so high that they outbalance the obscenity, so that its publication is for the public good?[22]

Lord Widgery, C. J., in *R.* v. *Anderson*:

> what is contemplated there [the public good defence] is that, if an article is found to be obscene, ... it is then for the jury to balance the merit and demerit of the article and conclude whether they find it acceptable or not.[23]

Lord Wilberforce in *D.P.P.* v. *Jordan*:

> the section [s.4] is dealing with a different range, or dimension, of characteristics from that with which s.1 is concerned. It is not raising over again the issue of 'deprave and corrupt' .... It assumes that, apart from what s.4 itself may do, the issue would be resolved in favour of 'deprave and corrupt' and, having assumed that, it allows a contention to be made and evidence to be given that publication of the material is, on specified grounds, for the public good.[24]

Burden of proof of obscenity, a question of fact, rests on the prosecution; burden of proof that, despite its obscenity, publication of the article is justified as being for the public good on the ground of its literary or other specified qualities, a question of merit, rests on the defence. And the jury, if it finds the article obscene, must then, if the public good defence is pleaded, determine the merits of the article and weigh them against its obscenity. The one court, as mentioned above, which found a difficulty in reconciling s.4 with s.1 and s.2 of the Act declared that a jury might find it hard to "understand how it is possible that if a book

---

21 n.2 above at 649–50.
22 n.5 above at 233.
23 n.12 above at 1158–9.
24 n.20 above at 779.

has such a tendency to deprave and corrupt it can be justified on any ground as being for the public good".[25] Salmon, L. J., went on to give his view how, in the absence of any guidance from the Act, a jury should go about considering the question whether, despite a book's tendency to deprave and corrupt those likely to read it, its publication might still be justified as being in the interest of literature, etc. They

> must consider, on the one hand, the number of readers they believe would tend to be depraved and corrupted by the book, the strength of the tendency to deprave and corrupt, and the nature of the depravity or corruption; on the other hand, they should assess the strength of the literary, sociological or ethical merit which they consider the book to possess. They should then weigh up all those factors and decide whether on balance the publication is proved to be justified as being for the public good.

One may wonder how a jury so directed is better off than one not directed at all. They have to supply values for each of four different variables ((a) the number of readers whom the book will tend to deprave and corrupt, (b) the strength of that tendency, (c) the nature of the depravity and corruption, (d) the literary and other merits), where supplying them can hardly be better than guessing or postulating. And then, in order to answer the question whether, despite its obscenity, the book's publication is justified in terms of its literary or other contributions to the public good, they have to ask themselves, given the value they have ascribed to (d), how many readers, for the sake of that public good, may legitimately be exposed to the likelihood of depravity and corruption, of what degree of likelihood and of what intensity of depravity and corruption. Can one really imagine a jury deliberating whether 20 people reduced to depravity and corruption is a cheap price to pay for a book of such literary interest, whether 200 is still a fair price, and whether 2,000 is altogether too much?

What the court did not do in that case (nor in any other, so far as I know) was to point out that the real defect in the Act was, not that it gave no guidance how the publication of material that

---

[25] n. 21 above.

tended to deprave and corrupt those exposed to it could nevertheless be justified as being for the public good, nor how a jury could be expected to produce a verdict based on impossibly complicated and unrealistic calculations, but that it set the jury the wrong question. Surely, the question at issue is, *not* how can the publication of the material both tend to deprave and corrupt and be *justified* as contributing to the public good, *but* how can it both tend to deprave and corrupt and *be* for the public good? Given that a work is (as under the Act it is) to be judged as a whole, and not on the basis of particular parts or passages, how can a book (say) both be of such high literary or other quality that it is in the public interest that it be published and also be one which will tend to deprave and corrupt those (or a significant number of them) likely to read it? Whatever is being asserted in the claim that it is for the public good, "on the ground that it is in the interests of science, literature, art or learning...", that a book be published is incompatible with the assertion that it will probably deprave and corrupt those likely to read it. The only kind of case in which the two assertions could be made without hitting each other head-on would be that in which a book produced for one class of reader was distributed in such a way that it was falling into the hands of another for which it was not intended. A textbook on human anatomy for use in medical schools might contain illustrations which would make it an object of interest in "adult" bookshops; but, if that is a problem to be dealt with, it is hardly to be dealt with by going after the author and publisher of the textbook.

What is wrong with the law on obscenity (still assuming that there should be such a law at all) is to be found, not in defects of draftsmanship in the Act, but in the thinking, or lack of it, behind the Act. There is an attitude that, if, for example, a book has a lot of sex in it, if the sex passages are lengthy, detailed, explicit and so on, then it had better have plenty of merit on the *other* side, i.e., as literature, if it is to be allowed. So, a *Decameron* gets through, a *Fanny Hill* does not, or previously did not. There are perhaps good aesthetic reasons for some restraint in the description of sexual encounters, but lack of aesthetic restraint there is hardly in itself corrupting. And it is interesting how sex gets confused in the minds of the public guardians of morality with the relationship of the persons concerned. There were no sex passages at all in *The Well of Loneliness*; there were a number in *Lady Chatterley's Lover*, but it is striking how heavily the prosecution relied on the adulterous relationship of the two persons, as though it were that relationship that made the book obscene, as though that relationship had not for centuries been a major theme of European literature. It appeared that Penguin Books, having been indicted for publishing a book that was more than usually frank about the physiology of human lovemaking, then found themselves in court being accused of having committed the crime of publishing an English *Anna Karenina* or *Madame Bovary*.

2.

I now want to argue that there *is* something corrupting about much that is published, that it is caught by the phrase 'tend to deprave and corrupt', that the scale of the tendency is much wider than anything that is considered either by the present Act or by the previous common law of obscene libel, and that it is at least arguable that the law should provide for the prosecution of such publications. The argument will involve a distinction between pornography and obscenity, to which insufficient attention has hitherto been paid.

There is a different notion of tendency from either of the two which have played a part in the history of the law on obscenity, and which have been used in the first part of this paper. According to the first notion that I distinguished, a statement of a tendency was a statement of what usually happens in given circumstances, according to the other it was a statement of what is likely to happen; the first is an empirical frequency statement, the second a non-empirical statement of probability. The third and different notion is that of a causal property of a substance or an event, which it may have consistently with its seldom, if ever, producing the effect, and with its being unlikely that it will produce the effect. In this sense, the thing can be said to incline or lean in the direction of producing the effect, even although, because of other factors that are present, there may be no danger of the effect being produced. This is, in no way, a stretched or figurative sense of 'tend': the thing is being said to head in a certain direction, which is compatible with its not succeeding, because of other factors, in getting far in that direction. There is *some* analogy here with one's being inclined to think that *p*, or to want that *p*. My being inclined to think that the next President of the USA will be a Democrat, or that the possession and use of marijuana should be legally permitted, is clearly less than thinking that..., and clearly more than simply not having made up my mind whether.... It is not having made up my mind, while at the same time leaning in the direction of.... And to report that that is what I am inclined to think is to say just that, leaving it open whether that is where I shall stay, or whether I shall go all the way in that direction and end up by thinking that..., or whether I shall turn around and go some or all the way in the opposite direction. The difference between a statement about a person's inclining or tending to think that... and a statement about something inclining or tending to... is that the former is not, but the latter is, a causal statement, ascribing a causal property to the thing, much what Locke in the *Essay* called a *power.*[26] The poison which I pour into the town's water reservoir does have a tendency to make the water from the reservoir unfit or unsafe to drink, even although there is no danger that it will – because of the counteractive factors: that the volume of water is enough to dilute the poison to an ineffective level; that the poison is detected and neutralised by the water authority; or that, even if not detected, it is neutralised by the normal chemical treatment of the water at the filtration plant. I have poisoned the water supply, even if I have not made it poisonous.

Parenthetically, J. S. Mill's foundation of morals, the Greatest Happiness Principle, "that actions are right in proportion as they tend to promote happiness, wrong as they tend to produce the

---

[26] Cf. *An Essay Concerning Human Understanding*, 2.8.8, 10, 23.

reverse of happiness",[27] might have been better appreciated if he had been understood to be using 'tend' in that way. He used it that way elsewhere too, e.g., in his evidence to the Commission on the Administration, Etc., of the Contagious Diseases Acts, on 13 May 1871. Arguing against the governmental claim that passage of such Acts led to a striking reduction in the number of women and girls engaged in prostitution, he, on the one hand, offered strong reasons for having "very great distrust in statistics altogether on that subject", and, on the other hand, asserted that "the mere taking away forcibly from the competition of a certain per-centage of the prostitutes for a certain time naturally tends to have that vacancy filled up by healthy persons from other quarters".[28] His offering it as a responsible opinion that removing a certain number of prostitutes naturally tends towards a certain result, while insisting on a lack of statistical evidence in support of (or against) the proposition that it usually had, or was likely to have, such a result, and adding that "the law which produces the tendency is as strong as any law in political economy", shows how he was using 'tend'.

It seems to me that much of what gets published today does poison the water supply, i.e., does have a tendency to corrupt the atmosphere of society – not just the minds and morals of those who read the publications; and, if the law should do anything about those publications, it is because of what they tend to do to us all, not because only of what they tend to do to those who read them. When Lord Devlin came out against the recommendations of the Wolfenden Committee on private homosexual conduct between consenting adults, his fundamental objection was that, if the recommendations were passed into law, that would constitute an outrage against society's positive morality, and so be destructive of society.[29] He got short shrift from his critics, who

---

[27] *Utilitarianism*, chapter 2.

[28] *Report of the Royal Commission upon the Administration and Operation of the Contagious Diseases Acts*, Volume 2 (1871), p. 733.

[29] Patrick Devlin, *The Enforcement of Morals* (London: Oxford University Press, 1965), pp. 13–15.

responded that the claim that legalisation of such conduct would be destructive of society must be either definitional or consequentialist; if the former, it was trivial, and if the latter, it rested on a causal hypothesis requiring the backing of empirical evidence – and where was the evidence?[30] I do not know exactly what Devlin's argument was meant to be, but it could have been one that steered a course between the Scylla and the Charybdis of those two objections, that the legalisation of homosexual conduct was the sort of thing, by its affront to positive morality, to be destructive of society, which would be compatible with its having no likelihood, thanks to society's built-in powers of resistance or whatever, of having any actual destructive effects.

An obvious objection might be raised at this stage: that, even if some publications have a tendency of the kind that I have mentioned (I have done nothing yet to show that they do, and I have not space to do more than generally indicate how they do), it would not matter, unless it were true that they also had a tendency to deprave and corrupt in one or the other of the first two senses. It does not matter what gets into the water reservoir, as long as there is no danger of it still being there in the water supplied to the customers. The law is concerned only with actual or potential effects of conduct on people and institutions, and should not spend its time and resources going after published material, unless it either does have, or is in some degree likely to have, harmful effects on people or institutions. To which I reply: (1) that is not an accurate statement of the law's actual concern, e.g., the law on attempt is not concerned with actual effects, nor even, sometimes, with potential effects; (2) it is a matter for discussion whether the law should tolerate or license activities performed with harmful intent, where there is no danger of the intent succeeding. When the personified laws of Athens told Socrates that the escape from gaol which his friends were asking him to make would be destructive of law, and that he would show himself to be

[30] Cf. H. L. A. Hart, *Law, Liberty and Morality* (London: Oxford University Press, 1965), pp. 48–50.

a "destroyer of law", they were making the point, not that he would in fact destroy or imperil any laws, but that he would show the sort of man he was, who would try to destroy the law to save his own life.[31] And further (3), I reply that what those publications actually do do to society not only is the evidence that they have the tendency, but is itself enough to make them objectionable; and that the law itself should take objection can, I think, be maintained.

It might be easier to get ourselves thinking more clearly about the whole issue of obscenity if we could do what I fear is, in practical terms, impossible, and have the words 'obscene' and 'obscenity' dropped altogether. 'Pornography' is a much better word for what the law on obscenity is trying to grapple with, and pornography is much easier to recognise and characterise. If I may remain in the realm of what is written, pornography is whatever exploitation of sex is written, with no joy but with contempt, and especially contempt for one or other of the sexes, usually women – the latter, because, almost always, pornographers are men. D. H. Lawrence put it as well as can be required:

> Genuine pornography is almost always underworld, it doesn't come into the open .... You can recognize it by the insult it offers, invariably, to sex, and to the human spirit.... Pornography is the attempt to insult sex, to do dirt on it.[32]

Chaucer, Donne, Rochester wrote plenty of lusty, lustful sex, but there was no attempt in them to do dirt on it – it was something for both participants to celebrate and delight in. Chaucer, it is true, did like to make dirty knockabout jokes, seaside postcard jokes, about sex, but that was to bring out the ridiculous side of sex, not to do dirt on it. A sad feature of pornography is that it never laughs. The lustiness of the copulatings recounted in *Moll Flanders* and described in detail in *Fanny Hill* has nothing contemptuous about it; such remarkable gusto and staying power

---

[31] Plato, *Crito* 53b–c.

[32] D. H. Lawrence, *Pornography and Obscenity* (London: Faber & Faber, 1929); reprinted in *Phoenix* (London: Heinemann, 1936), p. 175.

may or may not be admirable, but they are too good-humoured to be condemned. The contrast between them and the dreary modern merchandise of porn in the girlie magazines could hardly be greater. Hard porn in the magazines is simply a coloured catalogue of a (predominantly) female meat trade, filled out with advertisements for sex gimmicks and gadgets, and with the poverty-stricken imaginings of male sex-fantasies. Attempts to argue their therapeutic value to the sexually deprived and inadequate aside (and they were very summarily brushed aside in *Jordan*),[33] it is hard to believe that they add anything to the welfare or gaiety of society. Whether they add something which we do not want added, and whether the law should provide for their removal and for the prosecution of their producers, is a further question.

I have called that material hard porn, because we have to recognise that plenty else that is published is also pornography. *Playboy* is not hard porn, but it is certainly soft porn, and with it, I think, should be classed the cookery books of gourmet sex, such as *The Joy of Sex*, and the clinical approach of authors such as Masters and Johnson who, as Lawrence said (writing then of Marie Stopes), "either kill sex altogether with too much seriousness and intellect, or else leave it a miserable disinfected secret". He made the good point too that comparative intensity of sex appeal had nothing to do with being or not being pornographic, and found "Boccaccio at his hottest... less pornographical than *Pamela* or *Clarissa Harlowe* or even *Jane Eyre*"; and for him Wagner's *Tristan und Isolde* came very close to pornography.

I confine my attention to the products of hard porn, for they raise in the sharpest form the question what the law's attitude should be to them and to their publishers. Should pornography, of such a kind, receive the same kind of protection of law as other publications enjoy, or should it be made the target of official prosecution? The argument for the first course depends on the principle of free speech, and is raised much more forcefully in the USA than in Britain, for in the USA people are all the time making

---

33 n. 20 above.

fanatical, not to say paranoid, appeal to the supposed power and scope of their First Amendment right. But, unless absolutely anything goes in the name of free speech, with no restrictions at all on the what, how, when and where of an utterance – and that there should be such absolute freedom is too silly a claim to take seriously – then, even if it is conceded that the right of free speech extends to cover what poisons the atmosphere (and I should not concede that), there are counterclaims which can weigh against, and which might conceivably outweigh, that of free speech. It is hypocrisy for a merchant of porn to present himself, as one of the chief American merchants did before he became a born-again Christian, as a champion of free speech. And it is ludicrously off-balance for a spokesman of the National Association of Broadcasters to lament as a blow against freedom a US Supreme Court ruling that the Federal Communications Commission had admonitory powers over a radio station which broadcast dirty language at a time when children might be expected to be listening. It is grotesque to claim that pornographers deserve the same protection of the law as other publishers get, and it is hardly believable that public policy makes it desirable that they should get it. One of the issues which the English law of obscenity has fought shy of is the question of intent, and in consequence under the present Act the *mens rea* required for the offence is little more than vestigial. A reason for fighting shy of intent can be the difficulty of proving it in court, especially if the definition of the offence makes it specific intent. But we can morally condemn the pornographer, not for what he is trying to do to his customers, but for what he is trying to do, and knowingly doing, to sex and to the relationship between men and women. He does, of course, meet a market demand, which it would be idle to pretend was wholly generated by supply, even if strongly stimulated by it. The freedom to have that demand met by supply is hardly a valuable one, the absence of which we would deplore if there were no suppliers; but should this freedom be suppressed by law? If pornography does tend to deprave and corrupt the atmosphere of society – and, although it is hard to prove, I would say that it does, by the way that it devalues the currency and language of sex – I can see no more reason that the customers of porn should be allowed to indulge their freedom at the expense of the rest of us than that the publishers of it should.

If the law on pornography is formulated as it is now, viz., to protect the customers of porn from what it does or tends to do to them, it seems to be trying to serve the wrong purpose; and I am less than enthusiastic about having such a law, looking, as it does, in the wrong direction. But if we can get the law changed, making publishers liable for prosecution for the publication of material which intentionally exploits sex by insulting it, and by degrading the parties to it, then I am inclined to support it. The hesitation which I express there is not hesitation about curtailing the freedom of expression. There is no more reason to think that freedom of expression, no matter what is expressed, is itself necessarily a good than there is to think that pleasure, no matter what it is pleasure in, is itself necessarily a good. It is not the hesitation about interference with the freedom of choice of readers, viewers and so on. Freedom of choice is already very properly interfered with in many ways on grounds of social, economic or aesthetic policy; there is no special reason why *that* freedom should be exempted from considerations which apply to others. And it is not the hesitation born of the certainty that such a law could be nowhere near 100% effective: below-the-counter porn would certainly flourish. But plenty of other law is good law, although its rate of effectiveness is well below 100%; and the pornography law would be in the company of that. My fear is rather of Grundyism, of the weapon which the law could be for the Mrs Grundys when they are in power, as, we have to face it, they sometimes are. If that danger could be minimised – and it could be reduced by requiring (a) that all action be by indictment, (b) that all trials be jury trials, (c) that the Act be so worded as to give a judge both clear and restricting guidelines in directing a jury – then such a law could be expected to be much of an improvement on what we have now. There is plenty of material around now, the tendency of which is no less insidious than the tendencies of toxic chemicals in agricultural sprays and herbicides, and of the sugar-coated rubbish of breakfast cereals; and its insidiousness is certainly no less for being less direct and less obvious than theirs. Memories of thalidomide are enough to embolden a government to come down on the chemicals. Whether one will have the courage to take on the cereal manufacturers and the children's lobby is much more doubtful. As to obscenity, or what, to circumscribe the issue more accurately, I have been calling pornography, the chances of a revising Act of the right kind are worse, I fear, than those of one of the wrong kind. A bill of the right kind would bring violent reaction from knee-jerk liberals; I should like to think that there would be enough more thoughtful liberals to answer them.

University of Virginia

A. W. B. SIMPSON

OBSCENITY AND THE LAW[1]

1. THE EXISTING LAW

At present the law governing 'obscene' material (one has to use some word to identify the subject matter of this paper, but I shall try to beg no questions) is covered by a disorderly and scattered body of law, ranging from the Vagrancy Act of 1824 through to the recent Protection of Children Act of 1978.[2] Everybody agrees that it needs tidying up, if nothing else. The principal working controls are however limited to three areas.

The first is customs control, based on powers originally conferred by the Customs Act of 1846, and now based on Acts of 1876 and 1952. Here what is prohibited is the import of "indecent or obscene prints, paintings, photographs, books, cards, lithographic or other engravings, or any other indecent or obscene articles." The test of indecency and of obscenity is not that of the

[1] This paper was written before the Home Office's *Report of the Committee on Obscenity and Film Censorship* under the chairmanship of Bernard Williams had been either written or published; this report has now been published by H.M. Stationery Office, London, as Cmnd. 7772, 1979. As a member of this committee I was somewhat inhibited in what I could say on the subject at the Lancaster conference, but I have not modified the pages for publication except in matters of detail or to correct errors. I have added some references to the report, hereafter cited as *C.O.F.C.*

[2] *C.O.F.C.* Appendix 1 sets out the law. Since then, the Indecent Displays (Control) Act of 1981 has introduced restrictions on the manner in which materials may be displayed in shops, at cinema entrances, etc. Further proposals which, if enacted, would impose controls on the activity of sex shops and sex cinemas are contained in the Local Government (Miscellaneous Provisions) Bill and the privately sponsored Cinematograph Bill, which have been introduced in the 1981/82 parliamentary session. A very full account of the law up to 1979 is given by Geoffrey Robertson, *Obscenity* (London: Weidenfeld & Nicolson, 1979).

M. A. Stewart (ed.), Law, Morality and Rights, 223–238.

Hicklin judgement[3] or that of the Obscene Publications Acts of 1959, 1964. The material need not have a tendency to corrupt or deprave; it can be 'shocking', 'lewd' to be judged obscene: it must offend against recognised standards of propriety. In the leading case it was said that 'indecency' is at the bottom end of a scale of impropriety, 'obscenity' at the top. There is no defence of public good.[4] The powers given by customs legislation are enforced and much material (including some commercial films)[5] is seized. Control is essentially by forfeiture, which can be challenged in court but commonly is not.

The second major area of control is based on the Obscene Publications Acts of 1959 and 1964. Here the test of obscenity is quite different. It is derived from the *Hicklin* judgement of 1868.[6] The article is deemed to be obscene

> if its effect or (where the article comprises two or more distinct items) the effect of any one of its items is, if taken as a whole, such as to tend to deprave and corrupt persons who are likely, having regard to all relevant circumstances, to read, see or hear the matter contained or embodied in it.

Notice that 'obscenity' lies not simply in the article itself, but in the context in which it is available. This test (also in a trivially modified form in the Theatres Act 1968) derives from the *Hicklin* judgement:

> The test of obscenity is this, whether the tendency of the matter charged as obscenity is to deprave and corrupt those whose minds are open to such immoral influences, and into whose hands a publication of this sort may fall.

The Acts embody a defence of public good "on the ground that it is in the interests of science, literature, art or learning *or of other*

---

[3] *R.* v. *Hicklin* (1868) L.R. 3 QB 360.
[4] *R.* v. *Anderson* [1971] 3 All E.R. 1152, *R.* v. *Stanley* [1965] 1 All E.R. 1035.
[5] E.g., recently *Empire of the Senses* (Ai No Corrida) had difficulty with the Customs and Excise.
[6] *R.* v. *Hicklin* (1868) L.R. 3 QB 360.

objects of general concern".[7] The principal object of the Act of 1959 was to protect literature and the arts: this object, after the decision in the *Lady Chatterley* case, has been achieved, so in an important sense the Act of 1959 was successful.[8] Enforcement is either by criminal procedure with jury trial, or by forfeiture proceedings which may be challenged before magistrates, but often are not. The legislation, though enforced rather sporadically, is in no sense a dead letter. Its enforcement is in part local, since different police forces place different emphasis on the subject. In part there is some national control exercised by the Director of Public Prosecutions.

The third method of control concerns films (excluding those shown in cinema clubs and certain other exempt categories),[9] and is wholly different in conception and working. Under legislation of 1909 (and now 1952) district councils can attach conditions to the grant of licences to commercial public cinemas, and must by law attach conditions prohibiting the admission of children to 'unsuitable' films. The normal practice has long been for councils to impose conditions adopting the system of grading operated by the British Board of Film Censors, which grades films as follows:

- U Suitable for general exhibition;
- A Suitable for general exhibition, but parents are advised that the film contains material they might prefer children under 14 not to see;
- AA Suitable for exhibition only to those of 14 years and over;
- X Suitable for exhibition only to those of 18 years and over.

---

[7] The form in the Theatres Act of 1968 misses the words in italics, and refers to "drama, opera, ballet, or any other art, or of literature or learning".

[8] As Professor Woozley and others have pointed out, it is not possible to say whether the publishers of *Lady Chatterley's Lover* were acquitted because the jury felt that 'obscenity' had not been proved, or because of the defence of 'public good', or because of some combination of these two possible grounds.

[9] For a detailed account see *C.O.F.C.*, Appendix 2.

There is in reality a further category or non-category – refused a certificate. Councils may, and sometimes do, reject the British Board's classifications, and the Board is a private body financed by the industry. It will be noted that the categories employed are not defined in terms that provide indications as to *why* certain films are to be graded X, AA, A or U over and above their 'suitability' for the age-group, and in the case of A the fact that parents might prefer under-14's not to see the film. The criteria actually employed are complex and rest largely on past precedents, modified by conscious new decisions taken by the censors. They include a decision as to whether the film is illegal only when the total withholding of a licence is in issue (i.e., at the X–no certificate boundary). A film may be illegal for contravention of a variety of laws (not including, e.g., customs legislation, since the *import* of the film is not at issue), the most important being now the Obscene Publications Acts of 1959 and 1964 – the 'tendency to corrupt plus public good defence' law – the Protection of Children Act (the film must include no *indecent* photography of children), and the Cinematograph Films (Animals) Act of 1937 (no cruelty to certain animals). A film may also be illegal, according to a Court of Appeal decision in 1976, if it is 'indecent',[10] but this is no longer the law since the Criminal Law Act (1977) applied the Obscene Publications Acts of 1959 and 1964 to publicly shown films.

2. THE HISTORICAL BACKGROUND

This very brief and simplified account of the existing law, or of such parts of it as are of principal practical significance, is not intended merely to show the muddled situation; more importantly this muddle proceeds from different approaches to the identification of the problem (if there is one) of indecency, pornography and obscenity, and to the mechanisms by which it can be controlled or suppressed. Now although the common law offence of

---

[10] *R.* v. *Greater London Council ex parte Blackburn* [1976] 3 All E.R. 184.

obscene libel dates back to *Curl*'s Case in 1727[11] (the work published being *Venus in the Cloister, or, The Nun in her Smock*), no sustained legal action against pornography operating through secular courts pre-dates the nineteenth century, when, from 1802 onwards, the Society for the Suppression of Vice instigated prosecutions for, amongst other things, pornographic books, prints and objects, which commonly included snuffboxes. In terms of legislation the Society was influential in procuring the ban on indecent exhibitions in the Vagrancy Act of 1824, and it may have been remotely responsible for the ban on the import of 'indecent or obscene' articles in the Customs Act of 1846. The idea that pornography emanates from abroad is a persistent theme; in 1817 Italians were thought to be principally to blame. This early incursion into the field produced no sophisticated definitions of 'indecency and obscenity', largely undefined concepts[12] which, having got into the legislation early, stuck there, being reproduced in later legislation; eventually they passed into postal legislation, remaining with us to this day. For sophisticated analysis of the nature of the evil we have to thank, I fear, the philosophers.

This charge needs some explanation.[13] The definition in terms of a tendency to corrupt and deprave is first found in the case law in Chief Justice Cockburn's judgement in the *Hicklin* Case in 1868. The idea came from the utilitarians, who argued that the propriety of particular actions should be determined by a consideration of the probable *tendency* of the general class of acts to which the specific act belonged. Probably through the influence of John Austin, who became in 1833 a member of the Criminal Law Commission, this notion was adopted in the sixth report of the Criminal Law Commission in 1841, which, in relation to publi-

---

[11] *R.* v. *Curl* (1727) 2 Stra. 788.

[12] The elaboration of the concepts of the criminal law is largely a modern phenomenon, being related to the development of institutions and procedures which generated more 'law'.

[13] I am indebted to my colleague, Mr R. J. Spjut, for drawing my attention to the historical origin of the *Hicklin* formula.

cations, argued that the law ought not only to restrain publications tending to a breach of the law by incitement to commit crimes, but also those "which tend to the subversion of religion, or, in general, to the destruction of the principles of virtue and morality, which are essential to good conduct, order and decency" and concluded that since it was not possible to *enumerate* such publications, the offence should be described *generally* by prohibiting the publication of "that which, being immodest and indecent, directly tends to corrupt and vitiate the morals of the public".[14] Their seventh report offered a draft

> Whosoever shall maliciously publish any libel expressing or signifying any obscene, lewd or immoral matter or meaning, tending to deprave and corrupt the morals of Her Majesty's subjects, shall incur the penalties of the 21st class.[15]

This all lies behind the *Hicklin* judgement, where there is a twist: the 'tendency' is no longer an additional characteristic which obscene, lewd or immoral matter must possess in order to be criminal. It becomes a definition of what counts as obscene (and therefore criminal).

There are two principal peculiarities in all this. The first is that the utilitarian theory – judge the acts as a class by their general tendency – is an appropriate theory of legislation, not of court decision; and because what is criminal is defined in terms of the general tendency of actions of the same class, the court is plainly being used as a legislator, and furthermore the jury is not being asked to judge the accused person's acts at all. The second principal peculiarity is the enormous extension involved in the notion of criminal responsibility. For the accused is to be convicted not because he has aided the commission of crimes, or incited them, or facilitated them, let alone caused them; he has merely done something which belongs to a class of actions which in general

---

[14] The Sixth Report of H.M. Commissioners on Criminal Law is reprinted in Volume 3 of *British Parliamentary Papers: Legal Administration and Criminal Law* (Dublin: Irish Academic Press).

[15] Also in the reprint, Volume 4.

tend to corrupt and therefore to make criminal or other anti-social conduct in some remote sense more probable to occur. Looked at in this way the *Hicklin* definition involves an anomalous and remarkable extension of criminal responsibility.

3. CRITICISMS OF THE SCHEME OF THE OBSCENE PUBLICATIONS ACTS

The original sense of the *Hicklin* definition – now embodied in a modified form in legislation – has been much overlain by modern case law, and it is now clear (I am sorry if this is 'astonishing') that a tendency to provoke sexual fantasies will suffice.[16] Lawyers call these 'libidinous and impure' thoughts. *En passant* there is a curious failure in the case law and many discussions of the subject to mention the fact that the one activity with which pornography is undeniably associated is masturbation; whether the taboo against this activity lurks behind the law I leave to speculation. Professor Woozley's criticisms of the 'deprave and corrupt' test centre on the contention that it is wrong to ask a jury to decide a question (does this material tend to produce this effect?) which, however formulated, will only be answered with any confidence if the jury has access to satisfactory evidence on the matter. Put simply, his point is that the jury can only speculate on the effects of dirty books. This type of objection to the formula is of course not one which would have worried the utilitarians; it is a by-product of the rise in the notion of social sciences, which held out the notion that causal explanations of social phenomena are in principle possible, and thus makes plausible the objection – where is your proof that dirty books cause crime (or whatever it is)? Here I merely wish to draw attention to

---

[16] *D.P.P.* v. *Whyte* [1973] AC 849. The working of the test is discussed in *C.O.F.C.*, Ch. 2; as in most areas of English criminal law the courts in fact do not apply a single test or concept, but a loose range of concepts. This phenomenon of muzziness has not, so far as I know, been explicitly recognised as a leading feature of the system.

three possible replies. The first is that, if dirty thoughts are the effect in question, the jury might know from experience of this; the second is that it is by no means clear that causal explanations of social phenomena are in principle possible, and more particularly where the effect in question involves voluntary human conduct; the third is that if we were to wait on scientific proof of social effects before legislating we might wait for ever, and the jury is only being asked to do what the legislature normally does – act in advance of proof.

Professor Woozley also criticises the idea, embodied in the Obscene Publications Acts and the Theatres Act, that literary merit, etc., can as it were outweigh the obscenity as tested by the tendency to corrupt test, so as to justify the publication in the public good. At present the correct practice is for the judge to ask the jury to consider first whether the material is obscene, and then to consider whether the merits of the material (which must fall under the categories enumerated in the legislation), as it were, outweigh the tendency to deprave and corrupt so as to make the publication justifiable in the public interest. Expert evidence is admissible as to the merits, but normally is not admissible as to the obscenity, and it is this rule which lies behind the two-stage direction. The artificiality involved is criticised by Professor Woozley, and as he says stems from the scheme of the Act itself – not the draftsmanship, but the thinking behind it. He argues that it is absurd to invite a jury to decide that a particular book, for example, is likely to corrupt and deprave a significant number of its potential readers, and yet that its publication is in the public interest. I am not here concerned to defend the legislation in question, but I am not convinced that there is anything objectionable *in principle* to the taking of a decision that something has both merits and demerits, and that the merits outweigh (without negating) the demerits. Where the demerits with which the law is concerned may include erotic fantasies alone, the point is more obvious still. Most practical legislative decisions (and, as I have said, the jury or court here acts as a legislator) involve some form of weighing of advantages and disadvantages. To sustain Professor Woozley's *theoretical* point it would be necessary to show that there was some sort of logical incompatibility between saying that, e.g., a book was both likely to corrupt some of its readers (in the peculiar sense explained) and likely, e.g., to reveal the horrors of war, in an artistically successful way. I can see no such necessary incompatibility. However, I agree that the Act expresses a misconceived view of the ideal relationship between eroticism and artistic expression.[17]

4. POSSIBLE THEORIES OF CONTROL

There are a number of different grounds upon which the law might be used to control or suppress pornographic or obscene material, and they are not always clearly distinguished. At the risk of some oversimplification they may be enumerated as follows:

I. *The protection of participants in the production of pornography*
Where children are used as models most people would surely agree that the law should intervene. In addition we do at present have laws governing the cruel use of animals, and the protective approach included in such legislation could of course be extended to include even the protection of adults who participate in making pornographic films, etc., even though they consent. The intervention of the law in this way will be related to beliefs about the harm caused, or likely to be caused, to the participants.

II. *The protection of the public generally from nuisance*
This approach hardly needs explanation, and its adoption does not require anything more than an acceptance of the fact that many people are shocked or disgusted by pornography, and they should be allowed to live their lives without having it obtruded upon them. Difficulties do arise, however, as to how thick or thin skinned the citizen ought to be, for nobody would wish to treat

---

[17] The reasons why I do not favour the existing 'test', or the 'public good' defence, are set out in the report of the Williams Committee.

everything that upsets or shocks individuals as a public nuisance. Some notion of legitimate offence is required here.

III. *The protection of the public generally from criminal conduct, or perhaps lesser forms of anti-social conduct*
Here the assumption is that pornography encourages rape, violence, etc., and the law intervenes on the same sort of basis as is involved in the crime of incitement. Here the problem is to show the supposed 'causal' effects of pornography.

IV. *The protection of the general quality of life, vigour of the civilisation or culture, etc.*
This type of approach, which is in one form advocated in Professor Woozley's paper, has the attraction of apparently bypassing the difficulties which have confronted approach number III, in that the proposition that the mere existence of pornography reduces the quality of life is presented by some as self-evident, the material objected to being defined in terms which appear to sustain this claim. It is often presented in metaphorical language, e.g., 'corrupt the atmosphere of society'. An example of the form of presentation involved is the contention that 'pornography' or 'obscenity' just is by definition material which degrades women. So defined it is plainly to be deplored and, the argument goes, ought therefore to be extirpated.

In presenting these four basic approaches to the question of control or suppression I do not mean to suggest that they are necessarily mutually exclusive. One could perfectly well, for example, adopt in part the policies set out in I, II and III. Furthermore there are certain countervailing considerations which might be thought important in considering legislation on the matter. In particular, firstly there may be *values* (such as free speech, or sympathy for those who appear to need pornography, or a respect for privacy) which limit the proper scope of the criminal law. Secondly, there may be *practical* limitations on what the law can achieve in this area. Thirdly, there may be secondary *consequences* arising from prohibition which are not desirable, even if prohibition is fairly effective. It would be possible to produce a more elaborate taxonomy of countervailing considerations than this, but my main point is that there usually are such considerations.

5. PROBLEMS OF SPECIFICATION

Before turning to Professor Woozley's argument, which is about 'hard porn', I must express briefly some doubt as to whether he has really addressed himself to the difficulties involved in specifying what this is. The use of expressions of this kind ('hard porn', 'soft porn') suggests that there exists a set of received distinctions within a general concept of 'porn', and further that 'porn' itself is a reasonably clear concept. Such a view is perhaps most plausible when applied to still photographs, in relation to which attempts of a not wholly unsuccessful type[18] have been made to produce anatomical criteria of 'sexually explicit material', though such tests have to have built-in exception clauses – e.g., for forensic or medical or educational purposes. Attempts to specify clearly and without reference to extrinsic factors such as context and intention a concept of 'porn' applicable to films and books have not been very satisfactory. Nor is it at all clear that there is even a majority agreement on the categories as applicable in real life; this is partially so because many people have never seen the more bizarre material which is obtainable and which caters for minority interests. It is perhaps worth mentioning briefly some of the factors which make it difficult to produce agreement as to what the definition should seek to include. Firstly, human beings differ both in their sexual proclivities and in their self-awareness. Hence, even material deliberately produced for erotic purposes is very varied, and the material which individuals find erotic is individually determined. Secondly, individual reaction to the contents of sex

---

[18] I emphasise 'not wholly' – the 'list' technique runs into difficulties discussed in a slightly different context in *C.O.F.C.* 9.23–28, and these render it ultimately unworkable.

shops (a loose definition indeed) can be very varied. Some material is disturbing, some physically repulsive, some ludicrous and comic, some merely in poor taste, and in relation to some it may be a puzzle to determine why it is there at all. Thirdly, in relation to all of these reactions matters of degree are involved; concepts of good taste and proper modesty, for example, differ. Fourthly, the individuals' views as to countervailing merits and values may differ. It would make life easier if there was an area as to which there was general agreement that questions of countervailing merit did not arise, but I am very doubtful as to its existence, or at least as to its extent.

It is perhaps not entirely surprising that the law, confronted with these difficulties, has not hitherto been very successful in the task of specification. Many critics of the existing law point this out, vaguely implying that 'the law' or 'the lawyers' are to blame. I find this unconvincing in the absence of specific suggestions for new definitions.

6. CORRUPTING SOCIETY

Professor Woozley's own approach is to suppose that there is a category of 'hard porn' which is objectionable because it 'corrupts the atmosphere of society', the point of this way of putting the matter being to contrast a diffuse general phenomenon with the corruption of individuals who use pornography. Insofar as he attempts to indicate what constitutes 'hard porn' he appears to have in mind some (not all) kinds of girlie magazines and their advertisements for gimmicks and gadgets. Leaving on one side the fact that the character of magazines such as *Whitehouse, Playbirds, Hustler*, etc., does not remain constant, his categorisation of such magazines as 'hard core' illustrates the variability of standards in these areas. Speaking personally, nothing in such magazines appears to me to fall into my category of 'hard porn', which I should reserve for such material as the more extreme sado-masochistic films (which include, for example, realistic and even allegedly genuine depictions in close-up of scalpings, castration, etc.) and the more gross depictions of child abuse and bizarre sexual perversions. Of course, it is perhaps not surprising that the more extreme material caters for minority tastes; only a limited portion of the population is interested in pictures of what are alleged to be girls (or boys) totally encased in rubber garments, though it is apparently the case that some sado-masochistic films can attract large audiences. This perhaps produces a paradox: if pornography does have the propensity to damage society, perhaps it is the softer material – that which is most widely desired and available – which ought to concern us most. But it is of course just at this end of the spectrum that the problems of definition are so acute.

Professor Woozley's ground for intervention falls into my fourth category, but he does not, I think, intend to bypass questions of evidence completely, as some who use this approach do. I have two basic difficulties with this. The first is that it is all so vague and imprecise, and with this goes a certain implausibility. Am I personally in any way the less happy because there are some dirty books for sale in Soho? I can see that people in Soho may be, but that is another point. The second is that if what is meant is that the society in which we live would in some general sense be none the poorer for the disappearance of *Whitehouse* (a view with which I shall not disagree), the same may be said for many other dreary and squalid features of our society, and I should be inclined to say that pornography is not obviously where one would begin in a cleaning-up programme. Once such a programme was instituted, it becomes difficult to see where the use of the criminal law would stop. If the criminal law is to be used to further general programmes of social hygiene, I begin to worry about the lengths to which sanitary zeal might go.

Professor Woozley envisages that the choice lies between suppression and licence. I am not convinced that these are the alternatives. His approach, as he says, inevitably raises the question of free speech, and the lengths to which one ought to go in protecting this value in society. If the law were to treat pornography primarily as a public nuisance issue and attempt to regulate the business so as to keep it away from those whom it offends, this collision between competing values is avoided. This line also has the attraction of practicability, and in the criminal law this is surely a virtue. This does not, of course, bypass the problem of specifying what needs regulation, but the significance of the test employed is greatly reduced, since it is not a vehicle for total suppression. There are of course other grounds upon which certain types of pornography might be entirely suppressed – for example, material which can only be produced by cruelty or human oppression and exploitation. The merit of analysing the variety of possible bases for intervention is that some may be found more generally acceptable than others, and to point to more workable laws. In a democracy, those are merits.[19]

7. THE SPECIAL PROBLEMS OF FILM CENSORSHIP

Professor Woozley's paper does not discuss the existing controls over the cinema, which, in the case of the commercial cinema, include a system of censorship (what American lawyers call 'prior restraint') as well as the *ex post facto* criminal liability under the Obscene Publications Acts. Films may be, and in fact are, refused certificates of any kind on grounds which are not directly specified by law. The British Board of Film Censors proceeds on the assumption firstly that it must not certificate a film which would, if shown, be illegal by infringing the Obscene Publications Acts (or other legislation); and secondly that it must not certificate films which would not be acceptable to public opinion, expressed through the District Councils, who may, of course, refuse to accept its certificates. Under this system in recent times films which are in no conceivable sense pornographic or obscene have been refused certificates (an example is the film of the Manson family), and films which were admittedly seriously conceived works of art (such as *The Empire of the Senses* or Pasolini's *Salo*)

---

[19] The recommendations of the Williams Committee follow this general approach; though this seemed likely when this paper was written, the matter was far from decided.

have also been refused certificates. Additionally, extremely violent films (not, at least overtly, sado-masochistic in character) have been uncertificated, typically Kung-Fu films. Indeed, the problem of violent material, which causes considerable concern, is largely a problem simply of cinema and television. Certain films are simply never submitted since the refusal of a certificate is known to be certain.

Plainly there is here an established system of administrative control of a highly effective character, whose existence raises acute problems over the legitimacy of the state censorship, exercised at the moment indirectly through District Councils and immediately by an entirely unofficial body established by the film industry. In order to obviate this system of control there have grown up numerous clubs, some entirely respectable in character, others purely concerned to enable those who wish to do so to see pornographic films, most of which are of almost incredibly low technical standards; such films are consequently unaesthetic. The existing system does exclude the public showing in Britain of commercially produced full-length films of higher technical achievement, and quite extraordinary nastiness, and I have no doubt that far worse films could be produced than any I have seen, given even better technical skill, though the clubs have reduced the effectiveness of the system to some significant degree. Control over short films (usually on 8 millimetre film) is of course very difficult to achieve, and the efforts currently used to exclude such films from the country probably achieve little more than an enhancement of the profits of the importers. The video-tape recorder will also increase the difficulties of effective control.

The existing controls over the cinema raise two special theoretical issues. The first is the problem of justifying prior censorship, which does not exist (though it might) in the case of literature and the theatre. The second (obviously connected) is the justification, if any, for the view that the cinema is *different*, and requires a more elaborate and more rigorous system of control. The theatre was, of course, subject to prior censorship until 1968, but this is no longer the case, and television has no external system of censorship, though there is of course a powerful internal mechanism in both the BBC and in Independent Television.

8. CAN PHILOSOPHY HELP?

Obviously, philosophers, insofar as they are intelligent people, can and do contribute to discussion of what ought to be done in this area by legal or other mechanisms. So many of the competing positions have now been stated and restated *ad nauseam* that I am not myself entirely clear however that they are capable of much more illumination; philosophers may find that they, like the rest of us, have little new to say. There are, however, as it seems to me certain questions to which philosophy may have something special and valuable to contribute in this overworked area; may I suggest two possible subjects? The first is the analysis of the application of the concept of causation to diffuse social phenomena, which is relevant for example to the discussion of such crudely phrased questions as "Does pornography cause crime?". The second is the analysis of the relationship between artistic expression and the pornographic, the erotic, the obscene, the disgusting (I have to add, *et cetera*); the investigation here belongs presumably to the philosophy of aesthetics.

Finally, a word about practicality and priorities. In general, I feel that laws which cannot be effective are to be avoided; it is of course a matter of degree how ineffective a law is before its existence is futile or positively harmful. I also believe that the criminal law, and the mechanisms for enforcement, should be used with a reasonable sense of priority. I have no doubt that there exist victims of pornography, whose lives have been rendered acutely miserable by it (I am not here concerned with subtle analysis of causation). But there are far more victims of other crimes of a more readily identifiable nature, and it does seem to me that we ought to be careful to place the problem of pornography in a scale of practical priority in settling on legislation about its control or suppression.

University of Kent at Canterbury

GEOFFREY ROBERTSON

OBSCENITY AND THE LAW IN PRACTICE

"Obscenity, Ladies and Gentlemen, is like an elephant. Difficult to define exactly, but you know it when you see it." With that despairing aphorism, juries are sent away to consider their verdicts at Old Bailey obscenity trials. In an age when one person's obscenity is another's bedtime reading, one must be thankful that our symposiasts are a little more discerning. Professor Woozley can, I am sure, recognize an elephant at 40 paces, but he very convincingly demonstrates how defective are the sights on the legislative weapons that we train on obscene publications. He urges us to hunt for different game – pornography – more easily recognisable by the insult it offers to womankind and its tendency to poison the water supply should it happen to fall in the reservoir. Professor Simpson, however, has some reservations about the nature of the beast, and he of all people should be able to know it when he sees it. As a member of the Williams Committee, he has been studying its habits for two years. He reports that different strains of pornography tend to do different things to different people, and suggests that we should make legal distinctions on the relative strength of its core – hard core, soft core – of course, for Professor Woozley it is all rotten to the core. After reading both papers, one yearns for the simplicity of the test propounded by Kurt Vonnegut's Senator Rosewater, who introduced his obscenity bill with the magisterial pronouncement, "The difference between pornography and art, gentlemen, is bodily hair."

Pornography offers many positions, some of them philosophic, and I salute the ingenuity of both our symposiasts. Although I recently wrote a book on the subject, both papers taught me things I did not know, and put ideas into my head that I would otherwise never have contemplated. (That process, by the way, is a prosecutor's definition of the tendency to deprave and corrupt.)

M. A. Stewart (ed.), Law, Morality and Rights, 239–248.

Professor Woozley's ideas, or his metaphors at least, have a respectable history. Our first Obscene Publications Act in 1857 was sponsored by a Lord Chancellor who equated pornography with poison, and in 1928 *The Well of Loneliness* was destroyed on the theory that it would prove more dangerous than a phial of prussic acid. In 1974 it was read over the airwaves as the BBC's 'Book at Bedtime' – the equivalent, I suppose, of poisoning the water supply in a hot and thirsty summer. Professor Simpson's approach may equally claim a distinguished pedigree. One might almost term his the Missionary position, in that it reflects St Augustine's warning that some evils must be endured, lest worse ills result from attempts at their suppression. What we lack is a full-blooded defence of the right to read anything under the sun, but I suspect Voltairians are in short supply in these days, when the traditional proponents of civil liberties are so eager to ban writing which stirs hatred against blacks and Jews, offends Christians, or promotes discrimination against women. Laws against moral corruption may be incompatible with free speech, but without them a society which wishes to tolerate minorities would be powerless to protect them against verbal or written assault by degradation, humiliation and defamation. It is these "new obscenities" which may raise more problems about free speech than the ideologically vapid fantasies which change hands in the pornographic marketplace.

But that, I am afraid, is another seminar – we have our hands full with pornography. Is it as easy to recognise as Professor Woozley makes out? The framers of the Obscene Publications Act certainly thought so. They described it in the Preamble as "An Act ... to provide for the protection of literature; and to strengthen the law against pornography". They thought they had obeyed the injunction of Sir Alan Herbert, President of the Society of Authors, when he told them:

> It is the other man you want to get after, the man who sits down and thinks "I want to make my readers as randy as I can, as often as I can...". The problem you have to face is to distinguish, shall we say, between myself and the other fellow.

That the Society succeeded in roasting the pig without burning its own house was due less to the wording of the "public good" defence – and I agree with all of Professor Woozley's criticisms of the drafting of Section 4 – than to the forensic ability of Mr Gerald Gardiner in the watershed case of *Lady Chatterley's Lover*. It is a matter of record that had *Lady Chatterley* gone down, Scotland Yard were ready to move against two other pieces of what they described as pornography: *The Ginger Man* and *Lolita*.

In so far as the 1959 legislation was an endeavour to isolate "pornography" as the class of writing which should be proscribed, it paralleled the objective of the US Supreme Court two years before in *Roth*'s case. There the court decided that material which appealed predominantly to prurient interests, and which was devoid of intellectual content, did not qualify as "speech" to which constitutional protection could be afforded. But on both sides of the Atlantic the distinction between "pornography" and "literature" was found to be much more elusive than had been imagined. The old formulae broke down entirely in the following decade when confronted by *Playboy* magazine's modish appeal to both intellect and instinct, by "soft-core" journals offering medical and psychiatric advice on sexual problems in a deliberately titillating but arguably therapeutic style, and by the underground press with its flamboyant revolutionary celebration of sex as a means of baiting a prudish political establishment. These publications were neither "pornography" nor "literature", and whilst they did not particularly edify the public, there was not much evidence that they were prone to deprave or corrupt either. In consequence they flourished in this grey area between pornography and literature, between public good and public corruption, and when lawyers sought to intervene they often made an ass of the law.

Professor Simpson raises a more fundamental definitional problem in relation to trashy titillators like *Whitehouse* and its ilk, which we would all recognise as having a "pornographic tendency". In 1977 one marketing survey estimated that this "soft porn", dispensed by four hundred wholesalers through a national network of over 20,000 newsagents and bookshops, is consumed by 27 million men and women throughout the country. For those involved in operating *any* obscenity legislation couched in generalisations, the question must be, not so much "where do you draw the line?" as "where do you *begin* to draw the line?". What has happened in practice is that local police forces, acting as though they've been inspired by Professor Woozley's paper, raid arbitrarily selected newsagents, seize all publications pertaining to sex on the shelves, and despatch them to the DPP's office at Queen Anne's Gate for advice on how to proceed. In the DPP's office the spirit of Professor Simpson takes over, and the material is solemnly sorted into what the DPP sees as good clean pornography on the one hand, which is sent back to the police, and the more bizarre strains of pornography which are ripe for prosecution.

But what test is applied by the Director? In practice, prosecuting authorities ignore philosophical distinctions and concern themselves instead with the physical incidents photographed or described. A book describing deviant behaviour, even if written with compassion and understanding for the participants, will be charged with obscenity long before a book whose heterosexual heroes display the most callous disregard for women. Stories may degrade women, or do dirt on sex, by depicting them as objects to be manipulated for fun and profit. But obscenity for most prosecutors hangs on simpler things, such as whether the penis is erect; whether a whip is in evidence; whether a lady in the picture is wearing a wedding ring or a dildo. Officials have their lines to draw and they draw them fairly consistently at the male groin. Nudity is acceptable and even artistic, but to erect a penis is to provoke a prosecution. Some ingenious publishers spend thousands of pounds to circumvent the DPP's rule of thumb in respect of male organs. They float them on water, tilt them over thighs, and in one case sent a naked skier over a ski jump so that his penis would flutter suggestively in the up-draught.

This pubic hair-splitting represents some sort of law which is workable in practice by government lawyers with heavy case loads as they flip through masses of erotica, but I am sure Professor Woozley would prefer rules of law to rules of thumb, and in the second part of his paper he offers a working definition. Pornography, at least I assume that strain of pornography which we should worry about sufficiently to prosecute, is described or defined thus: "whatever exploitation of sex" (and stopping there, I suppose everything published about sex is a commercial venture and in that sense an exploitation of the subject) "is written, with no joy but with contempt" (whether it is joyful or not may depend upon your sense of humour, and most participants in hard core pornography seem to be enjoying themselves); and he goes on "especially contempt for ... women, because almost always pornographers are men". But what about Linda Lovelace and Fiona Richmond? I'm sorry, but this time I don't think D. H. Lawrence will stand up in court. These words 'contempt', 'insult', 'do dirt on sex', just seem to me too strong to catch the execrable prose and the clinical nature of the photographs of anonymous couples engaged in predictable rituals which form the real core of pornography.

But Professor Woozley argues that pornography does tend to pollute the English clime, when it is imported from Scandinavia under casks of Danish bacon, and I see some force in his argument that we should shift the emphasis in the law from the effect on likely readers to the effect on society as a whole, on social standards and proclaimed ethical values. He is quite right to criticise the present test of obscenity for forcing juries to speculate about unverifiable causal effects. If pornography tends to lower the tone of society, are we not justified in doing something about it? Well, yes; but that something need not take the form of imprisoning its purveyors. We could express societal disapproval by restricting its availability to licensed shops with discreet fronts, using gaming legislation as our model. I suspect this sort of solution might be congenial to Professor Simpson, but Professor Woozley wants us to get after the pornographers with criminal sanctions, to imprison those who "corrupt the atmosphere of society".

Are we entitled to imprison those who corrupt the atmosphere of society? The most familiar justification for the intervention of the State in matters of personal morality has been provided by Lord Devlin, who refers to the existence of a "public morality" which should be enforced by legislation, even if no harm is done by individuals who deviate from it. To adapt this argument, pornography should be proscribed because it undermines marriage as an institution of "the good way of life", or because salacious elements of any sort are excluded from *the* good way of life chosen by this particular society. This argument unjustifiably assumes that society's present laws protect the *best* and the *only* "good way of life". In a morally pluralistic society there may be a number of good *ways* of life which do not threaten one another's existence. And it may well be that *the* "good way of life" for society as a whole involves *toleration* of different kinds of sexual morality, including that of the gay bachelor and the pornography fancier, which do not harm other members of the same society.

Besides, I do not see how Professor Woozley's reformulation can avoid the realities of popular permissiveness which are already reflected in jury acquittals of pornographic material. At present, material charged as obscene must be tested by "the current standards of ordinary decent people". The jury, as a "microcosm of democratic society", must first identify the contemporary standards of its society, and then apply them to the publications at issue. The problem with this approach is that the notion of "community standards" is ambiguous. There are "standards" in the sense of precepts, laid down by the good and the wise, which most people respect but less manage to follow. Precepts such as premarital chastity and religious observance remain social standards, although they may be more honoured in the breach than the observance. Articles in many books and magazines attack moral precepts, but are nevertheless acceptable to a large segment of the population. This material falls within the tolerance of "popular standards": what the ordinary person is prepared to accept, and what a significant portion of the population wishes to consume. Under any test, whether it is "a tendency to deprave or corrupt" or "a tendency to further the exploitation of women", jurors will inevitably be aware of popular standards, and of the climate prevailing in publicly available entertainment, and this awareness will influence their response when they are invited, by any form of words, to set the lowest standard of all: the standard above which a person is entitled to publish without going to prison.

I suspect that Professor Woozley's approach would prove even kinder to pornographers than the present law. He seeks to locate criminality in an *intention* to pollute the atmosphere of society. Now this is not a very popular argument these days: see the House of Lords judgement in *Whitehouse* (the other one) v. *Gay News*. There is, as Lord Diplock points out in a rather stinging dissent, a fear that evil scribblers will hoodwink juries by pretending to have pure motives. The answer, of course, is that cross-examination should help juries to see through such pretences. The real problem is that most incorrigible pornographers sincerely believe in the value of their work, and some are able to wax quite eloquent about it. They are well up on the latest Danish statistics and the findings of the United States Presidential Commission, and they are waiting to scour the Williams Report for every crumb of scientific comfort. They will have an answer to every difficult question, because plausible answers do exist in the research, and they will proclaim their genuine intentions to elevate and enlighten a public whose minds have been polluted by ignorance.

If Professor Woozley's specific reforms pose too many problems, it does not follow that the thrust of his paper should be rejected on the grounds of expediency so coolly argued by Professor Simpson. Historically, it is obviously true that we can never eradicate pornography of any hue or core, but that does not solve the question of whether or not we ought to try. The problem with the present law, and perhaps with any solution which pivots upon a criminal trial, is that these deeply emotional, often intuitive, issues of sexual morality cannot be handled by language, nor by lawyer's verbal and analytical skills. "Moral corruption" cannot be described, in the sense that murder or theft can be described, in a general definition which will give a litmus result – positive or negative – when applied to any factual situation. The law against theft, expressed in the words "It is an offence to take property belonging to others", has an indisputable central meaning: it can be matched with the statement (a verbal projection of facts evidenced by witnesses or uncovered by cross-examination) that "John Smith took the television set belonging to Peter Jones", to form the syllogistic conclusion "John Smith has committed an offence". But when the major premise is "It is an offence to deprave and corrupt", the verbal projection "John Smith has published homosexual contact advertisements" requires the jury to supply a further value-loaded premise of its own making before John Smith can be convicted of obscenity. Obscenity laws, as Professor Simpson points out, are really directives to judges and juries to make their own law, to supply some verbal denotation of the phrase 'a tendency to deprave and corrupt', before matching that unwritten law – the law of their own particular sexual morality – with the defendant's conduct.

Obscenity trials reflect the inability of traditional modes of criminal adjudication to comprehend the issues which can arise in the decision to censor. Criminal law has developed as a method for obtaining the truth in a world of fingerprints, alibis, police informers, blood stains, and the dog that doesn't bark in the night. These are facts able to be tested: the evidence can be weighed; the credibility of witnesses can be shaken by confrontation. The machinery of the criminal law is geared to adjudicate disputes about *facts*. Obscenity cases call for decision, not about truth or falsity, but about which of two plausible opinions is to be preferred.

I believe that the only realistic and workable solution must be to move towards an administrative system rather than a form of control which relies upon criminal law. It is time that the written word was freed of all constraints other than those imposed by existing laws of incitement to crime, disorder and racial hatred. Pictorial pornography should not be prohibited, but restricted to discreet outlets where it would be available only to adults who sought it out. The decision to restrict would be made on clearly defined criteria by a Classification Board. Such a system would reduce the role of the criminal law from the only form of control to a subsidiary adjunct of a fair and open administrative control, modelled perhaps on existing gaming controls. Distributors would face prison only if they knowingly disobeyed a classification or deliberately sought to evade the system, and trials would in consequence be confined to issues of fact rather than matters of opinion.

For those who see censorship in absolute terms, as a reflection of society's lack of confidence in itself, these reforms will have scant appeal. Conversely, those who fear that tolerance of pornography will demean and diminish the quality of life in society may not be much impressed by a proposal to legalize the availability of sexually explicit materials for consenting adults. At least there can be no objection to licensing laws which prohibit profit-making enterprises from advertising sexual wares in a manner calculated to embarrass many citizens going about their ordinary business. Assaulting passers-by with gratuitous erotic appeals is an invasion of their privacy, quite apart from any insult to their taste; but it is a misuse of language to claim that sexually explicit material kept in a locked drawer in a private home, or on a shelf of a soberly-fronted sex shop, is an environmental threat. Sexually explicit literature may serve as a boon to the lonely, the ugly, the aged, those who are forced by circumstances or by personal unattractiveness to live without love and companionship. Some "adult" magazines disseminate a rudimentary form of sex education, combating ignorance of the sexual act and increasing popular knowledge of the possibilities of sexual pleasure. A system of control which requires responsible management of bookshops and cinema clubs presenting a modest front to a public street far from schools, churches and council flats deserves a try, based on a law which echoes the sentiments of Mrs Patrick Campbell that "It doesn't matter what you do in the bedroom as long as you don't do it in the street and frighten the horses."

A final comment on the question posed by Professor Simpson: "Can Philosophy help?" I hope not, because the best solution is always the one which raises the least philosophical problems. But please don't despair just yet. My most recent courtroom appearance prior to this conference was to obtain bail for a man charged with – wait for it – conspiracy to corrupt public morals. Yes, the DPP is true to form: in 1959 it was Shaw and the *Ladies Directory*, in 1969 *International Times* and its gentlemen's directory. In 1979, it is an organisation called the Paedophile Information Exchange and a directory, it is alleged, of underage gentlemen. So dust off your mildewed copies of the Hart/Devlin debate, and check the going rate for witness fees. By a remarkable oversight – one which will be remedied, but perhaps not in time for this case – expert evidence may be admissible on conspiracy to corrupt public morals charges. And who better to define public morality for a jury than experts in philosophy? The last conspiracy to corrupt public morals case was the notorious *Oz* trial, featuring philosophical evidence for the defence from Richard Wollheim and Ronald Dworkin. I remember a little difficulty over Professor Dworkin's qualifications: when told that Dworkin had succeeded the great H. L. A. Hart, the judge interjected "Who's he?". When that was explained, the Old Bailey jurist grudgingly conceded: "Oh, very well then. How do you spell this H. L. A. Hart?"

So perhaps Professor Woozley need not have bothered to argue for a law against corrupting the public atmosphere, since we already have it, intention and all. But then again, the history of conspiracy to corrupt public morals may well provide the most powerful objection to the proposals in his paper.

A. D. WOOZLEY

CONCLUDING COMMENTS

My paper was concerned with exploring the conceptual unsatisfactoriness of the current English law of obscenity, as laid down in and practised under the Obscene Publications Acts of 1959 and 1964. The subsequent publication of the Williams Committee's report,[1] to which Professor Simpson alludes, might be thought to have outdated my discussion, because the whole position has changed. But it has not. Some (not all) of my doubts apply to the committee's proposed law; and in any case, the government has so far not accepted the committee's recommendations,[2] so that

[1] *Home Office: Report of the Committee on Obscenity and Film Censorship*, Chairman: Bernard Williams (London: HMSO, 1979. Cmnd. 7772). Figures in parentheses refer to the numbered paragraphs of the report. There is now available an abridged text: *Obscenity and Film Censorship*, edited by Bernard Williams (Cambridge: Cambridge University Press, 1981).

[2] This was made very plain by the government spokesman in the parliamentary debate on the Indecent Displays (Control) Bill on 30 January 1981. That Bill, which has now passed into law, is not directly relevant to my subject, since it dealt solely with matters of packaging and not with the availability of what is packaged. Although it was a private member's Bill, government officers assisted with its revised drafting, so that one might read some significance into the fact that the word 'indecent' is used throughout in preference to the word 'obscene'; there is, however, no attempt to define 'indecency'. If the new Civic Government (Scotland) Bill, published on 6 November 1981, bears any analogy to the government's thinking on the corresponding English legislation, it is to be noted that it continues to propose that "any person who makes, prints, publishes, or offers for sale or distribution, or has or keeps with a view to its eventual sale or distribution, or sells or distributes, any obscene material shall be guilty of an offence". That current Scottish law on the subject is in just as much conceptual disarray as English law is well demonstrated in Lionel Barber's commentary on a recent Glasgow Sheriff Court case in *The Scotsman*, 16 July 1980, and by G. H. Gordon, 'Shameless Indecency and Obscenity', *Journal of the Law Society of Scotland* 25 (1980): 262–9.

M. A. Stewart (ed.), Law, Morality and Rights, 249–255.

the law remains, at present and in prospect, as it has been.

The principal changes recommended by the committee relevant to the discussion at the Royal Institute of Philosophy's conference are:

(1) The whole terminology of 'obscene', 'indecent' and 'deprave and corrupt' should be dropped, having outlived its usefulness (9.21).

(2) The law should rest partly on the prohibition of harm (10.2), partly on restriction to protect people from the offensiveness of the public display of pornography (9.7):

(a) Material should be prohibited, if it appears that harm has been done to participants in its production (10.6);

(b) material should be restricted, in the manner of its display, marketing and sale, so as to avoid giving offence to those who do not wish to be confronted with it (9.10–19).

(3) Restricted material should be defined as material (of specified kinds) which is offensive to reasonable people (9.36).

(4) There should be no exemptions on the ground of intrinsic merit (9.41).

(5) There should be neither prohibition nor any restriction on the printed word (7.22).

Other recommendations deal with live performances and with the cinema; radio and television were excluded from the committee's remit.

In what follows, I want to raise three matters about the present law and about the Williams report.

First, the offence of publishing an obscene article is an atypical crime, in that its definition contains no intentional element, and consequently no *mens rea.* That was a change brought about by the 1959 Act from the previous situation under common law, in which what the accused intended or knew came into the reckoning of whether his publishing the article constituted the offence of publishing an obscene libel; under the current Act, if the defence is not available to him that he had not examined the article before publication and had no reasonable cause to suspect that it was obscene, he is judged solely by the effect which it is likely to have. Thus, the offence is, in effect, one of strict liability, with the limited qualification that the accused may plead ignorance; but the onus of proof that it was both ignorance and reasonable ignorance rests on the defence – unlike other crimes, where the onus of disproof rests on the prosecution. Not everybody who is accused of being a pornographer is a pornographer; and it is unfair that he should be tried more disadvantageously than somebody accused of another offence. On the Williams proposal the same result need not be produced, but it probably will unless in drafting the bill care is taken to prevent it. If the offence is going to be that of publishing a prohibited article or publishing a restricted article outside its prescribed limits, it will be easy to disregard the accused's intent. As long as *mens rea* remains what it is for other offences, obscenity should not be treated differently; in this respect, at least, Scottish law has the advantage over present-day English law.

Secondly, obscenity is an atypical crime in that it involves personal judgment in a disturbing way. In other cases, a jury may have difficulty in making up its mind in the face of hard questions of law or hard questions of fact owing to unclearness of evidence or unreliability of testimony; but what they are trying to get at are the facts which are there independently of their trying to get at them, and they will end up by getting them right or getting them wrong. In an obscenity trial things are different: whether or not an offence has been committed is not determined by correct answers to questions of law and fact. After a jury (or a magistrate, if the proceedings are for forfeiture only) has tried to answer the impossibly difficult causal question what effects the published article is likely to have on those likely to be exposed to it (in practice, as the Williams report indicates (2.10), that question has in recent years been much ignored), it has an assessment to make, viz., whether the effect is one of depravity and corruption. Although the Act says nothing about it, judges have told juries that they are not to make their own moral judgment, but are to judge according to the moral judgment and standards of "ordinary decent people".[3] The question might now be thought to be one of social fact, to be answerable by the methods of market research and public opinion polls; but that route is closed by the Act's rule that the jury may not hear expert testimony on the question which they have to decide. As a jury cannot be supposed to be qualified either to answer an empirical question without the evidence or to have privileged access to the evidence, they are in effect being told to do what they are also being told not to do, viz., as ordinary decent people to make their own judgment whether the effect is one of depravity and corruption. Obscenity is thus in the eye of the beholder, where the beholder is the court. Again, the situation would be unlikely to be different under Williams, unless the legislation provided for the admissibility of evidence as to what offends reasonable people; otherwise the court (a magistrate) will be being invited to play its own moral hunches. It is anomalous that there should be an offence so defined that the question whether conduct falls under the definition should actually, as well as by verdict, be determined by a court. It is one thing for a verdict to be performative (that it must be); it is another thing for it to be constitutive also.

Finally, there is the issue of freedom of speech. There are those who hold that any law at all on obscenity is objectionable as an interference with free speech, and they will think that their objection is largely met by the Williams recommendation that the printed word be exempted altogether; but not entirely, because nonverbal material will be liable either to restriction or to prohibition. We have to ask what it is about speech that makes its protection so important. If speech is valuable as the expression and communication of ideas, must it always be more valuable than anything, no matter what, that may compete with it? And is speech coextensive with the spoken or written word? It would be surprising if the answer to the first had to be an unqualified Yes, because it would be surprising if any value is always, no matter what, to be prefer-

[3] Lord Reid, *Knuller* v. *D.P.P.* [1973] AC 435, 457.

red to all others. Even if it were true that people should always be allowed to say what they want, it would not follow that they should always be allowed to say it when and where they want; there are good reasons, of safety, reciprocity, etc., as well as of offensiveness, why they should not. If the written word (and spoken word, on record or tape?) is to be liberated altogether, then the libertarian's quarrel with Williams can only be over any speech that extends beyond verbal communication. Arguably, there is some; but incontestably much, and almost incontestably most, non-verbal pornography is not intended as the communication of ideas, and has not the remotest interest in questions of truth, however far the notion of truth is stretched; it is a simple causal stimulus, of an entirely physical kind. It and freedom of speech do not even reach each other.

The whole question whether or not the law should, in effect, license some degree of pornography is not an easy one. On the one hand, there is some analogy with prostitution: as Mill pointed out, from the fact that the law ought to tolerate women becoming prostitutes, if they want to, it does not follow that the law ought to tolerate people becoming brothel-keepers and pimps, if they want to. On the other hand, is the activity of the pornographer any worse than the activities of many other entrepreneurs in a capitalist society which we do not dream of making criminal? Those who make it their job to persuade others into spending or speculating themselves heavily into debt are at least as undesirable members of society. How much worse is the exploitation of sexual weakness than the exploitation of covetousness and greed?

Let me conclude with two comments specifically about the discussion at the RIP Conference. Some of the participants seriously misunderstood and misrepresented my paper in one respect. I was taken to be recommending a change in the law which would make being obscene be the having a tendency to deprave and corrupt..., in the sense in which I argue in Part 2 of my paper that pornography does have a tendency to deprave and corrupt. That suggestion was rightly criticized for its indeterminacy: it would be even easier for defendants to get off than it is now. But it is not what

I was suggesting. I was not proposing either a legal *definition* or a legal *test* of pornography, as Mr Robertson might be thought to have implied at one point in his Chairman's remarks; indeed I explicitly said that I was not. What I was doing was emphasizing a social feature of pornography, which might make it desirable to legislate against it. *How* what is to be legally determined to be criminally pornographic is to be determined, I left open in my paper.

Secondly, in some of his comments on the utilitarian roots of the language of 'tending to deprave and corrupt', Professor Simpson has overlooked the ambiguities to which I drew attention. The terminology of 'tending', which Professor Simpson illustrates by several quotations from the reports of the Criminal Law Commission, certainly is Austinian, and can be found fairly widely in Austin's lectures on *The Province of Jurisprudence Determined.* I would take issue, though, with Professor Simpson in his criticism of the utilitarian theory there involved, namely that it leads to a court being required to legislate rather than to judge the conduct of the accused person. Of the two meanings of 'tend' which I distinguished in the first part of my paper, if the first one is adopted – namely, the sense of that which *usually*, or *most often*, depraves and corrupts – then I think that the remarks which Professor Simpson makes certainly do apply. If we take the phrase that way, the accused has to be convicted if his publication belongs to a class of publication of which it is true that most members of that class do have that effect, with no consideration given to the question whether his particular publication belongs to the majority which do have the effect or to the minority which do not. How much the courts have used that sense is not for me but for a legal historian to say; but if that *has* been their use, the paternity order which Professor Simpson has asked for, fathering it on the nineteenth-century utilitarians, is surely invalid. Neither Austin nor J. S. Mill meant that by 'tend'. Austin tells us, in the Second Lecture, what he means by 'tend': that although the tendency of an act does indeed require treating it as a member of a class, a statement of tendency is a statement of *probability*, not a statement of frequency. On this second interpretation, the current statutory definition of obscenity escapes Professor Simpson's objection; but the law is still open to my objection, that it requires a jury to render a verdict in the absence of any evidence that could possibly make it a reasonable verdict. In the second part of my paper I introduce a third meaning of 'tend', and suggest both that it is a meaning which very clearly Mill, if not Austin, actually used; and furthermore that it is one which, while it will not be used in phrasing legislation, enables us nevertheless to express more accurately what it is about pornography that makes it a subject of possible legislative or judicial or administrative interest.

University of Virginia

PART V

REVERSE DISCRIMINATION

RICHARD H. S. TUR

JUSTIFICATIONS OF REVERSE DISCRIMINATION

> No social order can compensate completely for the injustices of nature.
>
> Hans Kelsen

> The tragedy of all political action is that some problems have no solution, none of the alternatives are intellectually consistent or morally uncompromising; and whatever decision is taken will harm somebody.
>
> James Joll

1.

The primary literature of reverse discrimination would furnish that style of philosophising which places language at the centre of concern with a treasure trove of instances. Even the definition of the phrase provides sufficient material for those whose interest, like Bentham's, is in dyslogistic or eulogistic terms, in what he called, in somewhat less jaw-breaking terminology, "passion-kindling epithets"; and Stevenson's notion of "persuasive definition", too, is well illustrated by the range of phrases used to refer to the central phenomenon. Thus the phrases "reverse discrimination", "positive discrimination", "preferential treatment" and "affirmative action" are widely, even undiscriminatingly, used. In general, it seems that those opposing the practice tend to use harsher phrases such as "reverse discrimination" or "positive discrimination" and those supportive in principle tend to use the softer phrases such as "affirmative action".

But not all usage treats the range of phrases as broadly synonymous. Thus one line of argument, canvassed by those who express concern for women and racial or ethnic minorities, seeks to

M. A. Stewart (ed.), Law, Morality and Rights, 259–294.

persuade us that "affirmative action" and "reverse discrimination" differ, that the former is a wider term than the latter and that at least some forms of affirmative action are both morally and constitutionally justifiable, whereas reverse discrimination, especially if defined in terms of quotas, is a quite specific form of affirmative action which is unjustifiable both morally and constitutionally. The *Bakke* decision, of which more later, is a case in point.

Again, some commentators seek to differentiate "reverse discrimination" and "positive discrimination". Thus one contributor "sharply distinguishes" a cluster of practices such as favourable taxation, or allocation of extra tax monies to specific purposes, direct cash payments to encourage private business, subsidised housing, pensions, guaranteed incomes, unemployment benefits, disaster relief and, in general, welfare payments, from "a kind of favoritism which is much more directly felt by the majority than the unequal distribution of government spending".[1] This is achieved by a deliberate attempt to hold open or reserve a number of benefits, sometimes by means of overt quotas, for members of the favourite group. These benefits most usually are places in employment, recruitment and promotion, and in education, especially in university and professional education. The author seems to believe that "favourable treatment" can be distinguished from mere "favouritism" on the ground that the latter "always results at least in the threat of fewer places being open to 'majority persons' ". He proposes to call the former "positive discrimination" which, he opines, is the term in use in Great Britain,[2] and the latter "reverse discrimination". His case is that "positive" discrimination, thus defined, is morally justifiable, though practically dubious; that is to say, such is the state of our existing social sciences that we cannot say with enough certainty that these programmes will have, in fact, the desirable effects attributed to

---

1 See Barry R. Gross, *Discrimination in Reverse: Is Turnabout Fair Play?* (New York: New York University Press, 1978), p. 18 *et seq*.

2 *Positive Discrimination and Inequality*, edited by H. Glennerster and S. Hatch (London: Fabian Society, 1975).

them. But "reverse" discrimination as thus defined is, he believes, morally unacceptable. This distinction is thin, insofar as even in the former case benefits are redistributed, albeit "losers" are less directly identifiable. Howsoever, one should notice that terms such as "positive discrimination" may undergo a sea-change in crossing the Atlantic and that the different phrases may hint at differences which do make a difference to our moral deliberations.

Nonetheless, this paper will use the phrase "reverse discrimination" as a generic term to refer to the phenomenon under discussion, not because its author is opposed to the practice – indeed precisely the opposite is emphatically the case – but because it remains the term in widest circulation which is instantly recognisable and which has the further advantage of stating the issue in its most rigorous form, including quotas. And reverse discrimination may be here defined as giving favourable or preferential treatment to individual members of ethnic or other minorities in the allocation of the burdens and benefits of society on the basis of perceived need.

It is widely defended on the basis that these very minorities have, hitherto, suffered such adverse discrimination as undermines any real opportunity of competing on equal terms. Defenders of the practice sometimes regard it as a necessary means to a distributively more just society. The overall thesis of this paper is that much of the reverse discrimination debate has been guilty of what might be called (with apologies to Ryle) a "category mistake"; that is, the debate has concentrated upon and been couched in the terminology of compensatory justice to the near-exclusion of distributive justice.[3] This thesis is in turn informed by the subthesis that the principle of compensation, particularly if appre-

---

[3] An interesting illustration of this is *Social Justice and Preferential Treatment*, edited by William T. Blackstone and Robert D. Heslep (Athens, Ga.: University of Georgia Press, 1978), which despite its more appropriate title collects together papers delivered at a conference entitled 'The Policy of Compensatory Justice for Women and Racial Minorities in Education and Business'. (This collection is referred to hereafter as 'Blackstone & Heslep'.)

hended legalistically, does not and cannot by tinkering with the mechanism be made to justify reverse discrimination.

The practice, however defined, also has opponents. It is widely condemned as racist or sexist, and even as paternalistic and patronising, though it might well be noted that advocates of reverse discrimination support the practice not *because* the favoured group are coloured or female, but because members of these groups have been discriminated against in the past or are currently discriminated against because of their colour or gender.[4] It is especially criticised on the ground that it disregards the allegedly basic rights of those not favoured by the practice, visiting an evil, or at least a deprivation, upon those in no way responsible for the prior discrimination. It is this last circumstance which founds the thesis of this paper that, although reverse discrimination may be justified, it cannot be justified on any argument being an isomorph of the justification of the Anglo-American law of tort.

The practice takes as its personal sphere of concern distinct minority groups, and in America this has meant primarily ethnic or racial groups on the one hand, e.g. Negroes, Chicanos, American-Indians, etc., and on the other hand, women. Despite legal[5] and moral[6] argument of impressive weight, American discussion and practice have excluded reference to the poor, such as might be identified in the U.K. by reference to socio-economic groupings. Nonetheless, some of the arguments relating to reverse discrimination could readily be applied to socio-economic categories, and the intuition of this, and all its heralds, may account for some of the

---

[4] See James W. Nickel, 'Discrimination and Morally Relevant Characteristics', *Analysis* 32 (1971/2), reprinted in *Reverse Discrimination*, edited by Barry R. Gross (Buffalo, N.Y.: Prometheus Books, 1977), pp. 288–290. (This collection is referred to hereafter as 'Gross'.)

[5] *San Antonio Independent School District* v. *Rodriguez* 411 US 1 (1973): see especially the impressive dissent of Marshall J.

[6] Richard A. Wasserstrom, 'The University and the Case for Preferential Treatment', *American Philosophical Quarterly* 13 (1976), reprinted in Blackstone & Heslep, pp. 16–32.

intense hostility and emotion which the very idea of reverse discrimination is capable of generating.

One should beware, however, of too readily believing that arguments relating to reverse discrimination can always be applied without modification where different groups are involved. Thus it may be easier to implement full-blooded reverse discrimination in the case of women than in the case of a specific ethnic group such as negroes, in that gender-based classification is necessarily bipartite, and there are no other groups waiting in the wings to claim like dispensations as there are in the case of ethnic classifications.[7]

Again, justification of reverse discrimination may turn upon one's perception of the historic disadvantage of different groups. Insofar as one perceives the historic disadvantages of racially defined groups, and especially of American Negroes, as far outweighing those of any other group, reverse discrimination could be justified in that single instance, but in no other.[8] Indeed it is just such a perspective which encourages the view that women's rights groups, by latching on to the head of steam for reverse discrimination in favour of American Negroes, have sapped its strength, trivialising the basis of the claim by the implication that women's historic disadvantages have been on all fours with those of American Negroes. As against which, supporters of reverse discrimination for women can point to their historic and legal disadvantages as admirably illustrated by Albie Sachs and Joan Wilson in their provocative book *Sexism and the Law*.

The material sphere of concern is, in principle, as wide as the sphere of burdens and benefits to be allocated. The potential ubiquity of the practice is itself further reason for the concern

---

7 See *Bakke* v. *Regents of the University of California* 483 US 265 (1978), *per* Powell J.

8 See Prince E. Wilson, 'Discrimination Against Blacks in Education: An Historical Perspective', in Blackstone & Heslep, pp. 161–175; and Rayford W. Logan and Michael R. Winston, *The Negro in the United States*, Volumes 1 and 2 (New York: Van Nostrand Reinhold, 1970–1971).

and emotion it generates. American experience has, however, tended to concentrate on two areas, namely education and employment, the centrality of which, even without the postulated cycle of deprivation, can hardly be disputed. Thus in hiring and promoting as well as in university admissions, reverse discrimination in favour of women and racial minorities has been fostered by Federal agencies. A complicating refinement is that of employment and promotion of academic staff, and we shall have occasion to consider in passing the special pleading which can be brought into play with regard to admission to professions, such as medicine, law and teaching.[9]

This paper concentrates primarily upon the racist, and suspends treatment of sexist, aspects. This is an administrative, not a moral, decision, taken on the basis that the legal history of racial discrimination in America is widely known and relatively non-contentious and therefore more readily assumed *en route* to a justification of reverse discrimination.

2.

De Funis v. *Odegaard*[10] is a case doubly to excite the interest of lawyers because it involved constitutional and legal issues relating to reverse discrimination and admission procedures of law schools. In 1971 Marco De Funis applied to the University of Washington Law School, but was rejected despite having college grades and a Law School Aptitude Test score such that he would have been admitted if he had been a black, a Chicano, an American Indian or a Filipino. De Funis asked the Supreme Court to rule that Washington Law School's admission procedure, requiring less exacting standards of minority groups, violated the Equal Protection Clause of the Fourteenth Amendment.

---

[9] See, for example, R. M. O'Neil, *Discriminating Against Discrimination: Preferential Admissions and the De Funis Case* (Bloomington, Ind.: Indiana University Press, 1975), chapter 5, reprinted in Gross, pp. 66–83.
[10] 416 US 312 (1974).

Thus the moral argument that, even if reverse discrimination (as practised by Washington Law School) does produce more good than harm, it remains unacceptable because it violates the "rights" of innocent individuals, was presented to the Supreme Court. Having initially accepted the case and having heard oral argument – the *amicus curiae* briefs, alone, ran to three volumes – the Supreme Court, somewhat perversely, declared the case moot, that is, it decided not to decide. De Funis had been admitted to the Washington Law School after a lower court had found in his favour, and the Law School had conceded that he would be allowed to graduate, whatever the outcome of the litigation. Given the importance of the issue involved and the widespread public concern, it is hardly surprising that this non-decision attracted considerable criticism.

Such critics included members of the Supreme Court itself, most notably Mr Justice Douglas, who, in his dissenting judgment, reached the merits of the case. He held that the Washington admissions procedures contravened the Constitution. He founded on the famous aphorism, reaching all the way back to *Plessy* v. *Ferguson*,[11] that the Constitution is colour-blind. He remarked, "A De Funis who is white is entitled to no advantage by reason of that fact; nor is he subject to any disability, no matter his race or color. Whatever his race, he has a constitutional right to have his application considered on its individual merits in a racially neutral manner." The Washington procedure was unacceptable to Mr Justice Douglas because it "did reduce the total number of places for which De Funis could compete – solely on account of his race".

Mr Justice Douglas, however, did take the view that admissions boards could consider an individual's prior achievements, even in the light of his having encountered adverse racial discrimination, and the circumstances that an individual is likely to use his (legal) skills to service poorly serviced communities. This, apparently, "would substantially fulfill the law school's interest in giving a more

[11] 163 US 537 (1896).

diverse group access to the legal profession". Thus is the *Bakke* decision prefigured in this judgement which contains more than a hint that a more subtle approach might achieve, constitutionally, the result aimed at by Washington Law School.

This more subtle approach is outlined in Archibald Cox's Harvard College *amicus curiae* brief and is known as the "Harvard Model". It emphasises a distinction between basic admission qualifications and selection criteria. It allows that within that large number of applicants who are admissible and capable of doing good work, race may tip the balance, simply because a black student may add something significant to the educational *milieu* not provided by a white on the basis that "diversity" is educationally desirable.

Given that a school must select a limited number from a pool of academically qualified applicants, a range of options is available. First, one might select students of the highest intellectual quality, treating formal educational qualifications as exhaustive and dispositive, on the grounds, perhaps, that education is solely concerned with challenging the intellect and increasing formal learning. Secondly, one might take a broader view of education, seeing it as "education for life" and not "education in books". Then, given some assurance of basic academic competence, such as is guaranteed by basic admissions qualifications, selection need not proceed solely on the basis of academic excellence. One might seek to realise a diverse student body drawing upon the widest possible variety of talents and interests and the most diverse social, economic and cultural background. Students learn not only from books and teachers, but also from each other. Thirdly, one might compromise, giving a high, but not exclusive, role to superior intellectual qualities, but allowing that equally marked superiority in other qualities will be enough to offset it. On the second and third of these options, membership of a minority race could be relevant, especially, as Cox observes, "at any institution which has been predominantly white for a long period".

The Harvard model seeks to combine features of the second and third options. Diversity once meant "students from California,

New York and Massachusetts; city dwellers and farm boys; violinists, painters and football players, biologists, historians and classicists; potential stockbrokers, academics and politicians". But a new conception of diversity has developed, to include students from disadvantaged economic, racial and minority groups. Thus race has come to be a factor in some individual admission decisions at Harvard College on the basis that just as "a farm boy from Idaho can bring something to Harvard College that a Bostonian cannot offer", so too "a black student can usually bring something that a white person cannot offer".

But diversity is to be achieved otherwise than by imposing rigid quotas or fixed minimum numbers of specific minorities. Clearly some relation between numbers and the benefit to be derived from a diverse student body obtains. Ten or twenty black students out of a total of a thousand or thereby would be mere tokenism and, probably, counterproductive. At Harvard College "many types and categories of student" are taken into account in pursuit of a reasonable balance. Although diversity is deemed more important in Harvard College than in Medical or Law School, it remains relevant in admissions decisions throughout Harvard University.

The combined impact of Mr Justice Douglas's dissenting judgement and Professor Archibald Cox's *amicus curiae* brief is that crude segregationist admissions procedures, even if they aim at aiding minority candidates, are struck at by the Constitution, but there is nothing in the Equal Protection Clause to debar education authorities from taking account of race among other criteria. Although this view did not have the status of a Supreme Court decision, it was widely regarded as a statement of how the Court would have decided had the case not been moot, and as an indication of how a like future case might be decided.

Bakke v. *Regents of the University of California*[12] is the like future case, and it was argued by the Supreme Court of the United States on October 12th 1977, and decided on June 28th 1978. The basic facts of this case are so well known as to obviate re-

---

[12] 483 US 265 (1978).

hearsal. At issue was the legality and constitutionality of a quota-based admissions programme directed towards minority groups. The Supreme Court had two related questions to consider:

1. Should Bakke's admission to Davis Medical School be ordered?

2. Can a University ever take race into account in admissions decisions?

It might seem that these two questions are logically related, in that an affirmative answer to (1) entails a negative answer to (2). But, as Holmes observed, "the life of the law has not been logic...", and the Court contrived to answer both questions in the affirmative.

Four members of the Court answered the first question affirmatively, and another four answered the second question in like fashion. It fell to Mr Justice Powell to reconcile these conflicting views by uniting, first, with the group supporting Bakke's admission and, secondly, with those insisting on the relevance of race as an admissions criterion, thereby creating two separate majorities.

And he squared this particular circle by arguing that, although Davis may be legitimately interested in a diverse student body, it cannot bring this about by reserving a specific number of places for preferred ethnic groups. He believes that Davis errs in its conception of diversity and that in pursuit of a "heterogeneous student body" one is concerned not solely with "simple ethnic diversity" but with a "far broader array of qualifications and characteristics". Consequently, to focus solely on ethnic diversity, as Davis does, is to limit the attainment of "genuine diversity".

But, praying the Harvard Model in aid, Mr Justice Powell takes the view that some other universities operate more sophisticated or subtle admissions programmes which, though taking account of race, do not rely upon assigning a fixed number of places to a minority group. Harvard is thus preferred to Davis because it "treats each applicant as an individual in the admissions process" and, consequently, the candidate who loses out on the last available place because of another receiving a racial "plus" will not (unlike De Funis or Bakke) have been foreclosed from all considerations "simply because he was not of the right color".

3.

Reverse discrimination and all that goes with it has excited much academic, primarily philosophical, comment. And this seems to be in part because of its capacity to bring to light inherent contradictions in our moral beliefs and principles. Just as the accretion of anomalies around a scientific theory may ultimately lead to a paradigm shift better to accommodate them, so too, reverse discrimination has gathered together a series of questions about utility, justice and individualism.

First, utilitarianism, as an ethical theory, is placed under even greater strain than usual. Perhaps no one (or rather, hardly anyone) has swallowed the doctrine entirely for some time. Clearly something is amiss with a doctrine which permits one thinker (Popper) to exclude revolution and another (Marcuse) to justify it.[13] Equally, utilitarianism can provide little guidance to someone contemplating suicide. What the "greatest happiness principle" leaves undetermined is the extent of the tract of future time which is to be taken into account. Thus, even if the various calculations were radically simplified or automated by, say, Texas Instruments coming up with a pocket version of Bentham's Felicific Calculus, the morally right action would not be uniquely determined. And this inherent weakness in utilitarianism's basic principle can never be overcome, because no principle can exhaustively determine the conditions of its own applicability.

Be that as it may, reverse discrimination has placed utilitarianism under further pressure by presenting in a painfully obvious form the old argument of utility versus justice, to reveal that even if

---

13 Karl R. Popper, 'Utopia and Violence', in his *Conjectures and Refutations*, 3rd edition (London: Routledge & Kegan Paul, 1969), pp. 355–363; Herbert Marcuse, 'Ethics and Revolution', in *Ethics and Society*, edited by Richard T. De George (Garden City, N.Y.: Doubleday, 1966), pp. 133–147; Kai Neilsen, 'On the Choice between Reform and Revolution', *Inquiry* **14** (1971), reprinted in *Philosophy and Political Action*, edited by V. Held, K. Neilsen and C. Parsons (New York: Oxford University Press, 1972), pp. 17–51.

continued adverse discrimination had desirable social consequences (both short and long term) it would still be unjust, and that even if reverse discrimination lacked such desirable social consequences it might still be just. Critics of utilitarianism, such as Dworkin, have not been slow to exploit this opportunity, arguing that whereas reverse discrimination can be justified by both utilitarian *and* ideal arguments, adverse discrimination can be justified only by utilitarian arguments.[14]

Conceptions and principles of justice also seem confounded by reverse discrimination. One popular, though somewhat uninformative, conception of justice turns upon the idea of equality, an idea in any case necessary if utilitarianism is to be made to work (i.e., Bentham's "one should count for one"). Yet reverse discrimination seems to urge that we abandon the principle of equal treatment in order to realise the principle of equality. One can readily argue for reverse discrimination as a device to equalise opportunity; that is, as a relatively minor adjustment in the operation of the meritocracy. Yet some more radical commentators on reverse discrimination see it as a device to sustain the inherent inequalities of the meritocracy, and advocate the sweeping away of such inequalities *en route* to a far-reaching equality of result.[15]

Again, reverse discrimination has thrown individualism into confusion with arguments couched in the terminology of compensation, that since certain groups have suffered adverse discrimination in the past, these groups should now receive more favourable treatment. This has occasioned a lively debate as to whether individuals or groups ought to be compensated and even whether

---

[14] R. M. Dworkin, *Taking Rights Seriously* (London: Duckworth, 1977), chapter 9.

[15] See Thomas Nagel, 'Equal Treatment and Compensatory Discrimination', *Philosophy and Public Affairs* 2 (1972/3), reprinted in *Equality and Preferential Treatment*, edited by M. Cohen, T. Nagel and T. Scanlon (Princeton: Princeton University Press, 1977), pp. 3–18 (this collection is referred to hereafter as 'Cohen, Nagel & Scanlon'); and Maxine Green, 'Equality and Inviolability: An Approach to Compensatory Justice', in Blackstone & Heslep, pp. 176–198.

group reparations are intellectually coherent.[16] Individualism has always been a characteristic feature of classical liberalism and the American tradition. It is therefore thought erroneous, even "slanderous",[17] to capture the label "liberal" to refer to reverse discrimination because, so it is alleged, the so-called "liberals" who support such programmes have in fact moved so far from a conception of and concern with *individual* rights towards collectivist concerns as no longer to merit the title. And when this "illiberalism" is linked to the circumstance that the most favoured means of achieving the goals of reverse discrimination is by Federal Government Agencies, such as the Equal Employment Opportunity Commission, then the whole reverse discrimination movement appears as socialist intervention and a threat to the full range of liberal values.

Any practice which can simultaneously embarrass the utilitarian, confound the egalitarian and challenge political individualism is worthy of study in its own right. But more: reverse discrimination is intensely practical, in that it is concerned with real, live social issues such as education and employment, providing a test-bed for the application of principles of social justice. It seems to me that no single issue is so broadly educative as is reverse discrimination – whatever one's moral judgement of the practice – since it unites philosophical, legal and political perspectives in an historical and sociological frame.

Arguments about reverse discrimination cover the full spectrum of philosophical debate, and this, too, accounts for the attractiveness of the topic from a professional philosopher's viewpoint. Arguments in favour of the practice can be variously classified.

---

16 See Roger A. Shiner, 'Individuals, Groups and Inverse Discrimination', *Analysis* 33 (1972/3); James W. Nickel, 'Should Reparations be to Individuals or to Groups?', *Analysis* 34 (1973/4); Alan H. Goldman, 'Reparations to Individuals or Groups?', *Analysis* 35 (1974/5), each reprinted in Gross, pp. 310–313; 314–320; 321–323 respectively.

17 See Lee Nisbet, 'Affirmative Action – A Liberal Program?', in Gross, pp. 50–53.

Gross, for example, lists eight categories, though some of them appear to evaporate upon a closer approach.[18]

One proposed distinction is that between empirical and ideal arguments.[19] Empirical arguments are primarily about means; they exhort us to perform certain actions or adopt certain policies because these will result in a definite state of affairs. Utilitarianism is widely regarded as the paradigm. Many reverse discrimination arguments operate on precisely this model, saying, for instance, that the practice increases the number of minority participants in crucial professions such as medicine, law or teaching, and that that state of affairs is, on balance, better for society as a whole than is its absence. Special pleading that reverse discrimination is necessary in order to provide black people with black teachers, black patients with black doctors, and black clients with black lawyers, in order that the black community be better serviced and provided with suitable role models to lift aspirations, fall into this category.

All empirical arguments are to some extent hostages to fortune and often we have little better than a speculative, though informed, guess. Often faith substitutes for knowledge. Further, behind all such empirical argument is the assumption that the resulting state of affairs is intrinsically valuable or a further means to an end state which is. For classical utilitarianism the "greatest happiness of the greatest number" is the significant end-state. Clearly no principle can be a test of itself and any proposed justification of the principle of utility must be non-utilitarian on pain of begging the question. It is dubious whether there really are, as Mill believed, "considera-

---

[18] Barry R. Gross, *Discrimination in Reverse*, pp. 32–33: "(1) Injustice to be compensated. (2) Equality of opportunity to be assured. (3) Equality of result to be assured. (4) Required for anything practical to be done for the discriminated groups. (5) What seems like reverse discrimination is really not. (6) Realization of social goal overrides satisfaction of theoretical principles of justice. (7) A great future good will come to society by the use of reverse discrimination. (8) Miscellaneous special circumstances purported to justify reverse discrimination."

[19] This purports to be a generalised version of Dworkin's distinction between utilitarian and ideal arguments in *Taking Rights Seriously*, chapter 9.

tions capable of determining the intellect", and utilitarianism, like any moral philosophy, must rest upon an assumed ideal state. Utilitarianism is, indeed, no worse off than any other monolithic moral philosophy in the essential weakness of the underpinning of its ultimate principle, although it sometimes appears so, because it is linked with a crisply empirical, anti-metaphysical epistemology wholly obnoxious to ideas such as the Good or Justice which cannot pay up in the hard currency of fact.

Even utilitarianism, therefore, seems to have an ideal aspect. Genuinely ideal conceptions and arguments overtly rely upon natural rights, upon justice and upon equality. Often, they are dismissive of end-states or results and hold out an *a priori* criterion such as equal opportunity, or the inherent worth of the individual human being.

The postulated distinction between ideal and empirical arguments informs the widely held view that in politics and in morals it is frequently necessary to strike a balance between expediency and justice, between general welfare and individual rights.[20] But often, maybe always, this is an exhortation to balance the unknowable and the incommunicable. Precisely what counts as general welfare depends upon tentative hypotheses of social causation, perhaps unverifiable even in principle, and tacit value assumptions. And justice, especially as canvassed by human rights philosophers, seems so intuitive as to be worthless. The image of the Platonic philosopher, one of the chosen few, intuiting Justice and being unable to communicate it, illustrates the point poignantly enough.

The proposed distinction hardly seems compelling. Ideal arguments have empirical dimensions and empirical arguments make ideal assumptions. Empiricists and idealists alike can be brought to agree that a policy which puts some, even many, quite admirable, even innocent, individuals at lesser or greater disadvantage may be justified because it makes the community as a whole better off,

---

20 An instance relating to reverse discrimination is Abraham Edel, 'Preferential Treatment and Justice', in Blackstone & Heslep, pp. 111–113.

though a utilitarian's conception of the extent of the disadvantage deemed acceptable may differ from that of one who defines justice in terms of the liberal tradition and the sovereignty of the individual person.

A rather more compelling distinction redounds upon the idea of deserts, and whether they are to be related to past conduct and events or based upon an *a priori* conception of human worth. The basic question of social justice is: Who should get what? One basic answer to this is that those who are good, i.e., those who behave according to a society's historical standards, should be rewarded and the bad should be punished. Such an answer seeks to allocate burdens and benefits according to individual behaviour. This answer, erected into the "fault principle", is the basis of the Anglo-American law of tort and of the criminal law of at least the western world. Intention, recklessness or negligence justifies reparation; *mens rea* is a necessary prerequisite of punishment. But these doctrines have never been implemented in their full purity in any legal system known to me. Strict liability has always played some role, justified by reference to the common good.

The fault principle is basically retributive. It assumes that wrongs should be adjusted, but otherwise that existing inequalities represent the proper ordering of actions, persons and things. It is this rather theological assumption that the *status quo* is just and that any changes to it must be referable to wrongful human conduct that underpins the cluster of "compensatory" arguments which seek to justify reverse discrimination.

But the compensation model is unfortunate. The principle has two aspects – crime and tort. If *X* commits a wrong he may be liable to criminal sanction and also to make reparation for the injuries suffered by his victim. The trigger for any re-adjustment is a "wrong". But what is a "wrong"? Unless one holds to an absolute morality valid throughout time and space, a "wrong" must be defined in culturally relative terms. Assume the validity of the fault principle. What follows for reverse discrimination? First, that those who have wrongfully discriminated on racial grounds ought to be liable to criminal sanction, and secondly, that those injured by such wrongful discrimination ought to be compensated, primarily by those wrongfully discriminating, but secondarily by society, say, on the model of the Criminal Injuries Compensation Board which operates in the United Kingdom, or through generalised social insurance.

Now the first problem this raises is whether racial discrimination, segregation, apartheid, prohibitions on racial intermarriage, etc., are "wrong". Ethnocentrism is the belief that the standards of one's own society are absolute standards. It is as much a vice historically as geographically. *If* racial discrimination was sanctified by the law and morals of the day, can we now project our norms backward to condemn those who lived according to the precepts of their time? This is, at best, ethnocentric. But it is also contrary to a widely accepted moral principle of the present age condemning retrospective liability.

But even if it is allowed that when blacks have in the past been discriminated against by whites a wrong has been perpetrated, the compensation model remains inadequate. Assume the wrong. Is compensation exigible? All legal systems of my acquaintance place some restriction on the extent of time which can be permitted to elapse before the remedy, the private right to recover damages for the injury or loss suffered, itself lapses. The moral philosopher finds the dimension of time problematic. Just what tract of future time is material may divide revolutionary and non-revolutionary utilitarians. The range of succeeding generations for which the present generation ought to have concern may divide philosophers into supporters and opponents of nuclear energy installations. Lawyers, especially private lawyers, are spared much of this anguish. A congeries of devices operates to limit the scope of past time to which legal organs need or may have recourse. Statutes of limitations of actions may cut away a right of action for recovery of damages. Prescription may operate negatively to remove private rights or remedies or positively to grant new rights. The doctrine of adverse possession is but one example.[21] Time, *per se*, may not

[21] "An occupation of land inconsistent with the right of the true owner ... actual possession in the absence of possession by the rightful owner, and

be a causal agent, but it is a legally or morally relevant factor, such that the mere passage of time may work a qualitative difference so that conditions which at one moment in time attract a specific legal consequence are mysteriously transformed into conditions which the law, if not condoning, refuses to act in cognisance of. And the law makes these arbitrary administrative decisions in pursuit of what Bentham, among others, sees as its sovereign virtue, namely certainty.

The lawyer, unlike the moral philosopher, escapes the question whether injuries done in the nineteenth century or in the first half of the twentieth century warrant compensation in 1979 or thereby. But the moral philosopher, if he is to be intelligible, must have at least a tacit conception of the relevant time sphere. One reason why arguments based upon compensation fail to make sense is that they fail properly to attend to this crucial aspect of their favourite analogy, the Anglo-American law of tort.

Another problem for compensation-based arguments is that of collective liability. Given that *A* wrongfully discriminated against *B* in, say, 1915 or thereby, is that any reason at all why the interests of *C* should now be sacrificed to those of *D* purely on the grounds that *A* and *C* are white and *B* and *D* are black? Collective liability is by no means impossible in law. The liability of a company to make reparation out of its assets is in effect a collective liability upon its shareholders, and war reparations make the population of an entire nation liable to repair wrongs perpetrated by a section of it. But it is unclear whether the nature of the groups involved in reverse discrimination arguments based on compensation have the integrity called for by the principle of collective liability. Unlike a company at national law and a state at international law, these groups lack legal personality.

These considerations suggest that the backward-looking, com-

---

without lawful title ... if the adverse possession continues, the effect at the expiration of the prescribed period is that not only the remedy, but the title of the former owner is extinguished" – *Osborn's Concise Law Dictionary*, 6th edition (London: Sweet & Maxwell, 1976).

pensatory justifications of reverse discrimination lack conviction and rest upon an insufficiently analysed conception of compensation. It therefore seems to me mistaken to seek to justify reverse discrimination now on the basis of alleged wrongs then. An alternative to this retrospective justification is the general justifying aim of the practice, namely a society committed substantially as well as formally to the proposition that equality of opportunity is a consummation devoutly to be wished. Given the overall aim of equal opportunity, the circumstances that some are disadvantaged by virtue of past discrimination and others are simply disadvantaged is hardly crucial. Vital only are the steps to be taken to maximise equality of opportunity. We ought to be less concerned with the apportionment of blame for the past and the present, and more with the means of determining the future. Advocates of reverse discrimination have been misled by the compensation analogy. Although superficially attractive and even plausible, it is ultimately untenable and harmful to the case for reverse discrimination because it furnishes opponents with an easy target.

Clearly one need not assume that justice is necessarily or exclusively compensatory, rectificatory or corrective. Justice is also distributive, concerned with the allocation of burdens and benefits, quite independently of the issue of wrongful behaviour. Distributive justice operates on some principle other than retribution and compensation for wrongs. This is sometimes obscured by talk of distribution according to deserts, e.g. *suum cuique* – "to each his due" – etc., but one can nonetheless radically separate that which is due on the basis of one's actions and that which is due on the basis of one's being.

Many debates about distributive justice are couched in precisely such terms. They hold that the very idea of a human being or a moral agent carries with it certain minimum necessary moral standards which are to operate even if contrary to the general welfare.[22] These include the idea that one ought to be able to

---

[22] Rawls' concept of "telishment" elucidated in his 'Two Concepts of Rules', *Philosophical Review* 64 (1955), is a good example in philosophical

participate in decisions affecting one's destiny and the idea that all human beings should be treated as equals.

Now I wish to suggest that it is this latter model of moral argument which ought to inform our attitude to reverse discrimination rather than the compensation model so widely canvassed. If reverse discrimination is justified, it is because it is a necessary means to realising that equality of opportunity sanctified by the belief that one's very humanity places limits upon what decisions can be taken concerning one's welfare and way of life. I am thus suggesting that the reverse discrimination debate has taken a wrong turning, tending always towards compensation rather than towards distributive justice.

4.

Crucial to one's understanding of the reverse discrimination debate is its American origin. The American legal system, the Constitution and the Supreme Court influence the mode of argumentation quite remarkably.

The ideology is as follows: The judicial office is understood as primarily concerned with the application of law according to settled rules and principles. Judges are not significantly in the law-making business, even if, as Holmes acknowledged, they do fill gaps by "interstitial legislation". Nor ought they to usurp the role of the legislature. In particular, they ought not to entertain questions of policy – that is for the executive branch of government with the approval of the legislature. Thus the judiciary interprets but does not initiate policy.

The reality is rather different even in legal systems such as those of England or Scotland where the House of Lords, the Court of Appeal and the Court of Session, though much more limited than

---

argument; Raskolnikov's deliberations and his personal tragedy in Dostoyevsky's *Crime and Punishment*, a particularly moving illustration in literature; Abraham Edel's 'Preferential Treatment and Justice' (cited above, n. 20), an instance within the reverse discrimination debate.

the American Supreme Court, have a considerably greater policy-making role than their members care to admit or is obvious on first glance.[23] But in America the policy-making role of the Supreme Court is profound and essential. The rare capacity to dismiss Federal or State legislation as unconstitutional means that the Supreme Court can in effect make the policy decision anew.[24]

Now, one writes "in effect" because in intention, from an internal point of view, the Supreme Court may not see itself as an agent of policy-making but as an agent of law application. Or, again, even if it does appreciate the policy impact, it may still require that it reaches its decisions by impeccably *legal* argumentation. Compensation, in the broadest possible sense of righting wrongs, repairing injuries and providing remedies, is a classic category of judicial activity, intervention and argumentation. Since courts are called upon to deal with policy issues, susceptible of solution merely by the application of judicial reasoning, legal rules and principles to the facts of the case in hand, courts must necessarily seek to present policy arguments in judicial categories. Thus an inherent tendency pulls the Court towards compensatory arguments when it is faced with reverse discrimination debates.

This contributes to legally infected arguments in moral debate. The distinction between law and morals is blurred precisely because of the remarkable role and function of the Supreme Court, which is a public forum – the significance of *amicus curiae* briefs bears this out – for the debate and synthesis of legal and moral principles. The Supreme Court thus functions in an educative role, setting the parameters and style of debate; and moral philosophers in America are much more likely to argue with the Supreme Court very much in mind than are their British counterparts to inform their arguments with the principles and predilections

---

23 J. A. G. Griffith, *The Politics of the Judiciary* (Manchester: Manchester University Press, 1977); Albie Sachs and Joan H. Wilson, *Sexism and the Law* (Oxford: Martin Robertson, 1978).

24 *Adkins* v. *Children's Hospital* 261 US 525 (1923); cf. *U.S.* v. *Darby Lumber Co.* 312 US 100 (1941).

drawn from the House of Lords. American jurisprudence is therefore more a mixture of moral and legal principles than its British equivalent.

One view of the role of the Supreme Court is that it applies the Constitution to the facts of the cases before it according to the strict, literal meaning of the words. This approach, often associated with Justice Black, takes the text as the primary referent and regards it as giving an intelligible rule for conduct. Another approach concentrates upon mediating principles which give somewhat more concrete meaning to the rather abstract ideals embodied in the text. This latter approach treats the Constitution as considerably more flexible than does the mechanical reliance upon the exact words and only the words. It *is* the judges who say what the Constitution is and their interpretation may vary over time. This is caught exactly by Chief Justice Marshall's widely quoted remark: "We must never forget that it is the *Constitution* we are expounding ... intended to endure for ages to come, and consequently, to be adapted to the various crises of human affairs".

The strictly textual approach may fail to provide intelligible rules of decision. The Fourteenth Amendment is couched in very general terms such as "due process of law" and "equal protection of the laws". The Court has written volumes on both phrases, and it is to these volumes – of case decisions – that one must turn in order to glean the mediating principles which inform judicial interpretation of the sterile phraseology of the text. Such a scrutiny may reveal that mediating principles themselves may undergo subtle and even dramatic change over time, according to the perceived needs of society and the moral and political philosophy of the members of the Supreme Court for the time being.

The question whether reverse discrimination is constitutional seems not to admit of an answer being directly read off the text. Rather, one must allude to mediating principles. One principle which is proposed for interpreting the equal protection clause is the antidiscrimination principle; that is to say, when explaining the meaning of that clause, lawyers and philosophers alike tend to suggest that it prohibits discrimination. But of course not all discriminations are prohibited. Even a well-ordered state must make distinctions, e.g. differential treatment of adults and children, of criminal and law-abiding, of sane and insane, etc. The discrimination principle must be understood as prohibiting "invidious" or "arbitrary" discrimination, which is usually understood as discrimination which is unrelated to a legitimate state purpose. The Constitution does not prohibit all discrimination, but it does place the burden of proof firmly upon the State that would enact discriminatory laws. The concept of a "suspect classification" is relevant. There are some classifications which *prima facie* seem so unrelated to any possible legitimate State purpose as to be inherently suspect. Race and gender are obvious candidates.

But even suspect classifications are not absolutely prohibited by the Constitution. Rather, a suspect classification automatically invokes rigorous judicial scrutiny and he who would utilise such a classification is called to account for it. In short, he must show that he seeks to realise a legitimate purpose, that the classification is a necessary means to its realisation and that no other less intrusive means are available. Consequently, one can argue that the Constitution does not prohibit all racial classifications. Indeed in the post-*Brown* period the question raised was whether racial assignment could be used to achieve integration, and by 1971 there was Supreme Court authority for the proposition that when racial assignment is linked to integration rather than segregation, it is constitutionally permissible.[25]

Thus an argument that the Constitution refuses to countenance any racial classifications flies in the face of judicial decisions. Indeed, one might wonder why either *De Funis* or *Bakke* raised such serious issues of constitutional principle, the point having already been conceded in *Swann*. Professor Fiss has argued, I think rightly, that an important distinguishing feature is scarcity.[26]

---

[25] *Swann* v. *Charlotte-Mecklenburg Board of Education* 402 US 1 (1971).

[26] Two articles by Owen M. Fiss, 'Groups and the Equal Protection Clause', *Philosophy and Public Affairs* 5 (1975/6) and 'School Desegregation: The Uncertain Path of the Law', *Philosophy and Public Affairs* 4 (1974/5), are

In the assigning of children to schools one is not preferring racially defined groups in the allocation of social benefits since all children will go to school, whereas in Law or Medical School admissions one is quite definitely depriving members of one race and preferring others. The racial classifications in *De Funis* and *Bakke* are thus harder to justify than those in *Swann*.

We have already seen how the Supreme Court appears to support the Harvard Model and condemn the practices proposed and operated for some time by Washington and Davis. The basis of its case, as explained by Mr Justice Powell, is that less intrusive means are open to universities than those operated by Washington and Davis. Mr Justice Powell, in *Bakke*, appears to regard the state interest involved as being the realisation of a diverse student body, and argues that racial classification is not geared to this end, nor is it the least intrusive means of realisation. But there is more to reverse discrimination than the realisation of a diverse student body, however desirable that may be. There is a conception of distributive justice associated with the idea of equal opportunity. And that too is surely a legitimate purpose, and a purpose more readily in keeping with the preamble to the Constitution of the United States, which alludes to "a more perfect Union", to the establishment of "Justice", to "domestic Tranquillity", and to "the general Welfare", than is the realisation of a diverse student body. And it remains an open possibility that full-blooded reverse discrimination, quotas included, is the least intrusive means of realising a state of equal opportunity, and as such constitutional.

If compensatory arguments are unsatisfactory one might expect them to have led the Supreme Court astray. They have. One can argue, consistenly with American constitutional jurisprudence, that there is no constitutional difference between Harvard and Washington/Davis.

---

among the best of the literature on reverse discrimination. They are reprinted in Cohen, Nagel & Scanlon, pp. 84–154; 155–191. His contribution has influenced this paper considerably, but nowhere more than in this and the preceding four paragraphs.

The Harvard Model is preferred by Mr Justice Powell because, unlike Davis, it pays proper attention to *individuals*. The loser in the competition for the last available place will not have been denied consideration simply because of his race. But, with respect, that is precisely what *must* happen at Harvard as well as at Davis insofar as race functions as a determining, even dispositive, criterion in competitive admissions decisions. Of course, the unsuccessful candidate at Harvard will not know whether he has lost out because he is white and Harvard wants to admit one more minority student to achieve a desirable "mix", or because he lacks the musical or athletic ability of another candidate.

The salient difference is that at Harvard the decisions are made on an intuitive, self-authenticating basis immune from external test or scrutiny, rather as a "just" decision is reached by a Platonic philosopher-king in the *Republic*, and not by way of the rational application of public rules to publicly acknowledged facts on the model of the judicial function in the nomocracy of the *Laws*. At Davis, admissions procedures were clear and determined by public rules, and candidates knew where they stood and could, in principle, understand how they had failed. The programme treated them with dignity and respect and was wholly open to public scrutiny. At Harvard, such is the diversity of the multi-track decisional process that no one can be sure why he had succeeded or failed. Because they are opaque, no one can readily complain that the admissions procedures have been improperly managed. Davis shows as much, if not more, concern for individuals. Its admissions decisions are transparent and it limits arbitrary whim, thus protecting the individual applicant.

But Mr Justice Powell, of course, meant much more than this. He believes that applicants at Harvard will not have been foreclosed from all considerations. But, again, this *must* be so. First, *all* those failing to reach the admission threshold are foreclosed. That means that the Harvard Model forecloses on minority candidates more vigorously than the Davis programme which *considered* (though it might still reject on academic grounds) minority candidates even if they had not attained the basic admission qualifications. To that extent, the Harvard Model is not a model of an affirmative action programme at all. Secondly, it is wholly wrong to say that some whites are not foreclosed upon at Harvard. The only differences between Harvard and Davis relate to precision and volume. At Davis all regular applicants (and possibly all white special applicants) were foreclosed from consideration for 16 of the 100 places. Harvard is committed in advance to securing an appropriate student mix, a commitment which openly includes *ethnic* diversity. Harvard cannot, even for one year, and even by happenstance, actually admit *no* racial or ethnic minority candidates at all; that would raise an almost irrebuttable presumption of traditional adverse racial discrimination. Nor will it admit only 10 or 20 such students out of a total intake of 1,100 for reasons developed in the *amicus curiae* briefs in *De Funis* and *Bakke*. Such would be mere tokenism and would isolate the minority students. Thus Harvard is committed to allocating at least 10 or 20 places, but in fact very many more given the "relationship between numbers and achieving the benefits to be derived". And it simply will not do for Professor Cox to remark that the committee does not set "a minimum number" of minority places. It may not do so formally, but it must have some tacit conception of the approximate "distribution among many types and categories of students" and apply that conception, however tacitly, to its admission decisions.

But this means that once X places have been filled (where $X = 1{,}100$ minus that figure tacitly conceived as appropriate for minorities, whatever it may be and however wildly it may fluctuate from year to year), white candidates are in effect foreclosed from any meaningful consideration. Mr Justice Powell wrote approvingly of the "fair and competitive" procedure at Harvard, but it is precisely at the point here indicated that the competition for places becomes non-competitive! Harvard may suggest and Mr Justice Powell accept, that at any one time all its places are open for free competition to all its applicants – but just as at Davis, there must be a number of places for which white applicants cannot meaningfully compete, even though exactly which places these are, and precisely how many there are, remains opaque.

Nor can the fact that Davis publicly established a quota (in the sense of an irreducible minimum and not an impassable maximum), whereas Harvard does so covertly, provide a difference upon which the Court could properly found. Mr Justice Powell observes: "That the Harvard approach does not also make public the extent of the preference and the precise workings of the system while the Davis program employs a specific, openly stated number, does not condemn the latter plan for purposes of Fourteenth Amendment adjudication ... there is no basis for preferring a particular program simply because in achieving the same goals that the Davis Medical School is pursuing, it proceeds in a manner that is not immediately apparent to the public." It would be a strange and wholly novel constitutional doctrine that that which is unconstitutional is rendered constitutional merely by being kept secret! All in all, Mr Justice Blackmun is dubious as to the soundness of the distinction. He writes: "I am not convinced, as Mr. Justice Powell seems to be, that the difference between the Davis program and the one employed by Harvard is very profound or constitutionally significant. The line between the two is a thin and indistinct one." Associate Justices Powell and Blackmun both acknowledge that the Harvard Model could conceivably achieve covertly what the Davis programme aims at overtly, viz. an adequate and guaranteed level of minority group admissions. But this potentiality is not itself unconstitutional because "good faith in its administration is practised as well as professed." Of course no one is challenging the "good faith" of *Harvard*. But one cannot properly make the constitutionality of a general model hang solely upon a particular matter of fact – namely, the "good faith" of the Harvard faculty. Sir Karl Popper, in his *Open Society*, observes: "Institutions are like fortresses. They must be well-designed *and* properly manned." But proper manning, *per se*, does not render an institutional model constitutional. The design of the institution must conform to the Constitution, and the Harvard Model, being at least potentially a covert replication of Davis, is either disqualified by the Constitution, or the Davis programme, by parity of reasoning, is constitutional.

5.

But the question is not solely whether one can find a constitutional difference between Harvard and Davis, but whether one ought to. And that is a question of morals. And, I submit, if the two are morally different, the difference favours Davis and not Harvard. If we look at the objective to secure an annual intake having an adequate racial and ethnic minority group membership, there can be little to choose between the two on any consequentialist morality except insofar as the consequences of secrecy may tip the balance.

But secrecy itself is challengeable. It is a strange moral principle which applauds the secret transaction of deeds the public realisation of which it condemns. There are standard examples in moral philosophy which develop the point. For example, suppose a university be bequeathed a substantial sum for a purpose dear to the testator but peripheral to the faculty. Suppose the issue for faculty vote is whether to "misapply" the whole or part of these funds to purposes more in keeping with faculty's priorities. There may even be good educational and social reasons for such a "misapplication". Nonetheless, "misapplication" might prejudice receipt of bequests from potential benefactors. Proper application of the fund may squander it or it may lie unused into the entire foreseeable future. Whatever a right answer may be in the circumstances, there is considerable agreement among moral philosophers that the advice "Misapply but keep it secret!" is wholly wrong. And it is wrong, because it is unjust to countermand the clear intention of the testator.

Writing of *De Funis*, Dworkin observed that the Harvard Model might be used to achieve the objectives of the Washington programme, and he added "But if this technique is used deliberately to achieve the same result, it is devious, and it remains to ask why the candid program used by the University of Washington was either unjust or unconstitutional."[27] That question survives the *Bakke* decision. Dean Rusk commented: "in one sense the Law School of the University of Washington was perhaps too formal, maybe too honest, maybe too candid with regard to the matters in the *De Funis* case; and I compliment them for it. But there would have been ways in which they could have handled affirmative action without embarrassing the judges."[28] *Mutatis mutandis* for *Bakke*. It is difficult to exorcise the suspicion that affirmative action is acceptable so long as it is secret! Certainly the *Bakke* decision supports such a view. But the idea of "open government" contains a moral value of considerable weight, no less in the government of universities that in the government of nations, and whatever virtues may grace the Harvard Model – and they are considerable – the decisive criteria and selection procedures are far from transparent.

The argument that Harvard and Davis differ little as to *result* does not entirely dispose of moral questions. Democracy is widely valued not because of its result but because of the sort of process it is, and adjudication, too, is often assessed by reference to so-called rules of natural justice and procedure rather than by reference to the content of the decision. One perspective on Washington/Davis is that it is excessively concerned with results and insufficiently alert to human values which should inform the process. Some seem to think that the separate procedures which characterise Washington/Davis treat individuals as "means only and not ends"; that it herds them into separate pens, like cattle, rather than assessing them individually as human beings, respectful of their personality. I do not, myself, share that perspective in that I do not see Washington/Davis as an affront to human dignity or as in any way productive of stigmata.

Nonetheless, perceptions of this kind coloured both Mr Justice Douglas's opinion in *De Funis* and Mr Justice Powell's in *Bakke*,

---

27 *Taking Rights Seriously*, pp. 223–239, at p. 225.

28 'Preferential Treatment: Some Reflections', in Blackstone & Heslep, pp. 154–160.

leading them to prefer the Harvard Model which, even if it produces like results, produces them by an altogether more sensitive procedure. And there is some validity in this moral stance. Nonetheless, the validity does not touch the issue of reverse discrimination and the explicit or tacit reservation of a number of places for the specified minority group. The fact that the total number of places at a university is divided up into sub-groups such as scientists, sociologists, lawyers and doctors, or minority and majority placement, does not, *per se*, entail anything for the treatment of those individual human beings who actually turn up on the doorstep whatever their aspirations and backgrounds.

It is difficult to assess the *Bakke* decision, given the "many opinions, no single one speaking for the Court". Certainly the Court decided that race can be taken into account in admissions decisions. But what is meant in detail is unclear. Mr Justice Powell refers to "a properly devised admissions program involving the competitive consideration of race and ethnic origin". Clearly he contemplates the Harvard Model. But that Model is hardly an affirmative action programme at all, because Harvard neither opens its doors preferentially to racial minorities, but asks all candidates to satisfy its admissions criteria, race counting, if at all, only at the stage of selection from a pool of qualified applicants; nor does the Model make any provision for ensuring sufficient minority representatives within the pool of qualified applicants.

It is rather difficult, then, to accept Mr Justice Brennan's statement that "the Court ... affirms the constitutional power of Federal and State Government to act affirmatively to achieve equal opportunity for all". It is certainly not true that the Court has approved full-blooded affirmative action on the Washington/ Davis model, though it is worthy of note that of the five Justices who entertained the question, four found such full-blooded affirmative action constitutional. The Supreme Court has not – at least, not yet – approved reverse discrimination.

Indeed, one might interpret the *Bakke* decision as an obstacle to reverse discrimination, in that it holds out as a national paradigm the Harvard Model which is not properly an affirmative action programme at all. Yet the Harvard Model is the preferred model. Such a preference must be a preference for, in the words of Mr Justice Blackmun, "the time when an 'affirmative action' program is unnecessary", that is, a society in which race-consciousness has become so benign and run-of-the-mill that one's race counts for no more, *but no less*, and participates in the definition of one's personality no more, *but no less*, than the full range of human characteristics that make up individual personality. Harvard says, in effect, that race *does not matter*, or at least that it does not matter very much in comparison with other significant personal characteristics. This is diametrically opposed to the Davis programme which treats minority race as of transcendent importance because both in the past and the present, unlike musical or athletic ability, minority race has attracted adverse treatment and promoted inequality of opportunity.

At Harvard race does not matter any more than, or any less than, other significant personal characteristics; it is but one factor among many and it attracts no paramount consideration. The Harvard Model, accordingly, is a model for a post-racist society, and as such it is infinitely preferable. But contemporary America is, emphatically, not a post-racist society, nor will it ever become such if adverse racial prejudice remains institutionalised in education admission and selection criteria and in recruitment and promotion decisions. As Mr Justice Blackmun puts it, "In order to get beyond racism, we must first take account of race".

The Harvard Model does not take account of race in the requisite sense, and it stands, therefore, not as a model, but a negation of affirmative action. It says only that it sometimes happens that race features in the assessment of an individual applicant and may even tip the balance in his favour, given the general commitment to diversity. It does not say that members of racially defined groups ought to find university places as a matter of priority as compensation for past, albeit diffuse, societal discrimination; or in order better to integrate such professions as Medicine, Law or Teaching, or better to integrate society in general. Such compelling state interests can be secured by the minimum necessary means, arguably race-conscious admissions programmes reserving a minimum number of places, quite constitutionally, provided that the causal and empirical assumptions can be discharged.

Race-conscious classifications, though suspect, and calling for rigorous scrutiny, are not automatically invalid. Such classifications can be validated by the purpose or goal aimed at. This is so by virtue of clear and long-established constitutional doctrine and not by virtue of the Harvard Model. Harvard's right to use race in its selection procedures flows from but does not exhaust that doctrine. There seems no good reason why compelling state interest should be restricted to countering societal discrimination, to diversity in the student *milieu*, or to integration of crucial professions and the betterment of their servicing of deprived communities. A post-racist society is a wholly integrated society. Reverse discrimination, even at higher levels of education, can plausibly be said to have an impact on integration in general. Rather than look backwards for discriminatory acts to justify "compensatory" reverse discrimination programmes, a state can look forward to greater social integration and more harmonious race and community relations. It can hazard a compelling state interest therein and it can hope to convince the Supreme Court that admissions procedures reserving a minimum number of places for racially classified candidates are the minimum necessary means to this end. Thus could reverse discrimination be morally and constitutionally justified, *Bakke* notwithstanding. The empirical leg of the proof remains demanding, but the entire argument exhibits a coherence absent from compensatory justification.

Reverse discrimination falls squarely within the realm of social policy along with such practices as compulsory purchase, protection of dockworkers' employment, redundancy payments, special privileges for first-time home-buyers, and inner-city regeneration fostered either by disproportionate rate support grants or by direct payments. Such issues are not obviously judicial, and judges are perhaps no better placed to reach decisions on them than is the politician, the moralist or the citizen. However, if such issues are turned over to the judiciary to determine, as is the effect of the

American legal system, then they will be dealt with primarily in judicial categories such as compensation.

The incoherence of compensatory arguments can be illustrated by a comparison of the *Bakke* with the *A. T. & T.* case.[29] The crucial issue in *Bakke* was the constitutionality of the overt quota-system of admissions operated by Davis Medical School. The Court apparently found that such a practice offended the Constitution. One writes "apparently" because of the diversity of judgements. The Court also found that race could be used as an admissions criterion and commended the Harvard Model.

Broadly speaking, the Court appears to have taken the view that, since Davis had not itself been guilty of adverse discrimination in the past, no case could be made for compensation and quotas were therefore unnecessary, the implication being that, had there been prior adverse discrimination, compensation would have been warranted and quotas might have been the appropriate mechanism. Quite why the interests of a De Funis or a Bakke are to be protected where a university has not discriminated in the past, but overridden where it has, is not stated. Yet this implication is confirmed by the refusal of the Supreme Court to entertain the *A. T. & T.* case.

This was an employment case involving an affirmative action override in recruitment and promotion to favour women and racial minorities, operated by an employer who admitted to having adversely discriminated against these groups in the past. Unions sought to have the consent decree founding the affirmative action override struck down as unconstitutional. The various courts which entertained the case all the way up to the United States Court of Appeals for the Third Circuit rejected the argument. And

---

[29] An employment case, involving an affirmative override procedure for recruitment and promotions, which was challenged on the basis of the Fourteenth Amendment by Unions seeking to protect the collectively bargained seniority rights of their members. The Third Circuit Court of Appeals upheld the affirmative override as constitutional on 22 April 1977 and the Supreme Court subsequently refused to grant a petition for a writ of *certiorari*.

by refusing to grant a petition for a writ of *a certiorari* the Supreme Court decided – at least for the time being – that the decisions upholding quotas should stand.

The crucial difference between *Bakke* and *A. T. & T.* seems to be the presence in the latter and absence in the former of prior adverse discrimination against members of the groups for whose benefit the quotas were proposed. And so the incoherence of compensatory arguments is now fully revealed. If *A. T. & T.* had discriminated against certain minorities, it may be right and proper that it should compensate those who have suffered, or at least that it should take steps forthwith to eradicate such discrimination. And, in conformity with the fault principle, it is right and proper that it bear the costs of such compensation or reforms. But in fact the costs of the affirmative action override are borne not by the employer who has discriminated adversely in the past but by union members whose seniority rights are overridden and who lose out on promotion to women and racial minority members. And, of course, it is as plausible to regard these unionists as innocent of past adverse discrimination as guilty of it. And even if one suggests that they have at least participated in the benefits of the adversely discriminatory practices, it fails to explain why precisely these individuals are singled out to bear the entire costs, whereas other whites, fortunately recruited or promoted before the operation of the affirmative action override, continue to reap full benefit of the adversely discriminatory practice without contributing to the costs of the remedy.

The compensatory arguments seem to allow the American legal system to provide a remedy where past discrimination is apprehended or admitted, but not otherwise. But it departs from the fault principle by arbitrarily fastening on innocent individuals to bear the costs of the remedy. Thus the compensatory argument ultimately destroys itself, being heir to the incoherence which infects its parent, the fault principle. The fault principle says that he who is responsible for a loss or injury should bear the costs of repairing it, and it adds, inconsistently, that if no one is at fault for the loss, the loss should rest where it falls; that is, the fault principle allocates some losses according to arbitrary fortune and not to fault.

But in the case of reverse discrimination the fault principle is doubly incoherent in that a remedy is provided only where prior adverse discrimination is proved, but then the costs of the remedy are borne by wholly innocent individuals and not by those practising the adverse discrimination. Nor can the principle ever begin to explain why a Bakke's interests are more worthy of protection than a union member's collectively bargained seniority rights. The current American situation is that quotas may be appropriate and constitutionally warranted in employment but not in education because, apparently, employers have admittedly discriminated whereas universities have not. This parting of the ways of employment and education is tribute to the power-hold compensatory arguments have upon the American judicial and moral mind. The argument remains incoherent for all that.

Reverse discrimination ought properly to be treated as social policy,[30] a practice deemed appropriate to bring about a more

---

[30] Terrance Sandalow, 'Racial Preferences in Higher Education', *University of Chicago Law Review* 42 (1975), reprinted in Gross, pp. 239–264, develops a similar argument. He holds that "the precise question posed by *De Funis* and like cases, however, is not whether preferential admissions policies are within the competence of a legislature, but whether they are valid when adopted by a university without explicit legislative sanction". Sandalow believes that "[a]lthough there is good reason to sustain preferential policies in any event, the grounds for such a judgment are far less compelling than they would be if the policies had received explicit legislative approval". He understands that "[t]he most compelling reason for sustaining preferential admissions policies is that they offer hope of ameliorating the nation's most enduring problem". He concludes that "... if judges are uneasy about resting constitutional interpretation upon such foundations [empirical, causal arguments about the kind of society we want], the remedy is not to fashion principles which mask the underlying choices. The remedy, rather, is candidly to avow the choices that must be made and develop doctrines that consign ultimate authority for these choices to the legislature, where in a democracy it rightly belongs." With nearly all this, I respectfully agree, but such is the American Constitution that judges must necessarily share "ultimate authority" in fashioning such principles.

equitable society, and not as a specific reaction to past wrongs. Supporters of the practice provide its opponents with gratuitous ammunition by adhering to compensatory arguments in favour of reverse discrimination. Justifications of reverse discrimination based upon isomorphs of compensation are internally incoherent, commencing with the principle that those who suffer a loss should be compensated and its corollary that those who have "caused" no loss should not suffer, and finishing up with the principle that some innocents should bear the cost of repairing some losses. Whereas justifications of reverse discrimination based on distributive arguments are vulnerable only to moral argument, those based on compensation fail to pass even the primary test of internal consistency.[31]

Oriel College Oxford

[31] The author would take this opportunity of thanking Professor G. S. Cowie, Department of Public Law, Glasgow University; Mr Christopher Coope, Department of Philosophy, Leeds University; and Professor Barry Gross, Department of History and Philosophy, City University of New York (York College), for most helpful comments on various earlier drafts of this paper.

ELIZABETH H. WOLGAST

IS REVERSE DISCRIMINATION FAIR?

1.

The defects in a compensatory justification for reverse discrimination are, as Tur argues, clear and crucial. That kind of justification yields the unacceptable consequences that innocent parties bear the cost of compensation while uninjured parties are compensated.[1] It also raises the question whether a whole racial subclass of a society can be blamed for the wrongs done another racial subclass. Then there is the matter of the relation in time between an injury and its compensation. These problems all point to compensation as an inappropriate form of justification for reverse discrimination.

Raising these difficulties is the first part of Tur's thesis. The second part is an explanation why compensatory justification should have been offered at all. In Tur's view, this is due to the role of the Supreme Court in the American form of government. Because the Court has its unique role of "justifying" legislation, those justifications tend to be cast in terms of legal precedent rather than in terms of social policy. The Court is not supposed to formulate social policy, but to pass on the constitutionality of legislation. Therefore it turns naturally to legal precedent, in this case to the tradition of tort law and the rule of fault. Were it not for this role of the Supreme Court, Americans could more easily justify reverse discrimination as social policy, as a means of more

[1] Some of these issues are raised by others, for example by Owen M. Fiss (cited by Tur), 'Groups and the Equal Protection Clause', *Philosophy and Public Affairs* 5 (1975/6): 107–177; George Sher, 'Justifying Reverse Discrimination in Employment', *Philosophy and Public Affairs* 4 (1974/5): 159–70; Robert Simon, 'Preferential Hiring: A Reply to Judith Jarvis Thomson', *Philosophy and Public Affairs* 3 (1973/4): 312–320.

M. A. Stewart (ed.), Law, Morality and Rights, 295–313.

fairly distributing the benefits of society. I will take issue with this conclusion. While I do not know whether the motive behind such programs is a commitment to distributive justice, there are profound difficulties in the way of giving such a justification. Other ideological commitments of a pervasive kind work against it. Indeed, a curious merit of the confusing and legalistic compensatory justifications is that they obscure from view a conflict which runs very deep and defies easy resolution.

2.

Justifying reverse discrimination brings to light what appears to be a contradiction. These programs have as their background and justification practices of bias against members of identifiable groups, chiefly women and racial minorities.[2] Such practices are called "discriminatory," meaning that members of those groups are prevented from obtaining benefits that they would have received if *either* they had not belonged to the group they do *or* their membership in that group had gone unmarked, unnoticed. They would have then had the same opportunity as others to obtain the benefits, which is to say an opportunity to compete on equal terms.

Behind this description is the assumption that discrimination is an evil principally because it interferes with fair competition. To let race or sex influence the outcome of a competition is presumably unfair, just as it would be unfair to let the color of

---

[2] I use the term "bias" here partly because "discrimination" against someone is naturally understood as an expression of dislike or aversion, aversion to the characteristic which identifies a person as belonging to the group they do. But in the case of women it is often untrue that they are denied positions because of dislike or aversion. They may even be viewed with affection by those whose attitudes are biassed. They may, for instance, fail to achieve positions they aspire to because of a perception that they are not serious. This does not constitute discrimination on the basis of sex (which would plainly be wrong) but discrimination on the basis of seriousness (which would seem justifiable). What is at fault is a mistaken perception.

someone's eyes influence it or the quality of one's grandmother's cooking. These factors are irrelevant to merit, and it is merit that should determine success.

Reverse discrimination, then, is a response to the injustice of allowing sex or race to influence competitions. But if this is the case, and what is desired is *fair* competition, then what is needed is a rigorous observance of competitive criteria.[3] What is needed is blindness with regard to sex and race – while reverse discrimination requires the contrary, the *noticing* of sex and racial characteristics and giving them affirmative weight in making decisions. Reverse discrimination thus provides for the *non*-competitive treatment of candidates from the groups which suffered injustice in the past. So that instead of establishing a fair competition, it introduces a new, though well-meaning, form of discrimination. If what was wrong before was that the competition was unfair, this is not a cure so much as another form of the disease. Justifying reverse discrimination seems to commit one to an inconsistent position.

The compensation argument is very useful here if it is not examined too closely. For just as you might give away a point in tennis to "compensate" for a wrong call in your favor, so (it might be said) we give advantage to those who were unfairly disadvantaged in the past. The compensation is moral, like giving away the point in a game. But the compensation analogy is not a good one; we are not in an ongoing tennis match nor are the players now the same as those who profited from discrimination in the past. It is not difficult to understand the claims of De Funis and Bakke that they were denied fair treatment. Reverse discrimination and fair competition seem to be essentially conflicting ideas about what is just.

Perhaps the concepts of fair competition and reverse discrimination can be reconciled by saying that reverse discrimination is

---

[3] This point is made by Alan Goldman, 'Affirmative Action', *Philosophy and Public Affairs* 5 (1975/6): 178–195, at pp. 182ff.

needed as a means toward *making* the competition fair.[4] The question is how this is supposed to work. What will show that the competition finally *is* fair? Will it be when blacks and women succeed in the same proportions as they stand in the whole population? Or when they succeed in proportion to their share in the applications? Furthermore, setting goals in this way may mean adjusting the criteria of success to achieve them and making this adjustment may seem no different in principle, no less an interference with fair competition, than the setting of quotas. One dimension of the problem is that setting the criteria for success may be bound up with one's perception of what qualities are relevant, and this in turn bound up with the group one belongs to. Criteria for success and the characteristics of winners form a circle. On the other hand, adjusting the criteria in order to influence the distribution of winners among different groups may be taken to cast doubt on the "real competence" of the groups for whose benefit the adjustment is made.[5]

Richard Wasserstrom is one writer who sees that the situation is complicated, having many dimensions.[6] Not least is the influence of stereotypes and models, an influence which is subtle and difficult to eradicate. Therefore his ideal society will not recognize sex or racial distinctions at all, but will be "assimilationist" with respect to both. "Reverse discrimination" is a justifiable instrument to achieving a just society, he argues, but once that society exists, such programs will be unnecessary. Competition will then be fair.

Wasserstrom has in mind an idea of a really fair competitive situation, one where sex and race are entirely ignored and affect no decisions, even personal ones. It is a society which is blind to

---

[4] Sher, for instance, sees reverse discrimination as a justified "way of neutralizing the *present* competitive disadvantage *caused* by those past privations and thus as a way of restoring equal access to those goods which society distributes competitively" (Sher, *art. cit.*, p. 163).

[5] This point is made by Goldman, *art. cit.*, p. 187.

[6] R. A. Wasserstrom, 'Racism, Sexism and Preferential Treatment: An Approach to the Topics', *U.C.L.A. Law Review* 24 (1977).

both race and sex, which is to say a society where these have no more importance than eye color has in our society. A weakness of this ideal however is that real differences in perspective, talents and interests may still emerge to affect the competition, skewing the proportion of benefits going to one group or the other. And if that happens, *will* the competition be fair? If not, what will show that it isn't ?

We need to examine and better understand the notion of fair competition if we are to make any progress here.

3.

By fairness, John Rawls has explained, he means what is meant "when one speaks of fair games, fair competition and fair bargains."[7] This is the concept which underlies our idea of justice. Others too compare aspects of society to games – in economics, in law and in social theory. What they suppose is that each individual plays in a comprehensive game which includes all the other members of his society, and plays to enhance his own position and satisfy his desires. To win rewards as a result of fair play in such a game is then a vision of justice, one that appeals to democratic and libertarian thinkers.

How precisely is fairness to be understood as a principle for society? Not all games embody the same kind of fairness: a race is fair if only the fastest runner in it wins; a tennis tournament fairly rewards the match's best player; a chess match goes to the player who is first to checkmate. Whoever plays best in such games ought to win. But other games work very differently – crap shooting, roulette and lotteries, for example. Here a person's skill doesn't enter in, and as far as the persons themselves are concerned, no one ought to win. All players supposedly stand equal and have equal chances. Besides these two kinds of games there are others, and intermediate types where both chance and skill have

[7] John Rawls, 'Justice as Fairness', *Philosophical Review* 67 (1958), p. 178.

some bearing on the outcome; but the two kinds I have illustrated raise some of the important questions which need to be asked about competition and social justice.

Competitions according to skill are clearly associated with non-random patterns of distributing prizes. The player who has a pattern of winning matches will, with some probability, win others; the man who loses consistently will in similar contests be likely to lose again. Many qualifications need to be put in here – e.g., that the player is playing in similar matches against opponents with similar skills – but a pattern is to be expected regarding both players. There are winners and there are losers. A pattern of this kind will not be associated with games of chance, and if such a pattern does emerge this is sufficient to cast some doubt on the fairness of the game. So as the games differ, the way that prizes are distributed will differ, so that a certain kind of result can be expected from each kind of game. If we heard that prizes at Wimbledon went to players who had consistently lost in similar matches, we would want to look closely at how that happened, just as when in a game of craps there is a consistent winner we want to look at the dice. There aren't champions at craps; there will most predictably be champions at tennis.

Suppose we consider the idea of "equal opportunity" in terms of these two kinds of competition. In a game of skill like tennis, an equal opportunity to play is only meaningful for people who can play, and an equal opportunity to compete in a big match still would rest on a player's qualifying for it. On the other hand, an equal opportunity to enter a lottery or play Bingo, if taken, is the same as an equal opportunity to win. This is not to say that an equal opportunity to compete in tennis may not be important for some black players, but the effect of such a policy could only affect a very small number of people and would not do much to redistribute society's goods. It is important to determine what kind of game our social system is being likened to if we are to evaluate the institution of such policies as equality of opportunity and reverse discrimination. It would be irrational to protest that the prizes of Wimbledon are concentrated in too few hands and to propose that they be distributed to past losers because they have lost, or given to representatives of the various areas represented by contestants, or to ardent fans who sit in the rain. These individuals are no doubt worthy in some sense and certainly part of the game, part of the contest and the tradition it belongs in, but they are not the winners of the match.

Where there are openings and choices to be made among applicants, there must be ways of making the choices. As Owen Fiss has said: "Let us suppose the state wishes to pick the best employees for a limited number of openings. That process inevitably involves choices. The state must discriminate."[8]

If the position is to go to the best applicant, then there should be criteria according to which candidates are compared and measured against one another. The competition in this case is like a competition of skill, and the result – the selection of one person for the job – will be done fairly if each individual is treated the same and the criteria applied consistently. If some other conception is involved – e.g., the job should go to the first who applies or to the neediest – then the decision is determined by other factors. And if it is to be done by drawing lots, the decision will be made still differently. What is fair to an applicant depends upon what rules govern the choice, and what *is* fair will be very different in the three cases. Yet equality of opportunity is often allowed to float ambiguously between various interpretations of the nature of the competition. The need for glosses is chronic. For instance, Tussman and ten Broeck, writing about the Fourteenth Amendment, say that

> The Constitution does not require that things different in fact be treated in law as though they were the same. But it does require, in its concern for equality, that those who are similarly situated be similarly treated.[9]

Though this sounds plain enough one has to wonder whether being "similarly situated" means joining the lottery or having six years

---

[8] Fiss, *art. cit.*, p. 109.

[9] J. Tussman and J. ten Broeck, 'The Equal Protection of the Laws', *California Law Review* 37 (1949), p. 344.

as a post-doc or being as poor as other candidates or what. These authors allow for criteria of "relevant differences" which would permit differences in treatment; but what if some of these are associated with race or sex? That would be too bad but there is no "equal protection" against it.[10] Everything hinges here on what kind of competition it is, what kind of game.

John Rawls defends inequalities of benefits if "it is reasonable to expect that they will work out to everyone's advantage, and provided the positions and offices to which they attach, or from which they may be gained, are open to all." But it is crucial to know *how* open to all, what kind of game we are considering, since otherwise the phrase is empty. Rawls gives us an answer: "Any offices having special benefits must be won in a fair competition in which contestants are judged on their merits."[11] This sounds now like the Wimbledon case: anyone can play if he is a superb tennis player.

I am drawing attention to the fact that "fair competition" and "equal opportunity" are ambiguous when applied to how we should treat people when dealing out scarce social goods unless we know what kind of game we are talking about. It isn't fair to pass the prizes of Wimbledon around, like the Secretary General's post at the United Nations, spreading them as widely as possible, no matter how much good this might do. But if the competitive game we play in our society is like tennis the pattern of winners and non-winners will likely continue, and the gap between the benefits of the two groups should continue to widen. But then there will certaintly be greater clustering at the extreme ends of the social scale. And at some point this process may lead to a

---

[10] The Supreme Court has worried about which sex-related criteria justify differential treatment and which do not, for instance in *Phillips* v. *Martin Marietta* (400 US 542 (1971)), and in *Diaz* v. *Pan American World Airways, Inc.* (404 US 950, 92 S.Ct. 275 (1971)). While viewing such criteria with suspicion the Court has refused to consider sex a "suspect classification" as it considers race.

[11] See Rawls, *art. cit.*, pp. 165, 169.

result that is morally intolerable. Can such a result then also be fair?

The central issue is this: the idea of fairness which goes with games of skill cannot be reconciled with a principle of distributive justice. The very *fairness* of such competitions will lead to a result which forces the question, what can be done for the losers? There is no way to answer without putting the game metaphor aside.

We regret the suffering and disadvantage that come to a loser when he loses, and just as we might give a booby prize to the worst competitor, we are inclined to compensate those at the bottom of the competitive ladder so that their losses will not be desperate ones. So after the winners have won we create programs for those who always lose. But this way of proceeding is a transparent stop-gap and plainly inconsistent. If the fairness of competition based on merit is selfevident then no compensation for losing is necessary or justifiable. We cannot have it both ways: either fair competition based on merit is justified or it is not. The question that needs to be addressed is whether this kind of fair competition *is fair*, taken as a principle for society.

4.

There have been numerous discussions about whether social and economic goods should go to those who merit them.[12] Among the defenders of merit as a principle for distributing benefits Gregory Vlastos makes a strong case. He begins by speaking about praise. A man, he says, "should not be praised for merit he does not have." To do so is to "violate the equal right of all persons to be praised in a sound currency if they are to be praised at all." Moreover he says, "praising for merit is something people like to do and do spontaneously... To try to suppress this practice would involve enormous inroads on personal liberty." There is some intrinsic

[12] Among the important papers in this debate I refer the reader to J. J. Thomson, 'Preferential Hiring', *Philosophy and Public Affairs* 2 (1972/3): 364–384, along with those cited in the text.

justification for recognizing merit even though praise is then distributed unevenly; and changing from the currency of praise to that of "economic reward, economic power, and political power", the justification of rewarding merit will remain the same.[13]

Whether people deserve jobs and wealth and privileges because they are qualified to do some job has been debated at length by various philosophers. The issue has led Richard Wasserstrom to challenge, not the connection between merit and desert, but the connection between *having an ability* and having merit. Between these two, he says, there is "tension rather than compatibility." No one merits having the talents he is born with, and so he cannot merit special rewards for having them.[14]

The debate about merit and desert is troubling for the reason that it takes place without a background and therefore the issue shifts as one puts first one background behind it, then another. If we are talking about deserving the prize at Wimbledon then the winner deserves it, the one who beats the others and is (therefore) the best (at this time). That is what deserving the prize means in such a context. A player who didn't really win wouldn't deserve the prize, but that is also to say he wouldn't merit it. In stating these truisms I am supposing of course that talent and skill are involved, abilities the players are born with and abilities trained by people whose care and advice are not deserved at an expense that is not deserved either. But deserving comes with the winning and not at any earlier stage; for it is only in the context of the game that we can talk about deserving in this way. It needs such a background.

If now you ask whether people deserve to have abilities, you are taking away the background, and now there is a question whether this makes any sense. A person doesn't *deserve* to be born to his

---

[13] G. Vlastos, 'Justice and Equality', in *Social Justice*, edited by R. Brandt (Englewood Cliffs, N.J.: Prentice-Hall, 1962), pp. 65, 69, 71.

[14] *Philosophy and Social Issues: Five Studies* (Notre Dame, Ind.: University of Notre Dame Press, 1980), p. 73.

particular family, but it is not *un*deserved either. It is a matter of luck or chance, more like winning at Bingo; you don't either deserve or not deserve the Bingo prize, so long as you are lucky enough to have the right numbers called. You don't deserve to win a lottery either – but that is not to say that when you win you *don't* deserve it, as if someone else did. Talk of deserving is out of place here.

When Vlastos talks about praising people we imagine a kind of background, i.e., one where people are doing things and other people are in a position to admire them. But imagine praising someone for winning at Bingo! What a difference from praising him for giving a good speech or winning at chess or growing a fine garden. In the one context praise makes no sense; in the other it is appropriate. So the question which Vlastos set out to answer, namely whether economic and political benefits should be distributed according to merit, still has to be given a background. When it has a background perhaps *then* we can say whether the answer is Yes or No. Offhand I don't know how to fill this in.

The ambiguity of asking who deserves what in an open-ended and abstract way is brought out by this example of Wasserstrom's:

> Suppose ... that there is only one resource of a certain sort in a community [e.g., a tennis court], and that some people are more qualified to use it than are others. ... Is it clear that the two best tennis players ought to be the ones permitted to use it? Why not those who were there first? Or those who will enjoy playing the most? Or those who are the worst and therefore need the greatest opportunity to practice? ... Each of these criteria appears to be as plausible a candidate for allocation as this idea of being the most qualified.[15]

The example shows very plainly how, when we change the background and look at the use of the court from different points of view, the criteria for its use seem flexible and full of various possibilities. Who deserves to use the court? That depends on how you are viewing it. In the abstract the question has no single answer, but many possible ones. People become qualified when some decision is reached about how to use the courts and criteria

---

[15] *ibid.*, p. 72.

are set up. And how is this decision to be made? Not by using some entirely primitive and fundamental sense of "desert", since there isn't any.

The point can be spelled out this way. In order to speak of desert or merit we need to presuppose some context – a game or a system in which people are ranked and one where individuals are measured against criteria. "Who deserves this or that?" is a question that can only be answered within a system of rules. Even when we say someone deserves a better lot than he has gotten we are thinking of a system in which virtue is rewarded, where people are ranked according to their characters. So the question who deserves to get into medical school needs also to be placed within a context: are we speaking of a school where academic records are the predominant criteria for entrance? Are we speaking of one where other characteristics – personality, a record of public service, for example – count as well? If someone has a good character he may deserve good things, but what would lead us to say that he deserves to be admitted to medical school? That question is too ambiguous standing by itself to answer.

Yet where criteria are laid down and understood, one *can* often speak of a person deserving to be successful; merit and desert both come into the case. Wasserstrom acknowledges that we sometimes take people's qualifications as the main criterion of selection, while in other cases it seems irrelevant.

> As among the applicants who desire to be neurosurgeons or commercial airline pilots, it seems defensible to make the process of selection depend heavily, if not solely, on their respective abilities. But the argument for doing so is not that they *deserve* to be selected because they are the most qualified.[16]

Wasserstrom reads more into "desert" here than seems necessary. As the person who plays best in a tennis match deserves the prize, so does the most proficient pilot deserve the job, other

---

[16] *ibid.*, p. 76.

things being equal. This carries no moral approbation, but only recognizes what kind of competition this is. For the rules of the selection process are supposed to guide one in making the selection, in showing who *should* get the job, and that I take to mean, who *deserves* the job. To choose a lesser qualified candidate and reject the most qualified would be unfair, assuming other things equal; it would betray the criteria laid down and not give the job to the one who most deserves it. In saying that ability has nothing to do with desert Wasserstrom carries his point too far. Sometimes it does and sometimes it doesn't.

Another way of sorting out the connection between qualifications and desert is given by Thomas Nagel, who denies that a connection between merit and desert exists. He says:

> Differential abilities are not usually among the characteristics that determine whether people *deserve* economic and social benefits (though of course they determine whether people *get* such benefits). In fact, I believe that nearly all characteristics are irrelevant to what people deserve in this dimension, and that most people therefore deserve to be treated equally.[17]

Part of what Nagel is saying is supported by my argument: people do not deserve economic benefits because of any set of characteristics. However my reason for saying this is that one cannot say *anything* about what people deserve unless there is some understanding what the background is, how they come to be measured and ranked. Without such a background *no one deserves anything*, but that does not mean they are undeserving either. To step from this conclusion to saying that therefore everyone deserves to be treated equally is wrong. It involves the same mistake as supposing that desert can be considered without knowing what it is desert with respect to, what the game or competition is.

Nagel sees that the problem with reverse discrimination policies is that they are instituted against a competitive background, leaving unchanged the underlying assumption that people are being

---

[17] T. Nagel, 'Equal Treatment and Compensatory Discrimination', *Philosophy and Public Affairs* 2 (1972/3), p. 354.

measured and ranked, and win or lose according to set criteria. With reverse discrimination programs we only transfer

> the same system of differential rewards, suitably adjusted to achieve comparable proportions, to the class of blacks or the class of women. If it is unjust to reward people differentially for what certain characteristics enable them to do, it is equally unjust whether the distinction is made beween a white man and a black man or between two black men... There is no way of attacking the unjust reward schedules (if indeed they are unjust) of a meritocratic system by attacking their racial or sexual manifestations directly.[18]

Competition according to any set of criteria is to start with an unjust and unfair way of deciding who gets what benefits. Changing the rules of the game will not change the competitive assumptions of the social system, which is at the heart of the problem.

In this argument Nagel comes near to identifying the reason why reverse discrimination presents such a problem to American political thinkers. If justice is related to fairness and fairness is understood to relate to a competitive outcome under some set of rules, then reverse discrimination at best muddies the rules under which an outcome was determined to be fair. It is still a competition but now it is one in which the fairness, taken in the sense of games, is corrupted. It is as if the results of a game played with scrupulous observation of rules were declared unfair since the outcome was too one-sided. But if the rules were followed, how could it not be fair?

The problem here is that fairness (as in a game) needs to be dissociated from justice (as in a social system). It is not a self-evident truth that justice in society is like fairness in a competition, particularly one of skill. That is the assumption that needs to be examined.

5.

Tur proposes that a principle of distributive justice would make a better premise for reverse discrimination programs. It is more

---

[18] *ibid.*, p. 357.

just to distribute social benefits widely: this is what reverse discrimination programs would do; hence they should be instituted. In a similar way Wasserstrom proposes that where differences in ability are small they may justifiably be subordinated to other criteria "to achieve a better result overall."[19] Thus, giving greater representation to minorities in colleges and the professions can be justified by the beneficial effects this would have on the community as a whole. There are minimum standards that everyone would need to satisfy, but above these racial differences could be taken into account – for a better society overall.

The problem with these two attempts is that they conflict with a system in which fairness to each individual is a fundamental social value. The idea here is that one should be able to determine with respect to any individual taken separately whether he has been treated fairly or not. Thus, suppose a college admits applicants on a variety of criteria, among them the diversity of the student body. The college believes this makes for a better result overall. Now diversity is not a criterion that an individual can satisfy, nor is a balance of the sexes, nor is geographic distribution. They are not criteria regarding which individuals can compete or be ranked; no applicant is better or worse according to them. Yet the criteria affect the choice of who is admitted. From an individual point of view, choices made using these criteria may seem arbitrary. They have nothing to do with his merit, and it is *that* which should be the issue. Is this kind of decision fair to individuals then?

Whether criteria pertaining to the whole society are fair to particular individuals is a curious question. Just as strange would be the question whether individuals "merit" the treatment they get as a result. Merit and success relate to competitions in a way that "a good overall result" does not. To ask whether an applicant from Minnesota *deserves* to be accepted because he is from Minnesota while one from Long Island (with perhaps higher qualifications) does not, hasn't clearly any sense. Criteria pertaining to a

---

[19] *Philosophy and Social Issues*, p. 77.

group don't concern merit and they are neither fair nor unfair to the individuals whose fate is determined by them. All that fairness to individuals requires is that all be treated alike *under the criteria which pertain to individuals*. There is no such thing as "treating them alike" when it comes to balancing the composition of the group.[20]

Now if the model for justice is fairness as applying to individuals, and this against a background of competition and rules, then it is not consistent to introduce a consideration like getting a better result overall, meaning a more just result. It is not consistent with this model to try to influence the overall result or distribution of benefits. So before the proposal of Tur, or those of Wasserstrom and Nagel, can be considered seriously we need to ask whether the game model should be modified or whether, as Nagel suggests, it should be thrown out altogether if distributive justice is to be brought in; and if the latter, whether we are willing to take this course.

To put the issue in perspective we should observe that American political thought has a traditional conception of how people in society are related. The conception is one of discrete and independent and autonomous persons, each moving on a path defined by its own interests, unrestrained in its "natural state." This conception is found in Locke's assertion that men are "by nature all free, equal and independent."[21] It appears more recently in John Rawls' description of society as a group of persons who have "roughly similar needs and interests, equal in power and ability to guarantee that in normal circumstances none is able to dominate the others." They have competing interests, desires which cannot

---

[20] Ronald Dworkin observes in his article 'Why Bakke has no Case' (*New York Review of Books*, Nov. 10, 1977) that college applicants are *usually* selected according to a variety of considerations, not all of them matters on which students can compete, and that the idea that admissions to graduate medical and law programs depends solely on "merit" is a myth. See in particular p. 12.

[21] *Second Treatise of Government*, paragraph 95. I neglect Locke's proviso partly because it was neglected by the tradition I am speaking about.

be satisfied without conflict with others, and out of such conflicts is the idea of justice born.[22]

The idea that society is a simple collection of individuals who are similar and independent I call "social atomism." It supposes that people in society are related in much the way molecules of gas in a container are – moving freely without interconnection. Within such a model it is evident that justice will concern the competition and from this idea we are led to the idea that justice will resemble the fairness of a game. Since the individuals in the model are all alike, rules which put them all on equal footing will be fair, and such a game will resemble a game of chance rather than a game of skill. One would expect the rewards of such a competition to be distributed randomly, not concentrated in the hands of a few.

The assumption that the units are alike and therefore equal in some natural sense is one which clearly leads to a difficulty, especially as disparities in wealth and power evolve from the initial equality of the starting point. Nagel expresses his concern over such development:

> The liberal idea of equal treatment demands that people receive equal opportunities if they are equally qualified by talent or education to utilize those opportunities. In requiring the relativization of equal treatment to characteristics in which people are very unequal, it guarantees that the social order will reflect and probably magnify the initial distinctions produced by nature and the past. Liberalism... with its meritocratic conception of relevant differences, seems too weak to combat the inequalities dispensed by nature and the ordinary workings of the social system.[23]

The liberal idea of equal treatment comes from the assumption that humans start on the same footing and should be treated the same. It is as if each were given a Bingo card or were allowed to pick a lottery number; there should be nothing to favor the chances of one over others. But this is an assumption not only about the players but about the kind of game they are playing.

---

22 Rawls, *art. cit.*, pp. 171, 175.
23 Nagel, *art. cit.*, p. 353.

And what if this assumption is false and a player can improve his position and that of his children, leaving others who are weaker competitors behind? The assumption of equality supports the idea of open competition; a restraint on the competition would be unfair under the assumption of equality. The reason the liberal idea runs into trouble, then, is that its assumptions lead it there; and it is not so much "too weak to combat inequalities" as it is stubbornly attached to a mistaken view of the nature of society.

A meritocratic society where no compensations are given to people without competitive skills will work to maintain or exaggerate the differences people are born with, and as the disparity grows many of us, like Nagel, become uneasy about the maldistribution of benefits and conclude that something is wrong. We address ourselves to the results; but if the system is fair in the first place we shouldn't need to patch up the results from a sense of fairness. And that very patching up will be perceived by some as *un*fair since it interferes with a competition which in a sense defines what is fair.

My argument is that reverse discrimination policies cannot be justified under this model, for the model supports an open unfettered competition among society's individual members. To tamper with the overall result and be consistent one needs to abandon some assumptions of atomism, principally the assumption of similarity and independence. Then room could be made for the consideration of what is best for the society overall or what is a fair distribution of wealth. Tur's and Wasserstrom's defenses of reverse discrimination are bound to fail without penetrating criticism of the underlying model.

The atomistic model can be seen to fail on a number of counts.[24] It fails to the degree that people are not autonomous but dependent on or responsible for others, and this is a "natural" feature of their lives from the time they are born. Parents seek the

---

[24] For a fuller discussion of the model and its failings, see my *Equality and the Rights of Women* (Ithaca, N.Y.: Cornell University Press, 1980), especially chapters 2, 3 and 6.

welfare of their children, teachers concern themselves with the good of their students, doctors are charged with care of their patients. The model fails too in its assumption that people are similar in both power and endowments, as the results of free competition bear dramatic witness. We have many reasons not to trust its implications.

On the other hand, it is not difficult to see why the assumptions of human equality and autonomy should have been made, for they give a theoretical protection against claims that the citizens should be governed by someone with a special right to do so. On the contrary, this model says that each person can see what his own interests are and pursue them accordingly; there is no need for one person to decide for or rule the others. But using the assumption of self-determination and independence as a model for how people relate to their fellows *in* society leads to inferences that are false and to consequences that are inhumane. The same assumptions that frustrate a justification of monarchy, unfortunately, also frustrate a workable conception of people living together socially.[25]

What is necessary is to reconsider what more appropriate assumptions can be made about humans and their relations in society. Under a more adequate model I do not think we would speak of programs which assist disadvantaged people in gaining favored positions as "reverse discrimination," nor would such programs even seem to conflict with a system which, in its fundamentals, we understand to be equitable and fair.

California State University at Hayward

[25] I neglect here the fact that Locke, who is a paramount atomist, thought it consistent with a justification of monarchy. My justification for doing so is that within the American tradition this juxtaposition seems an anomaly.

JENNY TEICHMAN

REVERSE DISCRIMINATION

The papers by Professor Wolgast and Mr Tur are scholarly surveys of material relevant to the subject of reverse discrimination. Mr Tur surveys court cases and legal decisions relating to such discrimination, while Professor Wolgast gives us an account of the views of philosophers. I will not comment on the facts so presented nor on the scholarship of the symposiasts (which is clearly extensive), my reason being that I am not completely competent to do so. Instead I will discuss four things which seem to me to emerge from the papers. One point is connected with Mr Tur's paper, one with Professor Wolgast's paper, and a third, which I in fact deal with first, is connected with the themes of both papers. I will also towards the end of my remarks discuss a question which Professor Wolgast merely touches on, and which Mr Tur does not refer to at all, but which nevertheless seems to me to be relevant to the topic.

1.

I think Professor Wolgast and Mr Tur might have done more than they did do to warn people off the term *reverse discrimination*. It seems to me that, in writing anyway, they accept this term too tamely. But it is a misleading term which has induced many people to jump to the conclusion that anything *called* 'reverse discrimination' by clever folk such as lawyers and philosophers must just *be* ordinary discrimination turned upside down: the same thing, but directed against a different set of human beings. Its defenders are then set the absurd and impossible task of trying to explain how this bad thing can be a *good* bad thing.

I would like to remind people *firstly* that not all the practices lumped together under the label 'reverse discrimination' are

M. A. Stewart (ed.), Law, Morality and Rights, 315–322.

controversial; *secondly* that while some activities connected with racial discrimination or with discrimination against women have parallels amongst the practices called 'reverse discrimination', very many do not – to take an extreme example, the activities of the Race Relations Board and of the Equal Opportunities Commission in no way resemble those of the Ku Klux Klan – and *thirdly* that the aims and purposes of 'reverse discrimination' are different from those of racial and sex discrimination. Of course some may object that reverse discrimination is similar *in principle* to discrimination according to race or sex: but this, I believe, is just because they *are* looking at words rather than at practices and aims.

Now of course the fact that the words 'reverse discrimination' are a misnomer and are misleading does not entail that the practices or even the aims are all right. That is a further question. As far as I can make out both Professor Wolgast and Mr Tur wish to say that some (possibly most) of the practices called 'reverse discrimination' are all right. So they need to refute certain familiar objections to the practices, and to consider any possible objections to the aims.

2.

From Mr Tur's survey of cases emerges the suggestion that objections to reverse discrimination are founded on a certain restricted model of what is just – a compensatory model. Thus Mr Tur implies, I think, that a different model of justice will enable us to overcome those objections. He implies that the idea of distributive justice will free us from at least some of the objections commonly made against reverse discrimination. I say 'free us from' because it is not absolutely clear to me whether Mr Tur would say that the logical objections can be *refuted* if we adopt a distributive model, or whether he would merely say that there would be fewer, or no, *legal bars* to reverse discrimination if we adopt the distributive model. But as the second alternative is the less interesting, and perhaps too the more dubious, I will assume that he intends the first.

The difficulties Mr Tur finds in the idea of *compensatory justice* do seem to me to be largely imaginary. They are caused by his giving the term *compensation* a much narrower sense than it in fact has. Mr Tur says that the idea of compensatory justice is unsatisfactory because it stems from the fault principle, and the fault principle, he suggests, has something wrong with it. For myself I can see nothing wrong with the fault principle, which simply states, according to Mr Tur, 'that he who is responsible for a loss or injury should bear the costs of repairing it, and... if no one is at fault for the loss, the loss should rest where it falls'. Now this principle simply tells us what to do in two different kinds of case (like the principle 'Feed a cold and starve a fever'). First it tells us what to do when someone is at fault; then it goes on to tell us what to do when no-one is at fault. I suspect that Mr Tur objects to calling the second kind of case a case of *compensation*. Any difficulty that might be felt about the fault principle could easily be overcome firstly by dealing with the verbal anxiety, i.e., by renaming the principle, perhaps as *the fault and no-fault principle*, and secondly by insisting that it is logically possible for compensation to be made for an injury by one who is not at fault and even when no-one is at fault. This can easily be proved by means of examples. The Criminal Injuries Compensation Board compensates victims of crime, but neither the Board nor the taxpayer is *at fault* here. Insurance companies compensate people for injuries caused by e.g. thefts and other crimes; they also compensate people for injuries caused by accidents: it would be absurd to argue that in the latter case the insurance company itself must be at fault, or indeed to argue that anyone is at fault. When the villages near Etna were engulfed by lava early in 1979, the inhabitants asked the Italian Government to compensate them for this Act of God.

Opponents of reverse discrimination often refer to the fact (if it is a fact) that no-one living now is responsible for the backward state of blacks and women. But this supposed fact does not at all rule out the possibility of compensation. Compensation is not the same thing as reparation. All reparation is compensation but not all compensation is reparation.

I conclude that the idea of compensatory justice has nothing wrong with it, and that it has not been shown so far that this idea could not explain and justify reverse discrimination.

Mr Tur suggests, I think, that the idea of distributive justice is more apt for explaining and/or justifying reverse discrimination than is the idea of compensatory justice. But it seems to me that distributive and compensatory justice complement each other: they are not separate self-enclosed systems of thought. Not all distributive justice is compensatory, but all compensatory justice is distributive in that it always involves a kind of re-distribution. For this very reason it turns out to be a good idea to bring the notion of distributive justice into the discussion, as Mr Tur has in fact done. It repairs a certain lopsidedness; and it also enables us to raise questions about aims. For instance, it allows us to ask the question: What after all is *wrong* with a state of affairs in which women and blacks have less say in government and public life than do white men? Is it wrong just because blacks are not as dumb as we thought they were, and that women aren't as lethargic as we thought they were? Is that *all* that's wrong with it? (I will return to this question a little further on.)

3.

Professor Wolgast, in her very first sentence, agrees with Mr Tur that a compensatory account of justice will not explain or justify reverse discrimination. In the course of her paper, though, she also refers to some of the difficulties found in the idea of distributive justice. This comes out particularly in her discussion of Nagel's opinions. On the whole she appears to prefer the notion of distributive justice to that of compensatory justice.

She notes an assumption found in some writers to the effect that 'fair competition' will bring about justice. She then argues, rightly I believe, that 'fair competition' is an ambiguous expression. She distinguishes two senses of the expression, the *roulette sense* in which a game is fair if and only if every player has an equal chance of winning, and the *chess sense* in which a game is fair if and only if the best player has the best chance of winning. Professor Wolgast says that a society which rewards people according to skill or merit is not guaranteed distributive justice – in fact, she says, meritocracies tend towards a maldistribution of goods and benefits. Thus she suggests that maldistribution could only be avoided if people were all equally meritorious and skilful; so that chess became as it were like roulette. However, since human society is not 'atomistic' (a *separate* point, I think), and since skills and merits never are equal, the roulette model cannot apply anyway. Whether Professor Wolgast thinks that maldistribution is more likely in a society which distributes goods according to merit than in one which distributes goods randomly as in roulette, is not clear, since she does not discuss the possibility of maldistribution in the latter kind of society.

Maldistribution can indeed occur in a meritocracy, but it could also occur in a roulette-style society. We need to distinguish two kinds of maldistribution: in the first kind the wrong people get the benefits, and in the second kind the right people get the benefits but the benefits are too big or too small; both kinds of maldistribution can occur in both kinds of society under discussion. Thus a meritocracy which adheres to the ideals of liberty cannot prevent the meritorious from syphoning off the benefits they have earned to the non-meritorious, through patronage, and free gift, and through Wills and Trusts. Hence a libertarian meritocracy needs an ideology which teaches that the heirs of the meritorious are themselves meritorious: for without such it must either give up liberty or else stop calling itself a meritocracy. A roulette-style society could just as easily syphon off benefits to non-players if it was libertarian in spirit. As to the other kind of maldistribution: in chess and also in roulette the rules determine both who is the winner and (in a given game or contest) what the prize shall be. The only way in which the prize can be too large or too small is for its size to be determined in some way that violates agreed procedures. In human society taken as a whole the rewards are not and cannot be fully determined in advance by pre-existing rules. It is quite possible for the reward to turn out to be non-existent, or, on the other hand, for it to be much larger than anyone could have predicted. Often enough the size and nature of the reward is determined by the winners after the game – as if a winning boxer were permitted to choose his prize-money after the knock-out. Thus the idea of maldistribution here is only partially tied to the idea of rules: it is partly also generated by ideas about social good and about equality of needs. Without these ideas, the idea of maldistribution (in the sense of rewards being too large or small) could not exist in the absence of pre-existing rules. It is obvious, I think, that maldistribution of this kind is not special to meritocracies. It could occur just as easily in a roulette-style society as in a meritocracy. Its causes are not special to meritocracies: they are, first, the fact that prizes and rewards are not determined in advance and so might turn out to be almost anything, and, second, the possibility that sometimes at least the size and nature of the prize is determined by the winner.

I conclude that maldistribution cannot be removed by de-emphasising skill and merit.

4.

Let us now consider the benefits whose distribution we want to be fair. It seems to me that not enough is ever said about the differences there are between different kinds of benefit; in fact it appears to be the mission of men like Rawls to blur and gloss these differences as much as possible. Some things which philosophers often call 'benefits' hardly seem benefits at all, to me, except *per accidens*. For instance, it is quite common for philosophers to describe jobs, particularly perhaps academic jobs, as 'benefits' or 'rewards' – as if universities existed for the sake of the professors and hospitals for the sake of the doctors! Work benefits the worker of course, but surely its main aim is not that – real work must be useful to others besides the worker. So work must not be botched. This applies to all work, not only to the work of airline pilots and surgeons. If your lawyer botches his job you might end up in gaol, and if your philosophy teacher botches his job he will spoil your brain. If work was of benefit to the worker only, it would probably not be work at all; it would be a sinecure.

On the other hand it is foolishness to suppose that skill is the only thing that matters in deciding how many jobs there shall be, and who shall have them. Work is not merely the activity which creates goods and services and benefits: it is also the activity which pumps the goods etc. around the community; and unless and until we invent a new pump, skill will remain only one of several factors that must be considered when deciding how many jobs there should be and who should have them.

Of course work does produce benefits for the worker as well as for others. There are first-order benefits, like money and status, and there are second-order benefits, which one might also call rights. Briefly, I call a benefit 'second-order' if it involves playing a part in deciding how society is to be run: this includes making decisions which determine how the first-order benefits are to be distributed. Some jobs have only first-order benefits; others have both kinds. Jobs which involve making decisions which determine how things shall be run include political jobs of all kinds, advisory jobs, the law, administration, etc. It is in my view a *serious* mistake to suppose that the reason why women and blacks should have such jobs is purely on account of the good pay and status that usually attaches to such posts. It is in a way a kind of accident that first-order benefits and second-order benefits go together. One can *imagine* a society in which the powerful people had to take a vow of poverty. If first-order benefits and second-order benefits were separated it would be more important that women and blacks had access to the second-order benefits than to the first-order benefits, for the second-order benefits are connected with the freedom and dignity of the individual, the group, and the society.

Consequently, although skill is an enormously important factor in the above jobs, it cannot be the only factor. Another factor is representation. The main reason why women and blacks should be getting into jobs such as politics, law, medicine, administration, and high-powered business endeavour, is the same kind of reason why, in India, most civil servants ought to be Indians: why, in Denmark, the P.M. ought to be, not the most suitable person in the world (= a form of colonialism perhaps) but the most suitable person in Denmark. Again, it is the same kind of reason as the reason why, if a Jew would prefer to employ a (relatively) dumb Jewish lawyer in preference to a (relatively) more able non-Jewish lawyer, then that option ought to be open to him, not only in Israel, but wherever there are Jewish citizens. The reason or reasons have to do with self-determination, and self-determination is an issue that arises not only between nations but also inside nations. Just how to describe the principles involved, and just how to settle the question about what to do when principles conflict (e.g., when the principle that work should not be botched conflicts, as is logically possible, with the principle of self-determination), would need a whole book.

Of course it will be argued that in Britain and the USA blacks are not a separate group requiring self-determination; and that women are not a separate group anywhere. But this, it seems to me, is a reason *for*, not a reason *against*, their being represented at all levels at which social decisions are made. If they were tourists it wouldn't matter: as they are or ought to be citizens it does matter.

New Hall Cambridge

RICHARD H. S. TUR

CONCLUDING COMMENTS

In my original paper I sought to argue that compensatory justice is simply the wrong model for justifying reverse discrimination and I *suggested* that distributive justice might provide a more appropriate model. Jenny Teichman, in her summary of the issues raised and discussed by Elizabeth Wolgast and myself, drew attention to one (though not necessarily the only) obscurity in my paper, namely whether I thought that adoption of the distributive model would allow one to *refute* the objections to reverse discrimination or merely render one psychologically freer to accept it. Now I certainly did not intend the first of these, and though I can see that the second is indeed a likely empirical consequence of my argument, I did not intend it either! Rather, operating at the level of criticism of the *style* of argumentation, I proposed something akin to a "paradigm shift", leaving it to experts in the area of distributive justice to exploit or explode my proposal.

Elizabeth Wolgast, in her very interesting paper, dealt with me rather generously and, much as I had hoped, turned attention to the nature of distributive justice as fairness to ask whether reverse discrimination could be justified by such a style of argumentation. Although sympathetic to my general attack on the compensatory model, she offered arguments which suggest that a distributive model has major difficulties to face. Ultimately, founding upon a rejection of social atomism,[1] she would press on to a vision of society in which neither compensatory nor distributive justifications were apt, rather as the Harvard model contemplates already a post-racist society. Other commentators, most noticeably Barry Gross, would insist that distributive justice, too, is simply the

[1] Cf. R. H. S. Tur, 'Anarchy versus Authority: Towards a Democratic Theory of Law', *Archiv für Rechts- und Sozialphilosophie* **63** (1977): 305–325.

M. A. Stewart (ed.), Law, Morality and Rights, 323–330.

wrong model for justifying reverse discrimination.

Now, if my critics are correct in their rejection of the distributive model, it might prove necessary to refurbish the compensatory model in order to justify reverse discrimination. If, however, my demolition of the compensatory model is well-founded, then one must either cast around for yet another model, and candidates seem rather thin on the ground, or seek to render the distributive model more plausible. This afterword offers some pointers, first, towards refurbishing the compensation model and, secondly, towards not so much a further model as a revised and fuller version of a model based upon distributive justice. This latter enterprise is much indebted to Elizabeth Wolgast's incisive and lucid treatment of fairness and to various comments offered by participants in the conference.

1. THE COMPENSATORY MODEL

Several of the contributors, not least Jenny Teichman, criticised what might be called the "legalistic" conception of compensation which I used. Granted, they said, that *if* one understands compensation within a tort lawyer's frame of reference then it cannot adequately furnish a justification of reverse discrimination. But why should one accept the tort lawyer's terms of reference? As Mrs Teichman countered: "All reparation is compensation but not all compensation is reparation". And this is fair comment. The lawyer has no exclusive lien on terminology. "Compensation" in ordinary and philosophical usage is a wider and looser term than I allowed. Examples include the Criminal Injuries Compensation Board whereby some victims of some crimes are "compensated" by the state although the state and its taxpayers are wholly innocent of the wrong which caused the loss for which the victim is "compensated".

Nowhere did "legalism" infect my argument more seriously than in my treatment of groups. I argued that those who thought that groups (rather than individuals) could not be compensated were wrong and cited legal examples to support my case. But then

I concluded that the groups contemplated by reverse discrimination simply were not the kind of group which could feature in my "legalistic" compensatory model because they lack the unity or integrity of a corporation or a state. Fortunately doubts on this point had already assailed me before I presented my paper, and I was able to pre-empt anticipated criticism with an example from the history of legal education which shows that different societies or different times might unify or integrate individuals into groups for the purposes of compensation rather differently from the way inheritors of the liberal tradition do today.

Bologna was the original law school. It became an international centre for legal studies. So much so that Emperor Frederick Barbarossa, in 1158, granted special privileges to its students. He promised them his protection during their journeys from their homes to Bologna. He exempted them from the jurisdiction of the city of Bologna and subjected them to the discipline of the professors – a rare privilege, for just as businessmen even today prefer commercial arbitrators to the courts of law so, in disciplinary matters, most students prefer professors to the police! Most important, he prohibited reprisals against students. In the Middle Ages it was considered lawful and just that a citizen of one community should be held responsible in a foreign city for any debts incurred by any citizen of his community. Therefore a student going to Bologna would run the risk of prosecution for the unpaid debts previously incurred in Bologna by his fellow citizens.

The exemption granted to students is less important from our point of view than the existence of the practice of reprisals generally, which exemplifies a principle of unification or integration of individuals for compensation purposes quite different from that contemplated by the liberal tradition. Why should I assume that the principles of the law of tort should be replicated in current moral thinking? There appears to be no good reason for such a belief. The moral philosopher might argue that implicit in our moral judgements are principles, including principles of unification and integration of individuals for the purpose of compensation as "moral entities", quite different in content from those implicit in legal thought. Some minority groups are just such entities, so his argument would continue, capable therefore of attribution of a range of moral characteristics, including, in this particular, the ability to suffer collectively and to be collectively "compensated" by way of favourable treatment of representative members. On such an argument such groups would have a moral right to be compensated, and that would provide a thoroughgoing justification for the practice of reverse discrimination.

This severance of compensation and legal argument would, however, attack my paper in another way. I was disposed to illustrate the inconsistent and morally unacceptable effect of the very model which I perceived as operating upon the judicial mind. My defence for adopting the tort concept of compensation is its intuitive familiarity to the judicial mind together with the circumstance that in American political thought and moral debate it is the judicial mind, through the medium of the Supreme Court, which tends to set the parameters of discussion. To that extent I was concerned to analyse and criticise a justification which, so it seems to me, is actually operative upon the judicial mind and which has adverse results.

Only later did I turn to an alternative model, and it is at this point that those who criticised my tort concept of compensation return with a model of their own in opposition to my distributive model. I set up a model – Model A ("tort" compensation), criticised it, and suggested an alternative model – Model B (distributive justice). My compensation critics offer a third model – Model C ("moral" compensation), as yet an ill-defined model, to replace Model A. But even my compensation critics conceded that I had demolished Model A. Thus the arguments towards refurbishing compensatory models are not really arguments between these critics and myself as to the substance of my paper. Rather they turn upon the proposition that arguments from moral compensation could do what arguments from tort compensation cannot do, namely justify reverse discrimination. Whether my model (A) or their model (C) is really *the* compensation model is thus exposed as a sterile verbal controversy, but I am indebted to such critics for showing that these two approaches were not sufficiently distinguished in my paper and for showing that I may have extrapolated from tort compensation to moral compensation rather too uncritically.

2. DISTRIBUTIVE JUSTICE AND THE ADJUSTMENT OF COMPETITION: DEFINING RULES IN THE LIGHT OF RESULTS

Were I to accept the claims of Model C, I would be spared the task of fortifying Model B. Elizabeth Wolgast's discussion of fairness provides a basis for understanding reverse discrimination. She ties reverse discrimination to the idea of fair competition and observes that they seem "essentially conflicting". Yet reverse discrimination might be an appropriate instrument for correcting unfairnesses which have crept into fair competition, though there are difficulties of detail. Further, as she acknowledges, the whole approach is vitiated by the non-transparency of "fairness". Philosophers frequently turn to a game analogy to elucidate but, as Professor Wolgast points out, "different kinds of game involve different notions of fairness". Thus chess-playing and crap-shooting are contrasted; one explains fairness in terms of merit or skill, the other, in terms of equal opportunity. Which is the appropriate social model?

It seems to me that both are, and that the social dilemma is: Where should one model stop and the other start? Or again: are there some social benefits which should be secured to all and others for which there should be competition? Suppose a society adopted the meritocratic principle as exhaustive. The results are described by Elizabeth Wolgast. Eventually it becomes clear that something has gone wrong; the outcome is "morally intolerable". Ought the meritocratic principle to be wholly abandoned and replaced by the equal opportunity principle? Well, though Professor Wolgast does not draw the conclusion so clearly, it is implicit in her citation of Judith Thomson's comment on university students having a right to good teachers that exhaustive allegiance to this principle, too, would have morally intolerable consequences.

It is easy to show that neither principle is suitable on its own when brought to the test of consequences. It is not at all easy to transcribe the point at which one should move over from the one model to the other. Nor can we turn to any neutral and absolute concept of fairness as a criterion. Adjusting competition rules, be they merit-related or random, may appear "a transparent stop-gap". But is it really? If we had access to an absolutely just cluster of competition rules, such tinkering would be a stop-gap and even irrational. But such is the nature of the human predicament that we are denied such access. The pursuit of justice in society is therefore a continuous and never-ending experiment, and societies adjust the principles whereby they seek to realise justice in the light of experience.

All persons, by virtue of their being, may have certain basic "rights" such as well-being and freedom. Beyond such rights, burden and benefits may be allocated according to behaviour, including merit. Whether a particular benefit falls into one or other system of allocation varies from society to society and over time. My paper could have been understood as seeking to remove access to university and the "learned" professions from the behaviour ("tort") system of allocation to the being ("right") system. But this oversimplifies. Doubtless education could be included as a basic right, but it is less clear that University education or Law or Medical School placements are.[2] If these are not basic rights, reverse discrimination cannot be justified by an appeal to such rights.

But we need not adjust our competition rules solely in the light of a concept of basic rights, though that remains a powerful candidate. We can argue that the undiluted meritocratic selection process has adverse results for crucial sections of the community and for society generally. Then we might seek to adjust the rules to modify the outcome. Any such adjustment is a hostage to fortune and may itself be re-adjusted in the light of further experience. Thus reverse discrimination need not be tied directly

---

[2] See Dworkin (cited in my paper) and Thomson (cited in Wolgast's paper).

to basic human rights and that is helpful because such rights are notoriously difficult to define or agree. As against which, the empirical leg of such justification remains difficult and ultimately can be "tested" only by experience. And identifying the results of competition rules as "intolerable" turns upon some fundamental moral proposition which may refer to "basic rights" such as equal opportunity.

Two concluding points may now be made. First, reverse discrimination is by no means the only instance of adjusting competition rules in the light of dissatisfaction with results. The law relating to monopolies and mergers, to restrictive trade practices, anti-trust laws in America, the development of *contra proferentem* rules in judicial interpretation of contracts, the implication by the common law of terms into contracts, contracts contrary to public policy, employee protection legislation and the consumer protection movement, etc., are all instances drawn from an area of the law until relatively recently thought to be determinate and certain, resting upon clear rules and principles, but increasingly discussed in policy terms.[3] Freedom of contract, the market economy and entrepreneurial zeal continue to be valued, but increasingly the idealised competition rules which defined the classical concepts are subject to adjustment as society perceives that some results of undiluted contractual freedom are detrimental to society at large or to particular groups.

The same process features in government's traditional response to periods of free collective bargaining. Here the competition rules are perhaps less widely accepted than even the rules defining freedom of contract and the free market, and certainly than the competition rules regulating admission to university and the "learned" professions; but even so, free collective bargaining remains for many a value to be maintained, and it is embodied in the current

[3] See P. S. Atiyah, *The Rise and Fall of Freedom of Contract* (Oxford: Clarendon Press, 1979); G. Gilmore, *The Death of Contract* (Columbus, Ohio: Ohio State University Press, 1976). See, too, EEC Treaty, articles 3, 113, 116 on "distortion" of competition and exploitation of dominant position.

Labour Law legislation of the United Kingdom. But, invariably, after a period of untrammelled free collective bargaining, government points to the results, not only inflation and unemployment, but also the unfair distribution of incomes achieved by free collective bargaining, and introduces, by statute or otherwise, an incomes policy, thereby changing, all too dramatically, the competition rules.

Perhaps such adjustment of competition rules in the light of results is a far wider feature of modern society than I indicate, and at least one writer suggests that such adjustment, by way of judicial discretion and open-ended standards, is a defining feature of what he calls "post-liberal society".[4] Be that as it may, suffice it here to observe that reverse discrimination is in no way unique once it is understood as the adjustment of competition rules in the light of the unacceptable consequences of the unadjusted rules.

The second concluding point is that this brief treatment of reverse discrimination as the adjustment of competition rules does not by itself provide a justification of reverse discrimination. What I have described is a mechanism, not a reason. Such a mechanism comes into play once results have been identified as unacceptable. If one believes that the existing competition rules for admission to university and for recruitment and promotion in employment have adverse results, adjustment is called for. Thus reverse discrimination is a rational response to a situation perceived as "morally intolerable", but its justification will turn ultimately on quite how intolerable one regards the results of the unadjusted rules. But opposition to reverse discrimination flows not only from a readiness to accept certain harsh outcomes, but also from a belief that these competition rules are the best approximation to absolute justice that society has, and much better than any *ad hoc* interventionism can attain. The reverse discrimination debate thus exhibits a clash not only of models of justification but also of conceptions of justice and political philosophies.

Oriel College Oxford

[4] See R. M. Unger, *Law in Modern Society* (New York: Free Press, 1976).

PART VI

DURESS

LORD KILBRANDON

DURESS *PER MINAS* AS A DEFENCE TO CRIME: I

The title calls for two definitions, or perhaps rather descriptions. A man acts *under duress* when another persuades him, by the uttering of threats, to commit a criminal act which, but for the threats, he would not have committed. The threats are threats of personal violence directed either against himself or against those with whom he has a close family connection. They would not, for my present purposes, include threats to expose the victim to ridicule, contempt, financial loss or criminal proceedings. Threats to injure a stranger, or even someone, such as the sovereign, whom the victim is under a public duty to protect, are not included. That is why this is a description rather than a definition; I am limiting the scope of the discussion to more manageable proportions. *Defence* can mean one of two things; I will take my illustrations from the crime of murder. First, if a man charged with murder shows that he killed a violent assailant who would otherwise have killed or seriously injured him, he is entitled to an acquittal. He has a good defence. To kill in such circumstances is not murder or any other crime. It is as lawful as is a killing by the public executioner or by a soldier in war. Secondly, if he satisfies the jury that he killed because he was subjected to intolerable provocation – for example, that he came on his victim and killed him in the act of adultery with his wife – he will be entitled to have the charge reduced from one of murder to one of manslaughter. His homicide was unlawful, but his culpability was reduced. He has a complete defence to the major charge, resulting in a verdict of not guilty, but not to the minor charge, to which he can plead provocation as a defence only in mitigation of sentence.

It is a commonplace that guilt of serious crimes – we have to exclude such offences as selling beer to infants – rests upon responsibility for a guilty intention. There can be no criminal act

M. A. Stewart (ed.), Law, Morality and Rights, 333–343.

without a criminal mind. The law will therefore not convict, let alone punish, insane persons or babies. How then, for example, does he who kills under duress stand in regard to guilty intention? His intention is plain – to kill as ordered. He has a motive too – though this is something with which the law is not commonly concerned. He formed the intention and carried it out in order to save his life or that of a near relative. But in so doing he acted in a way in which he would not have acted except under what he regarded as compulsion. *"Quamvis, si liberum esset, noluisset, tamen coactus voluit"*, as the civilians have it.[1] The act, as an act, he knew to be unlawful, though to say he knew he was wrong to commit it would be to beg the very question we are discussing. Is he, perhaps, to be regarded as a mechanism actuated by him who threatened, just as if the latter had physically forced the former's finger to press a trigger? If he is, guilty intention does not arise, because the threatener, not the threatened, committed the act. But this proposition seems to be ruled out by the very efficacy of the threat; the man threatened always had the choice between sacrificing his own life and that of his victim. He chose to do one wrong thing in order that another wrong thing might be avoided. It was a real choice, and one does not make that any less true by emphasising how difficult a choice it was, or how unreasonable it is to demand a high degree of heroism from the ordinary man. It was the fact of the reality of the choice which made the threat so horribly effective. The man may have had to choose between exposing his own children to the prospect of violence, and agreeing to kill the father of someone else's children. *Ex hypothesi* he chose the second of the alternatives.

The same considerations, to my mind, affect an analogous defence, that of *necessity*. Necessity is by some legal authorities distinguished from duress upon the ground that the latter is an instance of compulsion by human, the former by natural forces.

---

[1] See Andrew McDouall (Lord Bankton), *An Institute of the Laws of Scotland in Civil Rights*, Volume 1 (Edinburgh: Kincaid, Donaldson, 1751), p. 255.

For my part, while I appreciate the verbal distinction, I have some difficulty in applying it to the question of criminal responsibility. How far is a man to be permitted to commit criminal acts in order to mitigate the effect on himself of some natural calamity which he cannot otherwise avoid, and how does that problem differ, if it does differ, from that which presents itself when he is faced with human action capable of overwhelming his moral judgment? The classic case was tried in England in 1884.[2]

> Three men and a boy escaped in an open boat from the shipwreck of the yacht Mignonette. After having passed eight days without food, the men killed the boy in order to eat his body. Four days later, they were rescued by a passing ship. On their arrival in England two of the men were tried for the murder of the boy. The Court of Queen's Bench declared emphatically that there is no general principle of law which entitles a man to take the life of an innocent person in order to preserve his own.

The men were convicted, but their sentence was commuted to one of six months' imprisonment.

I have been quoting from Professor C.S. Kenny's *Outlines of Criminal Law*, the last edition for which that very learned author was personally responsible.[3] There follows what I find a most significant passage:

> The defence of necessity, however, can only be important where ... there is a prescribed minimum of punishment. For in all others every English judge would take the extremity of the offender's situation into account, by reducing the sentence to a nominal penalty. But in continental countries (where a minimum is frequently set to punishments) the necessity of averting grave bodily harm is often raised as a defence. See the penal codes of Italy, Germany, Hungary, Switzerland, Spain, Belgium.

This appears to me to be applicable with precisely equal force to the defence of duress. It will be noticed that in my paper I have been taking illustrations, as people always do, from the law of murder. The two recent cases which have no doubt given rise to

---

2 *R.* v. *Dudley & Stephens* (1884) L.R. 14 QBD 273.

3 C. S. Kenny, *Outlines of Criminal Law*, 12th edition (Cambridge: Cambridge University Press, 1926), pp. 75–6.

this debate, first *Lynch*[4] in the House of Lords, second *Abbott*[5] in the Judicial Committee of the Privy Council, were both murder cases carrying mandatory sentences. I took part in both these appeals, and will say something about them in a moment. But if, on the one hand, murder did not carry a mandatory penalty, or if, on the other, duress as a defence were to resemble provocation, giving rise to a change in the degree of criminal responsibility attributable to the accused, rather than resembling self-defence, giving rise to complete exculpation as being justifiable homicide, I hardly think this problem would be enjoying its current popularity in philosophical and legal circles.

There are certainly to be found in the reports, though they are rare and not particularly impressive, cases other than murder cases in which duress has been held a complete exculpatory defence. Examples are theft (or receiving) during political unrest in Ireland,[6] and even treason during the civil war of 1745/6.[7] Necessity, if it be (as I think it is) a close analogy, has been even more rarely set up as a defence, and textbook writers are forced into inventing fanciful debating-society possibilities. Kenny asks about the man who goes off at night to fetch the fire-engine on a bicycle which has no lights. But, as I have said, he has his feet on the ground when he says that only in the case of a mandatory penalty does the question arise in a practical sense. An antiquarian example, which I ventured to quote in *Lynch*, is the Scots common law of burthensek, under which a man charged with a theft which would be capital could plead that he took only as much food as he could carry away on his back. Hunger was his necessity. But here too, according to Hume,[8] the effect of the plea was not exculpatory, but mitigatory. The plea would save the prisoner's life.

---

4 *D.P.P. for N.I.* v. *Lynch* [1975] AC 653.
5 *Abbott* v. *The Queen* [1977] AC 755.
6 *A.G.* v. *Whelan* [1934] I.R. 518.
7 *R.* v. *MacGrowther* (1746) 18 State Trials 391.
8 David Hume (Baron Hume), *Commentaries on the Law of Scotland Respecting Crimes*, 3rd edition, Volume 1 (Edinburgh: Bell & Bradfute, 1829), pp. 55–6.

When, under the heading of necessity, it is a question of balancing public utility, as opposed to personal advantage, against the commission of a crime, I would respectfully agree with a view expressed by Professor G. H. Gordon.[9] He begins by quoting a French commentator:[10]

> Le délit nécessaire ne peut ... être considéré comme un acte antisocial; il a été socialement utile, si le bien sauvegardé était supérieur à celui qui a été sacrifié, et socialement indifférent, s'il était de valeur égale.

He goes on:

> This, it is submitted, is an appropriate approach, provided that the calculation includes the negative value of lawbreaking in arriving at the equivalence of values. Where the values are equivalent necessity should operate as an excuse. Any system of law must, however, endeavour to avoid the occurrence of a situation of this kind, and normally the negative value of the crime involved will tip the balance.

This is probably the true conceptual distinction between necessity and duress.

Until fairly recently, there was unanimity in the common-law world on this – that neither duress nor necessity was a good defence to a charge of murder. An exception was to be found in a South African case,[11] but South African law is not always classifiable as a common-law system. Then came a case in 1968 in South Australia,[12] in which the Chief Justice, in a dissenting judgment, expressed the opinion that duress might be a defence to a charge of complicity in murder, but "I do not think duress could constitute a defence to one who actually kills or attempts to kill the victim." This leads me to the two appeals to which I have referred.

Lynch was convicted in Northern Ireland in 1974 on a charge of murder in the following circumstances. He said that he was ordered

---

[9] G. H. Gordon, *The Criminal Law of Scotland*, 2nd edition (Edinburgh: W. Green, 1978), p. 422.

[10] H. Donnedieu de Vabres, *Traité de Droit Criminel et de Législation Pénale Comparée*, 3rd edition (Paris: Sirey, 1947), p. 224.

[11] *Reg.* v. *Hercules* 1954 (3) SA 826.

[12] *Reg.* v. *Brown & Morley* [1968] S.A.S.R. 467.

by a dangerous gunman, under threat that if he did not obey he and his family would be killed, to steal a car and drive it with the gunman and his associates as passengers. On the journey the object of the expedition was made clear to Lynch. He was ordered to stop at a certain place, where the other men got out and killed a policeman who was working in his garden. The actual assassins made their escape, but Lynch was arrested. He was charged with murder as a principal in the second degree, as the English and Irish phrase goes, or accessory, an offence which carries the same mandatory punishment as for a principal in the first degree. He pleaded duress, but the judge told the jury, and the Court of Criminal Appeal held that he was right, that duress was not available as a defence to an accessory to murder. The House of Lords, by a majority, held in 1975 that this was a misdirection in law, and ordered a new trial. Lynch was tried again; evidence of duress was admitted as setting up a relevant defence, and he was again convicted.

The second case came from Trinidad. Abbott had been convicted and sentenced to death on a charge of murder as a principal in the first degree. The evidence was clear, and supported by his own admissions, that he and some associates killed a young woman in circumstances of ferocious brutality. Abbott's defence was that he had done what he did at the orders of one Malik, a dangerous character who has himself since been hanged for murder, under the threat that non-compliance would mean the death of Abbott and his mother. The trial judge and the Court of Appeal held that duress afforded no defence to such a charge, and in 1976 the Judicial Committee of the Privy Council held, again by a majority, that the direction given to the jury was correct.

The first thing I must say about these appeals is that in *Lynch*, in the House of Lords, I was in the minority with Lord Simon of Glaisdale, and that in *Abbott*, in the Judicial Committee, I was in the majority with Lord Hailsham and Lord Salmon, the latter of whom prepared the advice which was given. I hardly think this is the place to discuss the rights and wrongs of the decisions, even if I could do so with a proper show of detachment. In *Lynch* I was convinced that such a defence had no foundation in the common law. Whether it ought to have is another matter. As an ex-Chairman of the Scottish Law Commission I have a sad distrust of judicial law reform. In the first place it is retroactive, though this does not much matter in allowing a criminal appeal. But the most important objection to it is that it takes place in the absence of all the wide consultations that, as experience taught the Law Commissions (a pretty elementary lesson, I would have thought), must precede and justify almost all recommendations for reform, let alone radical changes in existing law. It is absurd to suppose that the rules governing the relevance of a defence to crime, especially murder, can be classified under what is sometimes called "lawyers' law", and left to lawyers, however eminent, to alter as they please. There are too many subsidiary questions outstanding. How many people may I kill with impunity in order to save my own life from human or natural enemies? May I put a bomb in an aircraft? Could the strongest man in the Mignonette's boat have justified eating the whole crew one after the other? How far is the defence available to a voluntary member of the Mafia or IRA who carries out, albeit reluctantly, the orders of his boss? On these and other topics, more social or ethical than legal, many would clamour to be heard, and the proper place for them to speak is Parliament. Much the same considerations applied in the Privy Council appeal. There was, for the case of a principal in the first degree on a charge of murder, not even a *dictum* from a common-law judge, as for an accessory there had been from South Australia, indicating that duress was a good defence. This defence has been introduced into Commonwealth criminal codes, basing themselves no doubt on English common law, but in all of them murder has been expressly excluded from the crimes to which it is applicable.

The second thing I would say about these appeals is that, to my mind at least, they leave the law in a highly unsatisfactory state. It is quite possible to maintain this, while at the same time accepting, if one wishes to do so, that both were rightly decided. But making that assumption, how can one rationally acquiesce in a distinction between what are not easily identifiable as separate crimes, namely, that of the man who strikes the blow and that of the man who helps him to make his blow effective? I can ask that question the more plausibly inasmuch as the distinction, such as it is, between the crimes of principal and accessory is not observed in the law of Scotland. How the cases of *Lynch* and *Abbott* would have been decided in Scotland is a matter for speculation. Let us hope that effective law reform may precede the raising of the question.

It should perhaps be mentioned that duress *per minas* can be an issue in civil proceedings. A contract is a consensual agreement which may be vitiated in the absence of a willing common mind shared by the parties. Infancy, insanity, fraud, sometimes mistake, may make that consensus false, and so may duress. This is now very rare indeed. But it arose in the Judicial Committee in 1976 in an appeal from New South Wales.[13] To put it shortly, one well-to-do businessman was proved to have said to another, in effect, "If you do not sign that contract I will have you killed." There was no doubt that such a threat could be sufficient to make a contract unenforceable; what the Board (of which I was a member) decided was that, there being a great deal of doubt about the facts, it was for the person making the threat to satisfy the Court that the threat had not influenced the making of the contract and this he had failed to do. The leading opinion was delivered by Lord Cross, a great master of equity. The distinction from duress in crime is clear; the victim of the threat has been forced to agree against his own interest, not against someone else's, to do something he would otherwise not have done. I do not think that law reform is called for here.

But in crime, that is not so. The twin cases of *Lynch* and *Abbott* make that plain, although it is not their conjunction alone that gives rise to uneasiness. The present situation, as we have seen, is that duress *per minas* is a good defence, by which is meant that if proved it will result in an acquittal, to a charge of any crime except murder as a principal in the first degree. My own opinion is that this rule goes simultaneously too far and not far enough.

---

[13] *Barton* v. *Armstrong* [1976] AC 104.

First, I see no ground for distinguishing murder from other crimes when the question in issue is the responsibility of the accused for his action. Murder is a crime with an enormous span in gravity, or degree of delinquency. It may indicate irremediable depravity, but then so may other crimes, which may indeed in public estimation call for severer penalty than some murders. Which is the lower in popular estimation, the man who kills in the course of a violent quarrel, or the habitual molester of children? The latter can, as far as the theory of the law goes, plead duress, and demand an acquittal on it, while the former cannot. Second, leaving murder out of consideration for the moment, I would analyse the effect of duress as weakening the resolution of the person threatened so as to influence him towards doing that from which, without the threat, he would have refrained. That seems to be another way of saying that his responsibility, his answerability for the wrong he commits, has been diminished. It is not to say that his responsibility has necessarily been extinguished. Duress, then, ceases to be a defence in the sense that proof of it leads to acquittal, and becomes a defence in the sense that he can plead it in mitigation – or in an extreme case remission – of punishment. We may observe the analogy with Kenny's remarks about necessity; obviously a judge assessing the appropriate sentence will have in mind any factor which may have gone to vitiating the accused's resolution and thus lessened his responsibility, which is the measure of his criminality.

Unfortunately this solution is inappropriate in the case of murder, where, in face of a mandatory sentence appointed by law, the judge has no power to give effect to mitigating circumstances. To my mind the most satisfactory way of overcoming the difficulty, and one which incidentally would solve some other problems facing the law, is to abolish the crime of murder. I suggested this in my dissenting speech in the case of *Hyam*,[14] pointing out that, since it is no longer punishable capitally, murder does not require distinction from other crimes which may attract vary-

[14] *Hyam* v. *D.P.P.* [1975] AC 55, 98.

ing terms of imprisonment, up to and including that appointed for murder. Murder and manslaughter should be merged in a new crime called unlawful homicide, subject to a discretionary penalty. I cannot say that the suggestion has, so far, been received with enthusiasm in legal or other circles, so perhaps it will not do.[15] A less controversial solution would be to extend the defence of diminished responsibility to include the results of duress. This doctrine was introduced, judicially, into the law of Scotland in 1867.[16] It is analogous to the defence of provocation, which I mentioned at the beginning. By it juries were permitted, in cases where they found that a person accused of murder, although not insane, was suffering from some mental handicap (I am using completely unscientific terms) which had had some causative relationship with what he did, to return a verdict of culpable homicide (*anglicé* manslaughter). This power juries widely exercised as a means of avoiding death-sentences; it is one of the reasons for the notable fact that there was no execution in Scotland between 1928 and 1945. The doctrine was introduced into English law by statute in 1957.[17] It would be perfectly possible, again by statute, to make duress a plea on which a charge of murder could be reduced to manslaughter, and there is a good deal to be said for the view that this would be a rational step, inasmuch as it would give effect to the proper conceptual nature of the effects of threats on the mind of the recipient and on his responsibility for acceding to them rather than facing the consequences of resistance. At the same time, provisions could be made, as in the Commonwealth codes to which I have referred, to take care of, for example, the situation where the accused has voluntarily placed himself in a position vulnerable to threats, or where he could, with

---

[15] For recent comment, see the Criminal Law Revision Committee's *Fourteenth Report: Offences Against the Person* (London: HMSO, 1980. Cmnd. 7844), p. 7, where, however, it is noted that my proposal has the support of the Law Commission.

[16] *H.M. Advocate* v. *Dingwall* (1867) 5 Irvine 466.

[17] Homicide Act 1957.

the exercise of reasonable firmness, have taken steps to frustrate the aims of the threatener and neglected to do so. But first it would be necessary to decide whether we want duress to be a defence to murder at all; this is not a legal, nor even a philosophical, but a political question. I do not know how the public would answer it.

I have omitted a topic which is often discussed along with duress and necessity, namely the defence of superior orders. This has been raised in a number of cases both in England and Scotland, let alone in connection with "war-guilt" trials. But I think it involves questions with which this paper is not properly concerned.

House of Lords

ANTHONY KENNY

DURESS *PER MINAS* AS A DEFENCE TO CRIME: II

I am honoured to be invited to reply to Lord Kilbrandon's paper on duress. The paper contains proposals of the highest interest for reform of the law. It is particularly interesting to hear these proposals from a noble and learned judge who has himself played an important part in the legal debate of the law of England on this topic. The present condition of that law, as he ably illustrates, is a very difficult one to justify. As Lord Kilbrandon modestly refuses to dwell on the judgements in which he took part, and as he assumed perhaps a greater familiarity with the cases in question than can be expected of the philosophers among his audience, I would like to spend some time on the present state of the law before considering the pros and cons of each of the proposals for reform.

First of all, it is commonly said in textbooks, and has from time to time been asserted judicially, that duress consisting in a serious threat to life and limb constitutes a defence in all except the most serious offences such as murder. Thus, the present Lord Chief Justice in the perjury case of *Regina* v. *Hudson & Taylor*[1] said:

> It is clearly established that duress provides a defence in all offences including perjury (except possibly treason or murder as a principal) if the will of the accused has been overborne by threats of death or serious personal injury so that the commission of the alleged offence was no longer the voluntary act of the accused.

Lord Widgery's language is a little ambiguous: is he contrasting voluntary action with actions that are reflex, or somnambulistic, or gasping admissions of an exhausted man broken by torture, or does he mean by "voluntary" actions unforced actions contrast-

---

[1] [1971] 2 All E.R. 244.

M. A. Stewart (ed.), Law, Morality and Rights, 345–353.

ing, say, with the reluctant action of a man sealing up a wad of £10 notes and putting them in an envelope to send to a blackmailer? It seems to be the common teaching of textbooks that actions under duress, even though they are voluntary in the first sense, are excusable if they fall short of involving crimes such as treason or murder. I am a little surprised to see Lord Kilbrandon apparently throwing doubt on the authority for this view. He writes:

> There are certainly to be found in the reports, though they are rare and not particularly impressive, cases other than murder cases in which duress has been held a complete exculpatory defence.

However, perhaps he is not here departing from the consensus about the existing law. Certainly, however, it seems that, if his reform proposals were accepted, the effect would be a tightening-up of the law in respect of less serious crimes. For he seems to make no exceptions to the proposed rule that duress, if proved, should lead not to acquittal but to mitigation.

I do not myself find this proposal attractive. The present state of the law on duress as applied to less serious crimes, such as theft, seems to me to reflect a wholesome scale of values which regards human life as more important than the protection of property. As the law stands at present, a bank clerk will not be sent to prison for handing over cash to a gunman who threatens to kill him if he does not. If society does not want bank clerks to be obliged to defend their tills at the risk of their lives, I do not see why courts should send them to prison – even for a mitigated period – for not doing so. This, however, is a comparatively minor point. The really interesting and difficult question about duress is the question whether it should provide a defence or mitigation to a charge of murder.

In the case of *Lynch*,[2] the victim of the threats of the IRA gunmen, the three judges in the majority decided that duress was available as a defence to an accessory or principal in the second degree. They were hard put to it to find English authority for their

---

[2] [1975] AC 653.

view; they had to reject a large number of authorities that on the face of it told against them, and they could find in their favour nothing better than a dissenting judgement in the Supreme Court of South Australia and a decision of a South African judge administering Roman-Dutch law. It was not the weight of legal precedents which brought them to their decision: it was their feeling that to exclude the defence of duress was unfair and inhumane. As Lord Wilberforce put it, "A law which requires innocent victims of terrorist threats to be tried for murder and convicted as murderers is an unjust law." The arguments to this effect can be reduced to two principal headings. The punishment of killing under duress, it is claimed, is unjustified as retribution and irrelevant as deterrent.

To punish people who have killed under threat to their own life, it is argued, is to demand a degree of heroism which the law has no right to exact from the ordinary citizen. In the words of Lord Morris, "The law must take a commonsense view and remember that the instinct and perhaps the duty of self-preservation is powerful and natural."

The infliction of punishment on those convicted of crimes is most commonly justified by the deterrent effect of the threat of punishment. But no threat which the law can make will weigh more with a man than his immediate and overriding desire to save his life from instant attack. The punishment of crimes committed under duress, therefore, goes against the principle of economic deterrence and should be abandoned in any humane legislature.

I have stated these arguments against excluding duress as a defence in general terms as applying to murder, whether committed as principal, or as accessory. In the case of *Lynch*, of course, the arguments were stated with reference only to killing as principal in the second degree and their Lordships took pains not to commit themselves on the topic of murder as a whole. But as two of the majority judges pointed out, when they found themselves in a minority in the case of *Abbott* in which duress was pleaded as a defence to a murder charge by an actual killer, the arguments had equal force in either case.

In the minority in *Lynch* were Lord Kilbrandon and Lord Simon of Glaisdale. Lord Kilbrandon agreed with the majority judges that there was something inhumane in refusing to allow duress as a defence or mitigation, but he thought that the law as it stood clearly took this inhumane view and it was not for five Lords of Appeal but for Parliament to change the law in a more humane direction. Lord Simon, while agreeing that any change in the law was a matter for Parliament, thought there was rather more to be said for the law as it stood.

The case for the existing law was put most eloquently by Lord Salmon for the majority in the later Privy Council case of *Abbott.*[3] To allow duress as a defence to killers, he said, might prove to be a charter for terrorists, gangleaders and kidnappers:

> A terrorist of notorious violence might e.g. threaten death to *A* and his family unless *A* obeys his instructions to put a bomb with a time fuse set by *A* in a certain aircraft, and/or in a thronged market, railway station or the like. *A*, under duress, obeys his instructions and as a result, hundreds of men, women and children are killed or mangled. Should the contentions made on behalf of the appellant be correct, *A* would have a complete defence, and, if charged, would be bound to be acquitted and set at liberty. Having now gained some real experience and expertise, he might again be approached by the terrorist who would make the same threats and exercise the same duress under which *A* would then give a repeat performance killing even more men, women and children. Is there any limit to the number of people you may kill to save your own life and that of your family?

The joint effect, then, of *Lynch* and *Abbott* is that duress is now available as a defence to murder if the accused is not the actual killer, but is not available if he is a principal in the first degree. I agree with Lord Kilbrandon that this is an unsatisfactory state of affairs because the distinction between principal and accessory in English law is not clear enough or strong enough to bear the weight which judges put upon it. To remedy the situation Lord Kilbrandon has two proposals. One is that the crime of murder should be abolished and should be merged, along with manslaughter, in a new crime called unlawful homicide. The second is that

---

[3] [1977] AC 755.

duress, like provocation, would be available not as an absolute defence but as one which will lead to mitigation of sentence. If the crime of murder is to remain, then duress should be a plea leading to a reduction from murder to manslaughter.

The proposal to abolish the crime of murder seems to me an attractive one only if we are sure that the death penalty will never be reintroduced. In present circumstances, when the reintroduction of the death penalty seems a possibility which is not at all remote, it seems to me desirable to continue to try to separate out a particular class of unlawful homicide as constituting an offence of unparalleled seriousness. But I do not wish to enter upon this argument in the present paper, but rather to consider Lord Kilbrandon's proposal in its more modest form.

Before doing so I would like to say something about one more recent case which is not mentioned by Lord Kilbrandon, *The Queen* v. *Charles Anthony Fitzpatrick* in the Northern Ireland Court of Criminal Appeal.[4] In this case the appellant was a young man who while sitting for A-levels joined the IRA believing a civil war to be imminent. He was trained in the use of firearms and carried out vigilante duty in the Antrim Road. But because his studies suffered he wanted to go away to England and asked to be released from the IRA. He was told by an IRA officer that if he left the country his parents would be shot and he was ordered to take part in a bank robbery. During the robbery he shot and killed a banker who tried to stop him. He was found guilty of murder and robbery. The defence of duress was offered, but the judge held that, having joined the IRA and voluntarily exposed himself to the risk of compulsion by the IRA to commit crimes on its behalf, the appellant was not entitled to rely on the defence of duress exercised by that organisation. The judgement of the trial judge was upheld by the Court of Criminal Appeal.

I understand that leave to appeal to the House of Lords against the decision in *Fitzpatrick* was refused by the Court of Criminal

[4] Unreported. I am indebted to Mr C. McCrudden for drawing this case to my attention.

Appeal. If we assume, however, that the law in England on this point is the same as that in Northern Ireland as decided in *Fitzpatrick*, we have the following over-all law on the topic of duress. First, duress which is not itself voluntary excuses from all crimes except murder by an actual killer. Second, duress which is the result of a voluntary action does not excuse from robbery and, therefore, presumably not from the more serious crime of murder. (In the *Fitzpatrick* case it was not suggested that the actual shooting was under duress, but only the robbery in the course of which the shot was fired.)

I am not sure whether Lord Kilbrandon would wish voluntary duress to be excluded from his proposal that duress should be a mitigating circumstance. In his remarks in *Lynch* he noted that an exclusion of voluntary duress was to be found in the codes of most jurisdictions which admitted duress as an excuse. He said "Such a provision figures in the codes; I do not see how it could become part of English law save by legislation." It does, in fact, seem to have become part of Northern Irish law without legislation; but perhaps Lord Kilbrandon would regard Lord Chief Justice Lowry's decision as being as much a usurpation of the functions of Parliament as the majority judgement in *Lynch*.

Such is the state of the law. Like Lord Kilbrandon I regard it as unsatisfactory. In particular there is an illogicality in the different attitudes which the law takes to duress and which it takes to necessity. As Lord Kilbrandon says, legal authorities distinguish necessity from duress on the ground that the latter is an instance of compulsion by human, the former by natural forces. The case of *Regina* v. *Dudley & Stephens*,[5] in which the shipwrecked mariners killed and ate the ship's boy, laid down that necessity did not entitle a man to take innocent life. Majority judges in *Lynch* do not seem to have regarded themselves as overruling *Dudley & Stephens*. It seems therefore that duress will sometimes excuse the

---

[5] L.R. 14 QBD 273.

killing of the innocent, but necessity never will. This is strange, as the case for disallowing duress as a defence is stronger than that for disallowing necessity.

There were, as I have shown, two principal arguments in favour of allowing the defence of duress: that it demanded heroism to give up one's own life rather than to take another, and that the deterrent effect of the threat of punishment would be neutralised in circumstances of duress. The argument for disallowing the defence of duress was that to allow it was to enable a gangleader to confer impunity on any of his subordinates whom he terrified sufficiently. The two arguments in favour of allowing duress are equally arguments in favour of allowing necessity; the argument against it does not apply in the case of necessity.

To my mind it seems that the way out of the illogicalities of the present situation is not the one proposed by Lord Kilbrandon. It is rather to overrule *Lynch*. The arguments used in *Abbott* and *Fitzpatrick* seem to me basically sound and those used by the majority in *Lynch* to be specious. Let us take first the question of moral culpability. It is true that to resist duress, or to refrain from taking life under necessity, may call for heroism. It does not follow that it is morally permissible to do anything else. Most of us most of the time can steer a middle course between wickedness and heroism, but in tragic circumstances – as for instance in concentration camps or in a natural disaster – we may be faced with a stark choice between the two. If the law punishes immoral actions done under duress or necessity then it is not being unjust or enforcing anything beyond minimum standards of morality. But of course, while it is a necessary condition for an action to be severely punishable by law that it should be an immoral action, it is not a sufficient condition; and to point out that killing an innocent person to save one's own life is wicked does not yet establish whether it should be a crime.

To settle this we need to consider the second of the arguments in favour of allowing duress, the argument about the inefficacy of punishment. This argument, it seems to me, fails to take account of the fact that law is itself a system of threats. Law and duress are, as it were, in the same business. In the words of Stephen[6] quoted in *Abbott*:

> Criminal law is itself a system of compulsion on the widest scale. It is a collection of threats of injury to life, liberty, and property if people do commit crimes. Are such threats to be withdrawn as soon as they are encountered by opposing threats? The law says to a man intending to commit murder, If you do it I will hang you. Is the law to withdraw its threat if someone else says, If you do not do it I will shoot you?
>
> Surely it is at the moment when temptation to crime is strongest that the law should speak most clearly and emphatically to the contrary.

If this argument is correct, as I think it is, it tells not only against allowing necessity and duress as defences, but also against allowing them as mitigations. In fact, if we were to consider nothing but deterrence alone, the conclusion to be drawn would surely be that crimes committed under duress should be more severely punished than normal crimes, since a more severe threat of punishment will be necessary to counterbalance the threats constituting the duress. If it be said that whatever penalty the law provides can always be matched by a sufficiently ruthless criminal, this might be met by allowing judges discretion, above a certain minimum, to add ever greater and more terrifying refinements of punishment to whatever threat had been made on a particular occasion. If we reject this bizarre suggestion, it is not because we regard deterrence as irrelevant to actions under duress but because we know deterrence must be mitigated by humanity.

But if humanity towards the criminal tells against increasing the penalities for crimes committed under duress, humanity towards the victims of criminals – actual and potential – tells against mitigating them. When the majority judges in *Lynch* said that "law which requires innocent victims of terrorists to be tried for murder and convicted as murderers is an unjust law", they begged the question by using the word *innocent*; and the sufferings of the indisputably innocent – the general public – seem likely to be in-

---

[6] J. F. Stephen, *A History of the Criminal Law of England*, Volume 2 (London: Macmillan, 1883), p. 107.

creased rather than diminished by adopting a lenient policy towards crimes committed under duress. For, to the extent that duress is a defence to murder, the discipline exercised over their associates by sufficiently ruthless gangleaders or terrorist chieftains is to that degree reinforced.

There will, of course, be particular cases in which the incarceration for life of one who has killed under duress or out of necessity would be inhumane and unnecessary. In such cases the executive can exercise the powers available to it to temper the sentences passed by the courts, as it did in the classic case of *Dudley & Stephens.* But the mitigation of sentence should not be something which can be counted on in advance by someone who is tempted to give in to threats and take innocent life. It is a very great misfortune to be placed in a situation where one must kill and suffer the consequences, or be killed oneself: any man must pray never to be thus placed between the devil and the deep blue sea. But if the law takes away the deep blue sea, a man will go wherever the devil drives.

Balliol College Oxford

A. E. ANTON

DURESS *PER MINAS* AS A DEFENCE TO CRIME: III

Lord Kilbrandon and Dr Kenny are united in their view that the present law of England concerning duress is unsatisfactory. The combined effect of *Lynch*[1] and *Abbott*[2] is that duress is available as a defence – leading, on its establishment, to an acquittal – in cases where the accused is an accessory to murder, but is not available where he is the actual killer. Dr Kenny says that "this is an unsatisfactory state of affairs because the distinction between principal and accessory in English law is not clear enough or strong enough to bear the weight which judges put upon it". Lord Kilbrandon asks, "how can one rationally acquiesce in a distinction between what are not easily identifiable as separate crimes, namely, that of the man who strikes the blow and that of the man who helps him to make his blow effective?".

The prescriptions which they respectively offer for this defective state of the law differ. Lord Kilbrandon points out that the moral culpability of conduct does not depend upon the label or juridical category of the crime:

> Murder is a crime with an enormous span in gravity, or degree of delinquency. It may indicate irremediable depravity, but then so may other crimes, which may indeed in public estimation call for severer penalty than some murders ... Second, leaving murder out of consideration for the moment, I would analyse the effect of duress as weakening the resolution of the person threatened so as to influence him towards doing that from which, without the threat, he would have refrained. That seems to be another way of saying that his responsibility, his answerability for the wrong he commits, has been diminished. It is not to say that his responsibility has necessarily been extinguished. Duress, then, ceases to be a defence in the sense that proof of it leads to acquittal, and becomes a defence in the sense that he can plead it in mitigation – or in an extreme case remission – of punishment.

---

1 *D.P.P. for N.I.* v. *Lynch* [1975] AC 653.
2 *Abbott* v. *The Queen* [1977] AC 755.

M. A. Stewart (ed.), Law, Morality and Rights, 355–364.

Lord Kilbrandon, in consequence, suggests that duress should never be more than a plea in mitigation of punishment. He deals with the special case of murder, a crime with a fixed penalty, either by the adoption of a new crime of "unlawful homicide" not attracting a mandatory sentence – a solution which he does not press – or by proposing that coercion, if proved, should have the effect, like provocation, of reducing the crime of murder to that of manslaughter or, in Scotland, to that of culpable homicide, in neither of which the penalty is fixed by the law.

Dr Kenny, on the other hand, accepts the existing state of the law as applied to "less serious crimes", such as theft, where the allowance of duress as a defence "seems to reflect a wholesome scale of values which regards human life as more important than the protection of property". He argues that if society does not want men to defend other people's property at the risk of their lives, the courts should not send them to prison – even for a mitigated period – for acceding to the demands of the coercer. In relation, however, to murder – and it is not clear whether he proposes to go further than murder – Dr Kenny would allow duress to be admitted *neither* as a defence *nor* as a plea in mitigation. He utilises, and perhaps lays greatest stress upon, the moral argument that, while to refrain under duress from taking life may call for heroism, it does not follow that anything else is permissible. But he utilises also two arguments of policy. He adopts Stephen's argument that the law itself is a system of compulsion operating through threats: the law cannot afford to allow these threats to be withdrawn in the face of opposing threats. He also argues that the suffering of the general public would

> seem likely to be increased rather than diminished by adopting a lenient policy towards serious crimes committed under duress. For to the extent that duress is a defence to murder, the discipline exercised over their associates by sufficiently ruthless gangleaders or terrorist chieftains is to that degree reinforced.

Both contributors place most of their emphasis upon duress in murder cases and both are agreed that coercion should not in such cases constitute a defence. They differ only in that Lord Kilbrandon considers, and Dr Kenny denies, that the fact of coercion should be taken into account in fixing the penalty for murder. I propose to revert to this point later. What is most interesting, however, is that Dr Kenny's approach leads him to distinguish sharply between coercion in murder cases and coercion in relation to what he describes as "less serious crimes". He does not meet Lord Kilbrandon's argument that the real issue is a man's personal responsibility for his actions and that, since this does not correspond with the category or label of the crime, there is no reason for applying a different rule in the two cases. Dr Kenny merely suggests that "the present law on duress as applied to less serious crimes, such as theft, seems to me to reflect a wholesome scale of values which regards human life as more important than the protection of property". I find it difficult to follow this argument: those who suggest that coercion should not be a complete defence do not expect that persons coerced will necessarily sacrifice their lives rather than breach the criminal law. They merely say that if they do breach the law, their expectations should relate to clemency rather than to exculpation.

Neither contributor in fact pays much attention to "less serious crimes". This is unfortunate, because murder is relatively infrequent, and murder committed under duress quite rare. The Fagans of this world, however, did not die with Dickens, and coercion remains common in relation to "shoplifting" (or theft). It is an ugly phenomenon both in the context of soliciting for prostitution and in that of offences committed in the course of industrial disputes. It is a vicious one in the context of the abduction of adults and children to secure a ransom. In all these cases our sympathy with the person coerced by threats tends to make us say that coercion should be allowed as a defence. I suggest, however, that this is undesirable as a matter of legislative policy.

My reasons are similar to the arguments adduced by Dr Kenny for saying that coercion should not be a defence to a charge of murder. He accepts Stephen's argument that, since the law itself operates as a system of threats, it cannot withdraw its threats in the face of counter-threats. If, in coercion situations, the law were to withdraw its threats, the temptation of gangsters to resort to coercion or of their associates to say that they were subjected to coercion would be greatly increased. This argument is crucial, and is as relevant in relation to some of the "less serious crimes" as it is in relation to murder. The issue may be focused by considering the law of perjury. Perjury as a result of coercion is a distressingly frequent feature of criminal trials today. In *Re Taylor*[3] Lord Widgery thought that it would be harsh to exclude it as a defence to perjury and that the acceptance or exclusion of the defence should depend on the real prospects of protection in the particular case. I doubt, however, whether this approach is acceptable. The obtaining of truthful evidence is essential in any criminal (or indeed civil) trial: it is required not merely to secure the conviction of the guilty but to reduce the risk of the conviction of the innocent. It seems wrong, therefore, to allow a witness to defend a charge of perjury on evidence, which may easily be fabricated, that he was coerced. This may seem harsh in genuine cases. To allow of such a defence, however, would be to strike at the very roots of the effective administration of justice. It strengthens the hand of the suborner to perjury and it increases the risk of witnesses succumbing to threats. The degree of moral innocence of the witness coerced can be reflected in a mitigated sentence.

I concede that this argument is not of general application in the field of "less serious crimes", but it is relevant in relation to several crimes apart from murder and, since an accused may be charged simultaneously with a variety of offences, it would be confusing for judges and jurors to require them to apply different sets of rules relating to coercion to different categories of crime. I suggest, therefore, that the law should be amended to declare that coercion is never admissible as a defence to crime. It might be objected that the law would then be demanding an unrealistic heroism. But the law would not be demanding heroism as distinct from hoping for it: it would merely be saying that the punishment of the unheroic should be adjusted to their moral culpability. It

---

[3] [1971] 2 All E.R. 244.

might also be argued that punishment is useless in such cases, because the remoter threat of punishment would be neutralised by the immediate threats of the coercer. This argument, again, goes too far, because it does not recognise the need for general deterrence or for the emphatic statement by the law of the boundaries of permissible behaviour.

But a further issue arises in relation to "less serious crimes". Since, under the present law, coercion is treated as a general defence applicable to all crimes, with the single exception of murder as a principal, it is defined in terms which might be thought to justify its application to other crimes of violence, that is, as including only threats of death or of grievous bodily harm. Yet there are crimes other than crimes of violence which, in their total effect on society, are hardly less serious than crimes of violence, including the dissemination of dangerous drugs and offences under section 11 of the Atomic Energy Act 1946 and section 13(3) of the Radio-Active Substances Act 1960. In relation to these crimes coercion other than by way of threats of violence may be sufficiently effective, including coercion by threats of exposure and coercion by threats of economic loss, such as the destruction of property or the destruction of a business. If the law is not to seem arbitrary and inconsistent it must broaden its definition of coercion to allow it to take account of such threats. It can best do so by adopting a concept of coercion which has regard both to the relative seriousness of the threats and to the relative wrongfulness of the conduct required of the person coerced.

My next point is merely an extension of this argument. Since at present, whatever the antecedent record of the person coerced and his personal circumstances, coercion is treated as a defence which, if established, will lead to the complete exculpation of the person coerced, the law takes a predominantly objective approach to the determination of coercion to minimise the risk of false pleas. It also applies rather arbitrary rules to exclude the defence in situations where the accused voluntarily exposed himself to a coercion situation or, when it was practicable to do so, failed to extricate himself from such a situation. The application of these arbitrary rules may occasion unease in cases like that of *Fitzpatrick*,[4] where the accused appears to have tried hard to leave the IRA. Such arbitrary rules would seem to be virtually inevitable where coercion is admitted as a defence. It would seem better, therefore, for the law to recognise the wide differences in the moral equations presented to persons in coercion situations and to abandon the principle that duress may be a defence. Punishment, as far as may be practicable, should be tailored to fit, not the crime, but the accused's moral culpability. If this is accepted, the aims of the law would be better secured by amending the law to broaden the definition of coercion and to allow the adduction of evidence of such coercion with a view to the court's mitigating the sentence to reflect the accused's culpability.

It is believed that this approach would accord better with the views of the ordinary man in the street, who is likely – a point perhaps implicit in Lord Kilbrandon's remarks – to regard duress as an excuse rather than as a justification. In a case of duress it is difficult, as Baker suggests,[5] to speak of the conduct of the person who acted under duress as being justified: the whole point, or nearly the whole point, of a plea of duress is to throw responsibility for conduct admitted to be wrongful upon the person who emits the threats. He, and not the person coerced, must take most of the blame for the wrongful actings. Duress, therefore, is in essence an excuse. It is true that in some cases the coercer may have threatened evil not to the person coerced but exclusively to an innocent third party, and here the person coerced may claim that his conduct was wholly justifiable. In practice, however, the waters are usually muddied by the fact that the coercer will have threatened harm both to his proposed agent and to the third party, so that the conduct of the person coerced may not have

---

4 See the Law Commission Report, *Criminal Law: Report on Defences of General Application* (Law Com. No. 83) (London: HMSO, 1977), pp. 5–6.

5 Brenda Baker, 'Acting under duress', *Canadian Journal of Philosophy* 3 (1973/4): 515–523.

been wholly altruistic. There is always at least a suspicion that the agent may have acted to save his own skin. The plain man, therefore, quite apart from questions of legal policy, may consider that coercion is more fittingly regarded as an excuse than as a justification.

It is sometimes objected in this context that self-defence is admitted as a defence rather than as a plea in mitigation. In *Lynch*, Lord Morris referred to this analogy and remarked:[6] "A person who is attacked is allowed to take reasonable steps to defend himself."

This analogy strikes me as being unhelpful. In Scots law, and possibly in other systems, the rationale offered for the plea of self-defence is that the attacker by his unlawful actings has forfeited his right to be protected by the law and, subsidiarily, and possibly less plausibly, that the person defending himself is acting *ad hoc* as an officer of the law. But in coercion cases the third party who has been harmed by the person coerced has not by his own actings forfeited his right to be protected by the law, and the person coerced cannot readily be regarded as acting under the authority of the law. In my view, therefore, it does not follow that because violence may be justifiable in cases of self-defence, it is also justifiable in cases of coercion.

A final question remains. In relation to charges of murder Dr Kenny says with some emphasis that "the mitigation of the sentence should not be counted on in advance by someone who is tempted to give in to threats and take innocent life", and suggests that the executive can exercise the powers available to it to temper the sentences passed by the courts.

This is a remarkably tough approach. It has been the tradition in all parts of the United Kingdom, even where utilitarian considerations point in a different direction, to allow the judges to temper justice with mercy. And I think it is both politic and right that they should continue to do so. It is politic that they should do so because of the known reluctance of juries to convict when

---

[6] [1975] AC at p. 671.

they know or merely suspect that the sentence to be imposed will be a harsh one. The proposal, therefore, risks being counter-productive.

But it is also right that the judges should be entitled to mitigate the rigours of the law. Coercion, if pleaded, is a matter going to the root of the culpability of the person accused and should be determined by the organ which hears the evidence. Traditionally, it has been the task of the judge, when imposing sentence, to consider, in the light of the evidence adduced before him, the past criminal record (if any) of the accused, and the submissions of defending counsel, what sentence is appropriate to the case before him. The judge has not done so in cases of murder because the facts constituting murder are so defined that, in the view of the legislature, only a severe mandatory sentence is appropriate. But even in murder cases, it has been admitted by the law that the defence of provocation, if established, will "reduce" the crime of murder to that of manslaughter or culpable homicide and so permit the court to side-step the requirement of a mandatory penalty. The court can adjust the penalty for manslaughter or culpable homicide to the circumstances of the case. It would be possible for the law to adopt the same approach in relation to coercion, and this was recognised by the majority of the Privy Council in *Abbott.*[7] They said:

> Any murderer who kills under duress would be less, in many cases far less, blameworthy than another who has killed of his own free will. Should not the law recognise this factor? A verdict of guilty of murder, carries with it a mandatory sentence, in this country life imprisonment, in other parts of the Commonwealth death. There is much to be said for the view that on a charge of murder, duress, like provocation, should not entitle the accused to a clean acquittal but should reduce murder to manslaughter and thus give the court power to pass whatever sentence might be appropriate in all the circumstances of the case.

I suspect that the victim of threats – if indeed he is aware of the relevant law – will seldom weigh its effects in a fine balance.

---

[7] [1977] AC at p. 768.

He will not be able to assume that, if sentenced, a mitigation of the sentence prescribed by the court would be any more lenient than a corresponding mitigation given in the exercise of an executive discretion. Moreover, there are objections of a practical nature attached to the exercise of an executive discretion. The executive must rely mainly on the transcript of the evidence and, if duress is not to be admissible in murder cases whether as a defence or as a plea reducing murder to manslaughter or culpable homicide, the relevant facts will not necessarily be adduced in court and are unlikely to appear in the transcript of evidence. As a matter of policy, moreover, I would share the hesitations of the judges in leaving this matter to the discretion of the executive. Coercion today is often a feature of quasi-political crimes and it seems inappropriate in those cases to rely on executive discretion. It is arguable, moreover, that, since a plea of coercion goes to the root of the responsibility of the accused, it should be a matter for the judicial rather than the executive organs of the State.

I conclude, therefore, that, however persuasive Dr Kenny's arguments may appear, they should be rejected in favour of a version of Lord Kilbrandon's approach. The law should provide:

(a) for a broader definition of coercion;
(b) that coercion should no longer be admitted as a defence to any crime or offence;
(c) that an accused should be required to give notice of his intention to rely on coercion and that, if he gives such notice, the facts relating to coercion should be admitted to proof; and
(d) that, if coercion is established –
  (i) in a murder case, it should reduce the crime to that of manslaughter or culpable homicide; and
  (ii) in all cases, it should be taken into account by the court in fixing the sentence.[8]

Scottish Law Commission

[8] I am indebted to Lord Hunter and to Professor Neil MacCormick for

reading this paper in draft. I am particularly grateful to Dr R. A. A. McCall Smith of Edinburgh University for allowing me to read his thesis, *The Defence of Duress* (1979). The responsibility, however, for the conclusions in this paper is entirely my own.

J. L. MACKIE

DURESS AND NECESSITY AS DEFENCES TO CRIME: A POSTSCRIPT

Lord Kilbrandon and Dr Kenny are agreed that the present state of the law with regard to duress is unsatisfactory. But Dr Kenny is dissatisfied with the solution Lord Kilbrandon proposes, and I suspect that Lord Kilbrandon is also dissatisfied with Dr Kenny's. Nor am I quite happy with either of their solutions. Yet I think that in their two papers can be found practically all the materials for a solution that is as satisfactory as a solution can be to a problem posed by situations which are intrinsically deplorable.

First, we can surely clear up the problem of the voluntariness and intentionality of actions under duress (or necessity) and the related question of responsibility. As Aristotle said, such actions are not voluntary simply or in themselves, but they are voluntary on the occasions and in preference to something else. For example, when a bank clerk hands over cash to a gunman, though it would be misleading to say simply that he hands over the cash voluntarily, it is correct to say that he voluntarily chooses this rather than the other of the two alternatives open to him: he voluntarily and intentionally hands over the cash rather than be shot. It is, therefore, appropriate to say that he is fully responsible for doing-*X*-rather-than-have-*Y*-happen. It is more accurate to ascribe to him full responsibility for this complex action, doing *X* subject to this qualification, than to say that he has diminished responsibility for doing *X simpliciter*. This holds at least for one who makes a deliberate choice; diminished responsibility may apply to someone who acts on impulse, being too frightened to make a decision.

If this is agreed, the second question is, what do we – that is, society and the law as a formulation of the demands of society – want people to do when they are, unfortunately, faced with situations that involve duress or necessity? Dr Kenny says that we do not want bank clerks to defend their tills at the risk of their

M. A. Stewart (ed.), Law, Morality and Rights, 365–369.

lives, and I would agree. On the other hand he says that we do want people to refuse to kill innocent people, or to assist in the killing of innocent people, at the risk and indeed at the certain cost of their own lives, and Lord Kilbrandon agrees and extends this also to cases of necessity: Dudley and Stephens should not have eaten the cabin boy. Dr Kenny does not say in so many words that we also want people to refuse to kill, or assist in killing, innocent people at the risk or at the certain cost of the lives of their relatives, but this is implicit in his approval of the decision on *Fitzpatrick* and his support for the minority view about *Lynch*. I think that Lord Kilbrandon would agree; for though his judgements in *Lynch* and *Abbott* were determined by his views about what the law was rather than by an opinion about what it should be, his proposal for the reform of the law allows duress and necessity to count only in mitigation, not to make otherwise criminal actions justifiable in the circumstances.

My main plea is that there should be clear-headed consideration of this second question; but let me state my own opinion merely as a contribution to this debate. I suggest that in cases of necessity we do want people sometimes to kill innocent people in order to save the lives of other innocent people; typically if more will be saved than will be killed. In these cases, as well as in cases of duress that resemble the bank clerk example, the necessity or duress would therefore count as a complete justification of what the agent does; it should be a defence, not merely a mitigation. A more controversial issue is whether necessity may entitle someone to kill innocent people in order to save the lives of some to whom he has special responsibility, e.g. his own children. What view one takes of this issue will depend on the relative weight one gives to the bonds that unite such smaller special communities in comparison with the quasi-contract of mutual respect for the lives of everyone in the general community. Since we are not likely to reach agreement about this, it may be better to compromise on the conservative view that necessity does not *justify* killing in this sort of case, or, *a fortiori*, in a case like *Dudley & Stephens*, though it may where the situation can be assimilated to one of self-defence or the defence of those for whom one has responsibility. So much for necessity. Where duress is employed to induce the agent to kill, or to help in killing, innocent people there is, as Dr Kenny says, a further consideration which significantly distinguishes duress from necessity. To allow duress as a defence strengthens the hand of the criminal who can employ such a threat. I suggest that this is so strong a general consideration that we should never regard duress, in contrast with necessity, as a justification for killing or helping to kill innocent people.

If some such rulings were accepted, we could go on to a third question: to what extent can duress (and, again, necessity which falls short of justification) count in mitigation? What makes this question difficult is the fact that whereas in most circumstances deterrent considerations and what we can roughly call retributive considerations – those that turn upon the degree of wrongness of the individual action in the concrete circumstances – go hand in hand, they tend here in opposite directions. As Sir James Fitzjames Stephen (quoted from *Abbott* by Dr Kenny) said, the purpose of deterrence would encourage us to increase penalties in cases where agents are under unusually strong temptation or pressure to commit crimes, as they are where there is either duress or necessity; but we all feel that a criminal action performed as a result of either duress or necessity – even though, in the range of cases we are now considering, it is not justifiable – is less bad than an otherwise similar action performed for other reasons, where these special motives are absent. Even if we do not agree with Lord Wilberforce and Lord Morris that it is unreasonable to demand the degree of heroism that would be required to resist such threats, even if society and the law do, as I have suggested, call for such resistance, yet we do not blame very much a person who fails to resist them. So in all these cases our notions about what the guilty person does not deserve argue for leniency, while the need for effective deterrence argues for increased severity.

In this paradoxical situation, it is not surprising that Dr Kenny wants to have it both ways; he would allow sentences to be reduced on grounds of humanity, but, in order to keep the deterrent force, he says that 'the mitigation of sentence should not be something which can be counted on in advance'. But I do not see how this sort of trickery can work. The fairness of treating like cases alike requires that either the courts in sentencing or the executive in commuting sentences should follow regular practices and adopt consistent policies and principles; if they do, it will inevitably be public knowledge what principles they adopt and what practices they follow, and people *will* be able more or less to count upon them. (In private discussion, Adrian Zuckerman has replied that this argument from the need for consistency and the inevitability of public knowledge does not apply where cases of the kind are very rare. Cases of necessity are indeed rare; but cases of duress, regrettably, are not so rare, and the argument therefore has force with respect to them.)

If we cannot, then, escape this dilemma, how are we to resolve it? First, it is quite clear that any proposal that sentences should be more than usually severe in such cases, in order to provide the extra deterrence that seems to be needed, would be intolerable and unworkable: courts are simply not going to follow policies that are in direct conflict with everyone's feeling about the degree of wrongness of what the criminals have done. Secondly, this same principle, that deterrence cannot be effective if it gets far out of step with what is generally felt to be the degree of wrongness or guilt, argues that duress or necessity should count in mitigation to some extent. On the other hand, if the answer suggested above to our second question were widely and publicly accepted – that is, if people in general were clear that society and the law *do* demand heroic resistance to threats where what the threatener requires is the killing, or assistance in the killing, of innocent people – then it would follow that those who failed to meet this demand for heroism would be felt to have acted wrongly, however sorry we might be for their misfortune in being faced, as most of us never are faced, with such a desperate choice; consequently, there would be limits to the degree of mitigation that could be expected. And, of course, the degree of mitigation would be less in so far as the agent had voluntarily, and with fair opportunity for foresight, got himself into the situation where he is ultimately faced with this choice. In short, the requirements of deterrence, in our dilemma, must give way to our general judgement about the degree of wrongness of the action, but this judgement itself should be a reflective one which takes account of more aspects of the problem than the immediate predicament of the victim of duress.

To sum up, the elements of the solution I am proposing are these. First, full responsibility for the *qualified* action. Secondly, clarity about what society and the law demand of agents in situations of various sorts: giving way to duress when the result is something less than the killing of innocent people may sometimes be justified, and necessity, though not duress, may sometimes justify even the killing of innocent people, so that either duress or necessity will sometimes, but certainly not always, be a full defence to crime. Thirdly, where duress or necessity is not a defence, it will still count in mitigation, despite the deterrent argument against this, but the degree of mitigation should be limited in so far as we recognize that heroic choices are demanded of those who find themselves in such unfortunate situations, especially if they have got into them voluntarily and knowingly.

University College Oxford

PART VII

PUNISHMENT

JEFFRIE G. MURPHY

CRUEL AND UNUSUAL PUNISHMENTS[1]

> Excessive bail shall not be required, nor excessive fines imposed, nor cruel and unusual punishments inflicted.
>
> Amendment VIII
>
> *The Constitution of The United States of America*

1.

What does it mean to say that the infliction of some punishment *P* is wrong *in principle*? Getting at this question is to get at the core of the Eighth Amendment ban on cruel and unusual punishments. I shall argue that the best way to explicate the concept of a punishment's being wrong in principle is through a *retributive* conception and justification of punishment – i.e., a conception and justification resting upon the concepts of justice, rights and desert (and *not* social utility). Before arguing positively for this, however, let me first briefly suggest why other ways of proceeding (other conceptions of cruel and unusual) will not work.

(1) *Literalism.* The only punishments banned are those which cause great physical suffering and which happen with statistical

[1] A somewhat longer version of this paper may be found in my book ***Retribution, Justice, and Therapy*** (Dordrecht and Boston: Reidel, 1979), pp. 223–249. (This book is referred to hereafter as *RJT*.) The best general treatment of the constitutional issues surrounding an application of the Eighth Amendment – with special focus on the death penalty – will be found in Margaret Jane Radin, 'The Jurisprudence of Death: Evolving Standards for the Cruel and Unusual Punishments Clause', ***University of Pennsylvania Law Review*** **126** (1977/8): 989–1064. My own treatment of the topic has been enormously influenced by her essay.

M. A. Stewart (ed.), Law, Morality and Rights, 373–404.

infrequency – i.e., punishments which satisfy the literal meaning of the words "cruel" and "unusual".[2]

This analysis, of course, is absurd. Would anyone seriously maintain that radical mutilation or disfigurement will become acceptable as a punishment if we do it under anesthetic and several times a week? Surely not. And does anyone seriously maintain that we can meet all the reasonable objections of those who believe that the death penalty violates the Eighth Amendment by suggesting that we execute painlessly and with great frequency? Physical suffering is a relevant factor and, if severe enough, may even be a sufficient condition for calling a punishment cruel. It is not, however, reasonable to regard it as a *necessary* condition – as the case of anesthetized mutilation demonstrates.

(2) *Historical Authority*. The only punishments banned are those which the Founding Fathers regarded as cruel and unusual at the time the Constitution was enacted.[3]

Surely this will not do either. Suppose that the Founding Fathers banned punishment *P1* from a realization that *P1* had horrendous property Q. Suppose further that punishment *P2* also had horrendous property Q but that the Founding Fathers did not realize this. Are we then to be prohibited from attacking *P2* on constitutional grounds even though we realize that it has the very same property the Founding Fathers most wanted to oppose? This would be a strange kind of historical piety indeed. (For this reason it seems to me incorrect to suppose that the issue of whether the death penalty is cruel and unusual punishment is closed merely because the Founding Fathers did not explicitly ban it.) In my view of constitutional intent, the Founding Fathers should be viewed as intending to formulate reasonable deontological side-constraints or restrictions of principle on the pursuit of majoritarian utilitarianism. Thus, whenever we can mount a good argument for a principled restriction, we are at least not wildly far afield of their

[2] See Chief Justice Burger's discussion (with respect to cruelty) in *Furman* v. *Georgia*, 408 US 238, 392 (1972) (Burger C. J., dissenting).

[3] *Furman* v. *Georgia*, 408 US 238, 418 (Powell J., dissenting).

intent – as we would clearly be if we tried to interpret the Constitution in terms, not of principle, but of some notion of wise or useful or efficient social policy. The Bill of Rights is not a document of policy; it is a document attempting to give us just or fair ground rules for the pursuit of policy.[4]

(3) *Consensus*. The only punishments to be banned are those which would be rejected as inconsistent with the moral conscience of the citizens of the society at a certain time in history – namely, the time at which the Court is actually considering the constitutional permissibility of a certain punishment. This is at least part of what it means to claim that the Clause "must draw its meaning from the evolving standards of decency that mark the progress of a maturing society".[5]

This consensus test is open to two interpretations. On one, it is irrational; on the other, it is redundant. First, let us suppose that the consensus is the sort one could discover by taking a random sample of citizen preferences – e.g., an opinion poll. It is, of course, ludicrous to regard the Constitution as sanctifying this kind of consensus. Probably the best test of what the citizens will find morally tolerable is that which is enacted by their representatives. But to say that a punishment passes the Eighth Amendment test if it has been enacted into law by a legislature is simply to abandon constitutional review of legislative enactments – i.e., to abandon the very point of having a Bill of Rights. One cannot use a right to check majoritarian excess if that right is interpreted in terms of majoritarian preference or tolerance. If tomorrow an opinion poll reveals that Americans are tolerant or even in favor of torture and mutilation, the Eighth Amendment will not have to be reinterpreted in light of that fact. Thus this kind of appeal to consensus is irrational.

A second interpretation of the consensus test is the following: A punishment will be rejected as cruel and unusual if it would be

---

[4] See Ronald Dworkin, *Taking Rights Seriously* (Cambridge, Mass.: Harvard University Press, 1977).

[5] *Trop* v. *Dulles*, 356 US 86, 101 (1958) (plurality opinion) (Warren, C. J.).

rejected as shocking the conscience, not of a majority of people selected at random, but of those citizens who are truly informed, educated, and morally sensitive.[6] There are two problems with this élitist consensus. First, it is very likely that the characterization of the élite will be circular and question-begging – i.e., we shall count as members of the relevant élite only those persons who hold the view we want to appeal to consensus to defend (opposition to the death penalty, perhaps).[7] Second, and more important, is the following problem: If genuinely enlightened persons all agree that some punishment *P* is evil and shocking to the conscience, it must be because of some property Q (pain, unfairness, degradation, etc.) which they have found in *P*. But then *P* is wrong because of property Q, not because of a consensus of enlightened judges. *P* is not wrong because there is a consensus against it: there is a consensus against it because it is wrong and can be demonstrated to be so by argument (the showing that *P* contains Q).[8] This reveals that the consensus is morally redundant. We can go directly to *P* and condemn it as wrong because we can see that it bears morally obnoxious property Q – i.e., we can be brought to see whatever it is about *P* that the élite sees which makes them form a consensus against it.[9]

---

[6] *Furman* v. *Georgia*, 408 US 360 ff. (Marshall J., concurring). Justice Marshall considers and rejects the opinion poll model and adopts a version of an élitist model involving a prediction of what people would deplore if fully informed.

[7] One is reminded of John Stuart Mill's "competent judge" test in *Utilitarianism* (Chapter 2). Mill attempts to show that contemplative pleasures are superior to sensual pleasures because persons who have experienced both (competent judges) prefer the former to the latter. Any person who has experienced both and does *not* judge in this way, however, would obviously pose a problem for Mill's test. How does he deal with this? In the following circular way: such persons reveal that they have lost their capacities for finer feelings and thus lose their status of competence.

[8] This, of course, is logically similar to Socrates's puzzle in Plato's dialogue *Euthyphro*: Is that which is pious pious because the gods approve of it; or do the gods approve of it because it is pious?

[9] The élite, of course, may be *epistemologically* relevant – i.e., they may get

(4) *Utilitarianism*. A punishment is to be banned as cruel and unusual only if it is more extreme than that required for the pursuit of a legitimate state end or goal. As Bentham might put it, the purpose of punishment is to cause pain to the criminal as a means of deterring him and others from engaging in anti-social conduct, conduct which undermines the general welfare. Any pain inflicted beyond what is required for these goals is simply the gratuitous inflicting of suffering and constitutes cruelty.[10]

In American law, the utilitarian interpretation of the cruel and unusual punishment clause has taken the form of the so-called "least restrictive alternative" test – i.e., a punishment is cruel and unusual (in the sense of being "excessive" – a crucial word in the total language of the Eighth Amendment) if it is more restrictive or intrusive than necessary to accomplish a legitimate state purpose.[11] For example: Capital punishment will be cruel and unusual if the same legitimate state purpose (deterrence of murder, say) could be accomplished with a less restrictive or intrusive punishment – e.g., long-term imprisonment.

There is insight in this test, and it can be reformulated in retributive language so as to represent a demand of justice rather than utility. For example, I shall later suggest that "excessive" can be interpreted as "lacking a reasonable *proportionality* to the seriousness of the offense" – where the legitimate state purpose is conceived to be, not simply deterring murder, but also insuring that the punishment for murder will be of a gravity justly proportional

---

us to see or appreciate some morally relevant feature which we otherwise might have missed but for their insight. Their attitude toward the feature is not what *makes* it relevant, however.

[10] Jeremy Bentham, *The Principles of Morals and Legislation* (1789), especially Chapter 14.

[11] "There is no reason to believe that [capital punishment] serves any penal purpose more effectively than the less severe punishment of imprisonment" (*Furman* v. *Georgia*, 408 US 305) (Brennan J., concurring). The general constitutional notion of the least restrictive alternative is articulated in *Shelton* v. *Tucker*, 364 US 479 (1960).

to the gravity of murder. And so too for other crimes and punishments.[12] When interpreted in a strictly utilitarian manner, however, the test simply will not work as an interpretation of the Eighth Amendment – and this for one very simple reason: It will not account for the paradigms, for the cases of punishments which everyone would agree are cruel and unusual: torture and mutilation. The Eighth Amendment does not tell us that torture and mutilation may be used only when required by a legitimate state purpose; it tells us rather that torture and mutilation may never be used *at all*, regardless of the state's purpose. It is this absolute or side-constraint nature of a constitutional ban which no utilitarian outlook can capture.

2.

I wish now to develop a retributive account of the concepts of cruel and unusual punishment which will account for why the ban on such punishments must be regarded as a side constraint or principled restriction on policy. A retributive theory of punishment is one which characterizes punishment primarily in terms of the concepts of justice, rights and desert – i.e., is concerned with the just punishment, the punishment the criminal deserves, the punishment society has a right to inflict (and the criminal has the right to expect). In this way the theory makes central the special moral status of persons – unique individuals who, because they are autonomous and responsible creatures, must not be used for the benefit of others (as we use objects or animals) but who must be regarded as inviolate. Human persons have that special value which Kant (the most illustrious defender of retributivism) called

[12] Consider persons in an "original position" of the kind described by John Rawls. It seems reasonable to suppose that they would choose a system in which penalties were no more severe than necessary to accomplish whatever purpose they set as reasonable. If Rawls is correct in claiming that choices in such a constrained setting yield principles of justice, then we have a nonutilitarian foundation for a least restrictive alternative principle.

dignity – a value which we respect when we address ourselves to them in terms of their unique characters and acts (i.e., what those characters and acts *deserve*) and not in terms of the general usefulness of treating them in certain ways.[13] The retributivist obviously does not want to ignore such utilitarian matters as deterrence and rehabilitation and incapacitation, but he insists that these values be pursued only after the values he regards as primary (rights, justice, and desert) have been secured. The intuitive idea, then, is that a cruel and unusual punishment is among the class of unjust punishments, of undeserved punishments, of punishments we have no right to inflict – regardless of utility. A general theory of the *just punishment* is thus what is required.

The basic worry here is not whether punishment of any kind is ever justified; this, though highly controversial, will simply be assumed here.[14] The worry for present purposes is this: Given that we are going to punish in some way, are there certain *kinds* of punishment or certain *amounts* of punishment or certain *procedures* surrounding punishment which are so objectionable as to be banned outright or severely limited for reasons other than utilitarian deterrence? All of these worries – kind, amount, procedure – may plausibly be regarded as covered in the Eighth Amendment – a claim (controversial with respect to procedure) for which I shall argue later in the paper. *P* is intrinsically the sort of thing (torture perhaps) which we simply should not do to a person. *P* is not intrinsically evil but this amount of *P* (30 years in prison for possession of one marijuana cigarette, perhaps) is too much of *P* for this sort of conduct. *P* is the kind of punishment which is likely to be administered in an arbitrary and capricious way.[15]
These are the three primary ways we are inclined to object to a particular punishment on grounds of justice (and thus oppose it

---

[13] For more on this, see my 'Rights and Borderline Cases', *Arizona Law Review* 19 (1977): 228–241, reprinted in *RJT*.

[14] It is highly doubtful that the state has a moral right to punish at all in a society which is highly unjust. See my 'Marxism and Retribution', *Philosophy and Public Affairs* 2 (1972/3): 217–243, reprinted in *RJT*.

[15] It has been argued, for example, that capital cases bring out the worst and

in principle) and thus are the primary ingredients of the Eighth Amendment ban on cruel and unusual punishments.

Stating all this, of course, is not to solve anything – but is only to set the problems for discussion. *Why* are certain punishments intrinsically objectionable? *How much* punishment is too much (or too little)? All punishments certainly can be administered in an arbitrary and capricious way, so what is it about certain punishments which makes such administration more likely?

Here traditional retributive theories are not as precisely helpful as one would like, though they do give us a start in the right direction. Retributivism, as a general justification for punishment, proceeds in the following way – a way drawn from the theory of Immanuel Kant.[16] Punishment is justified primarily by backward-looking considereations – i.e., the criminal, having engaged in wrongful conduct in the past, *deserves* his punishment. It would be unjust for him not to receive it. In receiving it, he pays a kind of *debt* to his fellow citizens – to those other members of the community who, unlike him, have satisfied the social obligation of reciprocity, have made the sacrifice of obedience that is required for any just legal system to work. Since all persons benefit from the operation of a just legal system, and since such systems require general obedience to work, it is only fair or just that each person so benefiting make the sacrifice (obedience or self-restraint) required and thereby do his part. Those who do not must pay in some other way (receive punishment), because it would be unfair to those who have been obedient if the criminal were allowed to profit from his own wrongdoing. (In this view a certain kind of profit – not bearing the burden of self-restraint – is intrinsic to criminal wrongdoing.) Hegel, who elaborated this Kantian retribu-

---

the most irrational in juries and judges. See Charles L. Black, Jr., *Capital Punishment: The Inevitability of Caprice and Mistake* (New York: Norton, 1974).

[16] I have elaborated this Kantian account more fully in my 'Marxism and Retribution', *supra* note 14. See also my *Kant: The Philosophy of Right* (London: Macmillan, 1970).

tive theory, argued that the criminal, who as a rational person could see that even he derived benefits from participation in a community of law, could be regarded as rationally willing (though not empirically desiring) his own punishment.[17] This being so, he deserves it in the sense that he has a *right* to it.[18] It is important to see that this theory grounds punishment on justice or fairness (i.e., justice demands that we inflict the punishment deserved, that we have the right to inflict, that the criminal has the right to receive), *not* on utility. The basic principle is that no person should profit from his own wrongdoing, and retribution keeps this from happening. If a person does profit from his own wrongdoing, from his disobedience, this is *unfair* or *unjust*, not merely to his victim, but to all members of the community who have been obedient – one reason why crime is an offense against the *state*.

I have attempted to defend this retributive outlook in detail in other essays, and I shall not go over this ground again here except to mention three general points in an attempt to counter the bad press the theory usually gets:[19] (1) The theory is not an attempt to give approval to such barbaric motives as a desire for vengeance or vindictiveness. The only motive behind it is the desire to do justice. Thus retributivism is not an irrational cry for more and nastier punishments. Indeed, if retributivism were followed consistently, we should probably punish less and in more decent ways; for we now treat many criminals in ways harsher than, in justice, they deserve. (2) Retributivism is built around a rather attractive (if controversial) model of human beings as free or autonomous creatures, as enjoying rights, and responsible for what

---

[17] See my 'Marxism and Retribution', *supra* note 14.

[18] For more on punishment as a *right* of the criminal, see Herbert Morris, 'Persons and Punishment', *Monist* 52 (1968): 475–501. This is reprinted in my *Punishment and Rehabilitation* (Belmont, Calif.: Wadsworth, 1973).

[19] The retributive theory of punishment is, fortunately in my judgment, undergoing a bit of a renaissance at the moment. For a careful discussion which generally deplores this, see Hugo Bedau's essay in the 'Symposium: The New Retributivism', *Journal of Philosophy* 75 (1978): 601–624. For my defense of retributivism, see Part Two of *RJT*.

they do. Surely this is more attractive than the "you are sick and helpless or like a child" model behind a therapeutic response to crime, or the "you can be used and manipulated for the common good" model behind utilitarian deterrence theory.[20] (3) Even many people who do not like the *name* "retributivist" are persuaded by considerations that are clearly retributive in nature. Suppose it was suggested that we punish negligent vehicular homicide with life imprisonment and first-degree murder with a couple of years in jail, and suppose this suggestion was justified with the following utilitarian reason: Conduct of the first sort is much more common and dangerous than conduct of the latter sort (we are much more likely to be killed by a negligent driver than by someone who kills us with the primary object of killing us), and thus we should use the most severe deterrents against those who are genuinely dangerous. If we object to this suggestion, as most of us would want to, that this would be unjust or unfair because it would not be apportioning punishment to fault or desert, we should be making a retributive argument. Thus even if the label "retributivist" repels most people, many of the actual doctrines of the theory do not.

Let us grant for present purposes, then, that the retributive outlook sketched above can provide a reasonable general justification of punishment in terms of its being unjust or unfair to allow criminals to be free-riders or parasites on schemes of social cooperation – something which would occur if they were not made to sacrifice in some way for not having made the required sacrifice of self-restraint. How will this help us in determining the *kinds* or *amounts* of punishment which will be tolerable – i.e., what alternative methods of sacrifice will be allowed, and which ones will be prohibited?

Here the guidance provided by the retributive theory is not as clear as one would like. Some version of the *jus talionis* ("like for

[20] For an argument that utilitarianism also tends to treat persons as children, see Adrian M. S. Piper, 'Utility, Publicity, and Manipulation', *Ethics* 88 (1977/8): 189–206.

like") principle seems initially tempting; but even Kant – one of its staunchest defenders – cannot consistently maintain it to the end. One immediate problem is that the principle cannot with sense be taken literally in all cases. Hegel observes "It is easy enough ... to exhibit the retributive character of punishment as an absurdity (theft for theft, robbery for robbery, an eye for an eye, a tooth for a tooth – and then you can go on to suppose that the criminal has only one eye or no teeth)".[21] Kant also sees that there is a problem in applying *jus talionis* to "punishments that do not allow reciprocation because they are either impossible in themselves or would themselves be punishable crimes against humanity in general".[22] With respect to rape, pederasty and bestiality, for example, Kant believes that imprisonment is inadequate as a punishment but that a literal return of like for like would either be immoral (e.g., the rape of the rapist) or impossible (e.g., we cannot by definition commit bestiality upon a human criminal). Thus he proposes castration for the former two offenses and expulsion from society for the latter. He admits, however, that this is not a literal application of *jus talionis* but only in some sense captures the intuitive "spirit" of the principle.

What is it to capture the "spirit" of the principle? Perhaps something like the following: The principle of *jus talionis*, though requiring likeness of punishment, does not require *exact* likeness in all respects. There is no reason in principle (though there are practical difficulties) against trying to specify in a general way what the costs in life and labor of certain kinds of crime might be, and how the costs of punishment might be calculated, so that retribution could be understood as preventing criminal profit.[23]

---

[21] *Hegel's Philosophy of Right*, translated by T. M. Knox (Oxford: Clarendon Press, 1952), p. 72.

[22] I. Kant, *The Metaphysical Elements of Justice*, translated by John Ladd (Indianapolis: Bobbs-Merrill, 1965), p. 132.

[23] One interesting attempt to work something like this out may be found in Claudia Card, 'Retributive Penal Liability', *American Philosophical Quarterly Monograph Series* 7 (1973): 17–35. According to Card, a retributively just punishment exposes the offender to hardship that is comparable to the worst

There are still serious difficulties here, however – the chief being that, once a literal reading of *jus talionis* is abandoned, its application "in spirit" seems to be largely a matter of intuition unguided by any systematic theory. Kant's favorite example of *jus talionis* is the penalty of death for the crime of murder – this in spite of the fact that the punishment for *almost everything else* is imprisonment, a punishment which can literally satisfy "like for like" only for the offenses of false imprisonment or kidnapping. And speaking explicitly of the death penalty, Kant argues that this punishment must be "kept entirely free from any maltreatment that would make an abomination of the humanity residing in the person suffering it".[24] The criminal's "innate personality", he claims, protects the criminal against any morally indecent treatment.[25] In suggesting that the state should never do anything to a criminal that humiliates and degrades his dignity as a person, Kant seems to be working toward a ban on those punishments that have been described as cruel and unusual – i.e., a principled ban on certain punishments (torture and mutilation?) even when the "like for like" principle would seem to require them. There is insight here, but how the insight is to be squared with his support of castration as a punishment is a mystery to me.

The principle of *jus talionis* has thus produced a bit of a muddle, and the explanation for this is the following: Though a conception of reciprocity explains why the guilty should be punished, it is not clear that this same principle will explain why like should be returned for like or even that the evil inflicted on the criminal should be of equal gravity with that which the criminal has inflicted on his victim. The criminal has acted unfairly and that is why he

---

that anyone could reasonably expect to suffer from such conduct were it to become general in the community. As Andrew von Hirsch has pointed out, however, this will not do "because it gives disproportionate emphasis to the potential harmfulness of the conduct, and relegates culpability to the role of a limiting principle" ('Symposium: The New Retributivism', *supra* note 19). Von Hirsch's essay is a reply to Bedau.

[24] *Supra* note 22, p. 102.

[25] *Supra* note 22, p. 100.

must be punished. But unfairness is unfairness, murder being no more *unfair* than robbery. Thus if murder is worse than robbery (and thus deserves a worse punishment), this cannot be shown on the basis of purely formal considerations. Consider, again, the punishment for rape if the "like for like" position is adopted. If it be argued that the position does not entail that we rape the rapist but only do to him something of *equal* evil, it can be replied that the question "What evils *are* equal?" does not admit of a purely formal answer. Thus a retributivism grounded on fairness can at most demand a kind of *proportionality* between crime and punishment – i.e., demand that we rank acceptable punishments on a scale of seriousness, rank criminal offenses on a scale of seriousness, and then guarantee that the most serious punishments will be matched with the most serious crimes, and so on. This ranking must be reasonable, of course, but there is no reason to suppose that it will be determined solely or even primarily by considerations of fairness – i.e., no reason to suppose that seriousness can be totally analysed in terms of fairness. In particular, considerations of fairness alone will not answer the question of which punishments will be allowed as the most serious. There will be substantive reasons for not allowing certain punishments (e.g., torture) even if these would satisfy a fairness principle of proportionality.

Let me say one other thing at this point about the concept of proportionality as applied to punishment. It can mean either (a) doing to the criminal something of equal gravity to what he has done to his victim or (b) making sure that the most serious punishments are applied to the most serious offenses, etc. So if the most serious punishment in a particular legal system is 20 years in prison and if this punishment is applied to the crime of murder, it could plausibly be argued that the proportionality demand stated in (b) has been satisfied, but not that stated in (a). And my argument thus far has been that (b), but not (a), can reasonably be derived from Kant's theory. At most a constrained variant of (a) might be derivable: (a*) do to the criminal something of equal gravity to what he has done to his victim unless this would require our doing something (e.g., torturing) to which there are serious substantive moral objections. If we allow such substantive restrictions, however, we shall be forced to admit that the decision to allow or not to allow *death* to remain as a system's most severe punishment cannot – contrary to Kant – be based simply on considerations of fairness or proportionality. We must at least reflect upon the possibility that our choice of this as a punishment will be constrained by other morally relevant properties of death.[26]

So far, then, we can get this much from Kant's theory: A punishment will be unjust (and thus banned on principle) if it is of such a nature as to be degrading or dehumanizing (inconsistent with human dignity). The values of justice, rights and desert make sense, after all, only on the assumption that we are dealing with creatures who are autonomous, responsible, and deserving of the special kind of treatment due that status. This is why animals can be treated wrongly but cannot be wronged, cannot be treated unjustly, cannot have their rights violated. A theory of the just punishment, then, must keep this special status of persons and the respect it deserves at the center of attention. And there are at least two ways suggested by Kant whereby, in punishing, we can fail to do this: First, we can employ a punishment which is in itself degrading, which treats the prisoner as an animal instead of a human being, which perhaps even is an attempt to *reduce* him to an animal or a mere thing. Torture is of this nature. Using Kantian language, one might say that torture is addressed exclusively to the sentient or heteronomous – i.e. *animal* – nature of a person. Sending painful voltage through a man's testicles to which electrodes have been attached, or boiling him in oil, or eviscerating him,

---

[26] As I shall later argue, the mere fact (if it is a fact) that people tend to *believe* that death is horrendous is not a morally relevant property of death. (What people believe about death is surely not a property of death at all.) Such beliefs about death, however, might be relevant in a Rawlsian "original position" in that they might prompt the rational choosers to place special constraints on its intentional causation.

or gouging out his eyes – these are not *human* ways of relating to another person. He could not be expected to understand this while it goes on, have a view about it, enter into discourse about it, or conduct any other characteristically human activities during the process – a process whose very point is to reduce him to a terrified, defecating, urinating, screaming animal. I cannot, of course, *prove* that it is wrong to treat people in this way; for the wrongness of doing this is more obvious than any premises which could be given to justify its being wrong. Anyone who did not see this could not be made to understand anything else about morality. For we have here a paradigm of not treating a person as a person – and thus an undermining of that very value (autonomous human personhood) upon which any conception of justice must rest.[27] It is unjust to be tortured, everyone has a right not to be tortured, no one has a right to torture, no one deserves torture – all these claims flow from a theory of punishment (such as retributivism) which takes seriously and makes central the special status of persons.

A second way in which a punishment can fail to show respect for the status of autonomous persons is through radical lack of proportionality.[28] An autonomous person has a right that his punishment be *addressed* to that status – to those unique features of his individual, responsible conduct which occasion the punishment. A punishment radically disproportionate to the seriousness of the offense is not addressed to that for which he is responsible and blameworthy and deserving of punishment but is necessarily addressed to something else – e.g., society's mere *dislike* of him or

---

[27] For an expansion of this sort of argument (or of a defense for not giving an argument), see my 'The Killing of the Innocent', *Monist* 57 (1973): 527–550, reprinted in *RJT*.

[28] I say *radical* for the following reason: Any departure from proportionality is less than ideal justice would demand, but it may be impossible to grade these matters in a very fine way. We should still want to condemn, however, cases where the gap in seriousness between punishment and offense is clearly too wide.

his conduct.[29] This, in my view, is how the concept of "excessive" found in the Eighth Amendment should be interpreted.[30] To the degree that a person is being punished out of reasonable proportion to the seriousness of his offense, then to that degree is he being *used* – not being punished as justice would demand.

But is not the amount of punishment prescribed for an offense a criterion for how serious the offense is? That is, is it not almost true by definition that the most serious offenses will carry the most serious punishments – the prescription of the punishment by society being an index of how seriously society deplores the conduct? This challenge, in my judgment, is to be met in the following way: A just society cannot criminalize conduct simply because it deplores that conduct; its grounds for deploring the conduct must be *reasonable*. Conduct such as homosexuality does not cease to be morally trivial and become morally serious simply because a majority of people *think* it is morally serious and deplore it. As the Supreme Court correctly held in the *Robinson* case: if narcotic addiction is a disease, then no reasonable society may criminalize it – no matter how much it may represent a status detested and deplored by many persons.[31] In a just society, therefore, punishment must be proportional to the *objective* seriousness of the conduct, not to its subjective seriousness – i.e., the degree to which it is held in disapproval by the society at large.

At present, of course, we lack a coherent theory of objective seriousness. Thus, except in extreme cases, it will be practically difficult if not impossible to guarantee just proportionality in punishing. For one who cares about justice, however, this lack will stimulate research and thinking in order that a reasonable

---

[29] Obvious examples here are severe punishment for drug use, or consensual homosexual activity among adults, or any other "victimless crimes".

[30] See *Lockett* v. *Ohio*, 98 S. Ct. 2981 (1978) (White J., dissenting in part and concurring in part). Justice White articulates both the utilitarian and the retributive analyses of "excessive".

[31] *Robinson* v. *California*, 370 US 660 (1962).

theory on these matters may be developed. The alternative is simply to stop caring about doing justice – hardly an acceptable outcome.[32] As I indicated previously, a theory of justice alone may not be able to tell us which offenses are most serious; it may require supplementation by a consideration of the substantive or intrinsic character of certain kinds of conduct. A theory of justice, however, can at least demand the following: that everyone has the right to have offenses graded in terms of individual fault or blameworthiness (i.e., desert) and not mere social utility, that other even substantive bases for grading be reasonable,[33] that punishments be graded on a comparable basis, and that there be a matching between seriousness of punishment and seriousness of offense. A theory of justice may not be able to supply all the details for ranking, but it can supply the framework.

Thus (by a process of deduction, variation, and free association) I have extracted the following from a generally Kantian account of retributive sentencing: A punishment will be banned in principle if (1) it represents a direct assault on the dignity of persons or (2) it is radically disproportional to the seriousness (the *objective* seriousness) of the conduct criminalized. Consideration (1) is, of course, more basic than (2) – i.e., certain punishments might pass the proportionality test but would still be rejected because they fail what might be called the "respect for persons" test. Thus the punishment of torture by an act of torture could hardly be faulted on grounds of proportionality, but it would still be rejected as

---

[32] Andrew von Hirsch has made a start toward developing a framework for a theory of objective seriousness. See his *Doing Justice: The Choice of Punishments* (New York: Hill & Wang, 1976). Though von Hirsch believes that such devices as the Sellin-Wolfgang survey technique for measuring degrees of seriousness have a use, he sees clearly that objective criteria for seriousness cannot be ultimately based on popular judgments. Von Hirsch has not (as I believe he would be the first to admit) given us very much, but he has given us a start – and a start in the *right direction* (toward just retribution).

[33] "Reasonable" may equal "would be chosen by parties in a Rawlsian original position".

an intrinsically inhuman method of punishment.

Both of the above notions – intrinsic heinousness and radical lack of proportionality – have a secure place in the interpretation of the Eight Amendment.[34] A ban on the first is clearly a part of the original meaning, and a ban on the second has been prominent in twentieth-century Eighth Amendment cases – including the recent *Coker* case, where it was held (incorrectly in my judgment) that death was too severe a penalty for the crime of rape.[35]

3.

What I wish to do now is to move the general account I have been giving into this area of considerable controversy – namely, the penalty of *death*. Given the above sketch of the concepts of cruel and unusual punishments, is it reasonable to regard the punishment of death as falling under this description? That is, are there good reasons why, on grounds of justice or respect for rights (rather than utility), we should accept an absolute ban or principled restriction against the penalty of death? Does it belong, in other words, in the same camp as torture, mutilation, or punishments of radical disproportionality? We have the right not to be treated as animals – in a dehumanizing way. We have the right to be punished with sanctions proportional to our offenses. Do we also have the right not to be punished with death? If so, is this because death is necessarily a dehumanizing punishment, or because it necessarily lacks proportionality with all possible offenses – or both – or for some new reason entirely?

It should be obvious at the outset that there is no reason to believe that a punishment of death will always fail to satisfy the

---

34 For an excellent survey of the history of the Eighth Amendment and its interpretation, see *Furman* v. *Georgia*, 408 US 314 (Marshall J., concurring).

35 *Coker* v. *Georgia*, 433 US 584 (1977). In my judgment, the Court erred in not considering *degrees* of rape and aggravating circumstances which might render a punishment of death proportional – a point well made by Justice Powell in the dissenting part of his judgment.

proportionality requirement. It would, of course, fail to satisfy this requirement for many offenses – but surely not for at least some acts of *murder*. (Kant's intuition seems correct here.) It is often said that, by making the criminal wait for a long time in terror and uncertainty before execution, we do something worse to him than any murderer does to a victim.[36] But this is just not so. What about the killers of Aldo Moro? Or suppose Patty Hearst's abductors had finally killed her? Are these acts not quite proportional to capital punishment? (It is also perhaps worth noting that much of the waiting is *chosen by the prisoner* while he files appeals.) Or what if the murderer tortured and mutilated his victim before the murder? We think of these activities as so horrible that we shall not even allow them as punishments, so surely their horribleness plus killing could be proportional to capital punishment – if anything, capital punishment might seem disproportionately *little* here. (A query: If torture and mutilation are so terrible that we will not allow them as punishments even when we do allow death, why then do we rank murder as an offense as *more serious* than torture and mutilation?)[37] Thus, if the concept of proportionality can be worked out at all, it seems that it should be possible to work it out for some acts of murder punishable by death.

Even when proportionality is satisfied, however, we shall not use a certain punishment if it is intrinsically degrading to the humanity of the criminal – e.g., we shall not torture the torturer. Is there perhaps, then, something intrinsically degrading, showing lack of respect for persons as persons, in the punishment of death

---

[36] Albert Camus argued in this way in his essay 'Reflection on the Guillotine'. One other serious problem about long delays is the following: during the delay a prisoner can in a very real sense become a "new person" by morally transforming himself. Is it fair that this new person be executed for a crime committed by a different and previous self? As I shall argue later in the paper, the possibility of self-transformation is a very good reason against the penalty of death.

[37] There is, of course, the utilitarian reason: we wish to give the torturer an incentive for not killing his victim after the torture session is over.

– so that it too could be banned even in cases where it satisfies the proportionality demand?[38]

Now it is easy to think that capital punishment is intrinsically degrading if we allow ourselves to be dominated by a certain picture of what capital punishment is like – e.g., the final part of Truman Capote's *In Cold Blood*.[39] But all that this may show is that brutalization may preceed and may accompany (as surrounding circumstances) the punishment of death.[40] This would be a reason for objecting to and changing those circumstances. But it

---

[38] There are three bad arguments (addressed to me in various public discussions) that the infliction of the death penalty is intrinsically wrong which – since they may be widely used – are perhaps worth a brief attack. (1) Punishing people by killing them *degrades us* – *we* are demeaned in the process. But we shall be demeaned by doing this only if doing it is wrong; it cannot be wrong *because* it demeans us. This begs the question. (2) "Two wrongs do not make a right" – a favorite cliché of Americans, particularly undergraduate students. This, of course, begs the question also. The very point at issue is whether capital punishment is a wrong. (3) We must defend the value of the "sanctity of human life" – a value compromised when we execute. This bare slogan is of little help, because it can plausibly cut both ways on the capital punishment issue. Looking at the condemned person, we shall cite sanctity of life as a reason for not killing him. If we look at the *victim* (of murder), however, we could just as well cite sanctity of life as a reason *for* capital punishment – i.e., our use of a punishment this serious is our way of expressing how seriously we take the crime of murder. With analysis, however, this slogan can be turned into an argument – one which I shall develop later in the paper. Even analysed, however, it will rest on a controversial assumption – namely that killing is morally worse than letting die. For a defense of this assumption, see my 'The Killing of the Innocent', *supra* note 27.

[39] This book (based on a factual murder and execution) was made into a successful Hollywood movie. Both the book and the movie depict two marginal human beings of unclear responsibility who, after being convicted of murder and sentenced to death, arouse our pity and compassion as they reveal both their humanity and animality in touching ways. Their route to death (except for their contact with Capote) is cold and impersonal.

[40] For more on the distinction between death and the terrible circumstances which may surround death, see my 'Rationality and the Fear of Death', *Monist* 59 (1975/6): 187–203, reprinted in *RJT*.

would not be an objection to death *simpliciter* as a punishment. For suppose we consider another picture: the final scene of Plato's dialogue *Phaedo*, depicting the execution of Socrates by self-administered painless poison amid discourse with friends and family – all those around, even the jailer, showing great respect. This seems, at least intuitively, to depict a humanized death – a civilized execution. In this way, thus, does death seem to differ from torture. Is it conceptually possible to depict Socrates at a civilized torture session, a humanized case of evisceration of Socrates, a way of sending high voltage through Socrates's testicles which shows respect for him as a person? The answer seems *no*.[41] In a variety of social contexts (e.g., euthanasia) people are now rallying around the slogan "Death with Dignity". This suggests that they intuitively grasp some distinction between death *simpliciter* (which is surely bad) and circumstances which could surround death which would make it, not just bad, but degrading. But can we imagine anyone, who understands language and knows how to think, suggesting the slogan "Torture with Dignity" as part of a campaign against the excesses of certain political régimes? Death may be brought about in a degrading way; torture *must* be brought about in a degrading way. Thus we could imagine devising ways to humanize executions, to design them so that respect for the criminal would be shown. We cannot (*logically* cannot) imagine devising humanized or civilized torture sessions.[42]

Thus it seems to me that it is by no means obvious that execution *in itself* is necessarily – like torture – a way of showing lack of respect for a person, a way of treating him as or reducing him to an animal. Thus death may pass both the proportionality test

---

[41] This is not to say that some persons – e.g., Church martyrs, soldiers who will not betray comrades under torture, etc. – cannot rise above the inherent degradation of what is being done to them. Their animal nature is being addressed, but they hold out for a very long time (perhaps until death) before allowing that nature to answer.

[42] We would be more inclined to regard as insane a person who voluntarily tortured himself than a person who voluntarily took his own life.

and the respect for persons test. If so, does this then show that the punishment of death cannot legitimately be opposed in principle, that we have no general right not to be executed by the state, and that opposition to the death penalty on principle is, at best, a kind of well-meaning sentimentality or, at worst, merely an illegitimate attempt to legislate our preferences for policy through the vehicle of constitutional law?[43]

In the remaining part of this essay, I shall present a defense for an answer *no* to this question. That is, I shall argue that a basic right of citizens in just societies is compromised by the death penalty and thus that there are grounds for a side constraint or principled restriction against it. My argument will support, in broad outline, a primary portion of the majority reasoning in *Furman* v. *Georgia* and later capital punishment cases.[44]

In what way did the Court hold capital punishment to be unconstitutional? Many arguments were given, but the one which comes through most clearly is the following: The death penalty is applied in an *arbitrary* and *capricious* way[45] – e.g., it tends to be used upon the poor and blacks and on almost no one else. Thus we are required on constitutional grounds to do *one* of the following: (a) devise ways to keep capital punishment from being applied in an arbitrary and capricious manner or (b) ban it outright.[46] Against the general thrust of this argument, two charges are immediately to be made: (1) *All* punishments (including imprisonment) are arbitrary and capricious in the way noted, but it is

---

[43] This is the suspicion expressed by Justice Rehnquist in his dissent in *Furman* v. *Georgia* – a suspicion shared by some of the other dissenting Justices.

[44] The major relevant cases, other than *Furman* v. *Georgia*, are: *Gregg* v. *Georgia*, 428 US 153 (1976); *Woodson* v. *North Carolina* 428 US 280 (1976); *Roberts* v. *Louisiana*, 428 US 325 (1976); *Jurek* v. *Texas*, 428 US 276 (1976); *Coker* v. *Georgia*, *supra* note 35; and *Lockett* v. *Ohio*, *supra* note 30.

[45] This is also the central argument of Charles Black's widely read book on capital punishment, *supra* note 15.

[46] The Justices are clearly divided on which alternative is preferable.

absurd to say that all punishments are unconstitutional. And yet the court decision might seem to commit us to this absurd conclusion.[47] (2) To call capital punishment arbitrary and capricious is to make a *procedural* objection to it, one which could best be expressed by the Fourteenth Amendment "due process of law" or "equal protection" clauses. Why then drag in the Eighth Amendment, as the Court did, in support of its decision? The Eighth Amendment, in banning cruel and unusual punishments, is surely *substantive* and not procedural in nature; and bringing it in simply muddies the waters.[48]

What I should like to do now is the following: Develop a principle relevant to the capital punishment issue which (a) breaks down a sharp substance–procedure distinction and thus renders the Eighth Amendment relevant and (b) distinguishes death from other punishments – especially imprisonment. That is, I want to meet both of the above objections and thus vindicate the major thrusts of the Court's reasoning.

What will the principle be? Recall that I am concerned with principles which rest on *rights* (i.e., with principles proper) and not with useful social policies. And what possible rights could be relevant to the kinds of punishment permissible other than the ones already mentioned (right not to be dehumanized; right to proportionality) and tentatively rejected for the death penalty? I shall suggest the following: *the right not to be dealt with negligently by one's government*, the right not to have one's basic interests

---

[47] Again, see Black (*supra* note 15) for a clear statement of and an attempt to meet this objection.

[48] "The Eighth Amendment was included in the Bill of Rights to assure that certain types of punishments would never be imposed, not to channelize the sentencing process. The approach of these concurring opinions has no antecedent in the Eighth Amendment cases. It is essentially and exclusively a procedural due process argument [dealt with and dismissed in *McGautha* v. *California*, 402 US 207] ... and it would be disingenuous to suggest that today's ruling has done anything less than overrule *McGautha* in the guise of an Eighth Amendment adjudication" (*Furman* v. *Georgia*, 408 US 399 and 400) (Burger C. J., dissenting).

threatened in casual and irresponsible ways by the state.[49] But is this not simply a statement of procedure; and, as such, how can it bridge the substance-procedure gap? To answer this objection, we can do no better than to turn to the writings of Judge Learned Hand, whose discussion of negligence in tort law will be useful for our present purposes:

> The degree of care demanded of a person by an occasion is the resultant of three factors: the likelihood that his conduct will injure others, taken with the seriousness of the injury if it happens, and balanced against the interest which he must sacrifice to avoid the risk.[50]

In other words, there is no such thing as negligence *per se* or in the abstract. Whether the steps I take to reduce risk (the *procedures* of my acting) are negligent or not will depend in part on the (*substantive*) gravity of the harm that might result. Thus what constitutes due care as a precaution against my hurting your mailbox may not come close to what constitutes due care as a precaution against hurting your eyes. And, in the criminal area, what constitutes due process with respect to a parking fine may not come close to what constitutes due process for a long jail term.[51]

How does this apply to capital punishment? In the following way: All trial, conviction, and sentencing procedures are subject to *error* – to the possibility that they will convict the innocent. And there are two kinds of innocence at stake here: those totally innocent of any wrongdoing and those whose conduct, though meriting convicting of something (e.g., manslaughter), does not

---

[49] Again, it is perhaps worth noting (for those who are impressed, as I am, by his theoretical machinery) that Rawls's contractors would surely adopt such a principle in the original position.

[50] *Conway* v. *O'Brien* (2 Cir. 1940) 111 F. 2d 611, 612. See also *United States* v. *Carroll Towing Co*. (2 Cir. 1947) 159 F. 2d 169.

[51] Mr Justice Harlan wrote: "I do not concede that whatever process is 'due' an offender faced with a fine or a prison sentence necessarily satisfies the requirements of the Constitution in a capital case" (*Reid* v. *Covert*, 354 US 1) (1957).

merit conviction of an offense of supreme gravity (e.g., murder in the first degree). Due process is an attempt to guard against both sorts of error. And what will be responsible (i.e., non-arbitrary and non-capricious) principles of due process for various criminal sanctions? How is the state to exercise due care instead of negligence in dealing with its citizens in terms of penal sanctions? Obviously, if Hand is correct, this question can be answered sensibly only if we have a reasonable view of the gravity of the (substantive) *harm* that might result from the error. Thus we have broken down the sharp line which supposedly separated substance and procedure, and the Eighth Amendment at least has a foot in the door. One objection to the Court's reasoning is thus met. But what about the other objection – that the Court's condemning of capital punishment as cruel and unusual because arbitrary and capricious logically must condemn *all* punishments in our society (even imprisonment) as cruel and unusual? Obviously, the objection can be met in only one way – namely, by showing that death is a *graver harm* than loss of liberty and that, therefore, higher standards of due care ("super" due process) must surround the former sanction.

Can this be shown? Perhaps not in all cases – particularly in the case of life or extremely long-term imprisonment. Studies of the effects of long-term incarceration in "total institutions" indicate that long-term confinement develops in persons an "institutional personality" – i.e., a personality with diminished affect, neurotic dependencies, loss of autonomy and mental competence generally, in short, a kind of death (of personhood).[52] If these studies are correct, then long-term incarceration will be a kind of slow torture and psychic mutilation and *should* no doubt be banned on Eighth Amendment grounds (something the courts may be moving toward in declaring whole prison systems in violation of the

---

[52] See Erving Goffman, *Asylums* (New York: Doubleday, 1961). See also my 'Rationality and the Fear of Death', *supra* note 40.

Eighth Amendment).[53] This being so, it is a *virtue* of the Court's analysis that its arguments against death also apply to long-term incarceration. If they applied to all incarceration (or even to long-term incarceration if it does not have the above consequence), however, this would indeed be an absurdity. So what is it about death *simpliciter* which makes it a graver harm than loss of liberty *simpliciter*? Is it that people *fear* death more? – surely not, since many people fear death less than loss of liberty ("Give me liberty or give me death!") because they value liberty as a primary good of greater value than life.[54] Is it because death must entail intolerable suffering or degradation? No. As I have previously argued, certain manners of death may have this defect, but not necessarily death itself. What then?

One of the most common claims made in defense of the claim that death is worse than loss of liberty is the claim that death is *irrevocable*. But this will not do. Everything that is past is irrevocable. If I kill you in error, I have indeed done you an irrevocable injury. But so too if I imprison you falsely for five years. Margaret Radin, in her excellent discussion of capital punishment, attempts to meet this worry in the following way:

> Of course, even one day in prison is irrevocable in the sense that all past events and their resultant effects on human beings are irrevocable. Yet, although it might be difficult to articulate, most people intuitively recognize a distinction between the irrevocability of everything and the irrevocability of death or mutilation. The latter is the strong sense of irrevocability referred to here. It encompasses irreversible deprivations of attributes or capacities essential to, or at least closely connected with, complete personhood.[55]

---

[53] It is not uncommon for federal courts to declare the prison systems of entire states (e.g., Arizona) to be in violation of the Eighth Amendment – the primary reason usually being overcrowding. But what is the matter with overcrowding? Presumably the effects it has on prisoners. But what if long-term incarceration has the same or similar effects?

[54] As noted above, attitudes toward death as opposed to other punishments could be relevant in the Rawlsian original position; but, unless these attitudes are absolutely uniform for all persons, it is hard to see how the application of the punishment could be fair – i.e., some will be more hurt by it than others. Again, one needs an objective account.

This will not work. Radin is trying to show that death is a greater evil than loss of liberty because death is irrevocable – that is, she is supposed to be analysing "grave harm" in terms of "irrevocability". But she is actually reasoning quite the other way around – i.e. analysing irrevocability (in the "strong sense") in terms of grave harm. But if we already know the harm of death is greater than the harm of loss of liberty, we do not need the concept of irrevocability at all. One suspects that her analysis is unhelpfully circular – a suspicion reinforced when we notice that a synonym for "irrevocable" ("irreversible") is used in the analysis.

Let me then simply step in at this point and offer my own suggestion: Death is a greater harm than loss of liberty because it is (a) totally *incompensable* and (b) represents *lost opportunity* of a morally crucial kind. First, the concept of incompensability.[56] This is a concept which obviously admits of degrees. Some harms which we do to people are of such a nature – e.g., damage to their property or income – that it makes sense to speak of totally compensating them for their loss. For other harms, we cannot totally compensate; but we can at least make a reasonable attempt. Loss of liberty seems to me of this nature. In a culture such as ours, we know what it is like – and it intuitively seems reasonable and acceptable – to set a monetary value on my time and labor. Indeed, I can reasonably *bargain* these away for money – as when I work for a living. Thus if I am imprisoned by the state in error, it is at least not intuitively absurd to suggest that damages be paid as a way of compensating for the resulting harm. (We cannot totally compensate, of course, but we can in some sense make a reasonable stab at it.) But what would it be like to be paid anything even

---

[55] Radin, *supra* note 1, p. 1022. Irrevocability is probably the most frequently cited reason in defense of the claim that death is more serious than loss of liberty. See Black, *supra* note 15. And Justice Marshall: "Death is irrevocable; life imprisonment is not" (*Furman* v. *Georgia*, 408 US 346).

[56] For an excellent discussion of the distinction between compensable and incompensable injuries, see R. Nozick, *Anarchy, State and Utopia* (New York: Basic Books, 1974), chapter 4.

resembling adequate compensation for being tortured, radically mutilated, or debased in some other way – for being deprived of my status of honor or dignity as a person? If these have a price, this means that in a very real sense I do not have them to begin with – a man whose honor has a price simply being a man without honor. Suits in tort law may be brought and won here, of course, but how many winners would really believe that they had been even close to adequately compensated? How many would have bargained for this "price" in advance? Let us now move to death: On a scale of incompensability, death does indeed seem at the top. It is both logically and empirically impossible to compensate me if I am executed in error. (A wrongful death action may pay off someone, but necessarily *not me*.) In contract law, we do not even *allow* people to bargain away for money their life or their personal integrity against torture and mutilation; but we do allow them to bargain away almost totally their personal liberty – e.g., by joining a volunteer army.[57] Should we punish people by doing *S* to them when we shall not even allow them to do *S* to themselves – even for pay?

The question, of course, is rhetorical; and I shall move from it to present the upshot of what I have been saying thus far. I have argued that death is like torture and mutilation (and unlike loss of liberty) in at least one important respect: that when we injure someone by killing him in error, we have done him an injury which is incompensable. Not so with imprisonment in error; for this is at least compensable to a significant degree. Thus in at least this one respect death is a graver harm than loss of liberty, and thus it is reasonable to require greater standards of due care or due process to prevent error in its application as a punishment. The Court was thus correct: The procedures which surround the punishment of death may properly be called arbitrary and capricious even if those same procedures are adequate for imprisonment.

---

[57] We do, of course, have the concept of a Faustian contract. But we also take these to be perverse.

But is this all? Is the only reason that death is worse than loss of liberty the fact that the former (when done in error) is totally incompensable and the latter (when done in error) is only partially incompensable? This does not seem correct – not as the *whole* story. Surely death is a worse injury than loss of liberty even when the punishment is *correctly* administered (i.e., not in error) – this being the very point, after all, of having death as the most severe sanction in one's arsenal of responses to crime. What this shows is that the person in favor of the death penalty for the most serious crimes (and reserving imprisonment for lesser crimes) *cannot consistently oppose the Court's reasoning in Furman v. Georgia*! For by his own admission, the death penalty *is* more serious than imprisonment; and thus, unless he wants (unreasonably) to quarrel with the claim that standards of due care or due process are in part a function of gravity of harm, he must agree with the Court that higher standards of review are required for the death penalty than for any other.

Why, then, might death reasonably be regarded as substantively more serious than loss of liberty? An answer to this question might help provide an interesting reason for why death is an incompensable injury – i.e., a reason more interesting than "You cannot compensate Jones if Jones is no longer around to be compensated".

Thus I shall now turn to the second point I want to make about death – that it represents *lost opportunity* of a morally crucial kind.[58] What I shall say here will be very brief; and it may also seem rather old-fashioned and romantically sentimental. Be that as it may, here it is: The most important thing within a human life (something stressed by philosophers from Socrates through Kant and by such other admirable and insightful individuals as Jesus and Tolstoy) is the *development of one's own moral character*, the development of oneself in such a way that one's life can honestly

---

[58] I have elaborated this point in great detail in my 'Rationality and the Fear of Death', *supra* note 40. I am very grateful to Ellen Canacakos for discussion of this closing portion of the paper.

be said to be coherent, meaningful, and perhaps even admirable. To use the language of Plato and Socrates, one might say that what is most important in a human life is not what happens when the *body* is confined but is rather any harm that may come to the *soul* – or, to use less metaphysically provocative language, harm that may come to those crucial attributes of moral character and integrity which are most essential to personhood. The development of a morally coherent personality is the most crucial task or project of any human life – a project which we all muddle through with various degrees of success or failure for our lifetimes. To block or interrupt this project (or to preclude one's ever having an opportunity to have a change of heart, reflect on one's life, and *start* such a project) is, in my judgment, the gravest harm that one can do to a person. Imprisonment (unless of such a nature or duration as to have profound effects on the inmate's mental health) will not do an individual this kind of harm – witness the number of inmates who in a very real sense have become "new people" while serving prison terms. But death, alas, provides no such opportunities and thus can certainly harm a person in this highly significant (one could say spiritual) way.[59] For death is the *loss* of significant opportunity (the opportunity to accomplish certain things, to treat people differently, to become a new person); and for many persons this must be the most terrifying thing about it.

His mental sufferings were due to the fact that that night, as he looked at Gerasim's sleepy, good-natured face with its prominent cheekbones, the question suddenly occurred to him: 'What if my whole life has been wrong?'

---

[59] I say *can* instead of *must* because some persons (e.g., Socrates and other exceptionally rare individuals) seem to have attained personal excellence prior to their execution. The Justices in *Furman* v. *Georgia* who seem to me closest to the view I am here articulating are Marshall and Brennan. Marshall (at 346) writes "Death, of course, makes rehabilitation impossible." And Brennan (at 272, 273) writes: "When we consider why [certain punishments] have been condemned, however, we realize that the pain involved is not the only reason. The true significance of these punishments is that they treat members of the human race as nonhumans, as objects to be toyed with and discarded."

It occurred to him that what had appeared perfectly impossible before, namely that he had not spent his life as he should have done, might after all be true. It occurred to him that his scarcely perceptible attempts to struggle against what was considered good by the most highly placed people, those scarcely noticeable impulses which he had immediately suppressed, might have been the real thing, and all the rest false ... 'But if that is so,' he said to himself, 'and I am leaving this life with the consciousness that I have lost all that was given me and it is impossible to rectify it – what then?' (Leo Tolstoy, *The Death of Ivan Ilych*)

Given the exceptional moral gravity of having one's prospects for a morally significant and meaningful life interrupted, one might well want to deny the state any right to do this – i.e., one might adopt a direct absolute ban on the penalty of death. For it is by no means clear that one can show respect for the dignity of a person as a person if one is willing to interrupt and end his most uniquely human capacities and projects. Thus, contrary to initial and plausible impressions of the kind sketched previously, there is perhaps a case to be made that the punishment of death is degrading after all. Even if one does not buy this, however, one must at the very least – given the considerations I have noted – have strong sympathy with the disjunctive position articulated by the Court – namely, that granting the supreme gravity of the penalty of death, the Constitution requires either (a) significantly more stringent standards of review for this penalty than for any other or (b) an outright ban on the penalty. Recent Court decisions requiring an elaborate consideration of mitigating and aggravating circumstances before a sentence of death may be imposed are an attempt to work with (a).[60] If this attempt fails – i.e., if it turns

---

60 *Lockett* v. *Ohio, supra* note 30. There is, of course, a social cost of having stricter procedures to prevent error – Hand's third factor in his algebra of negligence. The primary social costs for criminal due process will be expense, court time, and – of course – the greater possibility that guilty and dangerous persons will be freed to prey again upon innocent victims and that others will be less effectively deterred from crime. I have had little to say about these matters – not because I think they are unimportant but because I wanted to see how far one could go via a different route. On the capital punishment

out that the standards of review surrounding imprisonment are really the best we can do – then we may be led indirectly into an outright ban on the death penalty. I am hoping for failure.[61]

> I have no pleasure in the death of the wicked; but that the wicked turn from his way and live.
>
> *Ezekiel* **XXXIII**, 11

Arizona State University

---

question, however, this issue will not be too central for the following reason: Probably no one would want to grant *less* due process than existed prior to *Furman*. But, even with that amount, executions had become so infrequent as to have (probably) very insignificant deterrence value. Studies seem to indicate that it is *certainty* of punishment (and not severity) which tends to deter. See Jack P. Gibbs, *Crime, Punishment, and Deterrence* (New York: Elsevier, 1975).

[61] Some criminals (e.g. the psychopathic killer) are perhaps best regarded as wild animals or other non-responsible natural forces of destruction. Such a way of looking at them is not to regard them as persons; but this is all right because, from the moral point of view, *they are not persons*. If drastic steps (e.g., execution) are advocated for them, this cannot coherently be regarded as capital punishment (since they are not responsible and thus not legitimately open to *punishment*) but must be regarded simply as painless extermination – something done in the same spirit in which we destroy a mad dog. I see nothing *intrinsically* wrong about such steps (i.e., see no reason for believing that psychopaths have a moral right to life); but the *practical* dangers of acting in this way (i.e., letting legal authorities – as in Nazi Germany – decide who is and who is not a person) are so grave that it is irresponsible even to consider this as a legal option. For more on this, see my 'Moral Death: A Kantian Essay on Psychopathy', *Ethics* 82 (1971/2): 284–298, reprinted in *RJT*.

M. D. A. FREEMAN

RETRIBUTIVISM AND THE DEATH SENTENCE

The late 1970s have been something of a watershed for capital punishment. The United States Supreme Court has been faced on a number of occasions with challenges to legislation authorising the death penalty. The Eighth Amendment of the Constitution which prohibits cruel and unusual punishments has been invoked in support of such challenges. In those Western European nations which have retained the death penalty there has been reconsideration and in some countries reform. Spain and Luxembourg have both recently abolished capital punishment. The Nordic countries, most recently Norway, have removed the ultimate sanction (which the death penalty is rightly or wrongly assumed to be) even in wartime. A number of men were guillotined in France as late as the 1970s but capital punishment was eventually abolished there in 1981. The Council of Europe and the United Nations may both take a stand against the death penalty quite soon. In Britain in 1979 and again in 1982 Members of Parliament have voted against the reintroduction of hanging by a surprisingly large majority. Outside Europe, however, executions remain an instrument in political battles. In Ghana no less than three former heads of state were executed in the summer of 1979. In Iran, revolutionary courts use a firing squad as a routine measure.

On the face of it there is a clear association between retributive philosophy and support for capital punishment. It was no less a figure than Kant who, in the leading classical defence of retributivism, asserted that 'whoever has committed Murder, must *die*'.[1] The decline of capital punishment in the period since the second world war may have been in part symptomatic of the decline in

[1] Immanuel Kant, *The Philosophy of Law*, translated by E. Hastie (Edinburgh: T. & T. Clark, 1887), p. 198.

M. A. Stewart (ed.), Law, Morality and Rights, 405–422.

support for retributivist philosophy. One commentator, writing in 1960, assured us that retribution was 'obsolete'.[2] But this can no longer be maintained. There has been a resurgence of faith in retributivism. Murphy's paper is just one instance of this phenomenon. However, far from supporting capital punishment, he uses retributivist philosophy to counter any suggestion that imposing the death sentence is permissible.

In this paper I examine Murphy's defence of retributivism both in the context of the revival of retributivism generally and *à propos* of the issue of capital punishment. I will argue that whether or not punishment can be justified in terms of retribution, no adequate model of what retribution involves has yet been constructed either by Murphy or by other supporters of the theory. This does not mean that retributivism is not worth working on. Like Murphy I agree that, if an adequate model can be constructed, it has more to commend it than utilitarianism, its principal rival.

1. RETRIBUTION – PAST AND PRESENT TRENDS

Kant, as Murphy notes, is the intellectual source of retributivist philosophy. (I stress 'intellectual source', for retributivism is also clearly rooted in the common sense of the man in the street.) Kant in his *Rechtslehre* stated:

> Juridical Punishment can never be administered merely as a means for promoting another Good either with regard to the Criminal himself or to Civil Society, but must in all cases be imposed only because the individual on whom it is inflicted *has committed a Crime*.[3]

Kant defines 'crime' narrowly. It is an '*intentional* Transgression'.[4] He probably, however, makes room for such acts as criminally negligent ones by including also a category of 'faults', uninten-

---

[2] H. Weifhofen, in *Nomos III: Responsibility*, edited by C. J. Friedrich (New York: Liberal Arts Press, 1960), p. 116.

[3] Kant, *op. cit.*, p. 195, italics original.

[4] *idem*, p. 32, italics original.

tional transgressions of duty which are 'nevertheless imputable to a person'. Kant also makes it clear that the only acceptable reason for punishing a man in a given manner and degree is that the punishment is 'equal' to the crime for which he is punished. He refers at this point to the *ius talionis*, which concept has dogged and befogged subsequent discussions about punishment. Kant also makes the point, in an oft-quoted and colourful passage, that upon the winding-up of civil society the last murderer ought to be executed, 'in order that everyone may realize the desert of his deeds'.[5] Desert is the linch-pin of retributivism.

The early contribution to retributivist theory of Hegel also cannot be ignored. From Hegel particularly the idea is found of punishment being the right of the criminal. 'Punishment is regarded as containing the criminal's right and hence by being punished he is honoured as a rational being.'[6] Hegel made the assumption, which many would dispute, that the action of the criminal was the action of a rational being. This idea has been restated with force by Herbert Morris. 'We treat a human being as a person', according to Morris, 'provided: first, we permit the person to make the choices that will determine what happens to him and, second, when our responses to the person are responses respecting the person's choices.'[7] Punishment, in other words, is a good to persons punished because they act on deliberate choices and know that in committing crimes they make themselves liable to punishment.

Retributivist theories did not take root easily in England in an environment dominated by the utilitarianism of Bentham and Mill. But through the writings of Bradley, Green and Bosanquet retributive theories did establish themselves in English philosophical thought.[8] Yet twenty years ago there were few glimmers left of

---

[5] *idem*, p. 198.

[6] *Hegel's Philosophy of Right*, translated by T. M. Knox (Oxford: Clarendon Press, 1952), p. 71.

[7] H. Morris, 'Persons and Punishment', *Monist* 52 (1968), p. 492.

[8] See *The Philosophy of Punishment*, edited by H. B. Acton (London: Macmillan, 1969), pp. 9–13.

this tradition. Retribution, rightly or wrongly, was identified with revenge and inhumanity. 'Punishment' was a dirty word and the 'serpent-windings of Utilitarianism', in Kant's graphic phrase, dominated penal thought as we tried the twin remedies of deterrence and rehabilitation. But deterrence as a penal aim has not worked. The evidence concerning the deterrence efficacy of capital punishment is particularly unconvincing.[9] High recidivism rates do not suggest that rehabilitation programmes have been very successful, though these have been doomed to failure by inadequate concentration of resources.[10] Liberals have also lost faith in rehabilitation. The 'right to be different',[11] to be free from the clutches of the 'therapeutic state', has commonly been asserted. Doubts have also been expressed as to the feasibility and moral propriety of behaviour modification, operant and aversive conditioning and the like, which were in fashion not long ago.

One objection that can be put to all these theories concerns their effectiveness. They are instrumental theories and, if their avowed aims are not successful, then, whatever their moral or other shortcomings, they must be considered to have failed. But theories of retributivism are not concerned with effectiveness, but with justice, desert and right. This, together with the swing back towards 'law-and-order', may go some way towards explicating the revival in the fortunes of retribution as a theory of punishment.

Historically, utilitarian justifications for punishment were 'a protest against the indiscriminate and ineffective use of the criminal law'.[12] They were advocated to limit retributivism.

---

[9] H. Zeisel, 'The Deterrent Effect of the Death Penalty: Facts v. Faiths', *Supreme Court Review* (1976): 317–343. See also S. J. Knorr, 'Deterrence and the Death Penalty', *Journal of Criminal Law and Criminology* 70 (1979): 235–254.

[10] R. Martinson, 'What Works? – Questions and Answers about Prison Reform', *Public Interest* 35 (1974): 22–54.

[11] N. N. Kittrie, *The Right to be Different* (Baltimore: Johns Hopkins Press, 1971).

[12] J. Rawls, 'Two Concepts of Rules', *Philosophical Review* 64 (1955), p. 7.

'Retributivism was seen as the conservative ideology of reaction, vengeance, and the worst human instincts, masked in a false rhetoric of high moral aspiration.'[13] Today retributivism has become a way of attempting to circumscribe utilitarianism. Before the re-emergence of 'pure' retributivism, theories which combined the retribution–deterrence approach occupied the stage for some years.[14] These argued that, whilst punishment as a general practice might be justified teleologically, the application of punitive measures to specific individuals could only be justified deontologically. This approach did not commend itself to retributive thinkers, for it countenanced the idea that only those who deserved punishment *and whose punishment would serve social purposes* should be punished. The convicted criminal, in other words, would be treated as a means to a social end.

Retributivism untainted by any association with teleological ideas is now before us once again. Three of the most influential of recent books on punishment present defences of the retributive doctrine.[15] The author of one of these books (Andrew von Hirsch) prefers not to have his view called 'retribution', because, he says, it is not a 'helpful term'.[16] But, whatever he calls it, and his colleagues in their introduction to the book do not shirk from espousing 'retributive purposes', it is clear that *Doing Justice: The Choice of Punishments* (the book in question) is a defence of retribution. Retributive thinking has also found its way into the reasoning of the United States Supreme Court as it has found itself having to grapple with challenges to the death penalty.[17] Many

---

[13] D. A. J. Richards, *The Moral Criticism of Law* (Encino, Cal.: Dickenson, 1977), p. 232.

[14] For example, H. L. A. Hart, *Punishment and Responsibility* (Oxford: Clarendon Press, 1968), pp. 35–61. Also see Rawls, *art. cit.*

[15] E. van den Haag, *Punishing Criminals: Concerning a Very Old and Painful Question* (New York: Basic Books, 1975); A. von Hirsch, *Doing Justice* (New York: Hill & Wang, 1976); G. Newman, *The Punishment Response* (New York: Harper & Row, 1978).

[16] von Hirsch, p. 45.

[17] For example, in *Gregg* v. *Georgia* 428 US 153 (1976).

philosophers have discovered themselves to be supporters of retributivist doctrine, some like Bedau[18] much to their own surprise. Most of the defenders of retributivism, Murphy included, are well aware of the difficulties of justifying punishment in terms of retribution. But problems in abundance still remain. It is to some of these that I now turn my attention.

2. WHAT IS 'RETRIBUTION'?

As indicated previously, the doctrines associated with retributivism are mainly a synthesis of ideas derived from Kant and Hegel. The new retributivists build upon these classical sources. But neither Murphy nor other contemporary defenders of retributivism define what they mean by 'retribution'. There is a tendency to take the concept for granted, rather as there is little attempt to define what is meant by 'punishment' itself.[19]

Murphy tells us that it is a 'conception and justification resting upon the concepts of justice, rights and desert', that it is 'concerned with the just punishment, the punishment the criminal deserves, the punishment society has a right to inflict (and the criminal has the right to expect)'. This is as close as Murphy comes to a definition of what retribution involves. It is a good deal further, it may be noted, than many other proponents of the doctrine. Van den Haag, for example, tells us that 'retribution is to restore an objective order rather than to satisfy a subjective craving for revenge'.[20] Other than telling us that proponents of retribution believe in legal punishment rather than in lynch law this tells us very little. Murphy goes a deal further, but his failure to elaborate on his central notions of justice, rights and desert leaves his concept of retribution over-vague and rather loose.

---

[18] H. A. Bedau, 'Retribution and the Theory of Punishment', *Journal of Philosophy* 75 (1978), p. 603.

[19] See S. Kleinig, *Punishment and Desert* (The Hague: Nijhoff, 1973), chapter 11.

[20] van den Haag, p. 11.

What Murphy means by 'justice' is not explained at all, despite the fact that he tells us that 'the only motive behind' the retributive outlook is 'the desire to do justice'. It is, he tells us, 'unjust or unfair to allow criminals to be free-riders or parasites on schemes of social cooperation – something which would occur if they were not made to sacrifice in some way for not having made the required sacrifice of self-restraint'. This view is not unlike similar reasoning to be found in Hart, Rawls and Morris.[21] But it is question-begging. The label 'criminal' is not itself unproblematic.[22] Whether or not someone is a criminal depends on a number of factors, including who he is, when he does or is supposed to do the act, what the consequences of that act are, whether anyone is sufficiently offended to do anything about it, etc. Criminal activity presupposes rules outlawing particular acts. It assumes that the rules infringed by the criminal will be enforced and enforced in such a way (i.e., not, for example, by administrative regulation)[23] as to ascribe criminality to the actor in question. Further, Murphy underplays the normality of crime.

The conception of 'schemes of social cooperation' is also not without its problems. I am not aware of any of these 'schemes' and so must assume that they play a role not unlike the 'social contract'. This is, of course, fictive and totally abstracted from the realities of social and economic life. Murphy's 'schemes' presuppose a high degree of value consensus, whereas the reality in today's advanced, technological, capitalistic societies is more pluralistic, conflictual and antagonistic. 'Justice' seems to operate then to protect existing rights. The theory is reminiscent of Hume's or Locke's or Nozick's notion of justice as established right, with a consequent strong emphasis on rights of property. That this is only one notion of social justice hardly needs elaboration.[24] It

---

[21] Hart, *op. cit.*, pp. 21–4, 180–3; Morris, *art. cit.*; J. Rawls, *A Theory of Justice* (Oxford: Clarendon Press, 1972), pp. 235–43.

[22] Cf. H. S. Becker, *Outsiders* (New York: Free Press, 1963).

[23] Cf. W. G. Carson, 'White-Collar Crime and the Enforcement of Factory Legislation', *British Journal of Criminology* 10 (1970): 383–398.

[24] But see D. Miller, *Social Justice* (Oxford: Clarendon Press, 1976).

is easy to stray into a discussion of social justice for that is what Murphy in effect does. He sets out to justify punishment in terms of retributive justice but his justification amounts to arguments based on a notion of social justice which itself is little more than a defence of the existing system.

The concept of 'desert' causes as many problems. 'Punishment', Murphy suggests, 'is justified primarily by backward-looking considerations – i.e., the criminal, having engaged in wrongful conduct in the past, *deserves* his punishment ... In receiving it, he pays a kind of *debt* to his fellow citizens...' But this is to assume that desert and the payment of debts are strictly comparable. Such an equation may be doubted. Debts are paid to compensate. Compensation is due to the victim of the crime and not to fellow citizens collectively. Running the concepts of desert and payment of a debt together glosses over the line between punishment and compensation. This is unfortunate.[25] In a later, and more satisfactory, passage Murphy equates 'blameworthiness' and 'desert'. As Honderich has carefully pointed out, what is meant by 'desert' has not been clearly stated by those who emphasise it.[26] In Murphy's case, it is appropriate to ask why the criminal should 'pay' a debt to his fellow citizens. Is it because it is, in other words, a way of satisfying the desires of others? Does it stand, to quote Stephen, to 'the passion of revenge in much the same relation as marriage to the sexual appetite'?[27] Certainly, debts are usually paid to satisfy someone. But to what extent is this compatible with pure retributive theory? This finds justification for punishing a man wholly in his past actions and a relationship between those and the penalty *'in so far as it affects him'*. To introduce notions of the effect of the penalty on others is to deviate from the pure stream of retributivism. Not that this is necessarily a bad thing to do: it is

---

25 Cf. R. Nozick, *Anarchy, State and Utopia* (Oxford: Blackwell, 1975), pp. 138–9.

26 E. D. R. Honderich, *Punishment: The Supposed Justifications* (Harmondsworth: Penguin, 1971), pp. 26–34.

27 Cf. J. F. Stephen, *A General View of the Criminal Law of England* (London: Macmillan, 1863), p. 99.

difficult to see, however, how Murphy can reconcile his notion of desert with retributivism. His equation of desert with blameworthiness is useful (though not necessarily consistent with the line on desert just discussed) because it enables excuses and defences to be taken account of. Further reference is made to this question later in the paper.

3. APPROPRIATE PUNISHMENTS

It behoves the retributivist who insists that the criminal should receive his just desert to indicate what are the appropriate penalties for particular offences. To make the punishment fit the crime is an all too obvious guideline and of real use in demonstrating such obvious mismatches as the death sentence for parking on double yellow lines or a £6 fine for a cold-blooded murder. But why? Is there any way of demonstrating the latter offence to be more deserving of a severe punishment than the former other than in terms of a calculus of harms? Can the ranking of offences, in other words, be based on anything other than considerations of utility? Murphy admits that the guidance provided by the retributive theory is not as clear as he would like it to be. The temptation to use some version of the *ius talionis* must, he concedes, be forgone. He accepts, rightly I think, that Kant himself, whilst espousing notions of *ius talionis*, lapsed into muddled thinking. Indeed, the very frailty of the *ius talionis* was demonstrated by Blackstone when he showed the impossibility of requiting fraud by fraud, forgery by forgery, or even death by death. 'The execution of a decrepit assassin is', he noted, 'a poor satisfaction for the murder of a nobleman in the bloom of his youth and full enjoyment of his friends, his honour, and his fortune.'[28]

Murphy concedes that retributivism cannot specify with any precision what is the appropriate penalty for a particular crime. His concern is with limiting penalties that others, utilitarians for

---

[28] W. Blackstone, *Commentaries on the Laws of England* (1765), Book IV ('Of the Proportion of Punishments').

example, might accept as appropriate deterrent measures. Bentham, after all, was not averse to the infliction of torture in certain instances.[29] Retributivists seem to be on stronger ground in setting out negative considerations than in laying down those to govern what the appropriate punishments should be. The explanation for this is that the proper scope of retributive arguments does not mandate any particular sanction.[30] Murphy is concerned with proportionality, with ranking acceptable punishments on a scale of seriousness. So are other contemporary retributivists. Van den Haag, for example, argues that punishment should be such that the pain or suffering inflicted by it is in keeping with the gravity of the offence. Newman, less precisely, is concerned that punishments should 'resemble the offences both in quality and quantity'.[31] Murphy argues, therefore, that 'a punishment will be banned in principle if (1) it represents a direct assault on the dignity of persons or (2) it is radically disproportional to the seriousness (the *objective* seriousness) of the conduct criminalized'.

How is the 'objective seriousness' of conduct to be assessed? Murphy admits that 'we lack a coherent theory of objective seriousness'. Is gravity such an objective, obvious property of crime that moral philosophers can lay down standards which are definitive? Or should we accept that such standards will vary with time and place? The crucial question is whose standards are decisive in grading seriousness of particular conduct. Criminal codes and the penalties they lay down are an expression of political interests. For a long time in England maiming a sheep was considered (that is, by those with the power to do anything about it) a more serious offence than injuring a child. Burglary and cognate offences are today considered to be more serious offences than the so-called 'white-collar crimes', even though the amounts of money involved in the latter exceed by a considerable amount those taken

---

[29] See W. L. and P. E. Twining, 'Bentham on Torture', *Northern Ireland Legal Quarterly* 24 (1973): 305–356.

[30] See Richards, *The Moral Criticism of Law*, p. 256.

[31] Newman, *The Punishment Response*, p. 198.

by more conventional criminal means. Social security fraud is regarded as more heinous than tax evasion. The political implication of grading of severity must not be underestimated.

Murphy is right to argue that our present absence of a coherent theory of objective seriousness should stimulate research and thinking in order that a reasonable theory may be developed. We need to ask what matters such a theory should take into account. Although Murphy does not really consider this question any further, others have attempted to do so. It may be instructive, therefore, to consider these attempts.

One interesting exploration of the problem is by Card.[32] She interprets the problem of proportionality in terms of what she calls 'the Penalty Principle' and 'the Full Measure Principle'. The former states, in part, that a punishment is retributively just only if it imposes on an offender a deprivation of rights to the extent of his 'evident culpable failure to abide by the law'. The latter requires that the hardship to which he is thus exposed does not exceed 'the worst that anyone could reasonably be expected to suffer from the similar conduct of another if such conduct were to become general in the community'. The Penalty Principle embraces the idea that criminal conduct is a function both of the offender's *mens rea* and the harm the conduct causes the victim. The Full Measure Principle is designed to ensure that a just punishment consists in 'a suspension or withdrawal of rights of the offender corresponding to his failure to respect such rights of others'. But how are we to measure the victim's hardship or loss of rights? What if the victim is unaware of the fact that he is a victim? Suppose he has not noticed that property has been taken from him. What of the 'victim' who turns the other cheek? What of the so-called victimless crimes? To what extent can we take into account the interest of the state as victim?

In assessing hardship, what do we take into account? Should we punish rape of a white woman by a black man more severely

---

32 'Retributive Penal Liability', *American Philosophical Quarterly Monograph Series* 7 (1973): 17–35.

than the equivalent act by a white man? What significance, if any, should attach to the identity of the victim? Should rape of a virgin be punished more severely than rape of a prostitute? Should we distinguish rapes which produce pregnancies from those which do not? What of the 'gang bang' rape? Should each of the participants be punished more severely because such offences are regarded (by whom?) as worse than ordinary rape or should the individuals involved be treated less severely, the total harm perpetrated being divided by the number of offenders? Is rape of a child worse than that of an adult woman? Is the age or the marital status of the woman relevant? Is a previous sexual relationship with the rapist a relevant consideration? What is, and how does one measure, psychological harm? Is the murder of someone dying of cancer less serious than the murder of a healthy person? Is the offender's knowledge of the victim's state of health relevant? Where does mercy-killing come in? Card does not have answers to these questions, nor is her theory adequate to begin to answer them.

A second approach is that taken by von Hirsch in *Doing Justice*. He maintains that 'severity of punishment should be commensurate with the seriousness of the wrong ... seriousness depends both on harm done (or risked) by the act, and on the degree of the actor's culpability'.[33] Von Hirsch relies on the techniques for measuring degrees of gravity of offences worked out by the criminologists Sellin and Wolfgang.[34] They rank-order criminal offences to the degree of severity, and they do this by means of a scale with 26 equal intervals on which they plot judgments drawn from a large sample of persons reflecting their assessment of amount and relative degree of harm done by a wide range of crimes. The scales are formalistic and inflexible and some strange consequences result. They provide, for example, no way of distinguishing murder from manslaughter, for harm is their criterion, not culpability. Von Hirsh says that his penalty scale would be able to make distinc-

---

33 von Hirsch, *op. cit.*, pp. 66, 69.

34 T. Sellin and M. E. Wolfgang, *The Measurement of Delinquency* (New York: Wiley, 1964).

tions between different types of homicide, but he does not show how. Harm in the Sellin-Wolfgang typography is a relatively neutral category. As such it is not very helpful to those trying to construct about it a theory of 'just deserts'. On their ranking a one-eyed man who loses his other eye suffers no more harm than another man whose rib is crushed without his lung being punctured, as death results in neither case and both victims require hospitalisation.[35] Few would, I think, find this bracketing satisfactory.

Von Hirsch is committed, by his reliance on the work of Sellin and Wolfgang, to emphasise harm and to relegate culpability. He does, however, take into account the number and seriousness of the offender's prior convictions in constructing his penalty scale.[36] Certain mitigating factors, notably altruistic motives[37] and provocations,[38] are also mentioned briefly. It is questionable whether consideration of the offender's previous record is compatible with retributivism. The retributivist is, after all, concerned with what the offender has done on this occasion. I would not quarrel with the intrusion of such non-retributivist ideas. The case for treating a first offender more leniently than a hardened rogue is a strong one, even where they have done the same thing. It is a defect of retributivism that such a consideration should be alien to it.

The incorporation of the Sellin-Wolfgang research by von Hirsch also raises questions about the value and validity of relying on public opinion in the assessment of appropriate penalties. If seriousness is a notion without objective quality, it is perceived seriousness that is at issue. Popular opinion can therefore not be ignored. However, so much depends on the precise wording of the attitudinal questionnaire. Much depends also on when the question is put. There is likely to be greater support for the death penalty after a particularly savage murder or terrorist bomb out-

---

35 *idem*, p. 191.
36 von Hirsch, *op. cit.*, pp. 84–88.
37 *idem*, p. 81.
38 *idem*, p. 100.

rage. Nor should the way in which public opinion can be manufactured by the media and agents of social control be ignored. There must also be some doubt as to whether the public fully appreciates the implications of its opinions.[39] Is, therefore, what is required informed public opinion?[40] Is it important to explain to prospective respondents what their expression of opinion involves – what is, for example, meant by 'murder'? Very few of those who favour the death penalty for murder would want to hang mercy-killers or those who kill in the course of a *crime passionel*.

Questions can also be raised about whether public opinion has any legal relevance in the determination of the appropriate criminal sanction. This is a rather different question from the one which asks what part public sentiment should play in the actual determination of guilt during a trial. Professionals do not have a monopoly of expertise when it comes to deciding upon guilt or innocence.[41] But the whole history and development of the criminal law has been away from blood feud and revenge. Capital punishment would never have been abolished in this country or probably any other had the public had its way. Capital punishment may be one of those questions on which public opinion must be considered but may be rejected by those ultimately responsible for making decisions about the public good.

I have concentrated in this discussion of appropriate penalties on the matter of harm. When the question of culpability is raised the retributivist faces further problems. How are we to punish

---

[39] See J. Cohen, R. A. H. Robson and A. Bates, *Parental Authority: The Community and the Law* (New Brunswick, N.J.: Rutgers University Press, 1958).

[40] See A. Sarat and N. Vidmar, 'Public Opinion, the Death Penalty and the Eighth Amendment', in *Capital Punishment in the United States*, edited by H. A. Bedau and C. M. Pierce (New York: AMS Press, 1976), p. 190.

[41] A point made by Lord Devlin in his recent Blackstone lecture at Oxford (November 1978). See P. Devlin, *The Judge* (Oxford: Oxford University Press, 1979), chapter 5. See also M. D. A. Freeman, 'The Jury On Trial', *Current Legal Problems* 34 (1981): 81–97.

attempted crime? The intended criminal's blameworthiness may be as great or even greater than that of his successful partner in crime. Why should the latter be punished more severely?[42] Retributivists who argue that the just desert for deliberate killing is death do not (at least I have found none who do) recommend capital punishment for attempted murder, though many a heinous, well-planned but bungled murder attempt is far more evil than a successful impulsive murder. It is difficult to see why the survival of the intended victim should make the crime less culpable. The utilitarian has fewer problems with this situation. Very few of those charged with attempted murder expected to fail to achieve their end, so that punishing attempted murder and murder equally would have the same deterrent effect. This is not to argue that punishment deters: I have already noted that the evidence on capital punishment is at best equivocal, and the high rate of recidivism for other crimes suggests that imprisonment does not deter. It is rather to put the case for treating completed crimes and attempted crime comparably. There is little or no moral difference between the two. If we take murder again, it is obvious that more intended murder victims survive today if only because of improvements in medical skills. Conversely, what of the victim who dies when with more acceptable medical attention he should have survived, or the victim who dies because, on religious grounds, he refuses a blood transfusion? And why is killing one person regarded as more serious (as it certainly seems to be by many retributivist proponents of the death penalty) than maiming dozens by planting a bomb in a place of public resort?

4. THE SEVERITY OF PUNISHMENT

The other problem the retributivist must confront is what is a serious punishment. What constitutes severity? How are punishments to be graded? It is difficult enough to compare two punish-

---

[42] See Hart, *Punishment and Responsibility*, pp. 129–31.

ments which are qualitatively similar but quantitatively distinct. On the face of it, a 20 years' term of imprisonment is twice as severe as one of 10 years. But, even if we ignore the vagaries of the parole system, we have no way of determining, short of public opinion polls and even then, whether severity is perceived in this way at all. On this matter the value of public opinion is very limited, for it is difficult to conceive of a questionnaire that could adequately test attitudes to different terms of imprisonment: at least one that could do so meaningfully.

The problem is accentuated when we try to compare the relative severity of qualitatively different punishments. Is 'six of the best' more or less severe than a detention or a suspension from school? Is being executed worse than serving a life sentence in prison? Mill for one did not think so.[43] Death, he believed, was less painful than the long-standing suffering associated with a lengthy term of imprisonment. Mill's reasoning is not very convincing. Most people would rather avoid death than long or perpetual imprisonment. That is surely why cases like Gary Gilmore's attracted so much attention.[44] Murphy is right to assert that, in addition to considerations of fairness, there are substantive reasons for not allowing certain punishments. He has no difficulty in ruling out torture as a punishment even for sadistic torturers themselves, though the problematic nature of 'torture' is not one he considers. It would be an 'intrinsically inhuman method of punishment', he notes. 'Justice', he argues, 'demands absolute side constraints against punishments which are intrinsically heinous ... This is required if we are to respond to criminals as *people* – as individuals with unique characters and degrees of responsibility.' Whilst in general agreement with this, I am not convinced that such a constraint need be absolute. Murphy does not see capital

---

43 See his speech in the House of Commons on 12 April 1868, reproduced in *Philosophy of Law*, edited by J. Feinberg and H. Gross (Encino, Cal.: Dickenson, 1975), p. 619.

44 On which see N. Mailer, *The Executioner's Song* (Boston, Mass.: Little, Brown, 1979).

punishment as intrinsically degrading. We can, I think, draw too much, and Murphy does, from what I suspect may be a rather idealised, somewhat romantic picture of Socrates's execution. Our concern should be with capital punishment as it operates, or has operated, or would operate again in our criminal justice systems. Justifications of practices in current social systems must be premised upon an acute analysis of the actual workings of those systems to be of any real value. Truman Capote, whom Murphy also quotes, should be more valuable to him in this context than Plato.

I do not believe that capital punishment can ever be anything other than evil. Nor do I think that Murphy has made out a case that capital punishment is conceptually all that distinct from torture. But Murphy, who believes he has, is forced into finding another principle which will enable him to condemn capital punishment. He claims to find this in the right he asserts we all have not to be dealt with negligently by our 'government' (I suggest he means 'state' and, indeed, he does tend to use the two expressions indiscriminately). Using principles drawn from the law of tort he argues that this duty of care increases the greater the potential harm is. This is a principle to which it would be difficult to take exception. But Murphy's reasoning thereafter is far from crystal clear. He argues that, as death is the greatest harm (he has already ruled out torture as an acceptable punishment), it follows that the greatest care is required before taking a decision which will deprive someone of his life. Death, he maintains, is the greatest harm that can be perpetrated on a person because it is totally incompensable and represents lost opportunity of a morally crucial kind. That it is incompensable is almost a truism. But why should anyone wish to compensate a person who has been executed and has received, in retributivist language, his 'just deserts'? He may, of course, have been innocent (innocent men have been executed). But that possibility aside (and even supporters of the death penalty concede that the danger of executing the innocent is a strong argument against capital punishment), the need for justifying compensation remains. It cannot be that the harm to which Murphy refers is error. We cannot compensate the dead but innocent, but why should we want to compensate those lawfully executed?

It is here that Murphy's lost opportunity doctrine assumes importance. The opportunity to which he refers is that to develop 'moral character'. Death certainly prevents any further development of moral character. So do abortion, conscription into the army to serve at the front (as in, for example, the first world war), some surgery performed on those mentally ill, and the administration of drugs like Prolixin and Anectine to prisoners. Murphy's thesis could doubtless be extended to cover such cases. But why should not forfeiture of life, even if this means sacrificing the possibility of moral improvement, be the 'debt' paid by the murderer 'to those other members of the community who have satisfied the social obligation of reciprocity, have made the sacrifice of obedience that is required for any just legal system to work'?

I am not convinced in other words that Murphy has made out a case which is compatible with retributivism for outlawing the death penalty. I do, however, believe that it may be possible to refine the doctrine further to a point where it becomes possible to reject the death penalty in all but the most extreme of cases. If tyrannicide can be justified, and I believe it can, then the execution of a despot is surely also permissible. If the July Plot against Hitler is morally justifiable then his lawful execution after a properly conducted trial would also have been. At the very least such a thesis could employ consequentialist arguments.

University College London

JOHN COTTINGHAM

PUNISHMENT AND RESPECT FOR PERSONS

Much of the recent work on the death penalty has been conducted within the framework of a deterrence theory of punishment, and I think it is fair to say that it has been very inconclusive. The great interest of Professor Murphy's essay is that it is a serious attempt to tackle the issue of capital punishment (and other extreme penalties) within an alternative, retributivist framework. Before looking at Murphy's arguments, however, I want to make two very brief preliminary points about the utilitarian deterrence model which he wishes to replace. The first point is that many of the standard objections to the utilitarian view are often far too swift and peremptory. According to Murphy, for example, the utilitarian says to the criminal, "you can be used and manipulated for the common good". Well, perhaps at the end of the day this traditional charge against the utilitarian can be made to stick. But the sophisticated utilitarian will have a fighting defence, and the verdict should not be pronounced before the arguments are heard. Many utilitarians, for instance, would here point out that punishment is not a matter of the arbitrary manipulation of individuals, but is an *institution* governed by certain rules; and there may be good utilitarian reasons why these rules should proscribe many of the more sinister kinds of 'using and manipulating' which Murphy has in mind.[1] The second point about deterrence concerns the question of whether it works. Here it is Mr Freeman who is guilty of being over-swift; indeed, he perpetrates a howler which crops

[1] Compare for example Bentham's arguments against 'afflictive', 'indelible' and 'ignominious' punishments, in *The Theory of Legislation: Principles of the Penal Code* (1759), Part III, Ch. 9. In many cases (e.g., parking tickets, or a penalty system in football) the charge against the deterrence theorist of 'using and manipulating' people seems to me misleading or just false.

M. A. Stewart (ed.), Law, Morality and Rights, 423–431.

up with depressing frequency in criminological literature. "Deterrence as a penal aim has not worked", Freeman announces. And later we find what is presumably supposed to be the evidence for this claim: "the high rate of recidivism ... suggests that imprisonment does not deter." But recidivism, of course, suggests no such thing. The fact that the once convicted embezzler is more likely to embezzle again as soon as he gets out of prison is no evidence whatsoever that the imposition of custodial penalties for embezzlement has no deterrent effect on the population at large. As for the sweeping general claim that "deterrence as a penal aim has not worked", this is just preposterous. A simple *Gedankenexperiment* strongly suggests that if the penalties for, say, shoplifting, were abolished, there would be, if not immediately then at least before long, a massive increase in freeloading at the supermarkets (if not a total breakdown in the retail system). Those virtuous and unworldly academics who cannot even conceive of being tempted to shoplift (though, with the recent substantial relative and absolute drop in academic salaries they must be getting fewer) should substitute other crimes (omitting a lecture fee on their tax return perhaps, or smuggling in some perfume for the wife), and reflect on how their conduct might vary if there were no, or much lesser, penalties to scare them into compliance. Common experience clearly shows us that in very many cases indeed deterrence can and does work.

Professor Murphy's purpose in his essay is not, I take it, to *defend* a retributive theory of punishment (he has done this elsewhere); rather, he is *presupposing* the viability of some version of retributivism and examining the consequences of such a theory for the evaluation of extreme penalties. However, if we are to 'presuppose' retributivism, then at least we need to be tolerably clear about what exactly we are being asked to presuppose; and here there is a crucial distinction to be made (one which was articulated with splendid clarity during the conference by the late J. L. Mackie) between *negative* and *positive* retributivism. The negative retributivist is concerned to insist on two limiting principles for punishment: it must not be imposed in the absence of criminal wrongdoing; and its amount must not exceed the degree of wrongfulness of the act. These limiting principles have a very strong appeal to all those who share certain fundamental intuitions about justice and individual rights. The positive retributivist, however, goes very much further than this and claims that the occurrence of criminal wrongdoing somehow provides a sufficient justification for the infliction of a penalty. This is a very much more controversial and difficult idea to defend (and I have argued elsewhere[2] that it is an ambiguous idea which breaks down on analysis to a number of quite distinct subtheories, none of which turns out under scrutiny to carry the justificatory weight it is supposed to bear). The relevant point for the present context is that when Murphy expresses his confidence that many of those who do not like the name 'retributivist' are in fact deeply influenced, in their outlook on punishment, by considerations of a retributive kind, he seems to be skating over this crucial distinction between positive and negative retributivism. For while it may be universally agreed, as Murphy suggests, that it would never be fair or just to punish negligent vehicular homicide with death while giving the first-degree murderer a short spell in jail, this agreement simply shows that there is a widespread commitment to the negative thesis which imposes limits or side-constraints on the institution of punishment; it does not show that there is a latent groundswell of support for the positive doctrines of retributivism.

Now to the main thesis of Murphy's paper. The central principle is that "a punishment will be unjust (and thus banned on principle) if it is ... degrading or dehumanizing (inconsistent with human dignity)". This principle is derived from the highly attractive Kantian notion of respect for persons. Thus certain kinds of torture (boiling in oil, eviscerating) are to be ruled out because they do not respect what Murphy calls the 'special status of persons'. Now although I think that Murphy has here put his finger on an important and valuable moral principle, it seems to me that it will not quite draw the line where he thinks it does –

---

[2] 'Varieties of Retribution', *Philosophical Quarterly* 29 (1979): 238–246.

that is, it will not necessarily rule out the kinds of 'cruel and unusual' punishments that the U.S. Eighth Amendment is presumably designed to prohibit. It seems clear that the traditional Muslim penalty of amputation of a hand for theft would be outlawed by the Eighth Amendment. And thank goodness for that. But why is such a punishment inconsistent with respect for persons? Cutting off someone's hand is certainly a pretty nasty thing to do to a person, but it does not radically interfere with his autonomy or status as a human agent. Those who are handicapped by the loss of a limb (for example the *mutilés de guerre* for whom certain seats are reserved on the Paris Métro) are certainly unfortunate, but their status as human persons is in no way impaired. Our worry about *cruel* punishments is surely that they involve the deliberate infliction of a great amount of suffering and distress;[3] but this is not the same as the worry about failing to respect someone as a person. Causing great pain does not necessarily entail failure to respect[4] (or else all abdominal surgery would be a violation of Kantian principles). Nor, incidentally, does the converse entailment hold. The kind of brainwashing technique described in Anthony Burgess's *A Clockwork Orange* clearly involved loss of autonomy and agenthood for the victim – he was permanently deprived of certain capacities for self-development; but little or no actual suffering was inflicted.

It may be that the wording of Article Three of the European Convention on Human Rights which prohibits 'inhuman and degrading' punishments is closer to the Kantian ideal than that of its U.S. counterpart. For if a person is not just made to suffer but is *degraded*, then indeed his status as a person seems to be under attack. Thus the European Court ruled against the United King-

---

3 *Pace* Murphy, even *anaesthetized* amputation would cause great suffering and distress, as anyone who has recovered from surgery done under anaesthetic would surely testify.

4 This partly depends on the degree of pain involved. I would of course agree with Murphy that subjecting someone to pain intense enough to reduce him to 'a terrified, defecating, urinating, screaming animal' is inconsistent with treating him as a person.

dom, with reference to the Isle of Man, that for an offender to be birched on the bare buttocks was a violation of his rights under Article Three.[5] The rationale for the Court's decision was, however, not entirely clear. One might have supposed that the compulsory stripping of the offender was the 'degrading' element – this was presumably what prompted the Isle of Man authorities to give an undertaking that if the Court permitted birching it would henceforth be administered 'over the ordinary cloth trousers'. Since this undertaking was to no avail in persuading the court to allow birching, the judges must presumably have taken the view that any corporal punishment by court order was intrinsically inhuman and degrading. In which case one may again ask 'Why?'. Beatings are painful; severe beatings are cruel. And this, it seems to me, is a good reason for prohibiting them. But are they 'inhuman' in the Kantian sense of failing to respect our humanity or personhood? It does not seem obvious that one must necessarily emerge from such an ordeal with one's autonomy or agenthood damaged. It is certainly true that during the course of such a punishment the person punished is in the position not of an agent but of a *patient* – he is having something done *to* him forcibly, against his will. But to make *this* the rationale for the prohibition against beating would make the scope of Article Three impossibly wide, since it is true of any punishment (compulsory incarceration, for example) that it involves the forcible inflicting of something unpleasant on the offender.

The most striking part of Murphy's paper is his discussion of the death penalty, where he adopts a position that is distinctly paradoxical, though none the less fascinating for that. The paradox arises from the fact that Murphy's aim is to show that the *retributivist* must outlaw the death penalty. Yet, firstly, the arch-retributivist, Kant, was (as Murphy allows) firmly in favour of capital

[5] This was the *Tyrer* case, decided by the European Court of Human Rights at Strasbourg on 25 April 1978 by a majority of 6 to 1. According to Article Three of the European Convention "no one shall be subjected to torture, or to inhuman or degrading treatment or punishment".

punishment for murder; secondly, Murphy concedes that the death penalty need not be (though it no doubt often is) disproportionate to the heinousness of the offence; and thirdly, Murphy admits that execution does not necessarily have to be performed in a brutal and uncivilized manner (cf. the death of Socrates). In spite of all this, Murphy argues that there is a retributivist argument for a 'direct absolute ban on the penalty of death', because death represents '*lost opportunity* of a morally crucial kind'. "For it is by no means clear that one can show respect for the dignity of a person as a person if one is willing to interrupt and end his most uniquely human capacities and projects."

It seems to me that the claim which Murphy is making here can be interpreted in two ways: on the first interpretation it is trivial, and on the second it is false. It is indeed true that if *S* is executed then *S* ceases to be a person, for the very obvious reason that he ceases to be. If *S* is dead, then, tautologously, he cannot develop his human capacities or pursue his characteristically human projects. (This is, incidentally, true even if the soul is immortal; for souls, if there are such things, are plainly not human beings.) However, Murphy's argument requires more than this analytic truth: it requires the proposition that to end someone's life is necessarily to fail to respect him as a person. This proposition seems to be false, as can be seen from non-punitive contexts. Suppose that Achilles, having defeated Hector, had said: "I will not kill you, since that would be to fail to respect you as a person. Instead I will lock you up in a cage and wheel you round the Grecian tents to be pelted with rotten eggs." From what we know of the noble Hector it seems clear that he would have preferred death to such humiliation. To spare the life of a homeric champion in such circumstances is, precisely, *not* to respect him; respect for the dignity of a homeric champion *requires* that he be killed if defeated in battle. There is of course a difference between this and the penal case, namely that judicial execution is generally (though not always – cf. Gary Gilmore) not regarded by the condemned person as welcome-in-the-circumstances. But to say that capital punishment violates dignity and autonomy because it is administered to an unwilling 'patient' leads, as we have seen, to the unwelcome consequence that any judicial punishment is a potential violation of dignity and autonomy.

It may be objected that I have been over-swift in dismissing the importance of the first, tautologous, interpretation of Murphy's claim that death interrupts and ends our uniquely human capacities. Could not Murphy argue that, although this is an analytic truth, it is not a trivial one? Does not the statement 'If *S* is dead he cannot pursue his autonomous human activities' succeed in unpacking precisely what it is about death that makes it universally feared and shunned?

I think that Murphy is quite right to underline this crucial fact about death – that it is the *end*; and this does indeed partly explain why execution is regarded as such a particularly severe and terrible penalty. But it seems to me that the connection between this point and the alleged threat to dignity and personhood is simply not made out by Murphy. An analogy may help to make this clear. When my infant daughter messes around with my typewriter, forcing down five or more keys at a time and causing them to become bent or jammed, she is *abusing* the typewriter. She is (or would be if she was old enough for this charge to be appropriate) failing to respect its function as a typewriter. But suppose that an engineer simply dismantles the typewriter. It is of course analytically true that this operation cuts off all possibilities for the typewriter to continue to perform its unique and specialised function: since, after the dismantling, it no longer exists as a typewriter it cannot any longer perform the *ergon* of a typewriter. But it simply does not follow, and in fact it would surely be false, to say that such dismantling, such cutting off of future possibilities, necessarily involves some kind of *abuse*. (Just in case anyone misunderstands, I am *not* saying that human beings are just like typewriters, or that human dispositions and capacities are like the dispositions and capacities of an inanimate object; the point is simply that the elimination of *X* as an existing entity need not necessarily involve the abusing of *X*.) So in the human case we still need an argument – and such an argument has not, so far as I can see, been supplied by Murphy – to show that the eliminating of *S* as a person involves a failure to respect *S*'s dignity or status as a person.

As a concluding exercise, I think it is instructive to consider how Murphy's intuition about the incompatibility of the death penalty with the Kantian principle of respect might stand up to a concrete example. Consider someone who has committed a series of appallingly evil acts – a Himmler or an Eichmann perhaps. It seems to me that a severe but wholly just judge – one who shares all Murphy's other intuitions about human dignity and personhood – might well address such a prisoner as follows: "I could say that your behaviour was not your responsibility; I could say that it was the result of a fatal genetic flaw, or a disastrous upbringing, or the social climate in which you found yourself. I could decide not to punish you at all, but to alter your personality, or 'cure' you. But if I am to treat you as a *human agent*, as fully responsible for the horrible and irredeemable wrongs you have done, then there is only one penalty that fits the bill – death."

I hope I have said enough to show why the central suggestion in Murphy's essay will not work. But let me end on a note of agreement by saying that my own personal position on the undesirability of capital punishment is in fact in accord with Murphy's. That is, I share Murphy's hopes that, given the realities of the judicial process and the mechanisms of judicial review, the courts will be increasingly reluctant to resort to the death penalty. In this connection there is a quite separate, and to my mind much more promising, line of argument to which Murphy and Freeman both refer towards the ends of their papers, namely that death is unique among penalties because it is both logically and empirically impossible to compensate the victim in case of judicial error. Since any human system of justice is liable to error, we might well wish to outlaw in advance a penalty which is such that we cannot even attempt to redress the wrong done by a miscarriage of justice. Such incompensatable miscarriages, as we all know, have occurred, and have resulted in what is perhaps the most sombre and appalling of all acts which the executive may be obliged to perform – the bestowing of that ultimate mockery the 'posthumous pardon'. Positivist retributivists have traditionally insisted on the maxim *fiat justitia, ruat caelum*: let justice prevail though the heavens fall. The incompensatability of the death penalty if it is imposed in error raises the question of whether we should not adopt what seems to me to be a far more important negative maxim – *ruat caelum, ne fiat talis injuria*: let the heavens fall rather than that such injustice should come about. A just penal system may well have to give priority, over the aims of deterrence and positive retribution, to ruling out the possibility of such an appalling wrong.

University of Reading

JEFFRIE G. MURPHY

CONCLUDING COMMENTS

Dr Cottingham's excellent paper was written some time after the RIP conference. It reached me only after I had already completed the following remarks, and too late for me to prepare a considered reply. I accept, from reading his valuable comments, that some parts of my argument will need to be revised and reconsidered the next time that I return to this subject. For the present, I shall concentrate on two lines of criticism advanced by Mr Freeman. Freeman takes me to task (1) for providing an insufficiently precise and persuasive account of retribution and (2) for failing to appreciate the moral complexities of torture.

(1) *Retribution*. Freeman dislikes my account of retribution for three main reasons: (i) It employs a "notion of social justice which itself is little more than a defence of the existing system" – a notion which is "fictive and totally abstracted from the realities of social and economic life" and which "presupposes a high degree of value consensus, whereas the reality of today's advanced technological, capitalistic societies is more pluralistic, conflictual and antagonistic." (ii) It follows Kant in using a *debt* metaphor with respect to punishment. But "debts are paid to compensate", and thus my account unfortunately blurs the distinction between punishment and compensation. (iii) It rests upon the concept of satisfying just claims. But the concept of satisfaction is utilitarian in nature, and thus my account departs from pure retributivism.

In the article itself I anticipate and respond to point (i). I shall here simply refer the reader to footnote 14 and to my article 'Marxism and Retribution' cited in that footnote. I also attempt to respond to this worry in my 'Three Mistakes About Retributivism' in *Analysis* **31** (1970/71): 166–9, reprinted in *RJT*. My basic argument is that retributivism provides a good justification for punishment only in a society that is just; and that to the degree

M. A. Stewart (ed.), Law, Morality and Rights, 433–435.

that a society is unjust (e.g., racist, unfairly inegalitarian, containing unjustified restrictions within its criminal code, etc.) then to that degree it lacks a moral right to punish. With respect to point (ii), my supposed confusion of punishment with compensation, I must simply reply that I think it is Freeman who is confused. It seems to me simply false that, when I pay a just debt to a person, I am *compensating* him. What in the world would I be compensating him for? Do we not compensate people for *injuring* or *harming* them? And do I injure or harm a person merely by being in his debt? These questions strike me as self-answering. Finally, Freeman's charge that I may not consistently use the concept of satisfaction (point iii above) simply involves, so far as I can tell, a pun on the word "satisfaction". I am interested in the concept of *satisfying a claim* (a just claim), and one can do this without providing any satisfaction (in the hedonic or utilitarian sense of pleasure) to the person whose claim is satisfied. (You pay me the debt that you owe – and thus satisfy a just *claim* of mine – but the payment leaves *me* saddened rather than satisfied. For I know that the money meant a great deal more to you who are poor than to me who is rich and that your pride would have been hurt had I said "Forget about it".) Claims, like commands, criteria, descriptions, and demands, can be satisfied without anyone getting satisfaction.

(2) *Torture*. My discussion of torture contains many problems, and I quite agree that it needs more work. I might have avoided some unnecessary criticism, however, if I had made clearer my intention to be talking about torture solely as an *institutionalized legal punishment*. Some acts might be legitimate to perform (e.g., in wartime battlefield emergencies) that might still be absolutely prohibited as legal sanctions. (Professor W. L. Twining, as I recall, made this point in discussion.) Given this important difference between "doing *X*" and "the State's doing *X* as legal punishment", I think Mr Freeman is being far too quick when he writes that "if the July Plot against Hitler is morally justifiable then his lawful execution after a properly conducted trial would also have been". If it is permissible to kill an ordinary combat soldier in wartime,

does it follow that it would be permissible to try and legally execute that soldier after the war? Freeman would surely want to answer *No* to this question, and thus he would surely want to rethink his seeming endorsement of the principle "If it is ever OK to do *X*, then it is OK to do *X* as a legal sanction".

I had wanted to show that death, like torture, is simply not the *kind* of harm or evil which we want the State to inflict as legal punishment. In attempting to show this, I tried to bring out some analogies between torture and death. Though I still think that my account points in the right direction, I have been persuaded (not just by Mr Freeman and Dr Cottingham, but by criticisms which Professor Twining and Mr Antony Duff were kind enough to send me) that the account needs considerably greater precision and elaboration before becoming adequate. Doing this in the present context is impossible, but I hope in a future work at least to do a better job and to show that the thoughtful comments I have been sent were not wasted.

Arizona State University

INDEX I: CASES

AUSTRALIA

CANADA

EUROPEAN COURT OF HUMAN RIGHTS

SOUTH AFRICA

TRINIDAD AND TOBAGO

UNITED KINGDOM

England and Wales

Scotland

[Northern] Ireland

UNITED STATES

INDEX II: PERSONS

[*Judicial status is indicated by italics*]

INDEX III: TOPICS